Finding your unique, God-designed purpose is like a magnet that helps pull you out of addiction into a life lived for him. A great adventure awaits you in this book.

TIM CLINTON, EdD
President of the American Association of Christian Counselors and executive director of the Center for Counseling and Family Studies at Liberty University

Whether you're struggling to get it all together or are at the end of yourself, this gem of a book offers gentle guidance and support along the way. It brings focus to the fact that we're all in the process of recovery—or need to be.

RON NIKKEL, MPS
President and chief executive officer of Prison Fellowship International and author of *Radical Love in a Broken World*

Without a doubt, we could have used Katie's home run insights during our five-year bout with denial, anger, worry, and depression, when Dave lost his arm and shoulder to cancer along with his beloved pitching career with the San Francisco Giants. We urge you to spend prayerful time with this realtime recovery model anchored securely in God's miraculous plan for your own life.

DAVE & JAN DRAVECKY
Founders of Endurance ministry and authors of *When You Can't Come Back*

A must-read for those in recovery who want God to use their entire story for his glory. And what a great tool for recovery coaches and sponsors to use with those seeking to know and do God's will.

ARCHIBALD HART, PhD
SYLVIA HART FREJD, DMin and certified Internet addiction coach
Authors of *The Digital Invasion: How Technology is Shaping You and Your Relationships*

Discovering your true purpose will unlock a new joy and a new peace in you; that's the treasure in these pages. You don't want to miss this daily, hope-filled recovery journey!

GREGORY JANTZ, PhD
Certified eating disorders specialist, founder of The Center, and prolific author of addiction-related books

To experience the joy of choosing sobriety and living with significance, read *The One Year Recovery Prayer Devotional* each day. You'll love it!

LES & LESLIE PARROTT, PhDs
Founders of the Center for Relationship Development and authors of *The Good Fight*

The One Year® Recovery Prayer Devotional

THE ONE YEAR®
RECOVERY
PRAYER DEVOTIONAL

365 Daily Meditations toward
Discovering Your True Purpose

Dr. Katie Brazelton

Bestselling Author and Founder of
Life Purpose Coaching Centers International®

Tyndale House Publishers, Inc.
Carol Stream, Illinois

From the Author

Some of the sayings and slogans I use in this book are common phrases used in recovery groups, whose origins date back to the 1930s. If you feel that I have quoted a slogan or saying that you think you might have been the first to coin, please let me know. I'll be happy to give you credit in my book for it if you can verify that you were the first to use that phrase, saying, or slogan.

The Twelve Steps of Alcoholics Anonymous are reprinted with permission of Alcoholics Anonymous World Services, Inc. ("AAWS"). Permission to reprint the Twelve Steps does not mean that AAWS has reviewed or approved the contents of this publication, or that AAWS necessarily agrees with the views expressed herein. AA is a program of recovery from alcoholism only; use of the Twelve Steps in connection with programs and activities that are patterned after AA, but which address other problems, or in any other non-AA context, does not imply otherwise. Additionally, while AA is a spiritual program, AA is not a religious program. Thus, AA is not affiliated or allied with any sect, denomination, or specific religious belief.

People experience and overcome addictions in different ways. This book is not meant as a substitute to medical advice or diagnosis by a trained medical professional who is familiar with your medical history and personal circumstances.

Visit Tyndale online at www.tyndale.com.

Visit Life Purpose Coaching Centers International online at www.lifepurposecoachingcenters.com.

TYNDALE, The One Year, One Year, and Tyndale's quill logo are registered trademarks of Tyndale House Publishers, Inc. The One Year logo is a trademark of Tyndale House Publishers, Inc.

The One Year Recovery Prayer Devotional: 365 Daily Meditations toward Discovering Your True Purpose

In association with literary agent Nancy Jernigan and the Hidden Value Group

Life Purpose Coaching Centers International and Life Purpose Coach are registered trademarks of Katie Brazelton.

The Twelve Steps for Believers and The P.U.R.P.O.S.E. Plan copyright © 2013 by Katie Brazelton. All rights reserved.

Cover photograph copyright © by Andrey Volokhatiuk/Veer. All rights reserved.

Author photo taken by Francois Booyens, copyright © 2011 by Francois Booyens Productions. All rights reserved.

Interior photographs of roads copyright © Valentin Agapov, Krivosheev Vitaly and Kochneva Tetyana/Shutterstock. All rights reserved.

Designed by Beth Sparkman

Edited by Jane Vogel

ISBN 978-1-4143-6442-1

Printed in the United States of America

22	21	20	19	
8	7	6	5	4

Dedication

This devotional is dedicated to two men of great faith, who
loved me beyond measure while I was writing it.
To my father, Charles, who passed away before this project was completed.
To my brother Chuck, who helped me process my deep grief.

Table of Contents

Introduction

I will be made well.
MARK 5:28 (ESV)

I pray that this devotional is like a trustworthy friend who walks with you, day by day, reminding you that you're not alone. May you experience life-changing breakthrough as you travel down the only assured pathway to recovery, which is Jesus Christ. May you get to know him more deeply and love him more faithfully than you ever imagined possible. May you learn to obey him more consistently, allowing him to inspire character growth in you beyond your wildest dreams.

I pray that you'll soon find that Jesus has led you to where your sobriety intersects with your intriguing life purpose. You might feel trapped in addiction, wishing instead that you were already living out God's tremendous plan for your life. You might vaguely remember having a life dream, a longing in your heart for significance, a burden to help others, or a fascination in your soul. Have those dreams vanished? Did life take a wrong turn for you when you got beat up emotionally or physically, you grew weary with worry, your sins were piled higher than your head, or you chose to worship an addictive idol?

Whatever's transpired, I promise you that God wants to get your attention, as he did with Saul, the atheist and Christian-killer, on the road to Damascus. Just as he loved Saul and all who've gone before you with their own hurts and debilitating habits, God loves you. Just think about Miriam, the gossip and backstabber of her own brother; David, the adulterer and murderer; Martha, the controlling complainer; Zacchaeus, the cheat; Peter, the Christ denier; and Thomas, the doubter.

This devotional, which deals daily with major recovery themes, will lead you back to the desires of your heart, to your individual purpose, to God's will and call on your life. Just as God called Noah to build an ark, Abram to go to an undisclosed destination, Sarah to be the mother of nations, Moses to lead his people out of Egypt, and Joshua to cross the river into the Promised Land, he's called you also to fulfill your own particular destiny. Just as God called John the Baptist to prepare the way for the Lord, Saul to open the eyes of the Gentiles, Peter to feed Christ's sheep, Mary Magdalene to tell the disciples that Christ was alive, and the apostle John on the island of Patmos to write a book, he's called you to leave a legacy that only you can leave. God wants to use you to do the *One Big Thing* that he planted in your heart eons ago.

When you hear your Creator's call, you have the option of being like Moses, who begged God to send somebody else, or like Jonah, who ran and hid. Or you can be like young Samuel in the Temple, who said to God, "Speak, your servant is listening" (1 Samuel 3:10), or like Isaiah, who said to the Lord, "Here I am. Send me" (Isaiah 6:8).

God adores you. You're his beloved and the crown in his hand. You're his child, friend, and masterpiece. He's your Great Physician, Refuge, Rock, Provider, Protector, and King. Trust him with your life. Lean into Jesus and cry, "Heal me and commission me, Lord—but don't let me make Purpose my new idol!" And ask God's Spirit to fall fresh on you, especially as you go through the next 365 days with this devotional.

As founder of Life Purpose Coaching Centers International®, I've come to understand two things well: first, that everyone is addicted to something; and second, that God wired human beings to want to know their life purpose, the specific reason they were born. I'm humbled to have had the honor of coaching countless people through recovery to discover and experience God's magnificent plan for their lives.

During my many years of recovery-to-purpose coaching, I've often used an acronym to spell out the word *purpose* to help remind hurting, broken, and lost people of God's unique plan for them. So I've organized this recovery devotional around the P.U.R.P.O.S.E. Plan. These seven principles start with putting God first and end with experiencing heart-pounding purpose.

THE P.U.R.P.O.S.E. PLAN

Principle I: Put God First
My primary purpose is to worship God with my life.

Principle II: Understand Biblical Truths about God's Will
I understand my recovery in the bigger picture of how God is redeeming the world.

Principle III: Rightly Tell My Recovery Story
I turn my past and present over to God to complete my future life's work.

Principle IV: Pursue Positive Practices to Maintain My Sobriety
I'm fully cooperating with God regarding his unique plan for my life.

Principle V: Opt Out of Self-Sabotaging Methods
I choose to live a life of recovery and purpose now.

Principle VI: Surrender All to Christ My King
When I empty myself of self, I'm able to be and do all God wants.

Principle VII: Experience Heart-Pounding Life Purpose
I'm living in the center of God's will.

Each one of us will remain adrift until we're aligned with God's masterful designs for our lives. The P.U.R.P.O.S.E. Plan helps those in recovery understand that experiencing God's will is absolutely essential because it moves the focus off all types of addictive behavior to his healthy, invigorating dreams for us. In Principle III: Rightly Tell My Recovery Story, I carefully unpack the Twelve Steps for Believers that I created after being inspired by Alcoholics Anonymous's original Twelve Steps. I did this because those steps, used in a small-group format, have proven themselves an effective tool for helping people in recovery understand and overcome their addictions. The first two weeks of this one-year devotional, January 1 through January 15, give you an overview of how the P.U.R.P.O.S.E. Plan interacts with the Twelve Steps for Believers.

For your convenience, on the following pages you'll find the Twelve Steps for Believers and the original Twelve Steps of Alcoholics Anonymous. For a complete list of major topics addressed in this book, see the appendix. My goal is that after you finish using this devotional as a tool toward your recovery, you'll have everything you need to continue practicing these principles and steps for years to come.

Shy of having Jesus Christ as your Savior and Lord, I know of no greater gifts than sobriety, godly relationships, and having a distinct purpose in life. God has assigned you a life message supported by a life verse and also a life mission, which is your passionate ache to serve a certain group of people. My prayer for you is that you'll feel his hand on your life like never before. I pray that you'll recover from your present addictive choices and welcome his glorious anointing on your future. And I pray blessings on your ordained journey to sobriety and on your unique purpose—that it will be full of God-honoring perseverance and pure joy.

The Twelve Steps for Believers

Where Recovery and Purpose Intersect

God has a unique purpose for me, and he wants me to recover and follow his plan for my life. Therefore . . .

One.   I admit that I'm powerless over my dependencies and that my life has become unmanageable.

Two.   I believe that God can restore me to sanity and help me follow his plan.

Three. I turn my will and life over to God's care.

Four.   I conduct a searching and fearless moral inventory of myself.

Five.   I admit to God, to myself, and to someone who's trustworthy the exact nature of my wrongs.

Six.   I acknowledge that I'm entirely ready to have God remove all my character defects.

Seven. I humbly ask God to remove my shortcomings.

Eight. I prepare a list of all the people I've harmed and become willing to make amends to them all.

Nine. I forgive those who've hurt me, and I make direct amends to the people I've hurt whenever possible, except when to do so would injure them or others.

Ten.   I continue to ask God to help me to take personal inventory and promptly admit when I'm wrong.

Eleven. I seek through prayer and Bible reading to get to know God and his unique purpose for my life, asking him for the power to carry out his will.

Twelve. I tell others about my spiritual awakening using these steps, while continuing to practice these steps in my own life.

The Twelve Steps for Believers were inspired by the Twelve Steps of Alcoholics Anonymous; however, they are not actually an adaptation. Rather, they were created specifically for this publication and should not be construed otherwise. Alcoholics Anonymous, which is a program concerned only with recovery from alcoholism, is not in any way affiliated with this publication.

The Twelve Steps of Alcoholics Anonymous

1. We admitted we were powerless over alcohol—that our lives had become unmanageable.

2. Came to believe that a Power greater than ourselves could restore us to sanity.

3. Made a decision to turn our will and our lives over to the care of God as we understood Him.

4. Made a searching and fearless moral inventory of ourselves.

5. Admitted to God, to ourselves, and to another human being the exact nature of our wrongs.

6. Were entirely ready to have God remove all these defects of character.

7. Humbly asked Him to remove our shortcomings.

8. Made a list of all persons we had harmed, and became willing to make amends to them all.

9. Made direct amends to such people wherever possible, except when to do so would injure them or others.

10. Continued to take personal inventory and when we were wrong promptly admitted it.

11. Sought through prayer and meditation to improve our conscious contact with God, as we understood Him, praying only for knowledge of His will for us and the power to carry that out.

12. Having had a spiritual awakening as the result of these steps, we tried to carry this message to alcoholics, and to practice these principles in all our affairs.

The Twelve Steps of Alcoholics Anonymous are reprinted with permission of Alcoholics Anonymous World Services, Inc. ("AAWS"). Permission to reprint the Twelve Steps does not mean that AAWS has reviewed or approved the contents of this publication, or that AAWS necessarily agrees with the views expressed herein. AA is a program of recovery from alcoholism only; use of the Twelve Steps in connection with programs and activities that are patterned after AA, but which address other problems, or in any other non-AA context, does not imply otherwise. Additionally, while AA is a spiritual program, AA is not a religious program. Thus, AA is not affiliated or allied with any sect, denomination, or specific religious belief.

Finding P.U.R.P.O.S.E. through Recovery Steps

How the Twelve Steps for Believers enhance P.U.R.P.O.S.E.

Finding P.U.R.P.O.S.E. through Recovery Steps

Thanking God That I'm Not God

O LORD, God of our ancestors, you alone are the God who is in heaven. You are ruler of all the kingdoms of the earth. You are powerful and mighty; no one can stand against you! 2 CHRONICLES 20:6

Have you recognized God's kingship yet and admitted your need for him, or do you still playact as if you are controlling the world? The Gospel writer Matthew tells us, "You're blessed when you're at the end of your rope. With less of you there is more of God and his rule" (Matthew 5:3, *The Message*). God's unequivocal majesty is the biblical foundation of the Twelve Steps for Believers, helping us resign as Ruler of the World, admit that we're powerless over our dependencies (Step One), and gratefully undergo a character makeover.

Are you ready to celebrate your recovery in a healthy, God-honoring way, by thanking him that you're not him and for the victory he's declared over the demons in your life? Celebratory parties of your past may have been marred by food-induced comas, alcohol-fueled gossip, drug-incited tirades, predictable police reports, or upstaging the Joneses, but this moment is about commemorating the joy of saying good-bye to all that. As Tom Peters, a wise management guru on the topic of success, has said, "Celebrate what you want to see more of."

After we get this party started of allowing God to be God, he has a beyond-belief surprise for you—an exceptional high, one that's key to your recovery. It's the thrill of discovering and fulfilling his will for your life. As a Life Purpose Coach, I can testify that this heart-pounding experience of having purpose assigned to your life is God's commissioning of a great artwork, a magnum opus, in you. It starts out as his precious gift to you of all the hope that purpose brings. Somewhere along the way, though, you realize that it's also your opus gloria, your finest symphony performed for his glory.

SOUL SEARCH

How do you feel about admitting that you're not God—in fact, that you're actually powerless without him? What small action step could help you explore his purpose-filled will for your life?

God of the spiritually blind, I'm not doing so well. In fact, I'm lost. Please come find me and open my eyes to your kingship and majesty.

Finding P.U.R.P.O.S.E. through Recovery Steps

Being Restored to Sanity

[God says,] "Call on me when you are in trouble, and I will rescue you, and you will give me glory." PSALM 50:15

This passage reminds us of the supernatural power God offers to those who are hurting. He yearns to take the grief-stricken from their dark place of hopelessness, a place from which they feel they might never return, and to give them hope. And "he who has hope has everything" (Arabian proverb). If you need God's comforting hope, especially because you're deeply saddened by the loss of your sober sanity, he wants you to know that "you're blessed when you feel you've lost what is most dear to you. Only then can you be embraced by the One most dear to you" (Matthew 5:4, *The Message*). To receive this blessing, practice reciting with conviction Step Two in the Twelve Steps for Believers: "I believe that God can restore me to sanity and help me follow his plan."

Years ago I heard an inspiring statement: "Don't tell God how big your storm is; tell the storm how big your God is!" The statement may have inspired or been inspired by the country gospel song "Tell the Storm." If we'd only get in the habit of doing that, we'd be reminded continually that our God wants to rescue us when we're in trouble—even when we're reaching for familiar idols or crutches.

If you find yourself in distress or facing dangerous circumstances, put your hope in God and call on him for help. And why not get in the habit every day, all day long, of asking God to lead you by his truth and teach you to do his will (see Psalm 25:5)? He'll rescue you from the insanity that is addiction, and then you can give him all the glory he's due.

SOUL SEARCH

What godly assistance do you need to resist an enticing obsession or compulsion? How might the comforting hope and help you receive from God embolden your quest to discover and fulfill God's calling on your life?

God of all hope, help, and comfort, I'm in distress, but I'm counting on your much-acclaimed faithfulness to rescue me and guide me into a daily restoration of my sobriety and sanity. Don't let that conviction waver in my darkest hours. I know you have the power to help me recover and answer your calling on my life.

Finding P.U.R.P.O.S.E. through Recovery Steps

Humbly Choosing God

Though the LORD is great, he cares for the humble, but he keeps his distance from the proud. PSALM 138:6

I'm convinced God will do anything for those who are meek, anything at all that's in their best interest. When we humbly understand who we are in relation to him, our lives begin to make sense with a newfound confidence in him, his power, and his ways. One of the wisest, most humbling decisions we can ever make is outlined in Step Three in the Twelve Steps for Believers. It reads, "I turn my will and life over to God's care."

And the only way to live under God's care is by making a faith commitment to his precious Son Jesus Christ. As Galatians 3:26 declares, "You are all children of God by believing in Christ Jesus" (NIrv). The process of choosing God, through Jesus, rids us of our sense of emptiness and dissatisfaction, and it releases us to live out the significance-filled destiny God has orchestrated for us. Not bad for a moment's work, even though it takes all eternity to show our profound gratitude! Beginning a personal relationship with Jesus is as simple as saying a heartfelt prayer like this: *Jesus, I believe that you died for me and that God raised you from the dead. Please forgive my sins. You're my Savior, my only hope. I open the door of my heart to you right now. Come live in me.*

With that fresh start, that new lease on life, your recovery can kick into high gear as you truly desire to follow God's will more and more each day. If you already know the joy of Jesus, pray now for those who don't yet understand that God wants them to invite his Son into their hearts.

SOUL SEARCH

What godly person could walk alongside you during times of joy, pain, and pending relapses in your sobriety? In what way could God's purposeful plan for your life be about helping others find freedom from addictive chaos?

Jesus Christ, my Higher Power, I humbly dedicate my life to you because that's God's will for me and I trust him wholeheartedly.

Finding P.U.R.P.O.S.E. through Recovery Steps

Confessing My Shortcomings

If we confess our sins to [God], he is faithful and just to forgive us our sins and to cleanse us from all wickedness.   1 JOHN 1:9

God blesses us when our hearts, thoughts, motives, and actions are purified from the pollution of sin. When I mentioned that to a recovery client in a coaching session, she said to me in an exasperated tone, "I'm about as clean on the inside as a train-hoppin' hobo is on the outside. I've grown so used to that mental picture of myself and my impure heart that when I inventory all my sins, I imagine myself wrapping them up in a dirty, blue knapsack that I tie to the end of a stick. By carrying my heavy load in that way, at least the despicable things are out of sight and out of mind for a little while each day."

I took a deep breath and suggested we take a closer look at the hope she had overlooked in Step Four in the Twelve Steps for Believers. It reads, "I conduct a searching and fearless moral inventory of myself," which means she was forgetting to balance her sin inventory with an examination of the good in her life. And I asked her if she was exhausting herself by trying to come clean of all her shortcomings, resentments, and sins—on her own.

Your knapsack of sins is too weighty for you to bear alone. Let God carry it for you, and let him suggest a fellow sojourner to travel with you awhile (Step Five). Then take a prayerful moment to tell God of your earnest desire to grow in character and answer his call on your life. That pure-hearted offering is sure to warrant a full-on, royal celebration, even for a hobo-sinner like you or me.

SOUL SEARCH

In what way is your heart right and pure, right now? What peace have you found in confessing a fault to a sponsor, accountability partner, or recovery coach—or what joy have you found in sharing a success?

Pure One, I don't want to "go it alone" any longer. Help me examine my life, express gratitude for my victories, and confess my shortcomings to you, myself, and a trustworthy soul.

Finding P.U.R.P.O.S.E. through Recovery Steps

Agreeing to New Beginnings

Those who have been born into God's family do not make a practice of sinning,
because God's life is in them. 1 JOHN 3:9

Volunteer firefighters, volunteer leaders in churches, volunteer candy stripers in hospitals, Big Brothers and Big Sisters—each of these freely chooses to help others, following the strict guidelines of their particular organizations. Likewise, when you were born into God's family as a true Christian, you freely agreed to submit to his commands. In the interest of full disclosure—in case you forgot to read the fine print in your lifetime, volunteer contract with God—his call to holy living is all-consuming. Following his strict guidelines is a 24/7 commitment, especially with stipulations like this: "Those who have been born into God's family do not make a practice of sinning, because God's life is in them. So they can't keep on sinning, because they are children of God" (1 John 3:9).

When we agree to launch into any new beginnings with the Lord, our greatest desire is to do what's right. We actually hunger and thirst after God and his commandments. Step Six of the Twelve Steps for Believers phrases it this way: "I acknowledge that I'm entirely ready to have God remove all my character defects." Step Seven adds, "I humbly ask God to remove my shortcomings." Do you hunger for right living or only to be free of addiction?

It's important to make sure you want to go the distance with God, obeying him, doing what's right, giving up your character defects, and following his unique plan for your life. First Peter 1:13-14 says that you're going to have to "think clearly and exercise self-control" and that you're not allowed to "slip back into your old ways of living to satisfy your own desires." Know that if you do choose God's ways, he'll rejoice over you with blessings.

SOUL SEARCH

What word or phrase best describes what it means to be entirely ready to submit to God (i.e., peace, trust, hope, trepidation, roller-coaster ride of emotion, undeserved celebration)? Which character defect will be the hardest, yet the most rewarding, for you to allow God to remove?

God who rewards humility, I submit to your control of my life and I humbly ask you
to remove my character defects. Life without these commitments is no life at all.

Finding P.U.R.P.O.S.E. through Recovery Steps

Rethinking My Actions and Reactions

God blesses those who are merciful, for they will be shown mercy.   MATTHEW 5:7

Who's the bane of your existence? Who's hurt you deeply or ruined your reputation? Who do you despise and want exiled to a lonely island? If nobody comes to mind at this precise moment, just wait five minutes to see if you fall into the sin of not being able to forgive someone! On the other hand, if you can answer those questions quickly with a specific name or names, you're not alone in your struggle. Personally, I find our passage about mercy challenging. I want it said of me, "You're blessed when you care" (Matthew 5:7, *The Message*). Who wouldn't want to be blessed for being caring and merciful? It's just that I tend to lose my kindness-mojo after a mean person lights my Bunsen burner of anger. I'd still like it said of me, "You're blessed when you can show people how to cooperate instead of compete or fight" (v. 9, *The Message*). But competition is my middle name. What's a wild-eyed, competitive, or impulsive person to do?

The Twelve Steps for Believers tell us exactly what to do. Step Eight reads, "I prepare a list of all the people I've harmed and become willing to make amends to them all." And Step Nine continues the sound advice with "I forgive those who've hurt me, and I make direct amends to the people I've hurt whenever possible, except when to do so would injure them or others."

So, whenever possible, as far as it depends on us, we're to show mercy to others and live at peace with them. We're to rethink how we typically act and react. We're to choose to put an end to hostility in our relationships with others and even with God. Period. End of story. But if a recap using a popular recovery-circle adage would help, we're to live above our circumstances and take the high road, remembering God's grace to us.

SOUL SEARCH

Is it easier for you to offer forgiveness or to ask for it—and why? How will mercy and peace help you do the work God has entrusted you to do on earth?

God who blesses, I do want to rethink all my actions and reactions; I want to offer forgiveness to those who've hurt me; and I do want to make amends for the harm I've caused others, whenever that's possible. Help me!

Finding P.U.R.P.O.S.E. through Recovery Steps

Making Time to Hear God's Will

Oh, that we might know the LORD! Let us press on to know him. He will respond to us as surely as the arrival of dawn or the coming of rains in early spring. HOSEA 6:3

Make time to sit with God, whether that's for spiritual self-examination or to get to know him, his ways, his plans to redeem the world, and his will for your life. And boldly ask him for the power to follow his will and to share your spiritual awakening with others. (These ideas reflect Steps Ten, Eleven, and Twelve in the Twelve Steps for Believers.) God would love to give you the inside scoop about who he is, who you are in relation to him, how to become more like his Son Jesus, how to proceed with your recovery, and what he's assigned you as your stunning life purpose. Through the time-tested practices of quiet introspection, reading his Word, and prayerful meditation, he'll guide you into a victorious life. Hosea testifies that God will surely do this for you, if you press on to know him.

Years ago, I asked our city's Master Planner to tell me the inside scoop behind the name of a nearby intersection, Antonio Parkway and Avenida de las Banderas, wondering if it was in honor of Antonio Banderas, the actor-singer. It was not. That led me to become intrigued with other intersections, such as Elizabeth and Taylor; Harrison and Ford; Rosa Parks and M. L. King Jr.; and my favorite, Stroke and Acoma. As you press on prayerfully to discover more about the world's Master Planner and his substantive will for your life, you'll learn of an intriguing intersection: Recovery and Purpose. Don't be surprised when others ask you for the inside scoop about how you got to that place of peace after the desolation of addiction. Some will be looky-loos, but others will want you to teach them how to live soberly there in the center of God's will.

SOUL SEARCH

Will you cruise through the intersection of "Recovery Road" and "Purpose Pathway" to satisfy your curiosity, or will you set up offices there on a bustling corner? With what welcome gift might God surprise you, should you decide to stay forever?

Master Planner of my life, teach me to press on to know you. Thank you in advance for responding as surely as the arrival of dawn and the coming of spring rain.

Finding P.U.R.P.O.S.E. through Recovery Steps

Answering God's Call on My Life

Give yourself (mind, body, heart, and soul) to God on your recovery journey, and he'll lead you to a festive celebration, a Purpose Party, that's been awaiting your arrival. This is one gala you won't want to miss; it's where he'll reveal more about your divinely ordained life purpose.

☀ Meditate on the Assurance of God's Word

Jesus said to the people who believed in him, "You are truly my disciples if you remain faithful to my teachings. And you will know the truth, and the truth will set you free." JOHN 8:31-32

LORD Almighty, blessed is the one who trusts in you. PSALM 84:12 (NIV)

☀ Humbly Talk with the Lord

Let God know that you want to recover, enjoy his overflowing love, and answer the call he's placed on your life. Tell him that you're ready to submit to his personalized plan for you.

Ask the Holy Spirit to suggest something specific that he'd like you to entrust (surrender) to Jesus now, and then prayerfully consider his recommendation.

☀ Take the *Life Purpose Coach* Challenge

Recovery flourishes when we celebrate God. Without him, addiction wins.

Take a few minutes to reflect on God's greatest attributes (that he is all-powerful, all-knowing, everywhere present, faithful, kind, holy, forgiving, fair, generous, purposeful, pure, tenderhearted, trustworthy, brilliant, personal, and worthy).

And praise him for three special gifts: (1) sending his Son Jesus Christ, your Higher Power, to die for your sins; (2) allowing his Holy Spirit to live in you; and (3) being intimately involved in your sobriety and in the unfolding of his magnificent plan for your life.

Then invite someone to pray for you (and possibly even join you!) during the next 357 days of this Purpose Party.

Finding P.U.R.P.O.S.E. through Recovery Steps
The P.U.R.P.O.S.E. Plan
Principle I: Put God First

Live your lives in a way that God would consider worthy. 1 THESSALONIANS 2:12

Paul urged the church in Thessalonica to put God first by living a life worthy of fellowship with their Creator and proving they belonged to him alone. God expects us to make him our highest authority; he'll not be pushed aside by any foolish god-idol we crave. Our primary purpose is to worship him with our lives—in all we think, say, and do. The insanity of addiction drowns out our Lord's voice when he says, *I am your top priority, your first things first. Before anything else in time, space, desires, obsessions, compulsions, possessions, and importance, I am he who has a spectacular plan for your life. And I am the first and last Word regarding your recovery steps and your paramount purpose in life. I'm your most vocal advocate and your primary asset. I am he who loves you unconditionally, and I am the supreme director of what's best for your sobriety.*

What's got you in a tug-of-war between right and wrong, good and evil, God and Satan? Is it an unruly addiction, an immoral struggle, an unethical choice, or an unhealthy behavior? When we put God first and love him above all else, everything in our lives falls into its proper place or falls by the wayside. George Müller, a German-born, Christian evangelist and orphanage director in England in the 1800s, describes our great reward for doing so: "Be assured, if you walk with Him and look to Him, and expect help from Him, He will never fail you."

Put God first and you'll step toward wholeness and significance-filled living. Make it a practice, then, to give him all the glory for your character transformation, which keeps you sober, because he's the only reason for it.

SOUL SEARCH

Who or what is your all, your everything? What action step could you take to live a more consistent life of recovery out of adoration for your Creator?

God whom I call "my first and foremost," forgive me for sometimes treating you as a minor player in my life, as a supplemental vitamin, as an auxiliary counselor, and as a subsidiary to my main business. All that changes, starting now, with my next step toward recovery!

Finding P.U.R.P.O.S.E. through Recovery Steps
The P.U.R.P.O.S.E. Plan
Principle II: Understand Truths about God's Will

O Sovereign LORD! You made the heavens and earth by your strong hand and powerful arm. Nothing is too hard for you!   JEREMIAH 32:17

The reason we exist is simple: to honor our Sovereign Lord. When we do that, our lives make sense, as if we're following the doctor's orders for a prescribed manner of wellness. But when we're out of sorts with our purpose and dying from the poison of addiction, God still offers himself as our healing antidote.

One of the greatest benefits of glorifying God and keeping him as our constant companion is that nothing is too hard for him, not even the straightening out of our messy, confusing lives. Like a child, we can brag to others, "My Dad's smarter, faster, and stronger than your dad." He's the simplifier of all things difficult—our decisions, commitments, and relationships; he's our endless supplier of all things healthy; he's our hope amid hardship. He begs us to stop beating our heads against a wall and to turn to him for advice, encouragement, and unconditional love. The more of God we inhale, ingest, inject, or get involved with, the better our lives. And unlike overdosing on drugstore medicine, we can never overdose on our purpose of worshiping God with our lives. Having too much of God is an oxymoron, a contradiction! More of him is our only sensible treatment plan.

Choose God as your powerful, restorative therapy, and watch him delight in helping you understand truths about his will and your unique purpose. Before you were ever born, he decided on your specific role in his Kingdom service, and this divine urge he's given you brings healing to your soul. It nudges you to lead a more deliberately sober life, beckoning you to fulfill your heart's desire and reigniting passion that inspires you to become a better you. The proof is when you can't wait to get out of bed in the morning to serve God! Never underestimate the curative powers of purpose.

SOUL SEARCH

Knowing that God is the solution to life's illnesses, what recovery problem can you entrust to him now? How has honoring God moved you toward sobriety and his will?

God who reserved an emphatic purpose for me, you're the cure for all that ails me. Revive me. Mend me. Strengthen me. Nothing is too hard for you.

Finding P.U.R.P.O.S.E. through Recovery Steps
The P.U.R.P.O.S.E. Plan
Principle III: Rightly Tell My Recovery Story

"Who can hide in secret places so that I cannot see them?" declares the LORD. "Do not I fill heaven and earth?" JEREMIAH 23:24 (TNIV)

God knows every detail of your life; no part of it is hidden in a secret place, so trust his promise to use your recovery testimony for good. To ask God for the right motives and right timing for sharing your addiction-to-sobriety journey, whisper this prayer:

Lord, help me write my testimony accurately, without being tempted to exaggerate any parts of it. Stop me from trying to shock people, gain their sympathy, or play the victim. Originate my thoughts from a transformed mind, authentic spirit, and peaceful heart. I know that's more than I can ever offer on any given day, so shape my testimony over the course of time in a way that will most honor you. Help me deliver my chronicle humbly and with a grateful heart for all you've done for me, so people are attracted to you—to your power, kindness, patience, and faithfulness. Let my only goal be to draw listeners to worship you as their Savior and Lord. You're the one redeeming the world, but I'd love to be your PBS (Public Broadcasting Service), when your "On Air" light prompts me to speak.

You can also pray from Psalm 139: *O Lord, you know everything about me. You know what I am going to say, even before I say it. Go before me, follow me, and place your hand of blessing on my head* (see vv. 1, 4-5).

Be assured that God will check your motives for wanting to commit your twisting plot to paper, which will help determine the timing of its delivery. (See April 15 and June 10.)

SOUL SEARCH

Whose testimony of a redeemed life has helped you? What would your top two motives be at this time, if you decided to share your testimony?

You who fill heaven and earth, my "his-story" is an open book to you. Let my rightly told testimony be usable in your hands, as I live out the plan you have for me.

Finding P.U.R.P.O.S.E. through Recovery Steps

The P.U.R.P.O.S.E. Plan
Principle IV: Pursue Positive Practices

Pay careful attention to your own work, for then you will get the satisfaction of a job well done. GALATIANS 6:4

God has been calling his people into his plan of redeeming the world for centuries. For example, Jacob heard God's will in a dream (Genesis 28:10-15), Elijah heard the Lord speak in a gentle whisper and then received instructions (1 Kings 19:9-18), and Nehemiah's heart was burdened to repair the wall and gates of Jerusalem (Nehemiah 1:2-11). Like the procession of field workers who have gone before you, you've also been set apart for God's good pleasure. Like them, you'll need to pay close attention to the particular task that he's delegated to you so that when you've served faithfully, you'll get the satisfaction of a job well done for the Lord.

One of the richest blessings of a personalized life purpose is that it motivates you to pursue positive practices in your life, starting with those that buoy up your recovery. A life mission's beauty and intensity prompt you to know God more intently, love him more deeply, and worship him more completely with your life. Ask the Holy Spirit to send you a sponsor, mentor, sobriety coach, or wise friend—someone who can save you time, energy, and angst on the adventure you're taking toward God and for God. Scripture teaches, "Though good advice lies deep within the heart, a person with understanding will draw it out" (Proverbs 20:5). Expect to find a person with godly understanding to help draw out all the truth you have in your heart.

SOUL SEARCH

What small step can you take to cooperate with God regarding your recovery work and life's work? To you, what's more important or rewarding than the process of healing, which promotes spiritual growth, right relationships, and doing God's work on earth?

Field Supervisor God, please send me someone who can help me do life well. I wholeheartedly desire to live a purposeful life for your glory, and I'm ready to make healing my top priority, but . . . (Okay, God, you know full well that a "but" negates everything I've just said, so it might be best to send an angel who knows how to handle hesitant cases like me!)

Finding P.U.R.P.O.S.E. through Recovery Steps
The P.U.R.P.O.S.E. Plan
Principle V: Opt Out of Self-Sabotage

"LORD, help!" they cried in their trouble, and he saved them from their distress. He led them from the darkness and deepest gloom; he snapped their chains.
PSALM 107:13-14

Cry out when you're in distress, "Lord, help!" Or for extra emphasis, pray as Hezekiah prayed when he was at death's door, "I am in trouble, Lord. Help me!" (Isaiah 38:14). Let God hear your cries, especially when you desperately want to opt out of self-sabotaging methods that are blocking his will for your recovery and your life mission. You'll definitely need his wisdom and strength to give up your most stubborn saboteur habits, the ones you've deliberately cultivated over the years to crush your own success. How accustomed have you grown to the spell cast by those subversive habits, which excuse you from the heavy-duty responsibility of living a sober, purpose-filled life?

Self-sabotage should be labeled "Everyone's Disease" because everyone uses it, at times, to get themselves off their hamster wheel of shame, guilt, and debilitating fear about not being able to deliver what's expected of them. It's so much easier to convince themselves (and, if all goes well, to convince others!) that they're justifiably not able to complete a task or uphold an agreement. After all, they're exhausted from their job (made worse by an addiction to late-night television); they're not the smartest person for a ministry task (exaggerated by the deadly comparison game they play); they're sick with a stomachache (aggravated by binge eating and purging); or they can't seem to find the application form (intensified by hoarding).

Any one of us, finding ourselves in a similar situation, can cry out with the disciples in the boat, who woke up Jesus, shouting, "Lord, save us!" (Matthew 8:25). And we can cry out with the woman who came and worshiped Jesus, pleading with him to cure her demon-possessed daughter, "Lord, help me!" (Matthew 15:25). We can trust that when we cry for help, help will arrive.

SOUL SEARCH

What causes you to sabotage God's best for your life? What helps you stop the insanity of self-sabotage?

All-sufficient God, I don't want to throw any more monkey wrenches into your glorious plans for my life. Don't let me destroy what you've envisioned for me.

Finding P.U.R.P.O.S.E. through Recovery Steps
The P.U.R.P.O.S.E. Plan
Principle VI: Surrender All to Christ My King

Everything comes from him and exists by his power and is intended for his glory. All glory to him forever! Amen.   ROMANS 11:36

The world can't compute God's extravagant generosity and enormous wisdom; his kind heart and omniscience are simply unfathomable. Need we wonder why he doesn't rely on our fabulous, amazing suggestions to rule the world? When our eyes are opened to his impressive résumé, we fall to our knees, surrendering and exclaiming, "Everything comes from him; Everything happens through him; Everything ends up in him. Always glory! Always praise! Yes. Yes. Yes" (Romans 11:36, *The Message*). Until then, God waits patiently for us to run out of other options. Some addicts have to hit rock bottom, but others are able to get with the program sooner.

Eventually you'll find yourself at a crossroads, needing to decide whether you'll surrender your entire life to God or not. This choice includes surrendering all people, places, things, and issues—including family and friendships, obsessions and compulsions, possessions and personal power, and life dreams and goals. With the perspective that you're merely a custodian, steward, and guardian of your life comes the realization that you're not God-Creator-Ruler. It's then, and only then, that you become ready to begin a lifelong journey of surrendering your past, present, and future to God, which he'll recycle for the good of all. You can also begin to grasp the value of surrendering your comfort zone, assured outcomes, blame rituals, immediate gratification, temptations, and anxiety, as well as your joy and accomplishments, to the one who watches over you. If you empty yourself now of any pride to which you've been clinging, it'll help you surrender to become all you can become for God, so you can do all he intends for you to do on earth.

SOUL SEARCH

What have you already surrendered to the Lord? How will surrendering all areas of your life impact your recovery and God-inspired assignment?

You who set your glory above the heavens, I pray now for a fresh outlook regarding your rule over my life. I pray for an eye-opening surrender experience, which will help me lean into my sobriety and your calling on my life.

Finding P.U.R.P.O.S.E. through Recovery Steps
The P.U.R.P.O.S.E. Plan
Principle VII: Experience Heart-Pounding Purpose

To live in the center of God's heart-pounding will for your life, refuse to dwell on your addictive past and impossible present. Let go of your worries, self-doubt, and excuses. Hold fast to the promise that God has a triumphant future planned for you as a healthy, passionate, purpose-filled person. Trust him with childlike wonderment.

☀ Meditate on the Assurance of God's Word

Did I not proclaim my purposes for you long ago?   ISAIAH 44:8

I cry out to God Most High, to God who will fulfill his purpose for me.   PSALM 57:2

Our purpose is to please God.   1 THESSALONIANS 2:4

☀ Humbly Talk with the Lord

Sit with God, telling him of your renewed commitment to accept his full-blown plan for your life. Mention, too, that you need his patience during times of brain fog.

Ask the Lord to lead you to people, places, events, and thought processes that will clarify his hard-to-believe, yet oh-so-true, purpose for you.

☀ Take the *Life Purpose Coach* Challenge

Sit where you can feel the Holy Spirit washing over you like a soft-splashing waterfall or a gentle-rustling breeze. Breathe deeply and savor this time of serene living. Offer to God's Spirit anything that's been robbing you of this type of peacefulness, whether that's a drug of choice, immorality, busyness, jealousy, anxiety, or the fear of never knowing the heart-warming purpose for which you were born. Once you name the peace-robber(s), claim the gift of the "Serenity Prayer," written by theologian Reinhold Niebuhr and adapted for use in Twelve Step groups:

> *God grant me the serenity to accept the things I cannot change,*
> *Courage to change the things I can,*
> *And wisdom to know the difference.*

P.U.R.P.O.S.E. Principle I:
Put God First

My primary purpose is to worship God with my life.

P.U.R.P.O.S.E. Principle I: **P**ut God First

Born to Love God

Jesus replied, "'You must love the LORD your God with all your heart, all your soul, and all your mind.' This is the first and greatest commandment."
MATTHEW 22:37-38

Faithfully working your recovery program has undoubtedly caused you to ask yourself, *What on earth am I here for?* Jesus pointedly answers your question in the book of Matthew, explaining your greatest purpose with no holds barred: "You must love the LORD your God with all your heart, all your soul, and all your mind." There's no getting around it: we were created to love God. All other purposes, activities, and desires in our lives are meant to pale in comparison. Sure, you might have some healthy, exhilarating hobbies and a vibrant ministry about which you exclaim, "I was born for this!"—but nothing is to rival your love for God, especially not some addiction, which is basically an idol. Consider the remarkable wisdom that's summarized in this Portuguese proverb: "To love God is the greatest of virtues; to be loved by God is the greatest of blessings."

As you move forward to explore God's love and his agenda for your life, know that few things can stir a deep, cherished love for him like understanding that he first loved you (see 1 John 4:19) and that you're the apple of his eye (see Psalm 17:8, NIV). Once you experience these truths, your reality changes from heartbroken, lost, abandoned, frantic, fractured, alienated, abused, and alone—to beloved, cherished, and friend of God (see James 2:23). Reciprocating his love is the reason you're on earth.

SOUL SEARCH

What one small step could you take now that would help you love God more passionately—with all your heart, soul, and mind? How will this effort cause you to celebrate your sobriety and live out the unique plan God meant for you to live?

God above all gods, thank you for first loving me, for keeping me as the apple of your eye, and for calling me your friend. Even though I'm struggling to learn how to love you above everything else, don't give up on me. Permeate my life with your love and teach me to reciprocate.

P.U.R.P.O.S.E. Principle I: Put God First

God Claims Me

I would not forget you! See, I have written your name on the palms of my hands.
ISAIAH 49:15-16

God wrote Jerusalem's name on the palms of his hands to proclaim to its people that he would never forget its descendants. May this passage serve as a reminder to you that God tenderly watches out for you, too, claiming you as his own. The inscription of your name on God's hands is a public pronouncement that he's ever mindful of you, that he's concerned with your safety and will protect you. It means that no evil force or ineffectual god can claim you; it means you have God's power available to you at all times because he cares deeply about every detail of your life—and especially about restoring you to wholeness and sobriety. This gesture is his physical display of affection and affirmation that says, "Be comforted in knowing that you are mine no matter what the circumstances of your life."

I was comforted when my orthopedic surgeon wrote his initials in blue ink at the base of my thumb prior to "trigger thumb" surgery. I'd been told about the "Sign Your Site" protocol that prevents a surgeon from performing a wrong site surgery. Apparently, there's a 25 percent chance a surgeon will cut into a wrong site during a typical thirty-five-year career. So I was thrilled to know that my doctor was watching out for me and marking the correct problem area before cutting into my hand. How much more reassuring and calming is it when God claims us for his own by marking our names on his hands?

SOUL SEARCH

What does God's claim on your life mean to you? Is it worth giving up the things that entangle you—grip you—so you can take joy in fulfilling his call on your life?

God who holds me close, thank you for choosing me and writing my name on the palms of your hands. Out of gratitude, I want to spend the rest of my life loving you with all I've got.

P.U.R.P.O.S.E. Principle I: **P**ut God First

My King

The LORD is a great God, a great King above all gods.   PSALM 95:3

In 2011, my thirty-two-year-old son, Andy, was hailed as royalty by his officemates after he ran a fifty-mile race through dozens of streams, hundreds of mud holes, and four deep snowbanks. He said that the insane part was a steep drop of four thousand feet within a four-mile stretch. His wife, sons, and I had a blast cheering for him that day, but once he was back to work, his friends actually bowed as he walked past. My kid might have been a big kahuna for a day or two, but our God is King forever and everywhere!

Are you tired of bowing to the strong-armed god of addiction who has enslaved you, abused you, and ridiculed you? Then turn to the God who is a great King above all other gods. The Hebrew word for "king" is *melek*, a title the Bible often uses for God. God wants you to know him as Yahweh-Melek, as God our King—the one who saves his people from their enemies (see Zephaniah 3:15). He wants to save *you* from *your* enemies, like alcohol, pornography, gambling, overeating, or [name your poison]. Because we live in a fallen world that's full of temptations and pain, we need to be reminded of our merciful King's power to free us from a paralyzed life. As we ready our minds for sobriety, we can do so with expectant faith because the King of the universe has the authority, strategy, and desire to help us.

SOUL SEARCH

In what way has Yahweh-Melek watched over you, helping you navigate the tough terrain of your life, such as compulsions or obsessions? How does this memory give you full confidence and much-needed peace that your King is watching over your recovery and his unique, intriguing plan for your life?

O King of all, allow me to get another glimpse of your unparalleled power and majesty. Remove all my desires to bow to any other gods who try to rule over my life. Save me from all my addictive ways, so I will move forward doing your will.

The Lord Who Heals

If you will listen carefully to the voice of the LORD your God and do what is right in his sight, obeying his commands and keeping all his decrees, then I will not make you suffer any of the diseases I sent on the Egyptians; for I am the LORD who heals you.
EXODUS 15:26

After my daughter, Stephanie, was born in 1982, I sank into a postnatal depression for months. During that time I could barely function, but I was blessed to have a loving husband and family members who helped care for our newborn, her two-year-old brother, and me. I remember praying often for the Lord to get me through the next minute as I watched the second hand on the clock slog forward. At one point I thought of ending the anguish, but I couldn't bear the idea of saddling my two babies with that lifelong burden. Finally I had a daydream about being rolled into a hospital emergency room where God met me with utmost kindness. He sat with me, summoned angels to minister to me, and asked me to trust him. At that moment I knew that I was going to pull through, that I was being healed because of God's good pleasure, and that I still had work to do on earth.

In our Exodus passage, God was talking to the Israelites on their way to the Promised Land. He described himself as Yahweh-Rophe, "the Lord who heals." He's not only our cure for depression, he's also our source of restoration to wholeness in every aspect of our lives. Ask him to heal the ugly wounds and unmanageable parts of your life so you can be wholly engaged in his Kingdom-building purposes.

SOUL SEARCH

In what way has Yahweh Rophe healed your addictive tendencies? What healing still needs to happen to make you more fully able to carry out God's incredible plan for your life?

My Lord who heals, you've made me brand new in so many ways already. I humbly ask you to continue to heal me from my depression, hard heart, fears, control issues, and self-destructive ways.

P.U.R.P.O.S.E. Principle I: Put God First

God Is My Refuge

God is our refuge and strength, always ready to help in times of trouble. So we will not fear when earthquakes come and the mountains crumble into the sea.   PSALM 46:1-2

God, our Refuge—our *Machseh*—wants us to run to him for safety and strength in every circumstance and terror of our lives, including self-inflicted pain and uncontrollable dependencies. He's our shield, our strong tower, our dwelling place, and our fortress during all the earthquakes we face, whatever form they may take.

I distinctly remember calling on God as my personal refuge and strength on February 27, 2010, after an 8.8 earthquake struck Chile, causing waves to race across the Pacific Ocean and threaten Hawaii, where I was living on a one-year writing assignment. Outdoor sirens began to blast, awakening me at six in the morning and warning everyone of a tsunami evacuation. Newscasters reported—and mainland friends texted—that there might be a series of eight-foot waves that would travel up to six hundred miles per hour on any given surge. As the governor declared a state of emergency, helicopters hovered overhead with their loudpeakers blaring instructions to residents. I was soon evacuated to my pastor's home, on higher ground, and prayed for God to keep us safe. As the much-feared waves began dissipating before reaching us, a state of calm was restored to the Islands, and the warning was officially lifted at 1:38 p.m.

In our daily tsunami-type lives, we must realize that *Machseh* is the one who would love to awaken us from our states of unconsciousness—our addictive stupors—and keep us safe and strong in his restorative plans. Listen for his life-saving call, reminding you that he's the only one who can dissipate your fears and move you to the higher ground of completing your work on earth.

SOUL SEARCH

In what ways have you given lip service to the fact that you trust God to help you escape the horrors of your negative behavior, codependence, and emotional triggers—without really allowing him to be your first choice as a refuge or fortress? What's your new-and-improved plan for truly connecting with the Lord?

My Refuge, my safe place, my hideaway—protect me in the stronghold of your love; keep me secure and strong in you; let me run to you for safety from all my deep, scary, unresolved issues.

P.U.R.P.O.S.E. Principle I: **P**ut God First

The Lord Who Bursts Through

They named that place Baal-perazim (which means "the Lord who bursts through").
1 CHRONICLES 14:11

The book of 1 Chronicles is chock-full of drama, much like the drama that rages in the dangerous battles you face daily. Whether you fight the demons of domestic violence, immorality, insecurity, or substance abuse, God can burst through the situation to help you, just as he did when King David fought against the Philistines. What's amazing is how simple the process was for David: he asked God to weigh in about a situation; God answered; David obeyed; and the battle was won. You can read it in 1 Chronicles 14:10-11:

David asked God, "Should I go out to fight the Philistines? Will you hand them over to me?" The LORD replied, "Yes, go ahead. I will hand them over to you." So David and his troops went up to Baal-perazim and defeated the Philistines there.

In light of that expedient process, I'm not sure why we don't ask God more "Should I . . . ?" questions about our next steps. If we did, then, like David, we could exclaim, "God did it! . . . He used me to burst through my enemies like a raging flood!" (v. 11).

Read verses 13-17 for another "bursting through" story that begins with David asking God what to do—and ends with "and the LORD caused all the nations to fear David." Let the passage cause you to recall when you've experienced God bursting forth to rescue you from dysfunction, conceit, shame, regrets, and harm. Then allow that recollection to give you confidence that the Lord is on your side and ready to declare you victorious.

SOUL SEARCH

Have you learned to seek God's advice in all you do, or are you still "winging it" as the commander of your own army? If you really believed that God would burst through to lead you down the path to recovery and into a life of integrity and purpose, what action step would you take now?

My Lord who bursts through, rescue me from my inner turmoil, deadly ways, and enemies. Teach me to ask you questions that begin with, "Should I . . . ?"

P.U.R.P.O.S.E. Principle I: **P**ut God First
Choosing God

Be amazed at who God is. Seek him, worship him, choose him, and study his character and his ways. Ask him to take away the confusion and desperation you feel. Invite him into the destruction and frustrations of your life, and ask him to be your cure and your hope for the future.

☀ Meditate on the Assurance of God's Word

Abraham named the place Yahweh-Yireh (which means "the LORD will provide"). To this day, people still use that name as a proverb: "On the mountain of the LORD it will be provided."   GENESIS 22:14

The LORD will be king over all the earth. On that day there will be one LORD—his name alone will be worshiped.   ZECHARIAH 14:9

The LORD is my rock, my fortress, and my savior; my God is my rock, in whom I find protection. He is my shield, the power that saves me, and my place of safety.
PSALM 18:2

☀ Humbly Talk with the Lord

Praise God, your Quieting Love, for sitting with you today and always (from Zephaniah 3:17).

Thank God for his provision, protection, grace, and wisdom in one or more particular situations you've faced on your recovery journey.

☀ Take the *Life Purpose Coach* Challenge

In your dark hours, when the weight of your sadness seems too heavy to bear, choose one name of God from the last seven days or a different one, such as Abba, Protector, Hope, or Comfort. For twenty-four hours, focus on that name, calling out to God to fill your greatest need in that area and to point you toward a life of healing and incredible purpose.

P.U.R.P.O.S.E. Principle I: **P**ut God First

Knowing Jesus

This is what God has testified: He has given us eternal life, and this life is in his Son. Whoever has the Son has life; whoever does not have God's Son does not have life.
1 JOHN 5:11-12

We engage in life and death choices every day. Some toy with death more often than others through substance abuse, bodily harm, or dangerous adrenaline rushes. But God testifies in 1 John that we're not to toy with the opportunity he's given us to choose eternal life or everlasting death. He emphasizes that accepting his Son results in life but rejecting Jesus results in death.

C. S. Lewis, prolific author and former agnostic, wrote in the book *Mere Christianity*:

A man who was merely a man and said the sort of things Jesus said would not be a great moral teacher. He would either be a lunatic—on a level with the man who says he is a poached egg—or else he would be the Devil of Hell. You must make your choice. Either this man was, and is, the Son of God: or else a madman or something worse. You can shut Him up for a fool, you can spit at Him and kill Him as a demon; or you can fall at His feet and call Him Lord and God. But let us not come with any patronising nonsense about His being a great human teacher. He has not left that open to us. He did not intend to.

You may have mouthed the words "Jesus is my Lord," but now it's time to take seriously the high value God places on having an intimate relationship with his Son, who can heal you.

SOUL SEARCH

In what way have your actions treated Jesus as a lunatic or liar? How do you feel about spending the rest of your life calling Jesus *Lord* and letting your sobriety verify that?

Life-saving Son of God, Jesus Christ, turn my eyes from all the shoddy gods I've fashioned by my own hands that are destroying me. Lead me straight to you and your power, victory, and sacred purpose for my life.

Jesus Is the Vine

[Jesus said,] "I am the true grapevine."   JOHN 15:1

The night before Jesus died, he told his disciples that he is the Vine, the Sustainer of life who provides nourishment to the branches (that's us), so we can live and produce fruit. He also said, "If you remain in me and my words remain in you, you may ask for anything you want, and it will be granted! When you produce much fruit, you are my true disciples" (John 15:7-8). So let's do a quick review of what we know so far:

- Jesus, the Vine, sustains you, the branch. (He gives you life and makes you holy.)
- He nourishes you for the purpose of producing fruit. (He has a plan for your life.)
- If you stay connected to him, you have his ear for all your requests. (Yahoo to that!)
- True disciples produce much fruit. (Those who love him can't do enough for him!)

Are you seeing a pattern here of a benevolent Life Giver and a faithful servant who is rewarded? Do you see the importance of maintaining an honest view of whether you are producing fruit or are dead on the vine?

Today's metaphor about Jesus as the Vine used to be just words on a page to me, until he showed me a picture of what I would look like as a fruitless, dead branch: I was a nameless, battered, heroin-addicted dealer-prostitute lying dead in a filthy gutter. At that moment, I understood the truth of that "Abide in Me" pictorial, because I know the decay, deceit, and despair that anyone, including me, is vulnerable to without Jesus. I know the sin, selfishness, and stubbornness within us that will kill us unless he sustains us.

SOUL SEARCH

In your wildest imagination, what fruit might you bear long-term connected to the sustaining Vine? What stance against relapse could this daydreaming inspire you to take?

Jesus, the Vine, apart from you I can do nothing. Your Word promises that if I stay connected to you, I may ask for anything, and it will be granted! What I want most of all is to remain in you so I can bear the fruit of whatever significant work pleases you.

P.U.R.P.O.S.E. Principle I: **P**ut God First

Christ Lives in Me

My old self has been crucified with Christ. It is no longer I who live, but Christ lives in me. GALATIANS 2:20

I wonder if the Christian hymn "Saint Patrick's Breastplate" was inspired by our Galatians passage. Both share the supernatural concept that Christ lives in us. You can judge for yourself, using this popular version of the original Old Irish lyrics that have been traditionally attributed to Saint Patrick:

> *Christ with me, Christ before me, Christ behind me,*
> *Christ in me, Christ beneath me, Christ above me,*
> *Christ on my right, Christ on my left,*
> *Christ when I lie down, Christ when I sit down, Christ when I arise,*
> *Christ in the heart of every man who thinks of me,*
> *Christ in the mouth of everyone who speaks of me,*
> *Christ in every eye that sees me,*
> *Christ in every ear that hears me.*

Whether Patrick wrote those words or not, he certainly experienced spiritual victory over a hellacious past that could have driven any young person away from Christ and straight to the bottle or other numbing potion. As a teenager living in Britain, he was captured by Irish raiders and taken as a slave to Ireland. Historians tell us that he worked as a herdsman for six years, growing in his faith, before escaping to reunite with his family. Later, he returned to Ireland as a missionary and is now recognized as the country's patron saint. Who responds like that? I might have been consumed with plotting revenge. And don't play innocent yourself! But do take some time to think through your ideal response to all that has plagued you so, like Saint Patrick, you exude Christlikeness.

SOUL SEARCH

When have you felt Christ by your side, comforting and restoring you or washing over you through the love of others? In what way does your life reflect that Christ lives in you and that you're ready to answer his call on your life?

My sweet Jesus, I know how you love to hear Scripture prayed back to you, so I offer you what we label as Galatians 2:20. And, I pray, too, the related words of our hymn.

P.U.R.P.O.S.E. Principle I: **P**ut God First

An Invitation to a New Life

I am counting on the LORD; yes, I am counting on him.   PSALM 130:5

The Lord invites us to leave our addictive lifestyle and be ushered into a brand-new life of healthy relationships, wise choices, renewed joy, and promises to claim. Once we accept the fact that he's our only hope and that we can actually count on him, we're guided into newness beyond imagination.

One Super Bowl Sunday afternoon, I felt as if I had been escorted into a brand-new world as I shopped in a Chinese supermarket. I was enjoying the showmanship and antics of fish cutters when a clerk invited me to sample a snack of pork rinds (salty chunks of pork belly that he called *siu yuk*). I stared at the young man as if he were trying to poison me. Finally he said something like, "Pigskin cracklings are popular for Super Bowl snackin'!" How could I not have known that? How far out of the hog-fat, pig-hide culinary loop was I? Apparently Spaniards, Brits, Filipinos, Cajuns, and New Yorkers have all been known to tout their crispy-skin-aholic tendencies! What an entirely new perspective for me.

And why not entertain a fresh perspective, especially regarding new ideas the Lord calls to mind during your Scripture meditation time, while you're working the Twelve Steps for Believers or on your P.U.R.P.O.S.E. Plan? Instead, we often ignore or even bolt from the new life God offers us, rationalizing that our old-life patterns are comfortable and familiar. It's likely that we've grown accustomed to the blame game, low expectations, rigidity, attention received from well-meaning rescuers, and nightmares. What freedom we can savor, though, when the Lord invites us to feast on a fresh perspective that's found only in him!

SOUL SEARCH

What familiar, old-life patterns have made you unwilling to taste the new life of sobriety and purpose that God has offered you? What step can you take now to savor freedom (e.g., phone a friend for encouragment or use a lifeline from your recovery group)?

Holy One, I'm counting on you to stop me from relishing my old, bad habits. I choose you and the brand-new life you've offered me, which is spiced with adventure and significance.

P.U.R.P.O.S.E. Principle I: **P**ut God First

The Way, the Truth, and the Life

Jesus told [Thomas], "I am the way, the truth, and the life. No one can come to the Father except through me." JOHN 14:6

Jesus is the only way, the only truth, and the only life that makes sense. He's the answer to our sin and our ticket into heaven, he's all the wisdom we need to stay sober, and he's our victory over death. Erasmus, a Dutch theologian, summed up the concept nicely when he prayed for grace to follow Christ as the Way, to learn from him as the Truth, and to live in him as the Life.

Oddly enough, I pretend that I'm leaning on Jesus, the Way, and following him down a pathway, while doing my Achilles' tendon stretching exercises. That may sound corny, but when you've got plantar fasciitis—that dreaded pain of a strained ligament in your arch—you need to stretch often each day, and those exercise breaks make ideal one-minute prayer times. While praying, my mind might flash to the worst plantar sting of my life, when I was on a long run with my gym girlfriends in the middle of nowhere. The arch tenderness came on so abruptly that I had to pack mud on the underside of my foot inside my sock, and my friends helped me limp to where I could get a ride home.

Whatever your pain might be—physical abuse, emotional bombshells, mental horrors, financial ruin, religious lies, or something unspeakable—Jesus wants to give you a ride home. You only need to say yes to his offer. He will repair your brokenness and use your pain to teach you better solutions than limping along.

SOUL SEARCH

When have you leaned on Jesus and followed him down the pathway to purpose, which he paved for you? What has specifically happened when you've gone off in your own direction, limping along, unable to heal yourself?

Jesus, the Way, the Truth, and the Life, give me clear direction and set me on a path to live a recovered life that's dedicated to you and your phenomenal plans for me.

P.U.R.P.O.S.E. Principle I: **P**ut God First

Jesus Is the Best Gift

What are mere mortals that you are mindful of them, human beings that you care for them?   HEBREWS 2:6 (TNIV)

Our passage tells us that God is mindful of us mere mortals and cares deeply for us. Have you ever thought about how we humans typically thank him, whose unmerited favor saves us daily from loneliness, futility, excuses, numbness, addictive behaviors, and defeat? We offer substandard thank-you gifts to him, don't we—ridiculous gifts of guilt-ridden tithes, halfhearted praise, and impurely motivated obedience? The only gift God wants from us is that we develop an intimate relationship with his Son, Jesus.

The problem of lackadaisical gift giving versus heartfelt offerings struck home for me recently when my pastor asked his congregants not to give his family any more gift cards. I felt like he was talking directly to me as he said in a kind voice, "My wife and I forget about them just long enough for them to expire. Instead, please invite us over for a meal, offer to babysit our children, or bake us chocolate chip cookies!" I had become one of those people who gave gift cards because they were convenient timesavers, even if they weren't what my friends really wanted.

We need to give our God the only gift he wants—for us to know his Son. Don't be surprised, though, when kindhearted God manages to reverse the blessing of your gift back to you!

SOUL SEARCH

What gifts of convenience have you tried to give God to thank him for being mindful of you on your recovery journey, instead of giving him the gift he really wants? What could you do now to thank God for continuing to free you from a life of hell on earth and for assigning remarkable purpose to your life?

Lover of my soul, I'm overwhelmed that you're mindful of me and care for me, a mere mortal. I want to spend the rest of my life thanking you by deepening my relationship with your Son. Teach me how to give you and myself that one-of-a-kind best gift!

P.U.R.P.O.S.E. Principle I: Put God First
A Relationship with Jesus

Nothing will impact your recovery and life's work as profoundly as a loving relationship with Jesus Christ.

☀ Meditate on the Assurance of God's Word

A hired hand will run when he sees a wolf coming. He will abandon the sheep because they don't belong to him and he isn't their shepherd. And so the wolf attacks them and scatters the flock. The hired hand runs away because he's working only for the money and doesn't really care about the sheep. I am the good shepherd; I know my own sheep, and they know me, just as my Father knows me and I know the Father. So I sacrifice my life for the sheep. JOHN 10:12-15

God loved the world so much that he gave his one and only Son, so that everyone who believes in him will not perish but have eternal life. JOHN 3:16

☀ Humbly Talk with the Lord

Invite Jesus to sit with you, as friends do at a coffee shop, so you can pour out your heart to him and hear his voice about decisions you're facing.

Thank Jesus for all the times he's saved you from the downward pull of addiction and showered you with love, renewed faith, and purpose.

☀ Take the *Life Purpose Coach* Challenge

I refused to have a relationship with Jesus Christ for a long time because I was so mad at God for hurting his Son. Today, I know that the truth is this: Jesus chose to suffer and die for us because of his incomprehensible love for us. Talk to someone about any mistaken beliefs you have that are stalling your recovery and life contribution.

P.U.R.P.O.S.E. Principle I: **P**ut God First

God's Beloved

You'll be a stunning crown in the palm of GOD's hand, a jeweled gold cup held high in the hand of your God.   ISAIAH 62:3 (*The Message*)

In God's eyes you are a stunning crown and a jeweled gold cup that he delights in showing off to others. Hold tight to that thought, no matter how low your self-esteem may drop after poor choices about food, liquor, or other life-numbing agents. He treasures you more than a precious gift, an heirloom, or a hard-earned asset that anyone would guard from being tarnished or stolen. He sees human beings as the best part of his creation: "We, out of all creation, became his prized possession" (James 1:18).

When my kids were young, they often whined for more of my above-the-call-of-duty, quality time. Judge me if you must, but if I was particularly exhausted from mothering, I'd respond calmly with, "You've pushed me beyond what I'm willing to give right now." No matter what shenanigans they'd pull to get me to change my mind, I'd keep to my resolve, until they realized the futility of their begging. But God is nothing like me. Psalm 121:3 informs us that he gladly stays up all day and all night so his beloved children can have 24/7 access to him. It says, "The one who watches over you will not slumber." No wonder we sing the old hymn "Your Ceaseless, Unexhausted Love," written by Ken Bible and Charles Wesley.

In fact, God's already proven that he'd do anything for us, including giving us this world to enjoy, giving us life-everlasting through his Son, and sending his Holy Spirit to guide us. Isaiah 62:4 reads, "No more will anyone call you Rejected, and your country will no more be called Ruined" (*The Message*). God wants you to understand that he adores you and that nobody can reject you or ruin you in his eyes—not on his watch: not yesterday, not now, not ever. Make no mistake about it: you're his beloved in whom he delights!

SOUL SEARCH

What step could you take to thank God for delighting in you? How could that step help heal you and engage you in the mission he established for you?

The One who watches over me, I'm continually flabbergasted at how much you love me and how available you are to me. Teach me to show my gratitude daily.

P.U.R.P.O.S.E. Principle I: **P**ut God First

God's Child

To all who believed him and accepted him, he gave the right to become children of God. JOHN 1:12

You may find it hard to believe John's words about your being a child of God; after all, you may have been labeled a lot of things, including a struggling believer who's an addict. If you doubt that our passage could apply to you, perhaps Paul's words in Ephesians 1:5 will convince you that God was thrilled to adopt you, even before he made the world: "God decided in advance to adopt us into his own family by bringing us to himself through Jesus Christ. This is what he wanted to do, and it gave him great pleasure."

My father-in-law adopted me into the Brazelton family in 1974 when I married his son, Gary. To this day, I love Pop for that. But he had a rather nonfatherly, yet funny, truism that he'd toss out after he'd botched a home improvement project at our place: "Oh, well, I can't see it from my house!" After all, if the plumbing he'd fixed, the concrete he'd poured, or the patio cover he'd built wasn't up to par, it wasn't really his problem once he was back in his own home in the next county. It was our problem.

Our heavenly Father has a different attitude: our problems are his problems, no matter how much hassle the restoration entails. His unconditional, paternal love includes his willingness to do a complete renovation of our mental, physical, spiritual, and emotional state, regardless of how much in disrepair our lives are and how long the rebuilding might take.

SOUL SEARCH

In what way have you acted like a loving child of the Most High God, bringing him great pleasure? What needs to happen now to make that behavior more consistent?

Abba Father, you know that I often feel like I'm the least worthy of all your children. I don't want to ask that you give me what I deserve, as that would be nothing. Instead, I ask that you give me the world by healing me from the fog of my compulsions and obsessions so I can use all my faculties, best attributes, and spiritual gifts to accomplish your far-reaching goals on earth.

P.U.R.P.O.S.E. Principle I: Put God First
God's Masterpiece

We are God's masterpiece. He has created us anew in Christ Jesus, so we can do the good things he planned for us long ago.   EPHESIANS 2:10

Even though our messy addictions often cause us to feel less than adequate, Paul tells us in Ephesians that we're God's masterpiece, his magnum opus, his great work of art. He says that we're made brand new by our life-changing relationship with Christ, in order that we might do the good things he calendared long ago for us to do. That word *masterpiece* is from the Greek word *poiema*, which gave us the English word *poem*. We're God's incredible poem, his work of genius that he personally crafted with great care and purpose. Even the psalmist David has his choir director sing about God's exceptional handiwork in creating us: "Thank you for making me so wonderfully complex! Your workmanship is marvelous—how well I know it" (Psalm 139:14).

You may want to offer a rebuttal right now that you don't feel like a divine masterpiece. You may worry that you've been a devious, conniving, manipulative, self-centered, lying trickster, much like the young, unruly Jacob in Genesis. If so, think about the fact that God loved Jacob so much in spite of his flaws that God continued to work with him to the point of submission. Like Jacob, hang on tight to God and cry out in faith-filled prayer, "Bless me!" (see Genesis 32:22-32), until you're assured of God's promise to rescue you from your self-imposed difficulties and the cruel opposition that others devise against his plan for you. After all, God sees you as his exquisite, amazing artwork, and his view of you is accurate. Expect him to bless you.

SOUL SEARCH

Because you are God's masterpiece, in what way could you acknowledge him as your magnificent Creator? What do you hope he created you to be and do for him?

Sweet Creator, it simply doesn't compute that you'd think of me, a recovering addict and habitual sinner, as your inspired masterpiece. But because you've created me in the image of Christ Jesus, I'm determined to take you at your word and do the good things you planned for me to do long ago.

A Victor

Every child of God defeats this evil world, and we achieve this victory through our faith.
1 JOHN 5:4

God decided that his children, who declare their faith in his Son, would be victorious over evil in this world. In his generosity, he even promised that we could be freed of the wickedness we ourselves initiate through our deliberate blindness, paranoid behavior, and delusions of power. Although we can't escape the struggle of being human and the pull of our lower nature and inherent weaknesses, we've already been declared victors in Christ! As we claim and reclaim that victory, moment by moment, every day for the rest of our lives, we defeat the world. We conquer its malevolent ways and our vicious cycle of acting out. John expands the idea of how this is possible: "The conquering power that brings the world to its knees is our faith. The person who wins out over the world's ways is simply the one who believes Jesus is the Son of God" (1 John 5:4-5, *The Message*).

Or as Paul wrote in one of my favorite verses, "In all these things we are more than conquerors through him who loved us" (Romans 8:37, NIV). This means that through the blood of the Lamb, our Lord Jesus Christ, we're able to overthrow our adversary, who's a smart, determined enemy. And although we must never forget how good Satan is at his career job, we must believe that we're overcomers who not only fight the good fight but also win with the help of the Lord.

My client Angie, who's a recovering controller, shared with me what helps her overcome: "I remind myself repeatedly that the victory has already been won in Christ. And I pray for humility and calmness, so I can hear the Holy Spirit's wise counsel."

SOUL SEARCH

What example do you like to share with others about how your faith has made you victorious, restored your dignity, renewed your joy, and guided you into God's plan for your life? What supernatural victory is next for you?

Conquering Jesus, you have filled my emptiness, removed my humiliation, and put me in reach emotionally with others. I'm more than a conqueror in you, my Higher Power.

P.U.R.P.O.S.E. Principle I: **P**ut God First

A New Creation

Anyone who believes in Christ is a new creation. The old is gone! The new has come!
2 CORINTHIANS 5:17 (NIrv)

How can we possibly comprehend that we're given new identities when we choose Christ, especially when we feel that our self-gratifying behaviors have made us such colossal disappointments to God? We may be able to grasp, somewhat, that Christ died to take away our sins, but living a resurrected life . . . well, that can seem downright ludicrous. And yet our passage declares that the old, wild creature in us really has gone and the new, fresh creation really has come. Indeed, we may live in an earthly body with all its fleshly desires, but when we trust in the Son of God, who loved us and gave himself for us, he guarantees us that our previous immoral and unspiritual condition has died and that we're made new in him.

Colossians 3:9-10 clarifies our role in the process this way: "You have stripped off your old sinful nature and all its wicked deeds. Put on your new nature, and be renewed as you learn to know your Creator and become like him." That tells us we must choose each moment to be renewed in Christ. In fact, God intends for us to realize that we have no life outside Christ. William Gadsby, a Baptist pastor and hymn writer in the 1800s, explains, "It pleases the Father that all fullness should be in Christ; therefore there is nothing but emptiness anywhere else." And Charles Hodge, a Presbyterian theologian, also of the 1800s, says it this way: "To be in Christ is the source of the Christian's life; to be like Christ is the sum of his excellence; to be with Christ is the fullness of his joy."

SOUL SEARCH

If you truly believed that you were no longer living your old, stagnant life, but that Christ reigns supreme in the new you, what behavioral difference would you notice? How would you describe your transformation to a struggling addict?

Resurrection and Life, stir in me a lasting desire to let you shine through the sober me. Raise me up to complete the meaningful work you have for me to do during my short time on earth.

P.U.R.P.O.S.E. Principle I: **P**ut God First

Christ's Friend

I no longer call you slaves, because a master doesn't confide in his slaves. Now you are my friends, since I have told you everything the Father told me. JOHN 15:15

Jesus loves us as his friends, even though we're often defiant souls who prefer addictive idols to him. When he prophesied about his death on the cross, he told us how much he loves us: "There is no greater love than to lay down one's life for one's friends" (John 15:13). In return, he asks us to show our love for him by obeying his commands. Yet what do we often do? We leave him and choose to follow destructive gods!

On April Fools' Day 1985, my husband, Gary, who was my best friend and the love of my life, unexpectedly announced that he was leaving our twelve-year marriage. I knew he was a jokester, but this soon proved to be no prank. As I threatened to lie down behind the car to block his departure, he pleaded with me to let him go, saying, "I've gotta live before I have another heart attack!" (He'd had an attack and triple bypass surgery five years prior on April Fools' Day, when he was thirty-four years old, and his cardiac surgeon had warned him then that he'd probably have to have another surgery within five years.) I was decimated by his announcement, departure, and soon-to-be-apparent infidelity, especially when his girlfriend asked our young children to call her "Mom." Within months, I dropped forty pounds; my counselor said that grief was eating me from the inside out.

The only reason I survived was that Jesus became my best friend, one who was willing to sit with me for hours, pray with me, and enlist angels on earth to help care for me. (See "Challenge" on February 5 for how to invite Jesus to be your best friend.)

SOUL SEARCH

How has Jesus' loving friendship seen you through your darkest hours of loneliness, fear, anxiety, physical pain, divorce, addiction, or withdrawal? In what way has Jesus been asking you, his friend, to obey his long-standing call on your life?

Dearest Forever-Friend, I respect you, but help me love and obey you, even to the point of laying down my life for you. I want to be willing to reciprocate your generous love, as a true friend would do.

P.U.R.P.O.S.E. Principle I: **P**ut God First
Who I Am

You are God's beloved, his child, his masterpiece, a victor, a new creation, and Christ's friend.

☀ Meditate on the Assurance of God's Word

In Christ the fullness of God lives in a human body, and you are complete through your union with Christ. He is the Lord over every ruler and authority in the universe.
COLOSSIANS 2:9-10

Thank God! He gives us victory over sin and death through our Lord Jesus Christ.
1 CORINTHIANS 15:57

This is the secret: Christ lives in you. This gives you assurance of sharing his glory.
COLOSSIANS 1:27

☀ Humbly Talk with the Lord

Ask God to open your eyes as to how he sees you so you can carry out his wishes for your life whenever, wherever, and however he'd like.

Invite Jesus to help you with your most pressing addiction issues that are causing you to disobey him.

☀ Take the *Life Purpose Coach* Challenge

In the devotional for February 4, in regard to my broken marriage I said, "The only reason I survived was that Jesus became my best friend." My friendship with Jesus deepened immeasurably as I read the book of Philippians, which taught me that he loves me in good times and in bad, in sickness and in health. I wrote out key passages (for example, chapter 1:6, 10, 21; chapter 2:3, 5, 10, 13; chapter 3:8, 12-14; and chapter 4:4, 6, 8, 13, 19) and read them often each day for one year. I challenge you to capture a dozen of your favorite Scriptures and to reflect on them frequently as you promise to cherish Jesus' love all the days of your life.

P.U.R.P.O.S.E. Principle I: **P**ut God First

Becoming Like Christ

They drank from the spiritual rock that traveled with them, and that rock was Christ.
1 CORINTHIANS 10:4

The Israelites drank from God's fountain, which was Christ, but they sure didn't act as if they were Christ-filled much of the time. We know that their temptations defeated them regularly during hard times in the desert. It's the same with us. We have Christ living in us, but we're defeated constantly by temptation, especially in our area of primary addiction. We could blame Adam and Eve for ruining the human condition so hugely. After all, their original sin in the Garden of Eden certainly destined us to a nasty fall that won't ever be completely rectified this side of heaven. When we feel worthless, for example, we overcompensate by becoming critical of others; when we ache for control over some aspect of our lives, we err on the side of impatience and perfectionism. These types of failure cause us to avoid Christ and tear ourselves down as colossal losers.

The truth is that, as children of God, we were created to resemble Christ. We're actually "hidden with Christ in God" (Colossians 3:3), meaning our spirits are forever safe and secure in a heavenly place, and the evil one can't destroy us. Living daily in this reality encourages us to resist temptation, rather than caving in pessimistically at the first sign of a devilish attack. We begin to develop a right view of self, understanding that human beings are imperfect but that God is patient with us, and that compassion must begin at home—with ourselves! We stop comparing ourselves to others, and we begin to live in gratitude, remembering that God has a regal plan for our lives. We lean into the joy that Thomas Merton (a Trappist monk who took the name Father Louis when he was ordained as a priest) described: "Be good, keep your feet dry, your eyes open, your heart at peace and your soul in the joy of Christ."

SOUL SEARCH

In what way are you becoming more like Christ? How has that pivotal work impacted your recovery and moved you toward the acts of service God chose for you to do?

Image of the invisible God, I thirst for you. Fill me with more of you, so I may resemble you more.

P.U.R.P.O.S.E. Principle I: **P**ut God First

Humility and Patience

Let me teach you, because I am humble and gentle at heart, and you will find rest for your souls.   MATTHEW 11:29

Has anyone, like your sponsor or a support group member, forewarned you of possible unpleasant repercussions of praying for humility and patience? I'm living proof of what tough lessons you can face when you utter those dangerous surrender prayers.

After I'd been a single mother of two young children for several years, I got laid off from my job. So in 1988, I started a housecleaning business to help support us and pay down my graduate school loans. As I finished cleaning each client's home, I put a flower in a kitchen vase and mints on the bedroom pillows, doing my best to present the WOW! factor of my hard work. But one day, I lost all enthusiasm during the drudgery of scrubbing an endless marble floor on my hands and knees in a rich family's home.

I looked up to heaven and shook my fist at God—raging at him: "You know how hard I've prayed for humility and patience. Is this how you decide to teach me those character lessons? How dare you? Well, is this humble enough for you, God—with me cleaning floors and toilets until I'm exhausted and my back is broken? How much longer do I need to wait patiently for you to provide enough money for me to make ends meet? I'm a decent, God-fearing woman who needs rest for her soul, so why are you treating me like this? And why did you insist that I get a stupid PhD? A lot of good that's doing me now!" I broke down in tears after my outburst, realizing that I was still filled with pride that criticized God's ways and with impatience that questioned his timing. My sordid sin of self-focus on I-me-my and "I want it now" was still haunting me. When would I learn?

SOUL SEARCH

In what way will focusing more on God and less on yourself further your recovery? Are you ready to let God inhabit more of your vision now, so you can get on with fully living out his benevolent goals for you?

Humble and gentle Christ, rid me of self-absorption so I might learn to renounce pride, resist impatience, and find rest for my soul in you.

P.U.R.P.O.S.E. Principle I: **P**ut God First

Boasting and False Humility

He must become greater and greater, and I must become less and less.   JOHN 3:30

John says that Christ is to become greater, and we're to become less. We often fight that logic, refusing to let God take a center-stage bow for all he's done for us. We get puffed up with pride, and we boast about our sober living or our ministry and mission.

One of the most eye-opening Bible stories about pride is Obadiah's account of the Edomites who looted what the people of Judah left behind when taken into Babylonian captivity. God said that the Edomites' pride had deceived them into thinking that they were so great, like the king of the mountain whom nobody could touch! God promised that he'd bring them crashing down from the stars to the earth—until they were weak and despised and their world collapsed. He was angry at the godless nation and certainly didn't mince words when he specifically reprimanded them for their obnoxious boasting about their evil actions: "You should not have gloated when they exiled your relatives to distant lands. You should not have rejoiced when the people of Judah suffered such misfortune" (Obadiah 1:12).

How does this type of ugly arrogance and gloating overtake people, including us? And just as important, how do we also fall into the trap of false humility, putting ourselves down (acting lowly about our accomplishments, gifts, or talents), in hopes of stirring up praise from someone or appearing spiritual to God or others? This "innocent-sounding," yet sneaky, disgusting sin deflects glory away from God to us. It's pride in disguise, used to impress someone, whereas genuine humility impresses others about God!

The reason we're overtaken by prideful ugliness and fall into these traps is that we forget the guiding principle that we're to celebrate God's greatness in all we do.

SOUL SEARCH

How much damage could boasting and false humility do to your recovery progress? What could such pride do to your future life endeavors that are intended for such incredible good?

Overseer of my soul, give me more opportunities to tell others how beautiful you are and how eternally grateful I am that you love me.

44

P.U.R.P.O.S.E. Principle I: **P**ut God First

Being Patient

Be strengthened with all his glorious power so you will have all the endurance and patience you need. COLOSSIANS 1:11

God will strengthen us with his glorious power so we can have patient endurance. Why then do we so often run out of patience and misplace our endurance when life gets in the way? In fact, what's a fairly patient and persistent person like my friend Fred, a 362-day-sober addict, to do when life won't let up? We join Fred at 10 a.m. on a Thursday, his day off work. As he prepares to throw in a load of his own laundry, he discovers that his son has not moved his washed clothes to the dryer or emptied the lint trap on the dryer. Discarding the lint reminds Fred that Friday is trash pickup day, but that his wife won't get home from her conference before dark to take her turn at moving the household bins to the curb. That's when he remembers the lawn needs to be mowed so the clippings can be hauled off too. When Fred tries to start the lawnmower, he realizes that his daughter forgot to get gas for it. As he jumps in the car to go get some gas, he notices that someone has left the car door ajar all night, and now the battery is dead. He begins to worry about getting to his midday recovery meeting on time. Life has interrupted his best intentions.

Fred's only wise plan for not becoming totally overwhelmed is to stop and pray for God to strengthen him pronto with his glorious power, including a sizable outpouring of patience and endurance. (He also needs a friend to give him a ride to his meeting and for his sponsor to prompt him to schedule a family discussion to rethink chores!)

SOUL SEARCH

What do you typically do when a "Fred day" gets in your way? How could you upgrade your reaction by choosing to stop and pray for God's glorious power?

My Strengthener, I ask you to grow my patient endurance so I won't get overwhelmed on my recovery journey. Strengthen me also for my life's work, which will be loaded with distractions, delays, debates, decoys, and dead ends.

P.U.R.P.O.S.E. Principle I: **P**ut God First

Patience with Self and Others

Be patient with each other, making allowance for each other's faults because of your love.
EPHESIANS 4:2

Let's start with the following reminder from Francis de Sales, an early bishop of Geneva, to be patient with ourselves, before we discuss being über-patient with the rest of the world! He wrote, "Have patience with all things, but chiefly have patience with yourself. Do not lose courage in considering your own imperfections, but instantly set about remedying them—every day begin the task anew." Although being impatient with ourselves is core to human nature, those in recovery are often also inordinately harsh with themselves. If we factor in low self-esteem, a feeling of powerlessness over circumstances, and mistaken beliefs like performance-based faith, we've got a volcano ready to erupt with impatience toward self. This sad conundrum of why we treat ourselves so poorly, so impatiently, can be addressed only by developing a right view of self. (See January 30 through February 5.)

How, though, do we develop a right view of others so we can exercise patience with them despite their annoying faults, poor choices, and non-saintlike conduct? My dad sure had a great way of explaining this concept to me in 1986, when I was giving him an earful about how evil my husband's girlfriend was for setting her sights on my man after her third divorce. After listening to me rant and assign 90 percent of the blame to her, my father shared this wisdom: "God loves her just as much as he loves you. We're all sinners, and God can never love us more or less than he does right now." I was stunned, but I did understand what he was saying about God's view of her. It now all boiled down to my praying for serenity (for a calming, untroubled peacefulness) to accept the things I could not change, rather than continuing to ramrod my way impatiently to a solution of my choosing.

SOUL SEARCH

In what circumstance are you most often patient with others? How can you develop more patience with yourself regarding your recovery steps and broader, life-purpose action steps?

God who searches hearts and minds, help me accept human imperfection in others and myself. I want more patience, but may I add . . . I sure need it now!

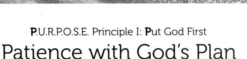

P.U.R.P.O.S.E. Principle I: **P**ut God First

Patience with God's Plan

Be still in the presence of the LORD, and wait patiently for him to act.   PSALM 37:7

Margaret Thatcher, who was nicknamed the "Iron Lady" as the first female British prime minister, must have been reading my mind when she said, "I am extraordinarily patient, provided I get my own way in the end." That's quite the opposite of our psalm, which commands us to be still before the Lord and wait patiently for him to act according to his own wisdom and timeline. Sometimes we must wait patiently for a spouse, as Ruth did for Boaz (see Ruth 3). Other times, we wait for a child to be born, as Rachel did (see Genesis 30:22); we wait to be absolved of blame, as Joseph did after an unjust rape charge (see Genesis 39–41); or we wait for healing, as Naaman did from leprosy (see 2 Kings 5). Sometimes we even wait for God's vision for our life to launch, as Paul did for years until people stopped fearing him (see Galatians 1:18). And how long have some waited for recovery from manipulation, drama, money abuse, nicotine, aggression, or sedatives?

What do you do if you've been taught to make your dreams happen, but you find yourself in God's purpose-filled waiting room? Consider these four options: (1) Remember that God's in charge of making his dreams for your life happen, not you! (2) Remain hopeful and connected. Despair and isolation could trigger a reaction to use and abuse, causing you to lose the sobriety ground you've gained. (3) Ask God to speak to you, directing your next steps, and (4) realize that he's preparing you for your journey by inviting you to rest up, build your character, and surrender your life to him. Regardless of his timing, he'll see you through with loving care.

SOUL SEARCH

When have you felt impatient about your recovery or about God's roughly outlined plan, annoyed that one or the other wasn't happening in the time frame you desired or perhaps even demanded?

Restorer of my soul, you know I've lost hope while waiting for you to work behind the scenes for my brighter future. Turn my thoughts to you and to your wise, perfect timing.

P.U.R.P.O.S.E. Principle I: **P**ut God First
Resembling Christ

Choose now to resemble Christ, especially as a humble and patient person, in the most challenging areas of your relationships, sobriety, and purpose-driven mission.

☀ Meditate on the Assurance of God's Word

The high and lofty one who lives in eternity, the Holy One, says this: "I live in the high and holy place with those whose spirits are contrite and humble. I restore the crushed spirit of the humble and revive the courage of those with repentant hearts." ISAIAH 57:15

I, John, am your brother and your partner in suffering and in God's Kingdom and in the patient endurance to which Jesus calls us. REVELATION 1:9

Scrub away my guilt, soak out my sins in your laundry. PSALM 51:2 (*The Message*)

☀ Humbly Talk with the Lord

Tell Jesus that you're now ready to learn whatever lesson you need for living humbly, without adding, "except for these lessons, Lord!"

Ask God to teach you to be patient with life, with yourself, with others, and with the unveiling of his plan. Mention several specific areas in which you most need patience.

☀ Take the *Life Purpose Coach* Challenge

Expect life lessons in humility and patience. Look for them on an overbooked flight, during a job layoff, in understaffed restaurants, at recovery meetings, or at home with odd family dynamics! In a journal, record a one-sentence description and the date of each lesson, along with what you did or didn't learn from it. After one month, note how many times you had to relearn a particular lesson. After the shock wears off, invite the Holy Spirit to crush any obstinate pride and impatience as you begin yet again to become more self-aware.

P.U.R.P.O.S.E. Principle I: **P**ut God First

Made Perfect by the Holy Spirit

How foolish can you be? After starting your Christian lives in the Spirit, why are you now trying to become perfect by your own human effort? GALATIANS 3:3

It always amazes me when I hear someone claim to be a perfectionist as if that's a good thing. The Holy Spirit indwells us when we become Christians, which makes it foolish for us to set about doing his work of perfecting us in Christ. Perfectionism can too easily become a sin of pride or legalism—especially if someone is attempting to earn a spot in heaven by doing everything ultraperfectly (including their recovery program!). Instead, we're to cooperate with the Spirit, who will perfect us in Jesus. Galatians 3:5 reads, "I ask you again, does God give you the Holy Spirit and work miracles among you because you obey the law? Of course not! It is because you believe the message you heard about Christ." Our spiritual growth and sobriety can happen only when we allow God's Spirit to do what we can't do ourselves.

Sadhu Sunder Singh, a missionary in the early 1900s, used a stirring analogy to describe the role of the Holy Spirit in our lives. He explained that those who live on the heights communing with God experience the Holy Spirit as a cascading river, going before them to cut a natural flowing course down the mountainside. But "those who devote little time to prayer and communion with God have to organize painfully," like canal diggers on flat plains who try to get water to flow. It appears that life is much easier when we let the Holy Spirit cause our destiny to flow right along of his own accord, rather than relying on our own painstaking work in life's trenches to get (poor) results.

SOUL SEARCH

In what way have you worked strenuously to become perfect and stay sober—and failed miserably? When have you relied on the Holy Spirit for a character makeover?

Spirit of the living God, I try to become more like Christ, but on my own I fail. How refreshing, instead, to live on the heights with you, allowing you to make your way of your own accord through my life, my recovery, and my destiny.

P.U.R.P.O.S.E. Principle I: **P**ut God First

Filled with the Spirit

Don't act thoughtlessly, but understand what the Lord wants you to do. Don't be drunk with wine, because that will ruin your life. Instead, be filled with the Holy Spirit.
EPHESIANS 5:17-18

Paul definitely hits both ends of the "Don't" and "Do" spectrum in our passage: don't act thoughtlessly or get drunk with wine, but do understand the Lord's will and be filled with the Holy Spirit. What a tall order he gives to the church in Ephesus and also to us. He wants everyone to be strengthened with power through the Spirit, putting on the new self, the new garment; he wants us to imitate God's love and walk wisely in a world of darkness. But what exactly does he mean in verse 18 about being filled with the Spirit, not wine?

We know the Holy Spirit came to live in us when we became children of God, so the command to "be filled" is not a prompting toward a secondary indwelling. Rather, Paul means that we're to clear out any debris from our inner lives that's hindering the powerful flow of God's Spirit through us. We don't want our spiritual pipes to become clogged with the encrustation of an intoxicated lifestyle. The word *intoxicated* actually stems from a Latin word meaning "poison," so Paul is cautioning us against poisoning ourselves with drunkenness.

What fills you controls you! So ask yourself what fills, influences, or dominates you. Is it darkness or light? Is it something outside yourself or the Spirit of God inside you? If you are controlled from the outside, confess it, so you can get on with your healing and the work God gave you to do on earth.

SOUL SEARCH

In what way do you think you typically interrupt the flow of the Spirit? What words would best describe trying to pursue God's goals for your life without the guidance of the Holy Spirit?

Most Holy Spirit, empty me of my inner debris and fill me, like a reservoir, with yourself.

P.U.R.P.O.S.E. Principle I: **P**ut God First

The Holy Spirit Prays

The Holy Spirit helps us in our weakness.   ROMANS 8:26

When we don't understand that we need the power of the Holy Spirit to make any beneficial changes in our lives, we get stuck in our addiction-related weaknesses, distractions, turmoil, and consequences. A prominent Christian evangelist, Rod Parsley, explains the Spirit's power in a creative manner: "The baptism of the Holy Ghost will do for you what a phone booth did for Clark Kent—it will change you into a different human being."

But how is this possible, to be granted such superhuman power to change? The apostle Paul explains that it's because we can rely supernaturally on the Spirit, who's right alongside us, even when we don't know how or what to pray: "He does our praying in and for us, making prayer out of our wordless sighs, our aching groans. He knows us far better than we know ourselves" (Romans 8:26-27, *The Message*). The precious Holy Spirit keeps us present before God, pleading for us believers in harmony with God's own will. He makes sure that every detail of our lives is worked into God's plan, including our recovery.

I was reminded about this concept of calling for help from a higher source when I was trying to activate my new Internet mobile device. The technician in a nearby retail store helped me for an hour to no avail. Finally, he made a phone call to corporate headquarters to get some guidance, only to be informed that the company was experiencing a nationwide Internet outage. That local technician had no way of successfully completing my service request until corporate restored power. We all need power from on high for whatever ails us!

SOUL SEARCH

If you could ask the Holy Spirit to intercede for you in one aspect of your sobriety, what would you request? Will you ask the Spirit for that favor now?

Holy Spirit of God, I don't deserve your kind attention, but I do want to live in harmony with God's will, both in this season of life and in my future, long-term assignment. Thank you for ushering me into those blessings.

P.U.R.P.O.S.E. Principle I: **P**ut God First

The Holy Spirit Is Clear

And I will ask the Father, and he will give you another Advocate, who will never leave you. He is the Holy Spirit, who leads into all truth.   JOHN 14:16-17

Jesus promised us that his Father would send his Holy Spirit to abide in us. This forever Advocate speaks truth into our lives, recommends particular "policies" for living a godly life, and pleads on our behalf. Other translations refer to the Spirit as our Comforter, Encourager, Counselor, Friend, Paraclete, Helper, Intercessor, Strengthener, and Standby, who helps us tackle any situation, even our worst addiction nightmares.

But notice that our passage begins with the word "and" in verse 16. Because that's a conjunction—a connector word—it signals us to look back at verse 15, which reads: "If you love me, obey my commandments." The position of these sentences tells us that (1) Jesus is expecting us to do our part by loving and obeying him, and (2) he will intercede on our behalf to ensure us his Spirit's help!

This Spirit of truth offers us clarity about our life direction and sobriety. Without his clear instructions, you might feel the way I did when I tried to put together a desk using its confusing assembly booklet. By the time I got to page 6 of 16, my eyes were crossed. It read: "Fasten the DESK TOP (G2) to the SMALL UPRIGHT (E2) and SMALL BACK (K2). Use two BLACK 1-15/16" FLAT HEAD SCREWS (LL). Turn Hidden Cams 210 degrees, not 180 degrees." I then guffawed at the incomprehensible French that stared at me from the next column, "Fixer le DESSUS DE BUREAU (G2). . . ."

I'm grateful that the Holy Spirit's guidance is nothing like my desk-building fiasco. Living with his wisdom actually makes our lives easier, especially when our Counselor-Strengthener helps us avoid sin: "So I say, let the Holy Spirit guide your lives. Then you won't be doing what your sinful nature craves" (Galatians 5:16). And less sinning will leave more room for doing the Lord's specific will.

SOUL SEARCH

When has a personal advocate in your life helped you? What do you like most and least about the clarity of truth?

My Advocate, I ask you to call truth into every situation of my life, especially into my recovery efforts. I need your step-by-step directions for building the future you've designed for me to enjoy.

P.U.R.P.O.S.E. Principle I: **P**ut God First

Bound by the Spirit

[Paul declared,] "Now I am bound by the Spirit to go to Jerusalem. I don't know what awaits me, except that the Holy Spirit tells me in city after city that jail and suffering lie ahead." ACTS 20:22-23

Oftentimes in our slow and rocky recovery, we don't act like Paul, who was bound to obey the Holy Spirit to the extreme of being jailed and suffering for the Lord. Instead, we act of our own volition with self-induced repercussions that are senseless, costly, and demoralizing. The apostle John is another great role model for us about the importance of staying in tune with the Holy Spirit. For example, when he was exiled to the island of Patmos for his outspoken religious beliefs, he worshiped one day in the Spirit and suddenly heard a loud voice like a trumpet blast. It said, "Write in a book everything you see, and send it to the seven churches" (Revelation 1:11). In obedience, John wrote the book of Revelation.

Many years ago, on an adventure with my teenage daughter and her friend in my car, I agreed to be bound by their one simple driving rule: to make only right-hand turns unless safety prohibited it. That odd agreement created a fun outing; we laughed ourselves silly as we got into one crazy predicament after another. The only problem was that we ended up at a dead end in a secluded area high up in the hills. One unclothed backside showed itself in the distance before we saw the "Private Property: Nudist Colony" sign and were able to make a sharp left turn out of there! Likewise, the rebellious journey of addiction may seem fun and harmless at first, somewhat like an adventure with odd predicaments. However, eventually we end up at a dead end and must find the quickest, safest route home, which is possible only by being bound by the Holy Spirit.

SOUL SEARCH

To whom, to what, or where do you feel bound (i.e., the Holy Spirit or, perhaps, "escorts," pills, the refrigerator, laziness, pouting, pornography, casinos, or liquor stores)? How has your attraction affected your life?

Spirit of counsel and of power, I'm sick of dead ends. I want to stay bound to you and not to a minigod. Lead me straight into God's incomparably generous plan for my life.

P.U.R.P.O.S.E. Principle I: **P**ut God First

Fruit of the Spirit

The Holy Spirit produces this kind of fruit in our lives: love, joy, peace, patience, kindness, goodness, faithfulness, gentleness, and self-control.   GALATIANS 5:22-23

Every waking minute of every day, we must choose between our deadly, sinful natures (including character defects, wrongdoings, the tendency to be a holy terror, and the wretched habit of enabling) versus the life-giving Spirit (who produces love, joy, peace, patience, kindness, goodness, faithfulness, gentleness, and self-control). Romans 8:6 confirms that we have a choice: "Letting your sinful nature control your mind leads to death. But letting the Spirit control your mind leads to life and peace."

But how do we let the Holy Spirit control our minds and our recovery choices? According to Jesus, it happens through consistent prayer (see Luke 11:5-13). In one of his best illustrations ever, Jesus creates a hypothetical situation to drive home his point: you ask your friend at midnight if you can borrow three loaves of bread because some late-night, unexpected company has shown up and your cupboards are bare. Even if your friend tells you to go away, eventually your shameless persistence will convince him to give you whatever you need. So Jesus is encouraging us to keep on prayerfully asking, seeking, and knocking on doors until we receive what we need (see Luke 11:5-8). He reminds us that even a sinful, earthly father knows how to give good gifts to his children. Then he says, "How much more will your heavenly Father give the Holy Spirit to those who ask him?" (Luke 11:13).

That's how we get all we need from the Holy Spirit: we simply ask God to give us the good gift of the Spirit of wisdom, understanding, counsel, might, knowledge, and reverential, obedient fear of the Lord (see Isaiah 11:2).

SOUL SEARCH

How has the Spirit's wise counsel helped you in the past? In what way could the good gift of the Holy Spirit help you now to stay sober and live out the legacy God has reserved for you?

Sweet Lord, hear my prayer: May "the grace of God the Father and the peace of our Lord Jesus Christ, through the fellowship of the Holy Spirit, dwell with us forever."*

---

* A prayer of John Calvin, a sixteenth-century Christian reformer.

P.U.R.P.O.S.E. Principle I: **P**ut God First
Listening to the Holy Spirit

Ask the Holy Spirit to reveal the truth of God's Word to you about your recovery issues.

☀ Meditate on the Assurance of God's Word

My Spirit remains among you, just as I promised when you came out of Egypt. So do not be afraid.   HAGGAI 2:5

Do not stifle the Holy Spirit.   1 THESSALONIANS 5:19

Do not bring sorrow to God's Holy Spirit by the way you live. Remember, he has identified you as his own, guaranteeing that you will be saved on the day of redemption.   EPHESIANS 4:30

I will send the Holy Spirit, just as my Father promised. But stay here in the city until the Holy Spirit comes and fills you with power from heaven.   LUKE 24:49

☀ Humbly Talk with the Lord

Thank God for his willingness to send the Spirit of truth to you (from John 15:26).

Praise God for the times you've chosen to live in tune with the life-giving Spirit, who has freed you from the power of sin and rescued you from death (from Romans 8:2).

☀ Take the *Life Purpose Coach* Challenge

Read Isaiah 30:1: "'What sorrow awaits my rebellious children,' says the LORD. 'You make plans that are contrary to mine. You make alliances not directed by my Spirit, thus piling up your sins.'" Then write a brief description of a plan you crafted or an alliance you made that was in sync with the instructions of the Holy Spirit. If you feel led to take a new action step about any plan or alliance, jot down your thoughts and share them with a sponsor, recovery coach, or trusted friend for input.

P.U.R.P.O.S.E. Principle II:
Understand Biblical Truths about God's Will

I understand my recovery in the bigger picture of how God is redeeming the world.

God's Plan

You can make many plans, but the LORD's purpose will prevail.   PROVERBS 19:21

Many Christians make megaplans based on their desire for happiness, safety, security, prosperity, spiritual growth, and significance. Their dreams may include getting a good education, finding a well-paying job they're passionate about, becoming physically fit, getting married, raising kind children and grandchildren, finding a Christ-honoring church where they can worship and serve, having a few close friends, going on a mission trip, enlarging their faith, and being available to their aging parents. If done in a godly manner with obsessions and compulsions turned over to the Lord, any one of these outcomes would create a richly significant life, one that is fruitful and blessed.

But the Bible is clear that the Lord's purposes for our lives will prevail, regardless of our own poor, good, great, or extraordinary plans. God assigns each of us seasonal roles and specific Kingdom-building work. Prayerfully consider what it would mean to follow his lead, doing so free from abuses in such areas as food, power, sex, or credit-card spending. Focus on the truth, privilege, and responsibility of having a unique, broad-reaching life purpose—one that is exclusive to you. Consider this claim from author Stephen Travis: "Noah was the first of many individuals who, apparently single-handed, have been used by God to carry out his purpose and to make a crucial difference in the world. . . . Even today people famous and unknown are making a difference in the world simply by trying to obey God. . . . They have refused to be bullied into believing that what they do makes no difference."

Yes, the Lord's plans triumphed for Noah, for countless others in Bible times, and for an untold number of other faithful servants since then—and the Lord's plan will triumph for you, too.

SOUL SEARCH

Who on your recovery journey has bullied you into believing that you will never make a difference in this world? How soothing is it to know that God's purpose will prevail in your life?

Kind Lord, you whose purpose is always right, noble, and victorious, make me mindful of the precise nature of your plans for me—that is, as much as I'm able to handle right now. More important, be my purpose; be the reason for my next breath.

P.U.R.P.O.S.E. Principle II: **U**nderstand Biblical Truths about God's Will

Eight Phases of God's Plan

We keep on praying for you, asking our God to enable you to live a life worthy of his call. May he give you the power to accomplish all the good things your faith prompts you to do.   2 THESSALONIANS 1:11

Our passage tells us that God has a calling on our lives—a specific plan for them. Things like false memories, victim mentality, lust, and refusal to make amends can slow the process way down, but you can anticipate eight phases of how God's plan unfolds: Calling, Hoping, Doubting, Believing, Doing, Waiting, Surrendering, and Birthing.

Calling: God calls you—maybe in a dramatic "Road to Damascus" way, as he did Saul (see Acts 9:1-31), or by giving you a vague impression that becomes a passionate ache in your soul. (See November 14 about sneak previews.)

Hoping: You feel hopeful and whisper a prayer accepting the assignment, wanting to believe that you've actually heard from God.

Doubting: Being human and plagued by confusion, questions, and delays, you begin to doubt God's call.

Believing: You come to know what you know, beyond a shadow of a doubt.

Doing: You begin countless action steps, thinking that your launch is imminent.

Waiting: You endure a severe test of waiting in the wilderness, a time that would test the patience of any saint! (See September 20–22 about reasons for the wait.)

Surrendering: You have a deep, confident expectation in God's miraculous power, and you commit to doing whatever it takes, however long it takes. You surrender all to Christ your King. (See Principle VI, starting on September 25, about surrender.)

Birthing: You walk into the "Promised Land" and receive the precious gifting of God's promises to you—or God has you pass the baton and receive something better.

We don't want to get ahead of God, but we do want to keep up with him by cooperating every step of the way to live a life worthy of his call.

SOUL SEARCH

Where are you on your journey through the eight phases? What character-building step would you like to take to support your recovery efforts and heavenly calling?

God of hope, I pray that you will enable me to live a life worthy of your call, helping me to cast aside all character defects that hinder my progress.

P.U.R.P.O.S.E. Principle II: **U**nderstand Biblical Truths about God's Will
Before I Was Formed

I knew you before I formed you in your mother's womb. Before you were born I set you apart and appointed you as my prophet to the nations. JEREMIAH 1:5

The popular 2010 movie *Eat, Pray, Love* attracted lots of attention for its universal theme: namely, that the purpose of life is a search for personal happiness. I'm sorry to disappoint, but life has so much more to offer us than happiness, which can be circumstantial, selfish, and fleeting. Although anyone, including addicts, would be thrilled to have a reasonably happy day, happiness can't be the central quest of our lives. Eric Hoffer, a non-Christian, American social writer, even commented, "The search for happiness is one of the chief sources of unhappiness."

God doesn't sit around heaven planning out how to make us happy and comfortable on earth, but he is committed to giving us great joy: the joy of knowing him and of completing the appointed tasks for which we were set apart before we were born.

I was thrilled when the main character in *Eat, Pray, Love* did learn some of the bedrock recovery principles for breakthrough living: forgive yourself, stop the guilt, quiet your fears, feel the pain until it passes, balance your life, and marvel at something. Personally, I love to marvel at the fact that, even though we may not have been foreordained to the office of prophet, as Jeremiah was, God *did* set us apart and appoint us (before we were born) to speak forth God's Word to whomever he called us to serve. He did create us to deliver our passionate life message to a certain group of people!

Also marvelous and incomprehensible is that he did this, knowing us as the stubborn, prideful, impatient, consistent sinners we are. So here's to eating, praying, and loving—I'm all for that—with the end goal being joy in the Lord and in his unique purpose for us.

SOUL SEARCH

Is it your wish to be happy or to know the God who formed you and appointed you to a specific task? In what way is your wish impacting your recovery process?

My Encouragement, I want nothing more than to know you, as deeply as you have known me before you formed me in my mother's womb and set me apart. Cleanse me of all my shortcomings so I may better serve as your appointed messenger to others.

P.U.R.P.O.S.E. Principle II: **U**nderstand Biblical Truths about God's Will

The Lord's Plans for Me

"I know the plans I have for you," says the LORD. *"They are plans for good and not for disaster, to give you a future and a hope."* JEREMIAH 29:11

It was Jeremiah's job to explain God's hope-filled plans to the Israelites when they couldn't see past their hard times in Babylonian captivity. He had to tell them that they'd be held captive for seventy years, after which God would do all the good things he'd promised. You may identify with the Israelites, feeling like your disastrous life, family secrets, and destructive cycles will hold you captive forever. Instead, share this hope the Lord gave to the Israelites:

"'In those days when you pray, I will listen. If you look for me wholeheartedly, you will find me. I will be found by you,' says the LORD. 'I will end your captivity and restore your fortunes. I will gather you out of the nations where I sent you and will bring you home again to your own land'" (Jeremiah 29:12-14).

I wonder what Jeremiah might have said in a tweet to the Israelites, using only 140 characters to explain God's entire message: U will b in Babylon 70yrs. Then God has gr8 future plans 4 u. Have hope. PRAY + he'll listen. Look for him + u will find him. $ + home later

That fun exercise made me think about Jack Dorsey, the American software architect who created Twitter in 2006, correctly predicting that Twitterholics would be addicted to news flashes in a short-message format. How much more important is it, however, that God created us, correctly predicting our future? Before time began, he foresaw our desire to emerge victorious over our pasts and dedicate our lives to his service. Now that's a news flash that's more than Twitter-worthy.

SOUL SEARCH

What tweet would describe how you're holding on tight to your own plans, pain, and escape hatches? What about how you're letting the Lord's purpose unfold in your life?

Eternal King, because of who you are and the power you wield, I'm excited to let you take my life in any direction, as you see fit. I trust you!

P.U.R.P.O.S.E. Principle II: **U**nderstand Biblical Truths about God's Will

My Legacy

Because we are united with Christ, we have received an inheritance from God, for he chose us in advance, and he makes everything work out according to his plan.
EPHESIANS 1:11

The inheritance that Ephesians talks about is Jesus—a legacy left to us in God's "will" and passed down to us and future generations of his descendants. We're abundantly blessed! We've hit the jackpot of fortune, the mother lode of riches. God has no greater gift to give than Jesus. Claiming our inheritance encourages us to keep on keeping on in our recovery efforts because we know that God will make everything work out according to his gracious plan for us as members of his family, whom he chose in advance.

Nichole Nordeman, a Christian singer-songwriter and a nine-time Dove Award winner, is inspirational when she sings "Legacy." It's a song about doing something eternally significant and loving with our lives by pointing people to our birthright, our Lord Jesus Christ:

I want to leave a legacy
How will they remember me?
Did I choose to love?
Did I point to You enough
  to make a mark on things?

I want to leave an offering—
A child of mercy and grace who
  blessed your name unapologetically
And leave that kind of legacy.

I can't sing, but I sure wish I could, because with my dying breath, I'd belt out that powerful message! Instead I must be content with whatever I can endow to the next generation about my inheritance, Jesus, based on the spiritual gifts and talents the Lord has bequeathed to me. God chose us and expects us to pass on the legacy of Jesus. What an honor for us and a saving grace for those we introduce to the Savior of the world.

SOUL SEARCH

What legacy are you leaving that points people to Jesus? How will your understanding that you were left an inheritance impact your day-to-day sobriety and your bold life purpose?

My Yahweh, I want to leave a legacy, an offering. I want to be a child of mercy and grace who blesses your name unapologetically. Help me to do so, starting with an immediate breakthrough from all that burdens me.

P.**U**.R.P.O.S.E. Principle II: **U**nderstand Biblical Truths about God's Will

My Life Verse

I have fought the good fight, I have finished the race, and I have remained faithful. And now the prize awaits me—the crown of righteousness, which the Lord, the righteous Judge, will give me on the day of his return. 2 TIMOTHY 4:7-8

Second Timothy 4 talks about fighting the good fight, finishing the race, remaining faithful, and winning the prize of a crown. But none of that's possible if you run the race in the wrong direction! Try this advice for a straight shot at victory: ask the Holy Spirit to reveal to you a Scripture verse—a life verse—that solidly confirms the direction and route God has mapped out for your life. This passage will not only become a motto for your God-designed, personal recovery plan but it will also assure you that you're not running toward the wrong unique life purpose. When all your plans are rooted in God's Word, as revealed to you by the power of the Holy Spirit, you'll emerge victorious!

My life verse, for example, is Isaiah 61:3, which is about helping people grow into all God created them to be: "They will be called oaks of righteousness, a planting of the LORD for the display of his splendor" (NIV).

Although it's impossible to know whether your life verse or your life mission will be revealed first, each will complement the other perfectly and be a focal point for your recovery testimony. To discover a verse that fits the theme of your life, begin with a prayer of expectation and stay tuned to God's Word.

SOUL SEARCH

What Scripture comes to mind as a possible life verse? Once the Holy Spirit reveals the perfect verse for you, will you memorize it, share it with your sponsor or support group, and reflect on it often to help you stay focused on the prize?

Spirit of Truth, I expectantly await the tandem confirmation that my life verse will give to my life mission—and that my life mission will give to my life verse. I also look forward to how the Scripture will illumine my recovery story.

P.U.R.P.O.S.E. Principle II: **U**nderstand Biblical Truths about God's Will

Cooperating with God's Plan

God's good plan trumps every evil plan of Satan's—every time. We'd be foolish, therefore, to try to rewrite God's trustworthy script for our lives. Decide now to follow
God's lead; ask him to cure your dangerous, deliberate blindness and help you learn to
cooperate with him one day at a time.

☀ Meditate on the Assurance of God's Word

*We must quickly carry out the tasks assigned us by the one who sent us. The night is
coming, and then no one can work.*   JOHN 9:4

God will make this happen, for he who calls you is faithful.   1 THESSALONIANS 5:24

*My dear brothers and sisters, be strong and immovable. Always work enthusiastically
for the Lord, for you know that nothing you do for the Lord is ever useless.*
1 CORINTHIANS 15:58

☀ Humbly Talk with the Lord

Be honest with God about your hesitancy to cooperate with him. Confess your tendency
to hang on to the hang-ups that guarantee you drama, sympathy, or a free ride.

Go to God for wisdom about your next steps toward sobriety. Ask him to share with
you in vivid detail his ideal scenario of a blessed recovery.

☀ Take the *Life Purpose Coach* Challenge

Get comfortable in your favorite easy chair or beach chair or on a long bicycle ride—and
daydream about what God might have in mind for your magnificent future. Let yourself dare to imagine what a major, lifetime dream would look like for you—as the new
and improved healed you—if that dream were dedicated to God's Kingdom-building
purposes. Trust the Giver of Big Dreams, who is ever faithful to deliver.

Two Universal Purposes

Christ died and rose again for this very purpose—to be Lord both of the living and of the dead.   ROMANS 14:9

Christ's distinct purpose in being crucified on the cross and rising from the dead was to be Savior and Lord of all. As he lived out this unique calling on his life during three years in his public ministry on earth, he actually modeled for us two universal purposes that all believers are to adopt: (1) like Christ, we're to give God all the glory for how he uses us; and (2) like Christ, we're to be holy (see March 1–4).

Traveling that road to God's glorification and our holiness can be a terribly bumpy ride for those barely clinging to sobriety. We know we're guilty sinners, especially in light of God's majesty. Frankly, we're not even worthy to join the seraphim in their praise of him who is all-powerful, let alone to do his work on earth. Yet God lovingly assists us to fit perfectly into our role of accentuating Christ's purpose on the wooden cross.

It's actually our job to cooperate with God and his plan to redeem the world as he raises each of us out of our own graveyard of hopelessness, and it's our joy to tell others how humbly grateful we are that he loves us and has offered us resurrected lives as his sanctified people.

SOUL SEARCH

What sin in your life has Christ covered by his blood on the cross? Gambling, bulimia, prejudice, manipulation, shoplifting, willfulness, sugar addiction, or . . . ? Once you accept that you've been set free, how might you help usher others into Christ's freedom, while deflecting all the glory to God?

Purposeful Christ, you died and rose to save a wretch like me. I invite you to be the Lord of my life. Teach me to accentuate your purpose by living a God-glorifying, holy life of purpose.

P.U.R.P.O.S.E. Principle II: Understand Biblical Truths about God's Will

Redeeming the World

God has now revealed to us his mysterious plan regarding Christ. . . . And this is the plan: At the right time he will bring everything together under the authority of Christ—everything in heaven and on earth.   EPHESIANS 1:9-10

The mysterious and wise plan of God is to redeem all who are powerless against sin by offering them faith in Jesus Christ as their Higher Power. The Bible is full of references to God's gracious plan of salvation through the death and resurrection of his Son, giving us complete confidence that "God's mysterious plan . . . is Christ himself" (Colossians 2:2). Another exceptional verse on this topic is Acts 2:23. It tells us that nothing Judas, Herod Antipas, or Pontius Pilate did was a surprise to God. All their actions were determined beforehand, according to God's plan to save the world through the Messiah. It reads: "God knew what would happen, and his prearranged plan was carried out when Jesus was betrayed."

Did you know that you're part of God's global plan to reconcile people to him through Jesus? I'll never forget when this reality hit me. I finally understood that I needed to be kinder and gentler, not just because of some humanistic reason that involved people caring for people. I needed to be kinder and gentler so my testimony would be more credible, so others would be attracted to the Jesus I carry in my heart.

It's our privilege to be part of God's plan to redeem the world; he invites us to spread the Good News about Jesus. And with great privilege comes great responsibility and accountability. Once we understand the privilege-responsibility-accountability factor, we'll never be the same. It mandates that we take steps to heal and, in God's timing, to help others heal.

SOUL SEARCH

If you could assign yourself a perfectly suited role in God's eternal plan (with his full approval), what would that be? Will you let God take control of your sobriety efforts so you can step into that role, as soon as possible?

Maker of heaven and earth, reveal to me the exact part you'd like me to play in your eternal plan to bring people to the knowledge of Jesus as their Savior.

P.U.R.P.O.S.E. Principle II: **U**nderstand Biblical Truths about God's Will

Glorifying God with My Life

All of us have had that veil removed so that we can be mirrors that brightly reflect the glory of the Lord. 2 CORINTHIANS 3:18

We learn in 2 Corinthians 3:7-18 that Moses' face shone so brightly with the glory of God that he had to put a veil over it when speaking to the people of Israel. Their minds and hearts were hardened, and they couldn't handle the stunning beauty of God. But if they had turned to the Lord and believed, the veil would've been taken away immediately. And we, who've had that veil removed, can see and reflect the glory of the Lord, even though our addictive behaviors often dull his reflection.

Our ultimate purpose is to glorify God with our lives. We're created to be mirrors that brightly reflect (bend back) his light to shine it on him. As we allow the Spirit of the Lord to work in us, we begin to worship God in all we think, say, and do—and we ache to help others do the same. Professional surfer Bethany Hamilton has certainly been deliberate about giving glory to God and steering others toward him. When Bethany was only thirteen, a shark bit off her left arm while she was surfing. Courageous, quick-thinking companions got her safely to shore. Her 2004 autobiography, *Soul Surfer: A True Story of Faith, Family, and Fighting to Get Back on the Board*, and 2011 movie, *Soul Surfer*, are great testimonies that bend back the bright light of the Lord onto him.

The *Westminster Shorter Catechism* (written in the 1640s to teach biblical truth) says, "Man's [and woman's] chief end is to glorify God, and to enjoy him forever." How kind of God to allow us to enjoy glorifying him!

SOUL SEARCH

How would you describe humanity's "chief end" to someone considering a recovery program? How has your definition moved you toward a daring encounter with the Master's plan?

My Blessed Ruler, I yearn to reflect your glory more every day. Prompt me to shine a light on your glorious throne in all I think, say, and do—and to help others do the same.

P.U.R.P.O.S.E. Principle II: Understand Biblical Truths about God's Will
Stealing God's Glory

[The Babylonians] said, "Come, let's build a great city for ourselves with a tower that reaches into the sky. This will make us famous and keep us from being scattered all over the world." GENESIS 11:4

Some attempt to steal God's glory by taking credit for his goodness; others do it by exalting themselves in the form of bragging, exaggerating, or maneuvering for a preferred position. The prideful Babylonians certainly tried to deflect God's renown to themselves. With selfish ambition, they began building the Tower of Babel, which was intended to reach to the heavens and make their name famous among the other nations. The Lord was displeased by this show of sinful pride. He said, as if talking to himself, "Come, let's go down and confuse the people with different languages. Then they won't be able to understand each other" (Genesis 11:7). Yes, because of the Babylonians' desire for renown among people, God caused them to babble and be scattered all over the world.

During the next few days, listen for how many times you hear yourself say "I" and notice how many times you feel entitled or attempt to be the center of attention. Listen for how often you name-drop or try to be in the know. You may be surprised by how often you've tried to make life and your life mission be all about you. They are not. You might even decide that it's way past time to get your face off the cover of your self-published magazine—especially when you consider how pride has contributed to a relapse in your recovery or has caused you to lash out at others. (And yes, I'm talking to myself, too, about my own issues with pride.)

SOUL SEARCH

In what way have you, like the Babylonians, dreamed of making a name for yourself? When have you taken credit for what God chose to accomplish through you?

King of Glory, I'm so very tired of my glory-stealing attempts. Stop me now. I'm ready to release all my pride, especially in the form of selfish ambition and glory seeking.

Be Holy

I am the LORD your God. You must consecrate yourselves and be holy, because I am holy.
LEVITICUS 11:44

Our Leviticus passage is phrased as a command from God, not as an option. Being holy means that we're willing to be set apart—consecrated—to do his will. It requires a dedication of our lives to him, no holds barred. That includes our daily rehabilitation: staying clean, stopping the bitterness, making amends, and releasing the shame.

Martha and Mary were both holy women who loved the Lord dearly and desired to do his will, but they had different priorities when Jesus visited their home. Mary sat at his feet, listening to his every word, whereas Martha felt a huge burden to feed him and the other guests. So Martha, the cook, griped to Jesus, "Lord, doesn't it seem unfair to you that my sister just sits here while I do all the work? Tell her to come and help me" (Luke 10:40).

Jesus' response to Martha indicates that Mary had discovered how to grow in holiness: by spending time with him. He replied, "My dear Martha, you are worried and upset over all these details! There is only one thing worth being concerned about. Mary has discovered it, and it will not be taken away from her" (Luke 10:41-42). Of course, faith without deeds is dead (as James 2:26 teaches), but those deeds can't take precedence over our relationship with Jesus. So when you're trying to decide, *Do I make dinner for my family or sit with Jesus?* don't call me! This is not easy counsel to hear or follow. I know you'd never guess that I'm a Martha, but some of my most treasured times in life are as a Mary. Other than the facts, you're on your own to strike a balance.

If you've noticed that your recovery process has begun to resemble a type A, Martha to-do list, watch out—or more pointedly, slow down, sit down, and soak up Jesus.

SOUL SEARCH

What would need to change if you decided now to pursue a life of holiness that included the joy and celebration of your recovery? What steps can you take so you'll be more prepared for the humanly impossible life mission God has in mind for you?

Lord my God, because you're holy, I want to live a life that is wholly consecrated to you. Help me cooperate with you as you make me more holy, one step at a time.

P.U.R.P.O.S.E. Principle II: **U**nderstand Biblical Truths about God's Will

God's Holy Priest

You are living stones that God is building into his spiritual temple. What's more, you are his holy priests. Through the mediation of Jesus Christ, you offer spiritual sacrifices that please God. 1 PETER 2:5

Could Scripture say any more clearly that God expects us to be holy priests, not an unruly people who attempt to deaden our pain with every known type of sedative, distraction, mind game, or mania? The prophet Isaiah and the apostle John, among other Bible authors, add their own resounding affirmation that we are priests:

"You will be called priests of the LORD, ministers of our God" (Isaiah 61:6).

"He has made us a Kingdom of priests for God his Father. All glory and power to him forever and ever!" (Revelation 1:6).

Being a holy priest means that you're to offer spiritual sacrifices that please God, including the living sacrifice of your Christ-mediated sobriety, seasonal life roles, and broad-reaching, lifetime assignment. It means that you're not allowed to think of yourself as a hopeless backslider, ground-zero rubble, or irreparably damaged goods. Instead you must accept that you're a living stone that God is building into his spiritual temple, with Jesus Christ himself being the chief cornerstone. According to 1 Peter 2:9, you've been called out of the darkness and set apart as a royal priest of God. In fact, Peter adds that you're God's possession, chosen for a holy purpose to show his goodness and light to others. What a huge responsibility; what an incomparable gift that a lifetime of gratitude could never repay.

SOUL SEARCH

How do you feel about being called a holy priest and being told to offer yourself—including your past mistakes, present worries, and future dreams—as a living sacrifice to God? In what way have you acted like a holy priest who showed God's goodness to others?

God's Messenger and High Priest Jesus, I ask you to use me as a living stone that helps build God's spiritual temple. Raise me up as a holy priest, a minister dedicated to you. Help me fix my eyes on you as my role model, especially when I'm afraid of what lies ahead.

P.U.R.P.O.S.E. Principle II: **U**nderstand Biblical Truths about God's Will
Two of My Universal Purposes

Expect to have your life turned upside down when you abandon your obsessions, compulsions, people-pleasing tendencies, and fear of vulnerability to take your assigned place in God's plan to redeem the world.

☀ Meditate on the Assurance of God's Word

God has made everything beautiful for its own time. He has planted eternity in the human heart, but even so, people cannot see the whole scope of God's work from beginning to end. ECCLESIASTES 3:11

They will be my people, and I will be their God. And I will give them one heart and one purpose: to worship me forever, for their own good and for the good of all their descendants. And I will make an everlasting covenant with them: I will never stop doing good for them. JEREMIAH 32:38-40

☀ Humbly Talk with the Lord

Glorify God by telling him you want nothing more than to be a conduit that moves people toward him.

Ask God to help you overcome a specific, unrelenting problem so that you may become more holy.

☀ Take the *Life Purpose Coach* Challenge

Ask God to remind you of a time when you accepted praise for an accomplishment without attempting to give him the glory or point people toward him (for example, you got a sobriety chip, organized a successful ministry event, gave a great speech, graduated from school, or rebuilt a broken relationship). If you can't think of a time you attempted to steal God's thunder, forecast a scenario for a situation in which it would be easy to get carried away with the accolades from others. Then script out and memorize your humble response to those congratulating you.

P.**U**.R.P.O.S.E. Principle II: **U**nderstand Biblical Truths about God's Will

God's Will

Don't act thoughtlessly, but understand what the Lord wants you to do.
EPHESIANS 5:17

A basic, God-designed tenet of human behavior is that people want to do what's right; healthy people don't set out to do a bad job or fall short or fail intentionally. For Spirit-led individuals, that principle is doubly true; they're eager to please God by doing the right thing. When they understand what's expected of them, they typically rise to the occasion rather than acting carelessly or thoughtlessly.

God has been unwavering about what he expects of all believers, specifically in regard to two more of his universal purposes: he wants us to love people as individuals and to love his church. Although one of those life directives might seem easier for you than the other, God does require both. When we're thinking coherently, avoiding any substance or activity that clouds our minds, we're able to understand how and why these purposes are important to God. (See March 7–10.)

On our best, obedient days, we're wise enough to pray with Paul that we'll humbly seek God's will in every aspect of our lives by asking, "What should I do, Lord?" (Acts 22:10). On our foolish days of making poor choices, we might barely be able to whisper the tax collector's prayer: "I am a sinner" (Luke 18:13). And on our worst days, when we don't feel like praying or obeying any of God's commands, including those that pertain to loving others and his church, our only hope is that God sends us a gentle reminder that Jesus is coming soon. That gracious prompt can certainly help us remember to choose Jesus, before we're asked to start 'splainin' (as Ricky would say to Lucy on *I Love Lucy*) any further misconduct!

SOUL SEARCH

What do you know to be true about loving others, loving God's church, choosing a victorious recovery, and discerning your critical work on earth? How do you feel about seeking humbly to do God's will in every aspect of your life?

Exalted God, you're without parallel. Thank you that you've stood by me in my haphazard approach to life. Send me a laser-sharp understanding of these two universal purposes you've given your followers—to love others and to love your church.

P.**U**.R.P.O.S.E. Principle II: **U**nderstand Biblical Truths about God's Will

Do What Matters Today

Love your neighbor as yourself.   MATTHEW 22:39

We know that one of God's purposes for us is to love others. We seem to know how to love people at arm's length—the impoverished in developing countries, prisoners' families, perhaps the homeless. But how does Christlike love translate into our daily actions with those closer to us—in our families, churches, neighborhoods, schools, workplaces, gyms, and recovery small groups? Do we do today what matters today and lovingly care for them? And to back up the train all the way to the station, how loving (versus self-deprecating, cruel, and intolerant) are we toward ourselves?

In 1993, I was given a rare opportunity to choose a destination retreat while my two teenagers were on an adventure of their own. My "holy-sounding" reason for heading to the tiny island of Malta was that I wanted to study the life of St. Paul where he'd been shipwrecked, but truly I was looking for any insights that would apply to *my* anger-filled, shipwrecked life. One day, after swimming in St. Paul's Bay (and praying the entire time, of course!), I spotted a small chapel and headed inside. There I met Mary, who was cleaning the floors; she invited me to her home up the cobblestone street to share lunch with her sister Josephina and her brother Jesus (sjeh-sus). I was soon in the presence of a holy family—Jesus, Mary, and Joseph(ina)! As we chatted leisurely over an authentic Portuguese meal, they reminded me that one of my main purposes in life is to love others, starting with loving myself. They asked me if I might have gotten so caught up in doing something grand for the Lord that I'd forgotten about enjoying my current roles, especially parenting. They refreshed my soul by saying that all my days had been ordained and that I was to embrace each day lovingly for the glory of God.

SOUL SEARCH

How are you doing with loving others and yourself in your everyday routine? How does loving someone amid the daily grind of life move you forward in God's plan for your recovery and future ministry endeavors?

God of endless love, I've heard this same message from the beginning: that we should love one another.* Create in me a more loving heart, O Lord.

---

* See 1 John 3:11.

P.U.R.P.O.S.E. Principle II: **U**nderstand Biblical Truths about God's Will

God's Presence

You have shown me the way of life, and you will fill me with the joy of your presence.
ACTS 2:28*

At first reading, Acts 2:28 appears to be nothing shy of Pollyannaism, which is a bias toward positive thinking that keeps you hunky-dory glad much of the time! *The Message* paraphrase of the verse is even more exuberant: "You've got my feet on the life-path, with your face shining sun-joy all around." But many addicts consider that a sickeningly sweet, optimistic outlook. How can sun-joy even be on their recovery radar when they often feel so defeated by the trials of life?

Only the context of our passage can help us make sense of what's really being said. Peter is preaching to his fellow Israelites at the Pentecost rally about Jesus the Nazarene, whom they nailed to a cross and killed. He says, "But God untied the death ropes and raised him up" (Acts 2:24, *The Message*). We learn that death was no match for Jesus because he was confident that he'd be resurrected. He knew that God, his Father, who was always with him, right by his side, would never allow him to rot in the grave.

To access joy during his horrific trials, Jesus dwelled on the full joy he'd have when elevated to the right hand of his Father in heaven, and he also focused on the joy of having his Father by his side on earth. Choosing to stay in the presence of God made him glad and confirmed his resolve to sing God's praises and do his will. We can have that type of joy and resolve for ourselves because Jesus sent his Holy Spirit to help us see God's face and live in his presence (see Acts 2:33).

SOUL SEARCH

Does the prospect of boundless joy in heaven sustain you during extreme trials on earth? In what practical ways can God's presence bring you peace now, as you struggle against the insanity of obsessions and move toward your godly purpose?

*My Great Reward, I pray that "you will show me the way of life, granting me the joy of your presence and the pleasures of living with you forever."***

---

* Peter, quoting from King David's psalm of confidence (Psalm 16:10-11) to comment about Jesus' confidence in being resurrected.
** Psalm 16:11.

P.U.R.P.O.S.E. Principle II: **U**nderstand Biblical Truths about God's Will

Stay Connected

As each part does its own special work, it helps the other parts grow, so that the whole body is healthy and growing and full of love. EPHESIANS 4:16

Christ is the head of his body, the church, which he supernaturally maintains. He promised that the gates of hell would not prevail against his church (see Matthew 16:18), and he has kept his promise. Neither deceptive tactics nor enemy schemes have been able to overcome it. Christ continues to make the whole body fit together, with each person contributing his or her spiritual gifts, natural abilities, personality, and life experiences to the health of the whole.

Just as those in recovery programs are instructed to stay connected with their sponsors or recovery coaches and "keep coming back" to meetings, we're instructed to stay connected to the body of Christ, to which the Spirit brings unity and oneness (see Ephesians 4:3). We help protect and unify our church when we love it and pray for its leaders and their families, as well as for our accountability partners, fellowship groups, Bible study teachers, and mentors.

Be extra careful not to catch Sunday Sickness, as described by an unknown author:

> Morbus Sabbaticus is a peculiar disease. The symptoms vary but never interfere with the appetite. It never lasts more than twenty-four hours. No physician is ever called. It is contagious. The attack comes on suddenly on Sundays. The patient awakens as usual, feeling fine, and eats a hearty breakfast. About 9 a.m. the attack comes on and lasts until about noon. In the afternoon the patient is much improved and is able to take a ride, visit friends, watch TV, work in the garden, mow the lawn, or read the Sunday paper. The patient usually eats a hearty supper and is able to go to work on Monday. This ailment is often fatal in the end—to the soul!

Be aware that recurrences of this disease often cause an individual to drift away from the Lord, fellow believers, and God's Word.

SOUL SEARCH

In what way has the church ministered to you? In what way have you ministered to the body of Christ?

Head of the church, I'm a wounded part of your body. Heal me miraculously, so all of me can serve all of you in precisely the way you destined me to minister.

P.U.R.P.O.S.E. Principle II: **U**nderstand Biblical Truths about God's Will

Gather in Churches

Through followers of Jesus like yourselves gathered in churches, this extraordinary plan of God is becoming known and talked about even among the angels!
EPHESIANS 3:10 (*The Message*)

What is this "extraordinary plan" that Paul talks about? Just this: "Both Gentiles and Jews who believe the Good News share equally in the riches inherited by God's children" (Ephesians 3:6). In most Christian churches today, Jew vs. Gentile is not a big issue. But what about "good Christian" vs. . . . well, those of us with something in our past (or present) of which we're ashamed? Paul reminds us that God's good news "is accessible and welcoming to everyone, across the board" (Ephesians 3:6, *The Message*).

What glorious news for anyone struggling with an addiction to a mind-numbing substance or behavior. The church is to be the safe haven for sinners! We get "the same offer, same help, same promises in Christ Jesus" (Ephesians 3:6, *The Message*) as the most respected saint. And God is calling us to "gather in churches" in part so we can share that extraordinary good news. Think about it: God wants addicts in his church.

If you've had a bad experience with church members who are judgmental, gossipy about your business, clique-driven, or an unhealthy influence on you, that's because church members are imperfect, not because God is pulling you out of church life altogether. You may even have come across a church whose pastor was preaching false doctrine from which you fled for your spiritual life. Good for you! But never forget that the Spirit of Christ loves his church, and he wants you to love it too. If you've been discouraged about church life, speak to the Holy Spirit about a church-based solution.

SOUL SEARCH

Have you allowed the shame and guilt of your past to keep you in isolation, away from supportive relationships in church? What can you do to love God's church more?

Lord Jehovah, thank you for creating a Christ-centered place for me, a church where I can worship, fellowship, heal, mature spiritually, serve in ministry, and discern and fulfill my life mission.

P.U.R.P.O.S.E. Principle II: **U**nderstand Biblical Truths about God's Will

No Eye Has Seen

Since the world began, no ear has heard and no eye has seen a God like you, who works for those who wait for him!   ISAIAH 64:4

The book of Isaiah is great movie-making material; it's got all the plot twists of any world-domination flick. The only problem is that we already know the end of the story: God wins! Even so, our particular passage is dramatic in its "if . . . then" script. It says that if we wait for God, then he will work for us. And to top that, it says that, since time began, nobody has heard or seen a God like him. This must be fiction: Jehovah, who is like none other, is going to work for recovering addicts, food junkies, lawbreakers, and sinners of every imaginable type. Amazing!

In Isaiah 46, God had compared himself with the Babylonian gods Bel and Nebo. He explained that he created us, carries us, and works for us, but the helpless gods of Babylon created nothing, must be carried, and can't help anybody, because they're not real. He says, "I will be your God throughout your lifetime—until your hair is white with age. I made you, and I will care for you. I will carry you along and save you" (v. 4).

So we have a choice to make: we certainly can continue to be counted among those disappointed people who worship the demigods of addiction that fill us with darkness. Or we can begin again in earnest to cooperate with our kind, powerful God, who's working for us, especially in matters of sobriety. Jean-Pierre de Caussade, a French Jesuit priest, gives his straightforward recommendation: "Each day you must say to yourself, 'To-day I am going to begin.'"

SOUL SEARCH

In what dramatic way do you need God's help for healing so you can move toward his most praiseworthy plan for your life? What can you do now to begin to abide by his wishes?

God of gods, I will wait for you alone to work on my behalf because other gods, the useless idols of addiction, are like "helpless scarecrows in a cucumber field!"*

---

* Jeremiah 10:5.

P.U.R.P.O.S.E. Principle II: **U**nderstand Biblical Truths about God's Will

God's Plan Is My Plan

Consider now how to make God's plan—that you love others and his church—your plan. When such devotion is difficult for you, remember that your loving obedience will invite blessings upon your recovery efforts and unique mission.

☀ Meditate on the Assurance of God's Word

No one has ever seen God. But if we love each other, God lives in us, and his love is brought to full expression in us.   1 JOHN 4:12

All of you together are Christ's body, and each of you is a part of it.
1 CORINTHIANS 12:27

I, a prisoner for serving the Lord, beg you to lead a life worthy of your calling, for you have been called by God.   EPHESIANS 4:1

☀ Humbly Talk with the Lord

Talk to God about his love for you and about how he purposefully designed your godly friendships to encourage your sobriety and specific life assignment.

Ask God to help you cherish, serve, and edify the body of Christ with an intensity you never thought possible.

☀ Take the *Life Purpose Coach* Challenge

To grow your Christlike love for others and for the church, experiment with several of these proven methods: (1) Suit up and show up. (2) Act your way into appropriate feelings, rather than waiting to feel like you want to act. (3) Hang out with encouraging role models who will disciple you and pray with you. (4) Resist criticizing yourself over your repeated failures; instead, get back on the bike and back in the pew! (5) Cultivate authentic relationships by showing genuine, Christlike interest in at least one person at each church meeting.

P.U.R.P.O.S.E. Principle II: **U**nderstand Biblical Truths about God's Will

An Approved Worker

Concentrate on doing your best for God, work you won't be ashamed of, laying out the truth plain and simple. 2 TIMOTHY 2:15 (*The Message*)

Paul encouraged Timothy to present himself to God as an approved worker—one who didn't need to be ashamed of his efforts but could honestly say that he gave God's assignment his all. Paul urged his protégé to study God's Word of truth thoroughly so he could explain it skillfully and accurately, keeping his listeners on the right path. Paul's mentoring and preaching goal was that all who belong to the Lord would come to their senses, turn from evil, and flee from Satan's snare. He wanted to raise up approved workers who bear the fruit of holiness as we share the gospel with those in danger (see March 14–17).

Reflect for a moment on how you've been held captive by the devil, so you can take in Paul's advice about how to escape captivity yourself and also help others do so. He warns,

- Refuse to become entangled in worthless, idle chatter and foolish controversies that foster strife and lead to more godless behavior (see 2 Timothy 2:16, 23).
- Flee from youthful lusts to pursue right living, faithfulness, love, and harmony with other faithful Christians of pure hearts (see v. 22).
- Don't be quarrelsome; instead be courteous and gentle in correcting others, in hopes that God will lead them to repent, know his truth, escape from the devil's trap, and do his will (see vv. 24-26).

To add to Paul's instructions, Georg Christopher Lichtenberg, an eighteenth-century German scientist, gave excellent advice: "Never undertake anything for which you wouldn't have the courage to ask the blessings of heaven." Isn't that the truth!

SOUL SEARCH

How could working Paul's list lead you to God's broader plan for your life? What step can you take toward sobriety now, so you're able to bear the fruit of holiness, rekindle the gifts God has given you, and share the gospel?

My Good News, disentangle me from chatter, controversy, lust, quarrels, and other godless behavior. Give me a gentle spirit that loves truth, and approve me for your work of spreading the gospel.

P.U.R.P.O.S.E. Principle II: Understand Biblical Truths about God's Will

Bear Fruit

[Jesus replied,] "You didn't choose me. I chose you. I appointed you to go and produce lasting fruit, so that the Father will give you whatever you ask for, using my name."
JOHN 15:16

We have been chosen and appointed by Jesus to produce the lasting fruit of holiness, a fruit that is rich in good works and is faithful in sharing the blessings of the gospel. This doesn't mean that we must try harder, go to church more, or do nice things for people out of guilt. It does mean, however, that we agree to give up everything, including our addictions, that can hold us back from reaching the great end for which Christians are chosen. This sobering call on our lives should also propel us to focus on the inordinate number of souls hungering for Christ rather than on our own personal desires, idle whims, useless gains, and distracting obsessions.

Harvesting fruit for the Kingdom isn't always easy, but it does bring great rewards. I liken it to the time my friend and I donned oversized, protective gloves and long-sleeved jackets to harvest wild blackberries off thorny bushes in Oregon. Our purple-stained lips proved we were serious connoisseurs of the messy fruit we ate from insecticide-free canes, but we also gathered enough berries to make the tastiest blackberry cobbler. Similarly, in our harvesting efforts for Jesus, some of our experiences will be thorny and messy, while others will be as sweet as cobbler. Regardless of how difficult or delectable the process, regardless of how inadequate we feel because of our personal transgressions, we've been appointed to do this work for the Lord. We're even encouraged to use Jesus' name to ask his Father for anything we need to do it.

SOUL SEARCH

In what way has an addictive lifestyle ever caused you to stop bearing the fruit of holiness in your life? How are you living out your purpose of gathering Kingdom fruit now?

Sower of good seed, help me be like a tree planted along a riverbank with roots that reach deep into the water, not bothered by the heat or worried by drought. Keep my leaves green and don't ever let me stop producing fruit. *

---

* From Jeremiah 17:7-8.

P.U.R.P.O.S.E. Principle II: **U**nderstand Biblical Truths about God's Will

Don't Lose Heart

Since through God's mercy we have this ministry, we do not lose heart.
2 CORINTHIANS 4:1 (NIV)

I used to think our verse meant that God mercifully gave each of us a purposeful, unique ministry, so we wouldn't become beaten down by a mundane existence and lose heart. And that wisdom sure comforted me, a woman about whom Saddleback Pastor Rick Warren had said, "Katie, you need a constant, intravenous drip of purpose running through your veins to keep you alive! We might have to hook you up to an IV on the church patio." We both chuckled, but I would've liked that delicious drip, just to counteract a depression about my purposelessness that followed me around every day in early 1990. You, too, may prefer my personal interpretation of our passage if you're heavy-laden with depression that's causing you to lose heart about how God could ever use the aimless, sobriety-challenged you.

As it turned out, I had understood the first part of the sentence correctly. It's definitely by God's favor that anybody, including those in recovery, would have the privilege of engaging in whatever ministry God decides is best for sharing his Good News. It was just the second part I'd misinterpreted. I realize now that the truth about "we do not lose heart" is this: it's God's mercy that keeps us from growing faint with exhaustion when our actual ministry becomes difficult; from becoming discouraged, despondent, and fearful when roadblocks to our ministry arise. If we remain focused on the one who blessed us with our ministry, we can hang on when the going gets tough (and ministry is guaranteed to get tough).

I pray you'll have all you need to serve in ministry: peace of mind in trying times, heart salve in emergency situations, and God-focused sobriety at all times. I pray you'll have "an unwearied effort," as the inscription over David Livingstone's burial place in Westminster Abbey reads: "For 30 years his life was spent in an unwearied effort to evangelize."

SOUL SEARCH

How does focusing on God's mercy in a specific area (e.g., in your ministry, family, recovery) help you counteract discouragement in that area? To whom in ministry could you offer mercy?

God who gives encouragement to those who get discouraged in ministry, give me an unwearied effort.

82

P.U.R.P.O.S.E. Principle II: **U**nderstand Biblical Truths about God's Will

Share the Gospel

My life is worth nothing to me unless I use it for finishing the work assigned me by the Lord Jesus—the work of telling others the Good News about the wonderful grace of God. ACTS 20:24

Paul, a previous Christian-killer, says that his life purpose was to share the Good News of God's grace. So if you ever worry that your addictive mistakes have made you unqualified to share the gospel, just call to mind Paul's rocky-road past. Or read about the Samaritan woman, a nameless divorcée who'd gone through five husbands and was living with a man when she met Jesus (see John 4:1-42). According to John's Gospel, this woman with a jaded history was the first person to whom Jesus openly revealed himself as Messiah (see v. 26), and his conversation with her is the longest private one with anyone on record. We read that after they talked, she immediately began to share the Good News with her entire town, and many accepted Jesus as their Savior. That makes her the first evangelist!

Once we sinners have a personal encounter with Jesus and hear him say, "I am the Messiah!" you'd think we'd automatically share our joy with others, as did Paul and the Samaritan woman. But let me be honest with you about the fears that blocked me for years: fear of rejection, of doing it wrong, of not having answers to theologically deep questions, and of being labeled a "Jesus freak." The only thing that eventually helped me was a seminar that presented lots of conversational ways to evangelize, including carrying a small, read-along pamphlet that does the hardest work for me. That tract frees me up to share my brief testimony and ask a few probing questions. Now when the Holy Spirit prompts me to speak with someone, I don't feel quite as conversationally challenged!

SOUL SEARCH

How can God use your jaded history for good when you're sharing Jesus with other sinners? If fear were not a factor and if you were blue-sky dreaming, what would be your ideal way to evangelize on a global scale?

Lord, give me what you are requiring of me. * *Shore me up with more of you, so my feeling of inadequacy doesn't overtake me.*

---

* A prayer of St. Augustine.

P.U.R.P.O.S.E. Principle II: **U**nderstand Biblical Truths about God's Will

Proclaiming the Gospel

Don't be afraid of suffering for the Lord. Work at telling others the Good News, and fully carry out the ministry God has given you.   2 TIMOTHY 4:5

In our poignant passage, the soon-to-be-martyred Paul is chained in a dark Roman dungeon, writing to his mentee, Timothy. You may know people today who've been imprisoned physically or emotionally, or those who are suffering for the Lord as they work to tell others the Good News and fully carry out the ministry God has given them. You might even have had that experience yourself. Or you may be sitting in a different type of dungeon, where you're chained to an addiction that's signaling the end of your life. May Paul's farewell letter, outlined below, help you hold fast to your faith in the face of your own trying times, whatever that entails.

The apostle tells us that, in all circumstances, we're to focus on God's grace, on the fact that we've been saved and called to live a holy life. This will give us hope. He says that we're to keep ourselves pure and to keep our eye on the task we've been assigned. This will fortify us with much-needed strength. In addition, we're to allow Scripture to teach, discipline, and train us to do good deeds. This will anchor us in truth. Such God-sent hope, strength, and truth help us guard our faith and ministry, so we can proclaim the gospel with intensity, even during times of personal adversity or suffering for the Lord. And we're not to be afraid of failing to persuade others; that is God's business, not ours. Until we're called home to be with the Lord, our sole concern is that we pour ourselves out as an offering to him.

SOUL SEARCH

In what way have you suffered for the Lord? With what spiritual habit (e.g., Bible reading, journaling, Scripture memorization, singing praise songs) do you typically keep watch over your faith, sobriety, and ministry-mission?

My Guardian, I'm broken, and I can't do the work of sharing your Good News without your help. Watch over me, and steel me with your strength.

P.U.R.P.O.S.E. Principle II: **U**nderstand Biblical Truths about God's Will

Strategically Placed

I will raise up Cyrus to fulfill my righteous purpose, and I will guide his actions.
ISAIAH 45:13

Who was this Cyrus, about whom Isaiah is prophesying as God's chosen one? He was a Persian king, a strategic, unstoppable general to whom God had assigned the privileged work of restoring Jerusalem and freeing his people from seventy years of Babylonian captivity.

But wait a minute—Cyrus was a heathen, a warmonger, and a cutthroat politician! If God chose to work through such a pagan to accomplish his will, surely he can use the likes of recovering addicts who worship a few select idols, right? Yes, it's God's prerogative to call into service anyone he pleases for the good of his people, even those who don't care to know him or obey him. He says that he does this so that "from the rising of the sun to the place of its setting people may know there is none besides me. I am the LORD, and there is no other. . . . I bring prosperity and create disaster" (Isaiah 45:6-7, NIV). Isaiah's prophecy (approximately one hundred and fifty years earlier) proved that Cyrus's success was from God Almighty.

Indisputable logic leads us to the wise conclusion that our best response to such a powerful God is a spirit of cooperation. On that topic, Darlene Wilkinson, ministry leader and *New York Times* bestselling author, writes, "First we look at our expanded territory and see how weak and helpless we are to accomplish what God has asked us to do. Next, we remember that God has strategically placed us right where we are for this time in history according to His plan. Finally, we recognize that it is God's hand upon us that is powerful. And we don't want to miss the opportunity to experience the greatness of our God." All to the glory of God's righteous purpose.

SOUL SEARCH

When have you chosen to be a Cyrus, ignoring the truth about God? Despite your shortcomings, what has God handpicked for you to reveal to the world about him?

Incomparable God, I want no god but you. Heal me and use me strategically in history.

P.U.R.P.O.S.E. Principle II: Understand Biblical Truths about God's Will
Committing to God

God's end-purpose will prevail, so commit yourself now to his universal purposes of bearing fruit and spreading his gospel. And don't lean on your own understanding of how to proceed. The Holy Spirit will lead you into all truth about how to manage your sobriety amid your ministry-mission efforts.

☀ Meditate on the Assurance of God's Word

Ask God to give you complete knowledge of his will and to give you spiritual wisdom and understanding. Then the way you live will always honor and please the Lord, and your lives will produce every kind of good fruit. All the while, you will grow as you learn to know God better and better. COLOSSIANS 1:9-10

What you heard from me, keep as the pattern of sound teaching, with faith and love in Christ Jesus. Guard the good deposit that was entrusted to you—guard it with the help of the Holy Spirit who lives in us. 2 TIMOTHY 1:13-14 (NIV)

☀ Humbly Talk with the Lord

Thank the Lord for the comfort you've received in knowing that his sovereign plan always prevails.

Respond to God's intervention in your addictive habits by offering him all your hopes, dreams, and schemes.

☀ Take the *Life Purpose Coach* Challenge

Go for a leisurely walk to reflect on the ways you've been self-medicating with any of these recreational excesses: shopping, eating, talking on the phone, using social media sites, gaming, sports, or watching television or movies. Confess these counterfeit ways with which you've been attempting to replenish yourself. Ask God to give you a new way to refresh your soul—for your own sake and for the sake of others you've been sent to refresh. Meditate on Proverbs 11:25: "Those who refresh others will themselves be refreshed."

P.U.R.P.O.S.E. Principle II: **U**nderstand Biblical Truths about God's Will
"This I Must Do" Assignment

I have come down from heaven to do the will of God who sent me, not to do my own will. JOHN 6:38

Jesus came to earth freely to accomplish what his Father had planned for him to do, not to do his own thing. His single-minded mission was to die for our sins, be raised from the grave to give us hope, and ascend into heaven to sit enthroned and prepare a place for us. You've also been commissioned with a "This I Must Do" assignment, meaning that you want to do it because it's your passionate ache, divine urge, heart's desire, and One Big Thing. This significant purpose is your unique way of guiding people into God's Kingdom. You must decide if you're willing to make critical, mid-course adjustments toward sobriety, so you can be better equipped to do this work. You'll want to pray fervently about accepting or declining this life-consuming commitment, which has eternal ramifications for yourself and others.

Cardinal John Henry Newman, who lived in the nineteenth century, wrote, "Everyone who breathes, high and low, educated and ignorant, young and old, man and woman, has a mission, has a work. We are not sent into this world for nothing; we are not born at random; we are not here, that we may go to bed at night, and get up in the morning, toil for our bread, eat and drink, laugh and joke, sin when we have a mind, and reform when we are tired of sinning, rear a family and die. God sees every one of us; He creates every soul . . . for a purpose."

It's a good thing that, before Jesus ascended into heaven, he reiterated a commitment to send his Holy Spirit to clothe us with power from on high: "Now I will send the Holy Spirit, just as my Father promised" (Luke 24:49). Lacking this supernatural help with our issues, obsessions, character faults, and roadblocks to our destiny, we'd be powerless and hopeless.

SOUL SEARCH

How do you feel about allowing the Holy Spirit to clothe you with power from on high to overcome your addictions? Will you pursue your God-designed, single-minded life mission with pure joy?

My Pathway to Purpose, only you can rescue me from madness and deliver me into your perfect will for my life. Please proceed swiftly.

Mission in This World

[Jesus prayed,] "In the same way that you gave me a mission in the world, I give them a mission in the world." JOHN 17:18 *(The Message)*

Just as God the Father gave Jesus a mission in this world, Jesus also gives you a specific mission—your "This I Must Do" assignment. You may be uncertain about it for a season or even try to ignore it for a long time, but you can't destroy God's plans. In fact, your mission might need to lie dormant during rough patches of your life, but it will be something you feel you can't *not* do before you die! If, in due course, you choose to disown it, God does have the option of reassigning it to a willing soul.

Jesus called these three people to serve in distinct, soul-winning ways. Listen to their passion as they describe their life purposes:

Lottie Moon, a missionary to China for thirty-nine years, said of her life's work, "If I had a thousand lives, I would give them all for the women of China."

Toyohiko Kagawa, a Japanese Christian who lived in a shed six feet square while helping the slum-dwellers of Kobe, Japan, said, "If Christ were here, he would help them, and so must I."

Shortly before Methodist preacher John Wesley died, he wrote a letter to William Wilberforce, encouraging him to be Parliament's voice for abolishing slave trading. Wesley wrote, "Unless God has raised you up for this very thing, you will be worn out by the opposition of men and devils. But if God be with you who can be against you?" Wilberforce succeeded.

We can only imagine how many sacrifices these servants of the Lord made to follow God's plan for their lives. I wonder how many times they felt like giving up, but didn't—and how many times they ran from sin, simply to honor their loving commitment to their godly mission.

SOUL SEARCH

Will you follow Jesus' example and do the will of God by embracing your mission in the world, however and whenever it's revealed to you? Will you prepare yourself by surrendering any shortcomings that are interfering?

My Bright and Shining Example, nudge me in the direction you want me to go. I desire to live a passionate life for you with my heart on fire for the mission you have reserved for me.

88

P.**U**.R.P.O.S.E. Principle II: **U**nderstand Biblical Truths about God's Will

Completing My Work on Earth

Jesus looked up to heaven and said, "Father, . . . I brought glory to you here on earth by completing the work you gave me to do." JOHN 17:1, 4

God certainly gave his blessed Son an imposing, death-defying assignment, whereas our custom-made tasks typically won't be the death of us. But might we cause the demise of our mission when we can't keep our addictive actions from compromising it? To cement the concept in my mind of how our reckless behavior could bring irreparable damage to our life's work, I've often imagined a missionary who was preaching the gospel with a cocktail and cigarette in hand, while punctuating sentences with foul-mouthed words and lewd remarks. That picture is so vividly wrong that it has stuck with me for years; what a dichotomy between God's good Word and the self-inflicted infirmities of slurred speech, a smoker's cough, and a filthy mouth. It's irreverent to treat our personalized ministry gift from God with such sacrilege.

You may feel as if you've ruined all your chances of ever having God trust you or help you launch into his desired work. When those discouraging thoughts overtake you, pause for a moment to tell him that you want to become trustworthy and that you want him to use you up for his glory. This type of "I'll do whatever it takes" extreme surrender statement will pull you back into the reality of who's in charge and who's not. God will be glorified, and you'll be well on your way to becoming a more faithful servant of the Lord, doing whatever character work he requires and whatever task he orchestrates.

SOUL SEARCH

How would you describe the gratitude you feel toward God for healing you enough to be able to participate in his unique plan for your life? What additional blessing on your sobriety might you request right now?

God, I want nothing more than to complete the work you gave me to do, so your glory will shine. Help me see my next recovery steps clearly so that I don't waste any more time avoiding the divine call you've placed on my life.

P.U.R.P.O.S.E. Principle II: **U**nderstand Biblical Truths about God's Will

God's Good Work

I am certain that God, who began the good work within you, will continue his work until it is finally finished on the day when Christ Jesus returns. PHILIPPIANS 1:6

Paul's phrase "the good work within you" refers to God's work of grace and faith in us, which regenerates us, heals us from our character flaws, and makes us pure and holy. He gives more insight into its meaning in Philippians 1:9-11, when he prays for the people of Philippi to love others sincerely, grow in their knowledge of the Lord, and live prudent, exemplary lives. He's talking about lives that Jesus would commend, lives that are rich in the fruit of the Spirit, lives that make Jesus attractive to all and glorify God. And, to be clear, Paul is saying that only God can do this good work in his people; we ourselves are too weak and too willing to yield to temptation.

Paul was speaking from personal experience about how God had begun a good work in him back when he was Saul the Christian-hater. By grace, God forgave him his murderous rampages, saved him from eternal damnation, called him into a ministry of grace, and equipped him for lifelong service. God even employed Barnabas, a Spirit-led man of faith, love, knowledge, and exemplary living, to mentor Saul for a full year (see Acts 11:25-26). Through one of the boldest discipleship assignments that God ever designed, Saul's character and knowledge of the Lord grew, and he began a respected teaching ministry.

Even when our spirituality pales in comparison to others like Barnabas and the newborn Paul, God still loves to do a good work of grace and faith in us. We need only to look to our Lord; he'll take care of the rest. No sinner, addict, or otherwise broken person is too lost or damaged for God to love and rescue. Think of it this way: those who are in the most dire straits will reflect the most glory for God when he makes them victors!

SOUL SEARCH

What evidence do you have that God is continuing the good work he began in you? What step can you take away from bad habits and toward faith, grace, and God's most enthralling purpose for you?

Almighty Father, I want to be your grace-filled, faithful servant; don't give up on me.

P.**U**.R.P.O.S.E. Principle II: **U**nderstand Biblical Truths about God's Will

What the Lord Wants

[Jesus said,] "If any of you wants to be my follower, you must turn from your selfish ways, take up your cross daily, and follow me." LUKE 9:23

Roman centurions conscripted Simon, a native of North Africa, to help Jesus carry his heavy cross to Calvary (see Luke 23:26). Simon must have asked himself, "Why me?" during that confusing life interruption, when he was forced to assist a condemned criminal. Well, in our focal passage, Jesus is blunt that following him (being his disciple) will mean carrying some type of old, rugged cross—and doing so unselfishly. Can you recall a time someone helped you shoulder an unbearable burden, such as a chronic illness, an unexpected divorce, or the aftermath of a natural disaster or corporate downsizing? What about a time you helped a friend with his or her splintery cross? And what about your willingness to take up your own hefty cross of choosing sobriety daily? Do you believe this is what the Lord wants of you and that he will send you a Simon to help you?

If it sometimes feels like you're carrying the weight of the world on your back, it might help you to think about what your humble, selfless journey could mean to others. For example, Simon of Cyrene served Christ in his hour of need by carrying his cross when no friend of Jesus had physically helped him since his arrest. We can only speculate what Simon's face-to-face encounter with Christ must have meant to Christ, to Simon, and to Simon's two sons and wife (each of whom is later mentioned as a Christ-follower). Reflect for a moment on what your encounter with Jesus could mean to you and yours as you respectfully carry your cumbersome cross of recovery. Shouldering such a burdensome load might feel like the hardest thing you've ever done, but it can also be among the greatest things you'll ever do on earth for yourself and your loved ones.

SOUL SEARCH

What backbreaking cross has Christ asked you to carry, and whom has he sent you to help carry it? How will bearing it kindly and steadfastly, rather than belligerently, further your recovery, bless others, and lead you to a life of deliberate purpose?

Christ, my Cross Bearer, you did for me what I wasn't able to do for myself: you saved my life. Now I lay my cross at your feet, admitting that I need your help once again.

P.U.R.P.O.S.E. Principle II: Understand Biblical Truths about God's Will

Days Ordained for Me

Your eyes saw my unformed body. All the days ordained for me were written in your book before one of them came to be.   PSALM 139:16 (NIV)

I can't imagine how God has previewed and overseen every single moment of every day for every person since Adam and Eve. I'm sure that looking after you was no walk in the park, but babysitting me; as an attention-seeking, middle child with control issues in a family of eight, should have been enough to do him in.

I had enormous, unrealistic dreams! I dreamed of being like Joan of Arc, who wielded control over an entire nation in a dramatic fashion! Reportedly, that French peasant girl had visions from God whose commands she obeyed; and presumably she was sane, even though skeptics doubted any divine call on her life. When God instructed her to rescue her homeland from English domination, she led the French army to several important victories during the Hundred Years' War. Like Joan, I wanted to ride into bloody battle on a horse with a sword—figuratively speaking. I wanted to sound some type of battle cry for God, assuming he had specific, anointed guidance for me.

In like-mindedness with someone like Joan, are you eager to live out the days God has ordained for you, days that are spent listening to his voice and obeying him immediately and passionately? I know you're not eager to be burned at the stake (as Joan was at age nineteen for alleged heresy), but what if you made a huge decision now to burn at least your primary sin of addiction at the stake? You'd certainly be making God's adult-sitting job easier!

SOUL SEARCH

In what way do you try to live out the days God has ordained for you in a manner that is pleasing to him? What could you do to increase your direct communication with God regarding his call to sobriety and his divine will for you?

Creator God, you know every detail about all the past, present, and future days of my life. "How precious are your thoughts about me, O God. They cannot be numbered! I can't even count them; they outnumber the grains of sand!"* Teach me to become your most remarkable rendition of me.

---

* Psalm 139:17-18.

P.U.R.P.O.S.E. Principle II: Understand Biblical Truths about God's Will

Purpose-Filled Living

God has a major, strategic plan that involves the sober, purpose-filled you living to honor him. Believing this truth may interfere with the personal agenda you've set previously for your life (financially, relationally, physically, or vocationally), but his way is always a far better way!

☀ Meditate on the Assurance of God's Word

Seek his will in all you do, and he will show you which path to take.   PROVERBS 3:6

The Canaanite woman prayed, "Lord, help me!"   MATTHEW 15:25

☀ Humbly Talk with the Lord

Praise God that he's helping you follow his will for your life. Invite him to be specific about what still needs to change to make you more loving, committed, and effective. Seek his will in all you do, and pray, *Lord, help me!*

Thank God that you can't see the whole scope of his work, which would cause your brain to freeze! Also thank him that, in his perfect timing, he'll reveal the next steps of your recovery marathon and his preferred plan for your life.

☀ Take the *Life Purpose Coach* Challenge

Make a list of the top three selfless things you'd do to grow God's Kingdom on earth if these support systems were in place: time, money, expertise, networks, volunteers, marketing resources, prayer support, political clout, advisors, and a public platform. Put an "X" by any of the three tasks you'd do even if it meant giving up your addictions. Put an "XX" by any that would be worth dying for—giving your all for them to come to fruition.

P.U.R.P.O.S.E. Principle II: Understand Biblical Truths about God's Will
Old Testament Purpose

Make your motions and cast your votes, but GOD has the final say.
PROVERBS 16:33 (*The Message*)

God has a reputation for creating "Must Do" assignments for his people and then sending his Holy Spirit to lobby votes for those projects! After such an impression from God's Spirit, you may have felt convicted about a particular healthy life dream. Or in the midst of incredible pain from self-loathing, sexual abuse, or a destructive action, you may have grown confused and gotten off target. Whether you're feeling convicted or confused, be assured that God's plan will be fulfilled. Consider these two Old Testament figures (and those on March 28 through April 1), who each felt pulled toward a particular ministry-mission for God.

A wealthy, respected woman from Shunem felt compelled to minister to the prophet Elisha by providing him with more than an occasional meal at her home. She said to her husband, "Let's build a small room for him on the roof and furnish it with a bed, a table, a chair, and a lamp. Then he will have a place to stay whenever he comes by" (2 Kings 4:10). And they did.

Nehemiah, a cup-bearer for King Artaxerxes of Persia, prayed for four months about rebuilding Jerusalem's walls, until he could no longer deny his burning desire to do so. Finally, Nehemiah said to the king, "If it please the king, and if you are pleased with me, your servant, send me to Judah to rebuild the city where my ancestors are buried" (Nehemiah 2:5). And the king granted Nehemiah's request.

Like the Shunemite woman and Nehemiah, we're to move toward God's will. Paul Tournier, a Swiss physician and pastoral counselor in the mid-nineteen hundreds, wrote, "The main thing in this world is not being sure what God's will is, but seeking it sincerely, and following what we do understand of it. The only possible answer to the destiny of man is to seek without respite to fulfill God's purpose." Seek it without intermission.

SOUL SEARCH

What, if anything, has been more spiritually satisfying to you than pursuing the seasonal or long-term work that God has placed on your heart? How has that satisfaction impacted your sobriety?

God of Abraham, Isaac, and Jacob, give me a clean bill of health—mentally, physically, and emotionally—and sign me up for whatever tour of duty you prefer.

P.U.R.P.O.S.E. Principle II: **U**nderstand Biblical Truths about God's Will

Noah, Build an Ark

God said to Noah, . . . "Build a large boat from cypress wood and waterproof it with tar, inside and out." . . . So Noah did everything exactly as God had commanded him.
GENESIS 6:13-14, 22

God observed that the world had become a hotbed of corruption, violence, greed, drunkenness, and gluttonous orgies. He grew sorry that he'd made the human race, so he decided to wipe out all living creatures in a great flood that would last forty days and nights. He instructed Noah to save his family of eight (himself, his wife, and his three sons and their wives), along with pairs of every kind of non-seaworthy animal, so the world could be repopulated with people and creatures later. Noah was to build a massive, three-story boat with animal stalls, which we can visualize today as having the floor space of twenty standard-sized basketball courts.

Can it be said of us (as it was said of Noah in Genesis 6:9) that we're righteous, blameless, and walking in close fellowship with God, or would it be more accurate to say that we're caught up in self-gratifying addictions and caustic ways? To put Noah's faithfulness and obedience into perspective, consider that this man spent 120 years building God's ark, although it's likely that he'd never before seen rain! This type of role model forces us to take an honest look at our lives to decide if we would have made the cut of those who boarded the ark for a full year, or if we would have been left behind to drown in our sinfulness. And just as important, we need to ask ourselves if we would have pleaded with others day after day for more than a century to have faith in God and heed his warning to repent.

SOUL SEARCH

How do you feel when you obey God and find favor in his eyes? If the great Flood had begun right now, instead of in Noah's time, what evidence could you present to God that the ark doors shouldn't close without you on board?

God of all the earth, teach me to walk in close fellowship with you and to obey your detailed instructions for my recovery and my life mission.

Abram, Go

The LORD had said to Abram, "Leave your native country, your relatives, and your father's family, and go to the land that I will show you." GENESIS 12:1

What if the entirety of the Lord's message to Abram were Genesis 12:1, in which he commanded Abram to leave most everybody behind and go toward an unrevealed destiny? I wonder if Abram would have gone. More particularly, has God asked you to leave your comfortable life, dreams of being famous, illegal activities, or regrets behind and head out on an unfamiliar spiritual journey to an unknown destination?

The next verse in Genesis 12 makes it clear that "leave" and "go" weren't all God had to say about Abram's call and his adventure into the unknown. The Lord adds, "I will make you into a great nation. I will bless you and make you famous, and you will be a blessing to others" (v. 2). Has God ever promised you anything of value as an added incentive for obeying his call and living a redeemed life—a holy, healthy, addiction-free life? Yes, he has!

You've been promised Jesus, our Morning Light, who brings peace: "Because of God's tender mercy, the morning light from heaven is about to break upon us, to give light to those who sit in darkness and in the shadow of death, and to guide us to the path of peace" (Luke 1:78-79). Ah, you're holding out for more enticement than Jesus and peace before you follow God blindly. You might, then, also hold out for more than hope, joy, strength, wisdom, courage, and purpose—all of which are promised on our road trip with God. Would you settle for a mansion, as is promised in John 14:2?

Don't let your heart be troubled as you head out on a journey of obedience; you'll be showered with unimaginable rewards!

SOUL SEARCH

How do you feel about obeying a call from God to be sober and faithful in exchange for the reward of character growth and a life of significance? Who or what has been urging you to hold out?

Morning Light, you promise so many rewards in exchange for my obedience. You're spoiling me with your love.

Sarah, You'll Be the Mother of Nations

I will bless [Sarah] richly, and she will become the mother of many nations. Kings of nations will be among her descendants.   GENESIS 17:16

God said that Sarah was going to play a key role in his divine plan: that he'd bless her with a son from whom nations would flow. He said that Sarah, who'd been barren all her life, was to become a mother at age ninety—making her a front-runner for the title of "Most Exhausted Parent Ever."

Although Sarah was chosen for this critical assignment, she was no angel. Like us, she had her issues, as noted in Genesis 12, 16, and 18. She was discouraged about unfulfilled promises from a decade earlier; she blamed God for her barrenness; and she circumvented God's plans by persuading her husband to have a child through her slave girl Hagar, thus creating a huge, political mess. She treated Hagar harshly; she eavesdropped on God's conversation with her husband, stubbornly refusing to come out of her tent; and she lied to God about laughing at his latest version of a ten-year-old promise. Enough said? God uses imperfect people, and he specializes in impossible situations.

Despite Sarah's shortcomings, sad heart, and nervous laughter, Hebrews 11:11 reports, "It was by faith that even Sarah was able to have a child, though she was barren and was too old. She believed that God would keep his promise." God sees your past, present, and future all at one time; he sees you as who he's destined you to become. No matter how bleak a situation may look to you, how dashed your hopes, or how long it takes for God to act, resolve now to constantly reaffirm your faith in God, who is always true to his promises.

SOUL SEARCH

What sober, fulfilling life has God promised you? What can you do to focus on God while you wait for his promises to unfold? (Just for fun: What personal hope about your own delays can you derive from a quick calculation of Sarah's age at her son's college graduation ceremonies?)

My Hope, help me grasp your response to Sarah's laughter: "Is anything too hard for the LORD?"*

---

* Genesis 18:14.

P.U.R.P.O.S.E. Principle II: **U**nderstand Biblical Truths about God's Will

Moses, Free My People

[God told Moses,] "Now go, for I am sending you to Pharaoh. You must lead my people Israel out of Egypt." EXODUS 3:10

Would you want a burning-bush experience like Moses had, where you stand on holy ground and hear from God about your future? That's a tough question, because as much as you might want to hear about how to live a healthy, recovered life of unique purpose, you might still say no out of fear of getting a Moses-size assignment. Your reply might be, "Who am I to do something great for God?" If so, you'd be singing out of Moses' hymnal. When he was told to escort an entire people group out of cruel oppression to safety and freedom, he protested, "Who am I to appear before Pharaoh? Who am I to lead the people of Israel out of Egypt?" (Exodus 3:11).

Moses had plenty of justification for his underlying fears. Although he'd been raised as Egyptian royalty, he'd been born a Hebrew, just like the abused slaves. Would his own people accept him? He had murdered an Egyptian man and then fled for forty years to hide in Midian tending sheep. Would he be punished if he returned? Regardless, his reputation was already ruined. And besides all that, he had a tendency to get tongue-tied. Too bad he had no clue that God could use his shepherding experience for the good of the upcoming Exodus. God's promise to Moses, urging him to take his place in history, is one for us to remember: "I will be with you" (Exodus 3:12).

God will be with us, too, when we're afraid and balking at our big assignment in life—the first step of which is consistent, Christ-centered, sober living that actually directs us to our God-willed destiny. We simply need to decide if we'll offer some excuse to God or accept what he's got planned for our lives.

SOUL SEARCH

Have you ever begged, "Lord, please! Send anyone else," as Moses did in Exodus 4:13? How will developing the habit of prompt, joyful obedience impact your recovery progress?

I Am Who I Am, send the healthy me to do your will, wherever you like, and to deliver your message to whomever. All I ask is that you'll be with me.

P.U.R.P.O.S.E. Principle II: **U**nderstand Biblical Truths about God's Will
Joshua, Cross the River

The LORD spoke to Joshua. . . . "The time has come for you to lead these people, the Israelites, across the Jordan River into the land I am giving them." JOSHUA 1:1-2

Would you have liked Joshua's job of getting the nation of Israel across the Jordan River into God's Promised Land? Those Israelites had enough recovery-type issues about control, stubbornness, fear, drunkenness, gossip, immorality, bickering, and idol worship to try the patience of a saint! To intensify your pressure, you'd have to follow in the footsteps of Moses, the one "whom the LORD knew face to face" (Deuteronomy 34:10). But stretching our faith is what God does with us. He commissions us to step into roles beyond our current abilities and to do impossible things, which always includes overcoming our own insecurities, addictions, and fears. He sets us at the edge of a Jordan River and tells us to cross it in blind faith with him so we can conquer imposing giants for him and lead others to the promise of a new life in Christ.

Do I faintly hear you saying something like "But I'm no Joshua. I've not been Moses' understudy. And basically, I'm a mess"? Well, let's talk about that. The Spirit-filled Joshua was certainly chosen, anointed, and commissioned. God even told Moses to lay hands on Joshua and to transfer some of his authority to him, so the whole community of Israel would obey him (see Numbers 27:20). The crux of the matter is this: like Joshua, you're Spirit-filled, chosen, anointed, and commissioned; and you have access to role models who can teach you to do whatever God wants. To cross the Jordan, however, you must be willing to accept the authority God transfers to your life.

Your job, your joy, is to work in concert with God, focusing on your sobriety and character transformation, not on your fears. The time has come to do God's will more fully; the time is now.

SOUL SEARCH

From what addiction would you need to be set free to fully engage in a Joshua-type role? If you knew God was committed to orchestrating your success, what group of people would you like to lead on his behalf?

My Commander in Chief, anoint me doubly—I'm excited. Commission me anew—I'm ready!

P.U.R.P.O.S.E. Principle II: **U**nderstand Biblical Truths about God's Will

God's Call to Service

Invite God to speak to you about his plans for your sobriety and his call to service.

☀ Meditate on the Assurance of God's Word

The LORD said [to Samuel about David], "This is the one; anoint him." . . . Samuel took the flask of olive oil he had brought and anointed David with the oil. And the Spirit of the LORD came powerfully upon David from that day on.
1 SAMUEL 16:12-13

[The Lord said to Jacob in a dream,] "The ground you are lying on belongs to you. . . . Your descendants will be as numerous as the dust of the earth! . . . What's more, I am with you, and I will protect you wherever you go. . . . I will not leave you until I have finished giving you everything I have promised you." GENESIS 28:13-15

☀ Humbly Talk with the Lord

Thank God that he loves you enough to have sent his Son to die for the stubborn sins of your addiction.

Ask the Holy Spirit to lead you to your anointed purpose in life in his good timing.

☀ Take the *Life Purpose Coach* Challenge

Imagine that Samuel has just anointed you with oil and that the Spirit of God has empowered you like you've never before experienced. Hear the Lord saying to you, "I am with you, and I will protect you wherever you go. . . . I will not leave you until I have finished giving you everything I have promised you." Consider how accurately this scene might reflect the truth of God's plan for your life that's actually spot on!

P.U.R.P.O.S.E. Principle II: **U**nderstand Biblical Truths about God's Will
New Testament Purpose

We are Christ's ambassadors; God is making his appeal through us. We speak for Christ when we plead, "Come back to God!" 2 CORINTHIANS 5:20

How do you feel about being Christ's ambassador and pleading with people—including those who are lost in addiction—to come back to God? Do you have any previous job experience as Christ's representative to those who are hurting? Any client testimonials on your behalf?

Many in the New Testament, like Stephen, Philip, John the Baptist, Peter, and Mary Magdalene, were Christ's emissaries, and they sang the powerful, Johnny-one-note song of "Come back to God" (see April 4–8). And they allowed God to make the decisions about how long and with whom they were to serve as Christ's advocates.

I've often wondered if individuals living back then were ever given a glimpse of the importance of their God-given assignments. For example, take Priscilla and her husband, Aquila, who were fellow workers with Paul in the ministry of Jesus Christ (see Romans 16:3). Did they even begin to understand their eternal impact in growing the early church? Logic tells us no, that they were just showing up for work and being obedient to go wherever God sent them on any given day. Looking back in time, though, gives us the advantage of understanding that all our actions—the God-directed ones and the ill-conceived ones—do have a positive or negative eternal impact. Each decision (whether to support or to subvert God's will) in our personal lives, homes, workplaces, congregations, or communities matters to him. In each case, our obedience builds up our faith and the faith of others or our disobedience tears faith down.

Have you been one to complain about the heavy responsibility you've been given in your difficult assignments? We must resist the urge to complain about our tough row to hoe. We mustn't be like Tevye, the main character in *Fiddler on the Roof*, who says to God, "I know, I know. We are Your chosen people. But, once in a while, can't You choose someone else?"

SOUL SEARCH

In what way has your reputation or smoldering secret regarding addictive substances or activities affected your role as an ambassador who's on a life mission for Christ? Who has helped you "Come back to God!" in the past?

Author of my story, thank you for allowing me to be your herald. What an honor.

P.U.R.P.O.S.E. Principle II: **U**nderstand Biblical Truths about God's Will

Stephen, Testify about Jesus

As they stoned him, Stephen prayed, "Lord Jesus, receive my spirit." He fell to his knees, shouting, "Lord, don't charge them with this sin!" And with that, he died.
ACTS 7:59-60

As one of the seven deacons of the early church, Stephen had a good reputation and was full of the Holy Spirit; he was a man of faith and wisdom who could be trusted to manage fairly the money and food for the Hebrew and Greek widows of the church. And he was "full of God's grace and power, performing wondrous miracles and signs among the people" (Acts 6:3-8). What a nice tribute to Stephen, but it makes any recovery testimony seem scandalous in comparison to this saintly church leader!

At least Stephen's story does have its own share of dramatic flair. He actually ended up on trial before the Sanhedrin when he was wrongly accused of blasphemy. Acts 6:15 reads, "Everyone in the high council stared at Stephen, because his face became as bright as an angel's." Led by the Spirit, Stephen refused to water down his teaching about the Savior; the crowd went crazy and stoned him to death.

This martyr's story gives us cause to reflect on three ideas:

- First, even if we're not eloquent speakers, we're called to speak up for the cause of Christ. (Has your God-gifted sobriety caused you to testify about Jesus, your Higher Power?)
- Second, even if we don't feel like we have the spiritual gift of martyrdom, we have been assigned a godly cause into which we're to pour out our lives. (Are you recovered enough to begin helping others to whom God is calling you?)
- And third, even if we'd rather not forgive those who've harmed us, we know that our healing involves saying something like "Lord, don't charge them with this sin!" (Have you been able to forgive others?)

SOUL SEARCH

To what parts of Stephen's testimony can you relate? When have you been led by the Holy Spirit to do something brave regarding your addictions or life purpose?

Lord Jesus, my life has been anything but dull. I ask you to turn all my drama and fears into Spirit-filled passion for you.

P.**U**.R.P.O.S.E. Principle II: **U**nderstand Biblical Truths about God's Will

Philip, Follow Me

[Jesus] found Philip and said to him, "Come, follow me." JOHN 1:43

Imagine that Jesus is speaking directly to you, a person who struggles with addiction, when he says, "Come, follow me." Would you do what Philip did and immediately go tell a friend that you'd found the Savior of the world (see John 1:45)? Jesus saw the evangelist in Philip, and he sees that foundational spiritual giftedness in you, too—even though you may not be able to see it just yet as a basic conversational skill.

Now imagine that you're Philip as one of the twelve apostles. Jesus tests your faith when he asks you where you could buy bread to feed all the people listening to him preach. You reply sarcastically that his question is absurd (see John 6:7). Jesus then begins to work with you long term to teach you to trust his infinite power in all matters. Yes, in all matters, including those of provision as well as your sobriety and sacred calling.

By Acts 6, Philip seems to have a hotline to God and be serving faithfully. What would that type of relationship with God do for you? Would it revolutionize the way you approach your recovery if you could simply pick up the phone, speed-dial God, get his yea or nay input on this or that, and request troops to protect you? And how would it feel to know that you were serving and discipling others faithfully on his behalf?

Later Philip received only minimal instructions for his next assignment: "Go south down the desert road" and "Go over and walk along beside the carriage" (Acts 8:26, 29). He obeyed immediately and was able to help the treasurer of Ethiopia understand Scripture and accept the good news of Jesus. Like Philip, will you go and walk alongside someone to whom God calls you, even if you don't exactly know where you're going?

It sometimes helps me to ask, "WWPD?"—"What would Philip do?" Three things we know for sure that he'd do: trust God, serve well, and go where commanded.

SOUL SEARCH

In what way is Jesus calling you, as he did Philip, to evangelize, disciple, and minister to those who are hurting? How do you feel about sharing the gospel or inviting someone to discuss his/her spiritual growth, even though you have recovery issues?

My Teacher and my Help, I want to follow you the rest of my life. Tell me to trust and I'll trust, to serve and I'll serve, to go and I'll go.

P.U.R.P.O.S.E. Principle II: **U**nderstand Biblical Truths about God's Will

John the Baptist, Prepare the Way

[Zechariah prayed,] "You, my little son, will be called the prophet of the Most High, because you will prepare the way for the Lord." LUKE 1:76

Zechariah certainly prayed knowingly, affirming that his newborn son would be a spokesperson for the Most High. Has anyone ever prayed over you—before, during, or after your most wayward days? Surely people have spoken harshly to you with warnings, admonishments, threats, and criticism, but do you have a cluster of family and friends who offer you encouragement and wise counsel that direct you toward God's will?

God is eager for you to be a spokesperson for him, just as John the Baptist was. Did you know that God's job description for you actually stipulates your duties as helping people find God and seek his forgiveness for their sins? Not to worry, though, about the minor details of how all that's going to play out, because by working a solid recovery program, you're becoming an expert in this area of asking for forgiveness, receiving it, and granting it to others. After all, how many of these statements do you repeat daily already?

- Forgive me as I learn to forgive (Step Nine in the Twelve Steps for Believers).
- My unforgiving heart causes me more pain than it does my offender.
- The most difficult type of forgiveness is forgiving myself.
- The flip side of forgiveness is resentment.
- "Forgive us our sins, as we have forgiven those who sin against us" (Matthew 6:12).
- Through Jesus, we have forgiveness for our sins (see Acts 13:38).
- There but for the grace of God, go I.

Like John, you could be the voice of someone shouting, "Prepare for God's arrival! Make the road straight and smooth" (Isaiah 40:3, *The Message*). Like John, you're filled with the Holy Spirit and with the ability to turn many people to the Lord their God. How do you share the Lord with others? One sober step at a time.

SOUL SEARCH

How would you feel if you knew people were praying for your recovery and for you to be unabashedly sold out for God? How would that affect your current choices?

Most High, heal me and empower me as a prayerful, Spirit-filled spokesperson for you! Send me into this world with a passionate message.

P.U.R.P.O.S.E. Principle II: **U**nderstand Biblical Truths about God's Will

Peter, Feed My Sheep

[Peter] said, "Lord, you know everything. You know that I love you." Jesus said, "Then feed my sheep." JOHN 21:17

During the emotionally and physically grueling night prior to Jesus' crucifixion, Peter brashly denied knowing his friend Jesus three times (see Mark 14:66-72). Later Jesus gave Peter three chances to be absolved from that heavy guilt by prompting Peter to profess his love for him. Our passage is Peter's third declaration in front of his peers. Christ was kind to let Peter have such blatant proof of his forgiveness and reconciliation to him. Anything sound similar to your recovery story? Has your relationship with Christ been on-again and off-again, stop and start, come and go, yes/no/maybe so?

In spite of our often-fickle behavior, Jesus knows we love him, just as he was already convinced of Peter's love. Earlier Peter had confessed Jesus as the Messiah, the Son of the living God, to which Jesus replied, "Now I say to you that you are Peter (which means 'rock'), and upon this rock I will build my church" (Matthew 16:18).

As for us, if we really love Jesus, then we'll listen carefully for and pursue diligently his personalized plan for our lives. He isn't demanding that we prove our love by scaling Mount Kilimanjaro's highest, volcanic peak on the very day it decides to erupt again; he's only asking us to follow his lead, step by step, down the specific pathway he lays out for us individually. Will you allow him to bring an action step to mind now—one you can take toward healing and a significance-filled life?

SOUL SEARCH

When have you felt that Jesus was giving you another chance to confess your love for him, possibly to keep you from growing too discouraged over your previous denial of his power? What's your favorite memory of Jesus in your life?

Patient Lord, I confess that I deny you often, and yet you forgive me repeatedly. Your patience with me, as I've struggled with addiction, has caused me to love you more. Lead me now to an obedient life.

P.U.R.P.O.S.E. Principle II: **U**nderstand Biblical Truths about God's Will

Mary Magdalene, Proclaim the Resurrection

Jesus said [to Mary Magdalene], "Go to those who believe in me. Tell them, 'I am returning to my Father and your Father, to my God and your God.'"
JOHN 20:17 (NIrv)

Mary Magdalene was one of the last people at the cross with Jesus, one of the few people to see where Joseph of Arimathea laid his body, and one of the first people at the tomb after he rose from the dead. Mark 16:9 reports that she was the first person Jesus chose to speak to after he had risen, and John 20:18 adds that she was the first person to proclaim the Resurrection. We must remember that all these privileges were given to Mary Magdalene, the one who'd been possessed by seven demons that Jesus expelled (see Luke 8:2).

How would you like to have received all the privileges afforded this forgiven sinner? Do you think that after Jesus healed you, your lifetime gratitude to him would have compelled you to stay with him at the cross and escort his bruised body to a hollowed-out rock cave? Could it be said of you now that you proclaim to others that he's alive?

Your own story of being bound by addictive forces might not involve seven demons, but it is a testimony of miraculous deliverance from evil, and it can be told as an encouragement to others worldwide for all time. And you can expect that when you're worried on any given day that Jesus has left you, he'll call you by name, just as he called Mary (see John 20:16). He'll meet you at your place of greatest sorrow and assure you of his presence.

SOUL SEARCH

If Jesus appeared to you right now, what words of encouragement would bless your recovery and what words of instruction would move you toward his admirable purpose for your life? Do you have someone who can offer you Christlike encouragement and guidance?

Rabboni/Teacher, I cling to the fact that you say you'll never leave me, not even for a second. I need you to teach me more about your truths, holiness, and boldness; I need your healing, comfort, and life instructions.

P.U.R.P.O.S.E. Principle II: **U**nderstand Biblical Truths about God's Will

God's Plan to Redeem the World

God doesn't need us, not even the sober us, to accomplish his plan of redeeming the world, so it's gracious of him to allow us to play a significant role. He designed us to desire to be part of a vision that is larger than ourselves—his vision—and for that, we can be eternally grateful. What small, inconsequential lives we'd lead otherwise.

☀ Meditate on the Assurance of God's Word

The disciples went out, telling everyone they met to repent of their sins and turn to God. And they cast out many demons and healed many sick people, anointing them with olive oil. MARK 6:12-13

The LORD had said to Aaron, "Go out into the wilderness to meet Moses." So Aaron went and met Moses at the mountain of God, and he embraced him. . . . Then Moses and Aaron returned to Egypt and called all the elders of Israel together. EXODUS 4:27, 29

☀ Humbly Talk with the Lord

Worship God for his brilliance in causing you to hunger after him and his vision for your life.

Ask God to give you obedient discernment regarding your next recovery step.

☀ Take the *Life Purpose Coach* Challenge

Get out of your same-old, same-old rut that's trapping you in ineffectual patterns and limiting how you see God's call on your life. Do something different that will stir up your creativity and get you out of your box. For such escapades, I've been known to sing my prayers aloud, switch brand loyalty, gaze at a picture upside down, or eat breakfast for dinner. Get creative and enjoy!

P.U.R.P.O.S.E. Principle III:
Rightly Tell My Recovery Story

I turn my past and present over to God to complete my future life's work.

Unpacks the Twelve Steps for Believers
May 1–June 11

P.U.**R**.P.O.S.E. Principle III: **R**ightly Tell My Recovery Story
God Works for Good

We know that God causes everything to work together for the good of those who love God and are called according to his purpose for them. ROMANS 8:28

God helped Paul overcome his past, and Paul encourages us in Romans 8:28 that God can do the same for us. The secret to this audacious overcoming is to love and obey our Maker. God is faithful to cause everything that happens in our lives to work together for a good outcome. One outcome might be our ability to see the truth about our alcohol dependency, lust, or power struggles, causing us to stop flirting with worldly desires. It might be that we begin to think with an eternal perspective about our actions or afflictions, causing us to embrace those practices that are good for our soul.

God's ability to use someone's traumatic past has even resulted in jaw-dropping good for an entire nation. We read in Genesis 37–50 that Joseph, the youngest son of Jacob, was sold into slavery by his jealous brothers and later unjustly accused of adultery and imprisoned. Because of Joseph's integrity and God-given ability to interpret dreams, he emerged at age thirty as Pharaoh's commander over the entire land of Egypt and began storing up crops for the upcoming seven-year famine. When his brothers finally bowed down to him, as he had foretold they'd do, Joseph said these insightful words to them: "You intended to harm me, but God intended it all for good. He brought me to this position so I could save the lives of many people" (50:20).

Like Joseph, we're not to get stuck in the past. Instead, we're to let God use it as a launchpad to the future he intends for us. Edmond Burke, an author and statesman, adds this simple reminder to let go and let God: "The past should be a springboard, not a hammock."

SOUL SEARCH

What evidence do you have thus far on your recovery journey that God is causing everything to work together for your good? In what way are you more of a springing-forward type person or a hammock-vegging one?

Never-Failing One, I want to overcome my past by allowing everything about it to contribute to my God-glorifying future.

P.U.R.P.O.S.E. Principle III: **R**ightly Tell My Recovery Story

Using My Grief

God is our merciful Father and the source of all comfort. He comforts us in all our troubles so that we can comfort others. 2 CORINTHIANS 1:3-4

God cares about the grief you've experienced, whether the circumstances are related to your addictions or simply because life is unfair and hard. Grief hunts us down in relentless pursuit after such circumstances as foster-care abuse, being homeless and hungry, a drug deal gone bad, a near-fatal car accident, cyberspace bullying, a military separation, or an unsuccessful adoption. Our passage tells us, though, that when life tragedies attack, God is the source of all comfort. And he asks that you give others the same comfort he's given you, recycling his love to them. He intends for you to lend a hand to others who are experiencing pain, including but not limited to that pain from which you're fairly well healed.

Suffering and grief decimate everyone's life at some point, making us all cracked pots. Whether our brokenness has been triggered by such sadness as date rape, foreclosure on a home, unfair treatment in our workplace, or the death of an unsaved friend, we're all hurting. Some of the walking wounded are obviously more expert at covering up their fractures—especially on Sundays at church, as they smile just long enough to collapse back into their cars!

And a word to the wise about the healing process: resist the temptation to cover up or ignore your hurts, because the lessons you avoid will come back to demand your full attention. God wants to use your past to shape and perfect you, so he won't let any lesson go unlearned. When you acknowledge and deal with your pain, you're forced to decide whether you'll surrender your anguish to God for him to use in his ideal plan or not. Don't be shocked when your grief lessons lead you to your life purpose. That is not to say you have to serve in your area of intense grief, but that your experiences will have perfectly prepared you for whatever spot God intends.

SOUL SEARCH

What grief issues are still festering in your heart, and which ones have healed? How has your surrendered past matured you spiritually, helped you recover from addiction, and given you a glimpse of your potential life mission?

My Comfort, bring your healing balm to my open wounds. Help me imagine the day that I'll have healed enough to comfort others in the same way you've comforted me!

P.U.**R**.P.O.S.E. Principle III: **R**ightly Tell My Recovery Story
Tiptoeing through Life

[Abraham] didn't tiptoe around God's promise asking cautiously skeptical questions.
ROMANS 4:20 (*The Message*)

Abraham didn't tiptoe around God's promise that he'd become the father of many nations. He sure could have spent his time worrying though, because Sarah had been infertile for decades and he was a century-old male. Instead, he came alive with grateful hope and shouted for joy over God's promise for his future. Why walk on eggshells around what is, or might never be, when we can step in tune to God's lively upcoming plans?

You might be tired of tiptoeing, literally, through your house because an abusive, alcoholic spouse or a volatile, rebellious teenager is sleeping. Carrying that type of stress is no way to live, especially if you can't even flush the toilet for fear of the next tirade. Now recall how you've tiptoed around the evil of your past to avoid the humiliation of being exposed. Instead of soft-shoeing around either your current or past circumstances countless times each day, perhaps it's time to flush the toilet!

What if a recovery program, where anonymity is a key principle, became your safe place to make some noise about what you've previously hushed? What if—by seeing that others are not tiptoeing around their issues—you realized you didn't have to either? What if you could go to a meeting and share your fear about your sleeping monsters or about an abortion, financial disaster, eating disorder, or your rage over a betrayal? What if participating in a small group there helped you understand that God wants to use your pain and sadness? What if wise counsel from a sponsor or recovery coach could keep you from greater harm to your body, mind, and soul? What if listening to a recovery testimony helped draw you closer to God, teaching you to trust and obey him?

SOUL SEARCH

What's got you tiptoeing through life? And what are you going to do about it now, so you can make some joyful noise regarding God's pre-orchestrated work awaiting you?

God who celebrates my recovery, I'm tired of tiptoeing around the evil of my past and present. Thank you for inspiring Christ-centered recovery programs, so I can openly give all my hurts and troubles to you to put to good use. One word comes to mind to express my grateful relief: whew!

P.U.R.P.O.S.E. Principle III: **R**ightly Tell My Recovery Story

My Extra Baggage

Travel light. Comb and toothbrush and no extra luggage. LUKE 10:4 *(The Message)*

When the Lord sent out seventy-two disciples to do his Kingdom-building work, he told them to travel light, not to take any extra suitcases. That was a command relating to their physical needs, but the principle applies to our emotional baggage as well.

Unresolved issues of guilt, jealousy, blame, sadness, and disappointment are emotional baggage that nobody needs to lug with them. Likewise, issues surrounding abuse, fear, and other trauma bulge from baggage, when it needs to be unpacked and left behind. And anger . . . well, my anger baggage had become too heavy for me to carry. I actually once stood at a local airport baggage-claim carousel and purposely allowed my two weighty suitcases to circle around the loop four extra times while I prayed nonstop for God to take that same weight of anger from me. Eventually I claimed my bags, but I left my trunk load of anger behind that day, asking God to stow it where I wouldn't ever find it again. As ridiculous as that may seem, it was a real turning point for me in eliminating my rage about my ex-husband, who'd left our marriage and then had the audacity to die, leaving me to raise our two young children.

What burdensome stuff are you hauling around that you want to ditch now? Your propensity to worry, overanticipate, lie, or cheat? Your vulnerabilities behind your three-pronged bad habit of cursing, smoking, and barhopping? Or perhaps your bags feel more weighed down with "I shoulda . . ." and "If only . . ." Consider, instead, that God wants you to travel light down the road to recovery so you can be the seventy-third disciple—a worker in his fields who helps with the harvest.

SOUL SEARCH

What "guilty conscience" suitcase would Jesus like to take from you now? What joy might that bring you?

Mighty One, I know that some of my baggage of past grief has given me an identity in the "Poor Me" Society and that asking you to stow my freighter trunk will change forever the way I see myself, the way others see me, and the way I interact with those you're sending me to serve. Praying for a new beginning, I'd like to trade in my unwieldy luggage for your joyful presence and the knowledge of your will for my life.

P.U.**R**.P.O.S.E. Principle III: **R**ightly Tell My Recovery Story

My Successes and Accomplishments

O God, in addition to everything else, you speak of giving your servant a lasting dynasty! You speak as though I were someone very great, O LORD God!
1 CHRONICLES 17:17

God had pole-vaulted David from hanging out with sheep to being king over Israel and annihilating his enemies. And now God was making David's fame rock solid, elevating him to a place of prominence in history. God was revealing that, purely out of the goodness of his heart, he was going to raise up one of David's descendants, one of his sons, to establish his kingdom firmly forever. David recognized that God had granted him great success and fortune in spite of his shortcomings. (And as onlookers, we know that David would commit many sickening sins after this.) First Chronicles 17:16 tells us that King David prayed in utter amazement that God would award him more: "Who am I, O LORD God, and what is my family, that you have brought me this far?" Is that a question you've asked God, too, as he's moved you from shocking transgressions into another chance at recovery? After all, God has done mighty things for you and also wants to do many through you.

Humble people try to avoid talking about their accomplishments; insecure people don't believe they've got much to brag about; and recovering addicts are well schooled about not attempting to be the center of attention. But sometimes God needs us to bring our applause-worthy moments to mind so we can remember how he's shaped and equipped us. For example, he may have given you a talent to play the piano or paint portraits; he may have anointed you with the spiritual gift of teaching or encouragement; or he may have afforded you opportunities to learn a new skill like snowboarding or fixing computers. Each of these types of triumph can be used to give glory to God, spread the gospel, and change lives spiritually. Each of them can add a small clue to the mystery of why God created you and why addiction is not an option.

SOUL SEARCH

For what success have you been affirmed? How could God use your victory to encourage your sobriety and establish the work of your hands?

O Lord God, who am I, and what is my family, that you have brought me this far?

115

P.U.**R**.P.O.S.E. Principle III: **R**ightly Tell My Recovery Story
My One-Minute Testimony

When the Father sends the Advocate as my representative—that is, the Holy Spirit—
he will teach you everything and will remind you of everything I have told you.
JOHN 14:26

The Holy Spirit, your personal Advocate sent from the Father, is available to teach you everything you need to know for leading a recovered life and helping others do the same. He wants to release you to be God's instrument to those still entrenched in chaos, secrets, promiscuity, or other types of hopelessness—assuming you're able to do so without relapsing.

In preparation for this high calling on your life, it's a good idea to reflect on how to write and present your one-minute testimony, which can be thought of as an "elevator speech." The time it takes an elevator to climb/descend a few floors may be all the time you have to present your story of God's mercy. Using these three topics in your testimony, be careful not to make it a preach-imony:

- your life before you met Christ or began to follow him more closely;
- specifically how you came to know him;
- your life after Christ, including what has changed and who he is to you.

This prayerful process includes seeking wise counsel about what parts of your testimony are appropriate to share during this season of your life. (See June 10 about writing your longer testimony.) It's equally important to check your motives for wanting to share your history. If any part of you thinks you might like getting some credit for your testimony regarding all the hard work you did to help save yourself, then it's best to wait until you've prayed that pride out of the equation and you've got only a humble desire to be a vessel in God's hands.

SOUL SEARCH

What facts might you consider including in your one-minute testimony? What trusted friend or sponsor could advise you and listen prayerfully while you rehearse aloud?

Advocate, as you prompt me to write my brief testimony, give me the right desire of obedience. Send me directly to those who need to hear the short story of how my life was spared for a purpose, and teach me to share my journey with utmost humility and gratitude.

P.U.R.P.O.S.E. Principle III: Rightly Tell My Recovery Story

Use All of Me

Have you invited God into your recovery attempts, knowing that he wants to use all of you for his work on earth?

☀ Meditate on the Assurance of God's Word

You keep track of all my sorrows. You have collected all my tears in your bottle. You have recorded each one in your book. PSALM 56:8

God had mercy on me so that Christ Jesus could use me as a prime example of his great patience with even the worst sinners. 1 TIMOTHY 1:16

☀ Humbly Talk with the Lord

Tell God that your spirit is being crushed under the heavy load of your emotional baggage (e.g., guilt, fear, jeolousy, hurt feelings, anger/rage issues from abuse) and that you need his immediate help.

Spend a few minutes admiring Jesus' healing power; revel in his kind willingness to make you whole.

☀ Take the *Life Purpose Coach* Challenge

We've all gotten stuck in a ruminating rut, which is the deadly mind game of replaying something in our past (e.g., rejection, accusation, abandonment, loss, physical harm, betrayal, crisis) as if it were in the present and we could affect the outcome. Satan's end goal in this bizarre tactic is to distract us from our sobriety and life mission by stirring up feelings of anger and depression in us. Instead, try this: recall something that you used to ruminate about—from which you've now been healed. Bring to mind God, the Commander of Heaven's Armies, as he met you at that dreadful place of your tremendous worry and handled the situation! Remember his power, love, and compassion during that difficult time of your life. Grab hold of that hope, and overlay it on a current situation. Envision the victory celebration that God has arranged for you in this additional circumstance.

P.U.R.P.O.S.E. Principle III: **R**ightly Tell My Recovery Story

Consequences, Regrets, and Ungodly Values

I am focusing all my energies on this one thing: Forgetting the past and looking forward to what lies ahead, I strain to reach the end of the race and receive the prize for which God, through Christ Jesus, is calling us up to heaven.
PHILIPPIANS 3:13-14

The apostle Paul laid out an excellent recovery model in our passage, recommending three steps that helped him move from the trauma of his life—some of which he caused and some that was wrought upon him.

First, do yourself a favor and stop dwelling on your past pain, which includes your faults, errors, consequences, regrets, ungodly values, and sorrow. Train your mind to let go of your unhealthy past, to forget about it, to leave it behind. Obviously, processing pain helps bring closure to it, so process it, and then put it to rest. As is said in recocvery circles, it's okay to look back, but don't stare. Second, look forward to your future, to what lies ahead. Once you get a glimpse of God's spectacular plan for your life, you'll desire to run toward it. Third, strain to finish the race. Focus all your energies on the racecourse and on the prize that awaits you. Bear down and go for it with every ounce of your being. Do so in a spirit of cooperation with God, as you prayerfully plug in to his wisdom, strength, and courage.

Author Aldous Huxley reminds us that we have an opportunity to mentally reframe our lives for the better, regardless of what has previously haunted us: "Experience is not what happens to a man; it is what a man does with what happens to him." We must change our default mode from dwelling negatively on our past to taking positive action steps that create a healthy future.

SOUL SEARCH

What have your past consequences, regrets, and ungodly values taught you? How will these valuable lessons guide you into making a timely recovery and a specific, eternal contribution?

God who focuses forward, help me briefly process my unhealthy past so I can forget it and look forward to all your goodness that lies ahead. I know this is a huge request on both fronts, so I thank you dearly for your help.

P.U.**R**.P.O.S.E. Principle III: **R**ightly Tell My Recovery Story

Tough Consequences

It's your sins that have cut you off from God. Because of your sins, he has turned away and will not listen anymore.   ISAIAH 59:2

Isaiah tells us that our sins can cut us off from God; one of the tough consequences of that estrangement is that God may ignore our cries for mercy. And our family, friends, boss, or pastor may choose to dole out additional consequences when we're unwilling to learn a critical life lesson. Exacting a high price may be the only way they can get our attention. Until our pain causes us to see the truth of a situation, you and I both know we won't change. The more we drag our feet stubbornly, refusing to listen to the voice of reason, the more painful the consequences to our reputations, income, health, relationships, freedom, careers, self-esteem, and future opportunities. The more we ignore God's truths and live outside his will, the more we choose to live defeated, sleepwalking lives.

On the brighter side, though, when we're entirely ready to have God remove our character defects, he'll lovingly reply with a personalized version of Zechariah 13:9, like this: *I will bring you through the fire and make you pure. I will refine you like silver and purify you like gold. You will call on my name, and I will answer you.* So if you've bought into the lie that you're alone or that you can't talk about "it"—whatever your horrendous "it" is—remember that your story is precious and priceless to God. Curl up in his arms and pour out your heart to him. He longs to say to you, *I love you to pieces,* and to hear you say to him, *I can't live without you.*

SOUL SEARCH

What's the toughest consequence you've faced? What valuable lesson did you learn from that situation that could help you address current rehabilitation issues and fulfill God's perfect plan for your life?

My Judge, I don't like facing hard consequences in my life, but I sure do understand the value of the ones you've initiated for my character upgrade. Thank you for loving me, especially through the consequences I've brought on myself.

Escaping Consequences

Be silent now and leave me alone. Let me speak, and I will face the consequences. . . .
God might kill me, but I have no other hope. I am going to argue my case with him.
JOB 13:13, 15

Our family, friends, and God don't usually allow us to escape consequences when we're on a merry-go-round of addictive behavior that brings suffering to others and ourselves. What a day to rejoice, though, when they do grant us a reprieve from a horrible fate after we've learned our lesson in earnest and made amends. Halfway through Job's story, we read that he expected no such reprieve for pridefully arguing his case before God. We have to rush to the end of the story to learn that, although Job was severely reprimanded for his attitude, he did escape consequences. In fact, "the Lord blessed Job in the second half of his life even more than in the beginning" (Job 42:12).

My oldest brother, Chuck, was seventeen when he escaped punishment from our parents for a prank he pulled on his seven siblings—and he loves to tell about it:

One Saturday night, I was put in charge of making dinner while our folks were gone. I summoned my seven "hungry wards" for a dinner of beans: pinto, garbanzo, red, black, white, and green. They took a big-eyed look at their plates and ran out the door screaming and scrambling in every direction! I spent several hours corralling them all back into the house and feeding them peanut-butter-and-jelly sandwiches. When our parents returned, they got an earful from the young'uns, who held an impromptu mock trial and recommended that I face the severe consequence of being grounded for a month. I'm sure I would've been punished for the fiasco, if our parents could have stopped belly laughing.

Although Chuck didn't deserve to be severely punished, we often do deserve the toughest possible consequences. When God holds court, though, he sometimes allows us to bypass punishment, offering us unconditional love and forgiveness.

SOUL SEARCH

How has your recovery-based understanding of consequences (those mercifully escaped and those paid at a high price) caused you to be a better person? How has it caused you to pursue the adventure God has graciously granted you?

Sweet Jesus, thank you so much for those times you have taken pity on me.

P.U.**R**.P.O.S.E. Principle III: **R**ightly Tell My Recovery Story

My Biggest Regret

Why does this people go backward, and just keep on going—backward! They stubbornly hold on to their illusions, refuse to change direction. I listened carefully but heard not so much as a whisper. No one expressed one word of regret. Not a single "I'm sorry" did I hear. They just kept at it, blindly and stupidly banging their heads against a brick wall. JEREMIAH 8:5-6 (*The Message*)

God's blunt and piercing words in our passage emphasize that he wants us to express sorrow for our bad choices, to actually say, "I'm sorry." We also need to stop the negative action and change direction. That's repentance! Instead of continuing to bang our heads against a brick wall, we work to set things right. Only then can we share with others how God's grace transformed us into a new person. This godly progression is the stuff of which great testimonies are made!

On the other hand, if we don't do much of anything about a particular regret, we guarantee ourselves quite a different outcome: shame and guilt. Remember Judas? Even Judas felt regret. Matthew 27:3 reads, "When Judas, who had betrayed [Jesus], realized that Jesus had been condemned to die, he was filled with remorse." Judas took action, too: he even returned the money he'd received for betraying Jesus (see v. 3). But he missed the next essential steps of seeking, accepting, and living out God's grace. God wants us to ask for forgiveness so we can put our regrets behind us and begin to walk toward the purpose he's carved out for us. We must decide if we'll succumb to self-hatred over our missteps or if we'll allow God to use our experience to form our character and bless others. We don't want it said about us, "Not a single 'I'm sorry' did I hear."

SOUL SEARCH

What's your biggest regret (e.g., adultery, unwed pregnancy, lust for power, anorexia, burglary, greed, or a prison record)? How has your dealing or not dealing with it affected the joy of living out God's plan for your life?

Precious Lord, I'm so sorry that I've continued to bang my head against a brick wall, blindly and stupidly. Save me, oh, save me from the self-hate I feel for my past regrets, and change my trajectory!

P.U.R.P.O.S.E. Principle III: **R**ightly Tell My Recovery Story
Future Regrets

You don't want to end your life full of regrets, nothing but sin and bones, saying, "Oh, why didn't I do what they told me? Why did I reject a disciplined life? Why didn't I listen to my mentors, or take my teachers seriously?" PROVERBS 5:11-13 (*The Message*)

We all regret holding on to certain outdated systems in our lives that don't work for us anymore. For example, we may regret the dead-end career that used to be so attractive or the backbiting friendship that used to look so promising. We may regret that we've never updated our parenting style, which had been effective when our kids were younger. And we may deeply regret that we've never challenged the current, nightmarish state of our sinful addictions, which used to seem more alluring and easier to manage. We hear ourselves mourn, *Oh, why didn't I do what my sponsor told me to do?* It's important to rethink all potentially defunct processes and listen to wise souls, so we don't face future regrets.

Case in point is that Benjamin Franklin, the first United States Postmaster General, never suspected that the once-vibrant postal service would now be antiquated. As more people go online to send cards, pay their bills, post photos, clip coupons, and read magazines, the volume of stamped mail has plummeted, thus triggering the layoff of postal workers nationwide and reducing the number of days mail is delivered. For those of us who never questioned the status quo of the old postal system, it's hard to digest how this could happen. However, those who saw the bleak outlook looming for decades and had the power to create solutions may regret not implementing change before it was too late.

If you've been duly warned of your own imminent ruin, you have nothing to lose by accepting instruction and creating solutions to implement change.

SOUL SEARCH

In what way are you operating in a defunct model of addictive behavior that is screaming to be transformed into a new recovery model filled with God's purpose? What necessary changes have mentors, teachers, and sponsors suggested you implement?

My Strength, I don't want to end my life full of regrets saying, "Oh, why didn't I do what wise instructors told me?" Help me rethink all areas of my life so I don't pile up more regrets.

P.U.**R**.P.O.S.E. Principle III: **R**ightly Tell My Recovery Story

Pearls of Great Value

The Kingdom of Heaven is like a merchant on the lookout for choice pearls. When he discovered a pearl of great value, he sold everything he owned and bought it!
MATTHEW 13:45-46

Luke 12:34 reminds us that whatever we select as our pearl or treasure sets the course for our lives: "Wherever your treasure is, there the desires of your heart will also be."

In addition to the Kingdom of Heaven, think about other valuable pearls that your heart has desired during your recovery. Is your priceless treasure serenity, accountability, or one of these?

- Community (see Romans 15:5)
- Wisdom (see Ecclesiastes 10:10)
- Kingdom Work (see 1 Corinthians 3:13)
- Knowing Christ (see Philippians 3:7-8)

Reflect on how such pearls can focus you on the goodness of God—and how they point you toward his undeniable will. Or is one of these worldly treasures of perceived value the true desire of your heart?

- Wealth (see Proverbs 10:2)
- Security in possessions (see Job 18:14)
- Fame (see Psalm 49:12)
- Power (see Isaiah 14:11)

God revealed to some African businessmen the hiding place of one of his treasured places for doing his work on earth. He led them to the abandoned mining town of Bulembu, Swaziland, which they bought and renovated as a Christian orphanage. With the extinction of the Swazi people by the year 2050 being widely predicted (due to HIV/AIDS), they felt compelled to act to save the small nation. During my brief time serving in Bulembu in 2011, it was evident that the leadership team cherishes these pearls of great value: the children, faith, hope, love, and God's call on their lives.

As you pray your way through sobriety, focus on what God values, and you'll find a priceless treasure.

SOUL SEARCH

What are your three most treasured pearls, and why? How might God rank these?

Heaven's God, teach me to value those things on which you place the highest value.

A New Beginning

How often have you and I wished we hadn't done all the evil we've done? Our only hope of sanity is focusing forward and letting God's new-every-morning compassion wash over us, detoxify us, and prepare us for our exciting future.

☀ Meditate on the Assurance of God's Word

Because of the LORD's great love we are not consumed, for his compassions never fail. They are new every morning; great is your faithfulness.   LAMENTATIONS 3:22-23 (NIV)

The hotheaded do things they'll later regret.   PROVERBS 14:17 (*The Message*)

Keep your eyes on Jesus, who both began and finished this race we're in. Study how he did it. Because he never lost sight of where he was headed—that exhilarating finish in and with God—he could put up with anything along the way: Cross, shame, whatever.   HEBREWS 12:2 (*The Message*)

I am El-Shaddai—"God Almighty." Serve me faithfully and live a blameless life.
GENESIS 17:1

☀ Humbly Talk with the Lord

Thank God for how he has used serious consequences or heart-wrenching regrets in your life to cause you to seek after brand-new values and a new beginning filled with purpose.

Ask God for advice about how to manage the residual consequences that linger from the days you pursued your substance of choice.

☀ Take the *Life Purpose Coach* Challenge

Imagine that you volunteer for a crisis hotline dedicated to preventing relapse in addicts. A caller gives you an earful about not being able to leave certain regrets behind. What would you say to encourage that person to get past those things and move into God's delayed plan for his or her life? (Which of your prayerful, wise, and pointed remarks also pertain to you?)

P.U.**R**.P.O.S.E. Principle III: **R**ightly Tell My Recovery Story

Right, Wrong, Confused, or Missing

You saw how the LORD your God cared for you all along the way as you traveled through the wilderness, just as a father cares for his child. Now he has brought you to this place. DEUTERONOMY 1:31

Your heavenly Father cares about all aspects of your life. He loves you regardless of what's right, wrong, confused, or missing in this season—or even if you need a serious do-over because of ghosts that chase you. Ask him for wisdom to help you clarify what's going well for you and what's not. It's important to get in this habit of seeking clarity, because it ignites gratitude in you regarding all the good things that are happening, and it also helps you find solutions and support systems for trouble spots. When you're willing to take a realistic look at your life, you're able to move forward more readily out of any isolated, wilderness areas into the hospitable, fertile future God ingeniously arranged for you.

Whether you've experienced painful trials, unfair suffering, humbling police encounters, senseless benders, or incredible success, bathe your history now in prayerful self-examination. This humble willingness to take an inventory of your life will improve your conscious contact with God and give you the knowledge of his will and the power to carry it out. Helen Keller shared this truth about how intense times, in particular, can make us better people, when she wrote, "Character cannot be developed in ease and quiet. Only through experiences of trial and suffering can the soul be strengthened, vision cleared, ambition inspired, and success achieved." Allow her words to encourage you when you feel discouraged.

SOUL SEARCH

When has God traveled with you through a wilderness, as a loving father would with his child? What clarity, gratitude, solutions, or support systems has your prayerful self-examination garnered?

Father, you're my shelter from the storm, my shade from the heat, and my sanctuary in times of trouble. You've traveled with me through the most extreme wilderness and have brought me now to this place where I can embrace my sobriety, live unapologetically for you, and follow your precious will for my life. Thank you so much for giving me my life back.

P.U.**R**.P.O.S.E. Principle III: **R**ightly Tell My Recovery Story

What's Right in My Life?

O LORD, I will honor and praise your name, for you are my God. You do such wonderful things! You planned them long ago, and now you have accomplished them. ISAIAH 25:1

God may be blessing you in extravagant ways right now, doing such wonderful things and accomplishing all he planned long ago for your life. For example, you may have stayed clean recently against all odds, or you may have learned a new spiritual habit that's deepening your faith. Perhaps you've taken a moral inventory or watched your love grow in a trying circumstance. If you were to take stock of your marriage, job, ministry, health, or life's work, you might be able to celebrate incalculable progress in one or more of those areas. The Creator of the world has done mighty things for you, and Isaiah reminds us to take the time to honor and praise our all-powerful, wise God for his generosity and miracles.

To fully engage in this question about what's right in your life, though, it's important to first remember the insanity of the days when you felt like you were herding cats through a car wash! Without that reminder of how far you've come, you may shortchange God for all he has done for you. Hush your mourning heart for a moment, so you can recount your blessings. Yes, thank the Lord for them one by one. And if need be, step out of any jaded cynicism you might be feeling, which is convincing you that nothing is going well in your life. And then plan to show gratitude for God's benevolence to you by sacrificially serving others who are still trapped in their hurts and bad habits. You'll be able to add that experience to your list of what's going well.

SOUL SEARCH

What's right in your life? Have you dropped to your knees lately to thank God for the kindnesses he has bestowed on you in one or more areas?

My Lord who provides, bring to my mind all the good you have caused in my life—so I can fully honor and praise your name. I humbly thank you for helping me to stop living a lie, for silencing the mean people who surround me, and for all you still plan to accomplish through me for your Kingdom.

P.U.**R**.P.O.S.E. Principle III: **R**ightly Tell My Recovery Story

What's Wrong in My Life?

Jesus told [a lame man], "Stand up, pick up your mat, and walk!" JOHN 5:8

The lame man whose story is told in John 5:1-9 had something major wrong in his life: he'd been ill for thirty-eight years and had no hope of a miraculous cure. Jesus asked him if he'd like to get well. "'I can't, sir,' the sick man said, 'for I have no one to put me into the pool when the water bubbles up. Someone else always gets there ahead of me'" (v. 7). The lame man was in a desperate situation until Jesus came along and healed him. Jesus wants to heal you, too, from whatever addictive behavior is majorly wrong in your life. Talk to him about it without rattling off a list of excuses, and listen for him to say, "Stand up." Don't be afraid of what has to change when you're cured; just stand up.

The other day, I hung up from a telephone conversation thinking, *Aargh . . . what's wrong with the picture of what just happened?* I had responded kindly, but firmly, to a sweet telemarketer by stating, "I'm not interested in your product. Please put my name and number on your DNC [Do Not Call] list." She started apologizing and got so flustered that it took her several more minutes to quit talking. Her sincerity caused me to feel sorry for her, and I ended up spending considerable time comforting her!

When consoling telemarketers and, more important, when stumbling on the path to recovery, learn to ask yourself, *What's wrong with this picture?* while you still have time to course-correct midstream. Even asking the question after the fact, though, can keep you from repeating the cycle of poor choices.

SOUL SEARCH

What's wrong with the current picture of your life? Has dark chaos caused you to put God on a DNC list regarding your healing and life purpose? Like the lame man, have you been without hope for so long that you don't expect any help with your brokenness?

Healer of my mind, body, and soul, I need you more than the air I breathe. Help me be honest about what's wrong in my life. I'm ready to be healed and to focus on the distinct life mission you've chosen for me. Call me to stand up and walk toward you.

P.U.**R**.P.O.S.E. Principle III: **R**ightly Tell My Recovery Story

What's Confused in My Life?

God is not the author of confusion but of peace.   1 CORINTHIANS 14:33 (NKJV)

Confusion clouds our judgment and can even make us physically sick. Just think about a time when a "love interest" of yours gave you mixed messages! That type of puzzlement can stump the savviest person and lead to a wide array of poor choices. God is not the author of confusion, but we are creatures of commotion because we live in a fallen world—in the devil's playground of secrets, trickery, and deceit. That's why we're so wise to follow this golden rule: when there's confusion, wait and spend time with God to hear his voice. Consider this: befuddlement might actually be a gift from God. Perhaps he's using it to cause you to prayerfully pursue his peace and comforting presence amid baffling trials. When you sit quietly with him, he can choose to disentangle the twisted ropes of your thinking, but at minimum, his presence grants you relief from running the universe.

Some common areas of confusion in your life may revolve around your past, thus posing questions about whom to forgive; how to repent appropriately from a carnal, selfish lifestyle; and how God can turn your history of lies into a testimony. Confusion may invade your present, preventing you from making decisions related to your spiritual habits, health, business, recovery program, and questionable hobbies. And it may consume your focus for your future, causing you to wonder whom to trust with your story and purpose-filled dreams; where to live, minister, or go on a mission trip; and what cause to champion—without, of course, allowing the cause to become an obsession.

Ask the Holy Spirit to help you search the Scriptures for answers and to send you wise advisors who bring clarity to situations you're currently facing. Pray that you won't try to manipulate the circumstances or control the outcome but that you'll rest easy in the Lord.

SOUL SEARCH

What's your greatest area of confusion? What do you recall about God's faithfulness in responding to something that perplexed you in the past, and how can that help you now?

You who hear prayer, please speak to me. Shine your light—actually, your flood lamp—on my confusion, and reveal your truth and clarity so I can make healthy, wise decisions.

P.U.**R**.P.O.S.E. Principle III: **R**ightly Tell My Recovery Story
What's Missing from My Life?

Depend on the LORD and his strength; always go to him for help.   PSALM 105:4 (NCV)

God cares about what you feel is missing from your life, about how you perceive you've been overlooked in one of the key domains of life: personal, family, faith, vocation, relationships, ministry, or community. He knows that your day-after-day yearnings can negatively impact your recovery process and prevent you from focusing on his glorious plans for you. Instead of living in the sadness of a paralyzed life, "depend on the LORD and his strength; always go to him for help." Take the time to have a heartfelt conversation with God; he certainly knows what's best for you.

If you feel you've lost out on parental love, personal joy, a spouse, children, or character development, ask him about those things. You can also ask him for a simplified lifestyle, a spiritual awakening, renewed creativity, more energy, or a new church family. Others may say of you that you're missing a support system, integrity, downtime, exercise, a budget, organizational skills, or a God-anointed dream. You may feel that you're in dire need of goals, clarity, purpose, income, courage, or hope. It's okay to put any topic on the table for discussion.

Should God decide, in his wisdom, to continue to withhold certain things that you perceive to be missing from your life, ask him to show you the bigger picture of how he plans to use your lack for his greater good. And listen for grace-filled answers that will ease your frustrations, make you whole, and teach you to focus your attention on what you do have and on how to help others who are hurting. The process will strengthen your recovery and could easily lead you right into God's winningest plan for your life.

SOUL SEARCH

What's missing from your life? In what way is that hurting your heart and tempting you to stuff down your pain, drown your sorrows, or otherwise numb yourself?

My Friend and Creator, help me live a life of gratitude for the many blessings you've so generously given me. I trust you to fill the hole in my heart with your presence. I bow to your sovereign will, whether you choose to deliver or continue to withhold what I perceive to be missing.

P.U.R.P.O.S.E. Principle III: Rightly Tell My Recovery Story

A Do-Over

Let me hear of your unfailing love each morning, for I am trusting you. Show me where to walk, for I give myself to you. PSALM 143:8

Thank heavens that our God is a God of a zillion chances. He encourages us to talk to him in the heartfelt tone of Psalm 143:8: *Let me hear of your unfailing love each morning—fresh and new. Give me another chance, a do-over, on this particular circumstance of my life: _____. I trust you to show me where to walk and how to handle this situation, so history doesn't repeat itself and so I can heal. I boldly yet humbly ask for this.*

If you're serious about getting a do-over, discuss it with God right now. He is definitely your best advisor on this topic. Whether you caused domestic violence, gambled away your life's savings, felt trapped by the demands of others, or were buried alive by vicious lies and deception, God is listening and wants to guide you.

You've heard the phrase "saved by the bell," which refers to getting a second chance. Widespread Internet fiction touts that the phrase originated because people were accidentally being buried alive. In anticipation of this unfortunate occurrence, loved ones would tie a string to a dead person's wrist in a coffin and attach it to a bell aboveground. You may have wished for such a huge second chance at life. In actuality, though, "saved by the bell" is a boxing phrase. A boxer can be saved by the ringing of the bell that signifies the end of the round, even if he's down and in the process of being counted out. If he recovers during the one-minute break, he gets a do-over in the next round! Similarly in life, you can pray that God will always ring the bell to save you, that even though you're down, he won't let anyone count you out.

SOUL SEARCH

If you were allowed a do-over on one recovery-related circumstance in your life, which would you choose and why? What have you learned about yourself that's going to make you a better servant-leader while doing the life work God has laid out for you?

You who show me the way, I ask for another chance to make things right.

P.U.R.P.O.S.E. Principle III: **R**ightly Tell My Recovery Story

Give Me Insight

Your heavenly Father would like to have a heart-to-heart with you about what's right, wrong, confused, and missing in your life—and about what you wish you'd get a chance to do again better. You've got God's full attention, so don't hold back. Ask for any insight that's especially related to your family, your sobriety, or your life mission.

☀ Meditate on the Assurance of God's Word

If you need wisdom, ask our generous God, and he will give it to you. He will not rebuke you for asking.   JAMES 1:5

O my people, trust in him at all times. Pour out your heart to him, for God is our refuge.   PSALM 62:8

We [Paul and his companions] were crushed and overwhelmed beyond our ability to endure, and we thought we would never live through it. In fact, we expected to die. But as a result, we stopped relying on ourselves and learned to rely only on God, who raises the dead. And he did rescue us from mortal danger, and he will rescue us again. We have placed our confidence in him, and he will continue to rescue us.
2 CORINTHIANS 1:8-10

☀ Humbly Talk with the Lord

Praise God for all that's right in your life, including your favorite blessing or miracle. Add a special word of thanks regarding any do-overs you've been granted.

Seek the Lord's insight about moving forward with your sobriety efforts and his remarkable plan for you, despite what's wrong, confused, or missing.

☀ Take the *Life Purpose Coach* Challenge

Ask God to fill you with himself as your chief source of wisdom and discernment. Then ask him to show you whom to invite to walk alongside you on your recovery journey toward a life filled with unimaginable purpose.

P.U.R.P.O.S.E. Principle III: Rightly Tell My Recovery Story

Living Sober

My health may fail, and my spirit may grow weak, but God remains the strength of my heart; he is mine forever. PSALM 73:26

Are you ready to admit that you're powerless over your dependencies and that your life has become unmanageable (Step One)? Are you ready to believe that God can restore your sanity and help you follow his plan (Step Two)? These resounding questions can be overwhelming unless you pray for strength of heart to claim your recovery and allow God to invade your thinking and actions.

Rahab, a pagan prostitute, claimed her new life by allowing God to invade her world. In acknowledging that God intended to give her city, Jericho, to Joshua and the Israelites, she said to Joshua's spies, "The LORD your God is the supreme God of the heavens above and the earth below" (Joshua 2:11). That was her turning point, when she realized she was powerless in an unmanageable situation and decided that she'd be better off if she trusted God as the strength of her heart. You can read her story in Joshua 2:1-24 and 6:17-25, but a great summary of it can be found in Hebrews 11:31: "By faith the prostitute Rahab, because she welcomed the spies, was not killed with those who were disobedient" (NIV). Rahab's newfound faith literally saved her life and her family members' lives.

What happened after the spies moved Rahab and her family to a safe place near their camp? God orchestrated that she would live among the Isrealites so she could grow in her faith! And we know from the genealogy of Matthew 1:5-16 that she married an Israelite and bore a son, Boaz. If we trace Rahab's family line through Boaz, we find that she was an ancestor of Jesus! Her expectant faith not only saved her life; it also reserved a place for her in Christ's lineage.

Andrew Murray, a South African pastor, reminds us, "Faith expects from God what is beyond all expectation." Do you expect God to save you, restore you to sanity, and guide you?

SOUL SEARCH

In what way has admitting that you're powerless been difficult for you? What would a "Rahab turnaround" look like for you?

Strength of my heart, I'm counting on nothing less than your faithful love of sinners to keep me from growing faint. Don't fail me now in my recovery process, or I won't live to praise you and fulfill the remarkable mission you've designed for me.

P.U.R.P.O.S.E. Principle III: Rightly Tell My Recovery Story

Step One: I'm Powerless

I admit that I'm powerless over my dependencies and
that my life has become unmanageable.

*Jesus had already commanded the evil spirit to come out of him. This spirit had often
taken control of the man.*   LUKE 8:29

The man described in Luke's story (8:26-39) was completely under the power of demons. That type of powerlessness over our lives is frightening, humbling, and maddening— and it can cause us to do crazy things. Perhaps you've experienced such helplessness and hopelessness after an unrelenting demon beguiled you into cutting, bingeing, scamming, or sex trading. Whenever you become trapped by evil, try to quickly remember that Jesus cares deeply about whatever problems you're struggling to overcome and that he's available to command the intruding spirit that's controlling you to leave.

Powerlessness reminds me of the Spinning Beach Ball of Death on our computers, the very one that just left my office fifteen minutes ago! You know too well that infamous, rotating wait-cursor that jumps onto your screen when an application is not responding. It's so dreaded by the masses that it's been nicknamed the pinwheel of misfortune, the rainbow wheel of doom, and the crazy ball from hell. It makes us feel trapped in an infinite loop of helplessness.

You may not know how to escape the cycle of misfortune, doom, and hell in your life that brings with it anger, boredom, fatigue, or loneliness, but Jesus knows how to help you. Simply approach him, as the demon-possessed man did: "As Jesus was climbing out of the boat, a man who was possessed by demons came out to meet him" (Luke 8:27). Yes, go meet Jesus now. Let him see deep into your heart—the place that cries for healing from a powerless, unmanageable life. Let him cast any demons into an abyss and restore your sanity so you can proclaim all the great things he's done for you.

SOUL SEARCH

What demon has trapped you in powerlessness? What's the hazard to your distinct life purpose if you don't meet with Jesus for help?

*My Burden Bearer, protect me from a life that has spun out of control. I turn my chaos
over to you and ask you to restore your sweet Spirit in me.*

P.U.R.P.O.S.E. Principle III: Rightly Tell My Recovery Story
Step One: Seeing Truth
I admit that I'm powerless over my dependencies and
that my life has become unmanageable.

Teach me to see what I still don't see. Whatever evil I've done, I'll do it no more.
JOB 34:32 (*The Message*)

What reason could people possibly have for not wanting to see the evil they've done? For one, if they saw it, they might feel pressured by Job 34:32 to say that they won't do the evil anymore. Another reason is that they might prefer the victim persona they have as a lost, shipwrecked soul, which gives them the attention they need. Or their disconnect from reality might have freed them from people's high expectations, created a distraction from their sorrows, or given them a modicum of control—no matter how much of a false smidgen of control that is. More than likely, their denial is a self-protective measure that keeps them from feeling mortified. But until we're able to see the evil and pain we've caused others and ourselves, we won't be able to recognize that we're powerless over our addictions. So our first step in making our lives manageable is to see the truth about our situations.

Twelve thousand years ago, ancient farming communities that milled cereal crops didn't know the truth, for example, about the value of bran, which is the lightweight, outer shell of a wheat berry. The miller crushed the wheat kernels, letting the bran fall to the floor; he then swept it up to discard it, much as a barber sweeps up hair. Today we know that bran is rich in dietary fiber and essential fatty acids—and that it contains protein, vitamins, and minerals. Ah, the truth continues to set us free, making some of us healthier and some in the health food market rich from selling wheat husks!

Like those who finally saw the truth about bran, we must be willing to see the truth about how powerless we are over our addictions.

SOUL SEARCH

What's the best thing that could happen if you asked God to reveal your shortcomings? What's the worst outcome for your life mission if you don't address your sins?

God of truth, teach me to see what I still don't see about my sins, so I'll understand how powerless I am over my problems and how unmanageable my life is without you.

P.U.**R**.P.O.S.E. Principle III: **R**ightly Tell My Recovery Story
Step Two: Choosing Sanity
I believe that God can restore me to sanity and
help me follow his plan.

*You will live in the fields with the wild animals, and you will eat grass like a cow . . .
until you learn that the Most High rules over the kingdoms of the world and gives
them to anyone he chooses.* DANIEL 4:32

The deadly progression of addiction can be halted only when we trust in God's power, rather than in our own efforts. Once we come to terms with the fact that we're not God, he begins to restore us to sanity through sobriety. Daniel 4 tells the story of King Nebuchadnezzar, who had a God complex that brought severe consequences. Verse 30 exposes the king's prideful heart when he says, "By my own mighty power, I have built this beautiful city [Babylon] as my royal residence to display my majestic splendor." Probably not such a good idea for Nebuchadnezzar to talk like that, especially when Daniel had just predicted what would happen if he did. (Pause for a moment to check yourself for any addiction to pride, any God complex, and any insanity about being the author of your own life plan.)

While those words were forming in the king's mouth, a voice called down from heaven, letting him know that he'd be driven from society to meet the fate described in our focal passage. This banishment was to last seven years—just enough time for Nebuchadnezzar to comprehend that the Most High rules over all. (Ask yourself how long it will take or already took for you to come to believe that a Power greater than yourself could restore you to sanity.)

At the seven-year mark, Nebuchadnezzar's sanity returned, and he declared what we all should say when we come to our senses: "I praised and worshiped the Most High and honored the one who lives forever" (Daniel 4:34). The king's advisers and nobles sought him out, and he was restored as head of the kingdom. (Think about how often you praise, worship, and honor the Most High.)

SOUL SEARCH

What will change if God restores your sanity and you follow his sobriety plan? What life dream might God want to restore to the humbled you?

King of heaven, your rule is everlasting and your Kingdom eternal. Your acts are just and true, and you are able to humble the proud. * *Humble me, restore me, lead me.*

* This was part of Nebuchadnezzar's prayer; see Daniel 4:34, 37.

P.U.R.P.O.S.E. Principle III: **R**ightly Tell My Recovery Story

Step Two: Second Chance

I believe that God can restore me to sanity and
help me follow his plan.

Fix your attention on God. You'll be changed from the inside out. Readily recognize what he wants from you, and quickly respond to it. ROMANS 12:2 (*The Message*)

We only get one life, and we need to make the most of it by asking God to rescue us from our cravings, schemes, and dependencies. Our Romans passage tells us that if we fix our attention on God, we'll be changed from the inside out. It indicates that now is "go" time—the time to recognize promptly and respond quickly to what God wants of us. Its urgency reminds me of the golden hour in emergency medicine: that short period of time during which rapid intervention prevents death after severe trauma.

The golden hour slipped away for Bryce Easley, a twenty-year-old Canadian who was a much-loved son, grandson, brother, and boyfriend. He drowned February 18, 2010, while snorkeling one hundred yards off Maui's Ka'anapali Beach. With tear-filled prayers, I watched the heroic efforts of the US Coast Guard, a search-and-rescue team, lifeguards, and the fire and police departments. Although hope faded regarding Bryce's rescue after the first hour, helicopters, boats, divers, and outriggers continued to search 2,700 square miles for his body for three days. Memorial services were held on the beach and later in his home church in British Columbia. Bryce didn't get a second chance at life, but you've been granted a golden hour.

You may feel as if you've been sucked under life's rough currents and that you're drowning in Internet pornography, terrors from your childhood, suicidal tendencies, scandal, or physical pain, but God is throwing you a lifeline of survival and significance. He's your only hope, and the time is now.

SOUL SEARCH

What will you do with your second chance at life? Will you fix your attention on God, allowing him to bring out the best in you as you become fully mature in Christ?

My Source of Strength, I'm in distress and drowning, but I'm holding on tight to you as my lifeline. Lift me out of the depths of my sin so I can accomplish what you put me on earth to do, which I know is to breathe your words of life into others.

P.U.**R**.P.O.S.E. Principle III: **R**ightly Tell My Recovery Story

Rest for the Weary

Jesus said, "Come to me, all of you who are weary and carry heavy burdens, and I will give you rest." MATTHEW 11:28

My friend Carol, who's a believer recovering from the addiction of taking care of her family of addicts, described to me how weary she was from carrying the heavy burdens of her dysfunctional family. Later she was able to find rest for her soul by making a conscious decision to spend more time with Jesus, simply sitting in his presence—often reading his Word and sometimes just weeping. She shared with me how repeatedly the Lord had laid on her heart in her quiet time to get some support, and how lifegiving that prompt from God had been.

After taking steps to be obedient in that regard, she said, "It's made a big difference for me to get understanding and encouragement at Al-Anon Family Group meetings. I had plenty of information, but I needed more than knowledge; I needed to admit I was powerless. In the AA community, I learned to let go and let God through surrender, faith, and trust. I received foundational assistance and learned how to live the Twelve Steps as a lifelong process with Jesus as my Higher Power."

Jesus is calling to the weary you; he wants to carry your heavy burdens; he wants to give you rest for your soul. Respond to Jesus by spending more time with him in quiet reflection. He'll be faithful to whisper timely advice that will heal your heavy heart, get you some much-needed support, and engage you in his perfectly crafted plan for your life. Do whatever you need to do to block out the whirlwind and noise of your life, so that only Jesus remains.

SOUL SEARCH

Do you tend to enjoy sitting quietly with Jesus, or do you see it as more of a burdensome requirement? Why do you think that's how you feel?

Jesus of the weary, don't stop carrying my burdens. I'm in such bad shape that I might even need you to hoist me over your shoulders and carry me like an injured lamb. Take me to a quiet place where I can be with you for a time of healing and rest. I'm sorry you've been my last resort; from now on, you'll be my first and greatest hope.

P.U.R.P.O.S.E. Principle III: Rightly Tell My Recovery Story
My Higher Power

When you realize that all your attempts to solve your problems have been ineffectual and that you're incapable of recovering on your own, Jesus, your Higher Power, will be standing by to help you make sense of your life again.

☀ Meditate on the Assurance of God's Word

Those who trust in the LORD will find new strength. They will soar high on wings like eagles. They will run and not grow weary. They will walk and not faint.
ISAIAH 40:31

[Jesus said,] "If you love me, obey my commandments." JOHN 14:15

☀ Humbly Talk with the Lord

Go to the Lord to admit that your life is out of control and that you've been deceiving yourself into believing you could stop your addictive behavior any time you wanted.

Ask God to send credible witnesses into your life—those who've come to believe and can testify that Jesus Christ restored them to sanity.

☀ Take the *Life Purpose Coach* Challenge

If you're in a season of denial, you may attempt to feel powerful by fixing someone else, by fighting an injustice, or by saving the world. Don't be tempted to do so, or you'll plunge deeper into avoidance of your own pain. Instead, grab a journal and make a list of all the good deeds that make you feel powerful and in control. Put a check mark by any that cause you to avoid your own problems. Make a decision now to pray about how to handle those checkmarked actions for the upcoming season, so you can focus on God's foremost plan for your life right now, which is recovery. If disengaging from certain projects becomes hard for you, remember that God wants you to heal now so you are able to make a significant contribution from a healthy perspective when he gives you a green light.

P.U.**R**.P.O.S.E. Principle III: **R**ightly Tell My Recovery Story

Faithful God

God has said, "I will never fail you. I will never abandon you." HEBREWS 13:5

Without the focal point of our Hebrews verse, you might feel it would be too frightening to make a decision to turn your will and your life over to the care of God (Step Three), let alone attempt to make a searching and fearless moral inventory of yourself (Step Four). So let's grab onto the promise given by our Scripture, which uses the phrase "I will never" twice in its brief remarks. God is giving you his solemn word that he'll never stop working on your behalf; he'll never disappoint you or miss the curative mark; and he'll never hang out a Going Out of Business sign. He won't let you down, fall down on the job, fall short, walk away, or steer you in a wrong direction. Failing you or abandoning you is never an option for him! He is smart enough; he is up to snuff; he is committed to you for the long haul; and he has processed all your prayers.

To put God's magnanimity into proper perspective, Blaise Pascal, a seventeenth-century philosopher, writes, "The God of the infinite is the God of the infinitesimal." Let this remind you that your faithful God cares about your biggest, overarching goals and also about the tiniest details of your life (moral inventory). In fact, he cares so deeply about your short- and long-term sobriety concerns that he's willing to sit with you around the clock for the rest of your life to guide you into your best possible life. You can trust in the simple, straightforward truth of 1 Peter 5:7, which instructs, "Give all your worries and cares to God, for he cares about you."

SOUL SEARCH

After being around a human being who failed you or abandoned you, how do you want to do life with others? After getting to know the one-and-only faithful God whose power is available to you around the clock, what do you think he'd choose as your next action steps toward recovery and investigating your unique life mission?

God of the infinite and infinitesimal, I testify that you've never failed me or abandoned me in spite of my unfaithfulness to you. Transform me into your faithful follower.

P.U.R.P.O.S.E. Principle III: **R**ightly Tell My Recovery Story
Step Three: Care of God
I turn my will and life over to God's care.

I have given you the choice between life and death, between blessings and curses. . . .
You can make this choice by loving the LORD your God, obeying him, and committing
yourself firmly to him.   DEUTERONOMY 30:19-20

The Lord God Almighty spoke through Moses to the Israelites reminding them of a decision they needed to make. Would they pick Option A: choosing him, loving him, and serving him—all of which would bring life and blessings? Or would they go for Option B: choosing to worship another god—a decision that would signal their ruin, spiritual death, and, assuredly, the accursed disaster that descends on those involved in evil. Moses even called on heaven and earth to witness their decision, and then he said, "Oh, that you would choose life, so that you and your descendants might live!" (Deuteronomy 30:19).

God used this stern language to make a deep, lasting impression on the Israelites and on us. Knowing our propensity to want a good life and to escape whatever misery we can, he reminds us of the deadly consequences of disobeying him and of being in bondage to a demigod. He cautions us to give up our self-will and to intentionally turn over everything to him—including our shame, secrets, fears, joy, dreams, and the grandiose thinking that creates the illusion we're in control.

Dependence on God and submission to his will bring us peace of mind, rest from weariness, and freedom from the horror of life-stealing addictions. We can either choose to resist God, keeping him at arm's length, or we can give up control to him for the rest of our lives and live in his favor. It's our decision.

SOUL SEARCH

In the past, what has prevented you from turning your life and will over to the care of the Lord your God? In what way do you trust God more now?

Life-giving Lord, of course I want your abundant blessings and hope poured into me, but more than that, I want you. Even if your favor and a dignified life mission weren't part of the package deal, I'd still choose to be sold out for you. May you accept my recovery efforts as a sacrificial offering to you, the Lord of my life, forevermore.

P.U.**R**.P.O.S.E. Principle III: **R**ightly Tell My Recovery Story

Step Three: 180-Degree Turnaround

I turn my will and life over to God's care.

Paul said, "And so . . . I obeyed that vision from heaven." ACTS 26:19

When Saul of Tarsus was traveling down the road toward Damascus, Jesus spoke from heaven, calling him into his service by confronting him with a decision to make about his future. Would Saul, a merciless persecutor of Christians, continue his violence against the church, trying his best to destroy it, or would he turn his will and life over to the care of God? Was Saul was on the fast track for Steps One, Two, and Three in the Twelve Steps for Believers program? In an instant he was asked to face the truth about his need for a Higher Power and the insanity of his prejudice and anger! And we know that Saul did turn his will and life over to the care of God through Jesus: "And so . . . I obeyed that vision from heaven" (Acts 26:19). Such radical obedience to God means that you obey your Maker immediately. It means that you can't continue in your evil ways of impulsive acting out or secret sins. Gone are the days of binge drinking, dry alcoholic raging, promiscuity, and antisocial behavior.

Saul explains how he was able to make the dramatic shift: "Even before I was born, God chose me and called me by his marvelous grace. Then it pleased him to reveal his Son to me" (Galatians 1:15-16). After a season of training, Saul began to use his Roman name, Paul, for the sake of his non-Jewish listeners. God wants to interrupt your patterns of behavior, too, changing everything that doesn't fully support his call on your life. You might not need a new name, but you can count on your newly grasped identity in Christ.

SOUL SEARCH

How do you feel about God orchestrating (or already having orchestrated) a 180-degree turnaround in your life? How do you feel about radical obedience to God, which means following the recovery plan and life plan he has laid out for you?

God who called me by his marvelous grace, I know I'm being sent like Paul to proclaim faith to those you've chosen and to teach them the truth that shows them how to live godly lives.* Thank you for this high calling, which gives me another reason to recover. And thanks, too, for crafting a unique approach of how I'm to do this.

---

* From Titus 1:1.

Step Four: Searching and Fearless Inventory

I conduct a searching and fearless
moral inventory of myself.

Go and sin no more.   JOHN 8:11

Can you imagine living in Jesus' day and being dragged before him in a public spectacle, like the woman caught in the act of adultery (see John 8:3-11)? How humiliating to have judgmental onlookers doing your moral inventory for you! I'm afraid that in front of a crowd, my tearful shame would have drowned out Jesus' words of forgiveness. How beautifully Jesus handled the situation when the religious teachers and the Pharisees said that Moses's law required them to stone the woman. He stooped down and wrote in the dust with his finger. What he wrote is a mystery; some scholars contend it was the names and sins of those demanding that she be stoned. Wouldn't that have been a classic Jesus response to reveal the truth so boldly and calmly? I can't wait to ask him about it one day.

The story continues, explaining that Jesus stood up and said to the crowd, "All right, but let the one who has never sinned throw the first stone!" (John 8:7). The accusers all slipped away, not one of them daring to condemn the woman. Then Jesus told her, "Go and sin no more."

If you've felt pummeled with rocks of moral accusation thrown at you by others, or if you've become ill over self-condemnation, rid yourself now of those reprehensible processes. They'll only make you feel more beat up, more bone tired, and more nauseous. Skip all that accusatory, busybody drama and ask Jesus and a trusted advisor for help with your personal inventory!

SOUL SEARCH

Will you ask Jesus to help you do a private searching and fearless moral inventory? What might it feel like to give examples of the flip side of your sins (for example, humility instead of pride, peace instead of anger, and integrity instead of dishonesty)?

My Redeemer, I'm ready now to discover my part in any given situation and to acknowledge my faults as well as character growth, but I can't do that alone. I need you more than ever to guide me in this process and toward the destiny you've mapped out for me.

142

P.U.R.P.O.S.E. Principle III: **R**ightly Tell My Recovery Story

Step Four: Carpe Diem
I conduct a searching and fearless
moral inventory of myself.

Repent! Turn away from all your offenses; then sin will not be your downfall. Rid yourselves of all the offenses you have committed, and get a new heart and a new spirit. EZEKIEL 18:30-31 (NIV)

Many things can cause us to turn our lives around and choose a different direction, whereby we actually repent or change our minds about habitual sin. For example, you might survive a traumatic experience that causes you to embrace a Jesus-honoring life, you might find a Scripture passage that convicts you to trust God with the torment of your soul, or you might even accept reproof about your lack of faith in God's ability to heal you from the bondage of addiction.

In January 2006, an unusual event caused me to take a quick inventory of my life—especially in the area of a broken relationship and amends. I had overslept one wintery morning and decided to skip my early jaunt on a nearby dirt trail that traces a rambling route around a behemoth crater below. Instead, I flipped on my television to a local news channel to see that a mountain lion had come up from that crater, crossed the trail I typically used, and was crouched on a neighbor's backyard fence. Call me a chicken or call me smart, but I never could get myself to go back down that pathway. I'd much prefer to err on the side of a healthy fear of danger. However, the incident stirred in me a predictable, "carpe diem" (seize the day) urgency to ask for forgiveness about a quarrel I'd had with my best friend, whom I called immediately.

What would cause you to repent, change your mind, or seize the day? Lamentations 3:40 suggests doing an honest, fearless, Step Four–type inventory to assess the good and the bad of your life: "Let us test and examine our ways. Let us turn back to the LORD." Why not take inventory now, before the lion of truth pounces out of nowhere? Why not seize the day for truth?

SOUL SEARCH

How is a spiritual inventory of your past and present God's gift to you? In what way does a personal inventory cause you to work toward God's future purpose for your life?

Honest God, I pray in concert with Psalm 119:29, "Keep me from lying to myself."

P.U.**R**.P.O.S.E. Principle III: **R**ightly Tell My Recovery Story

Rewards of Repenting

Resist the devil, and he will flee from you. Come close to God, and God will come close to you. JAMES 4:7-8

Our reward for resisting the devil is that Satan will flee from us; our reward for drawing close to God is that God will come close to us. Sounds like doctor's orders for how to live a recovered life. It's an offer we can't refuse! But why then do we often snub our heavenly Father's offer and prove the rest of James 4:8 right: Our "loyalty is divided between God and the world." It's obvious that we love our addiction idols, as well as God.

When Zephaniah called God's people to flee from evil and draw close to God, the prophet laid out their responsibilities and potential rewards. He said that if they sought the Lord, followed his commands, did what was right, and lived humbly, perhaps the Lord would protect them from his anger (see Zephaniah 2:3). Did they repent? No. Was it because the offer of a reward came with a "perhaps" clause that they lost motivation?

No, Zephaniah listed for them specific, impressive rewards the Lord was prepared to give. Allow me to list them, as if these are the rewards you'll receive for seeking the Lord and choosing sobriety: your enemies will be dispersed; the Lord himself—the King of Israel—will live with you; your troubles will be over; you'll never again fear disaster; a mighty Savior will take delight in you and calm your fears; your oppressors will be dealt with severely; the helpless you will be rescued; you'll be brought back home with glory and fame; you'll receive a good name of distinction; and your fortunes will be restored (adapted from Zephaniah 3:14-20). For rewards like this, we're foolish not to repent!

It's said that hindsight is 20/20, like looking in life's rearview mirror with perfect vision. With all the hindsight we have about the great rewards God gives, why is it still so hard for us to wash our hands and purify our hearts (see James 4:8)?

SOUL SEARCH

When has the devil fled from you? In what one way could you wash your hands and purify your heart now, so you can move forward with God's call on your life?

King of Israel, my greatest reward is you; all else is gravy!

P.U.R.P.O.S.E. Principle III: **R**ightly Tell My Recovery Story

In Relation to Him

As you develop right thinking about God and who you are in relation to him, lean into the hope of your sober future and invite right thinking about your sins.

☀ Meditate on the Assurance of God's Word

Search me, O God, and know my heart; test me and know my anxious thoughts. Point out anything in me that offends you, and lead me along the path of everlasting life. PSALM 139:23-24

He personally carried our sins in his body on the cross so that we can be dead to sin and live for what is right. By his wounds you are healed. Once you were like sheep who wandered away. But now you have turned to your Shepherd, the Guardian of your souls. 1 PETER 2:24-25

His unfailing love toward those who fear him is as great as the height of the heavens above the earth. PSALM 103:11

☀ Humbly Talk with the Lord

Praise God that he's willing to take you from where you are today to where he wants you to be.

Ask the Holy Spirit to direct you to a Scripture, person, event, or crossroads that will move you toward the care of God, a searching and fearless moral inventory, and your burgeoning life mission.

☀ Take the *Life Purpose Coach* Challenge

Recovery is a team effort of positive influencers, sober friends, and a wise sponsor, along with accountability and prayer partners. Prayerfully commit to enlisting one such person within the next twenty-four hours. Don't go on this long hike alone.

P.U.**R**.P.O.S.E. Principle III: **R**ightly Tell My Recovery Story
Becoming Ready

O my God, I am utterly ashamed; I blush to lift up my face to you. For our sins are piled higher than our heads, and our guilt has reached to the heavens.   EZRA 9:6

Let's pause for a moment to allow our hearts to catch up with our brains. We've discussed the indisputable facts that we're not God and that we have no power to stop the insanity of addiction without his help. We've reviewed the importance of committing ourselves to God's care and openly examining our lives by doing a searching and fearless moral inventory. We know to proceed with humility to Step Five, which is admitting to God, to ourselves, and to another human being the exact nature of our wrongs. And, we understand that Step Six won't be easy, as we become entirely ready to have God remove these defects of character. Although any such steps can create unwelcome vulnerability as we expose our shortcomings, worse yet may be the unexpected angst we feel about abandoning our old, comfortable patterns.

Instead of worrying, pray with Ezra, a man of integrity: *I'm utterly ashamed that my sins are piled higher than my head.* As tough as that advice might sound, this act of humility will move you from denial to an accurate view of yourself as a sinner, like the rest of the human race! Then as new challenges chase you, you'll be positioned to praise God, who loves you in spite of your debilitating addictions. As you live this recommended life of gratitude more consistently, you'll experience a deeper trust in God's power, thrilled that he's offered to guide you into wholeness, serenity, and integrity. Keep this Japanese proverb in mind as you proceed: "Fall seven times, stand up eight"— remembering that it's God who will help you stand up again.

SOUL SEARCH

When have you fallen and felt the Lord helping you regain your footing? How would you feel about writing down one particular story along those lines, so it can help you and others in the future?

God who sees my sins and calls me to a life of sobriety, give me strength to stand back up and become a purpose-filled person for you. I want to follow your utterly amazing and splendidly significant will for my life.

P.U.**R**.P.O.S.E. Principle III: **R**ightly Tell My Recovery Story

Step Five: I Admit

I admit to God, to myself, and to someone who's
trustworthy the exact nature of my wrongs.

Blessed are the pure in heart.   MATTHEW 5:8 (NIV)

"Blessed are the pure in heart"; blessed are those who openly examine their faults and confess them—to God, to themselves, and to a human being who's trustworthy. This personal examination or moral inventory is like doing a large, household cleanup project. Consider, for example, what it would feel like to call your local waste management company with a list of everything you want them to pick up: bulky items like a mattress, e-waste like an old computer, hazardous waste like car oil, green waste like branches, or even extra bundles of recycling and trash. You're told that the driver won't come inside your home or garage to demand that you relinquish any items, but you can dump curbside any old stuff you'd like hauled off.

That's a good picture of how God deals with your sins. He won't coerce you into giving up any of your old garbage, but he does offer curbside pickup of all unneeded and trashy items, including your shame, guilt, toxins, and deadliest patterns. In fact, he specializes in the disposal of all things hazardous to your spiritual, mental, and physical well-being. Such a major overhaul project requires that you crave God's greater good for your life, followed by an honest appraisal of what goes and what stays. Then the junk can get hauled off and the good can remain. Are you ready to admit to God and to yourself the exact nature of your wrongs?

SOUL SEARCH

When might be a good time to call on God, as the only reliable waste management expert, to dispose of your most unrelenting sins? How do you feel about the out-with-the-old portion of your life?

Lord, I confess my sins and thank you that all my guilt has gone out with the trash. I'm praying earnestly for a fresh, uncluttered perspective about how to grow my character and answer the calling you have on my life.

P.U.**R**.P.O.S.E. Principle III: **R**ightly Tell My Recovery Story

Step Five: Admitting More

I admit to God, to myself, and to someone who's
trustworthy the exact nature of my wrongs.

*David confessed to Nathan, "I have sinned against the LORD." Nathan replied, "Yes,
but the LORD has forgiven you, and you won't die for this sin."*   2 SAMUEL 12:13

King David of Goliath fame was a musician, poet, and influential leader who united
the tribes of Israel into one nation, but he was also a grievous sinner who committed
adultery and murder. And yet God loved him beyond measure and patiently waited for
him to confess his guilt to the prophet Nathan—and to accept stern consequences. Then
God rolled out his unbelievable plan to send our Savior through David's family line.
Just as God chose David, a forgiven sinner, to be an ancestor of Jesus' adoptive father
Joseph, he also chooses us sinners to play major roles in his eternal plans.

You may dread being fully known by another human being because of the grievous
nature of your own sins. You may struggle with becoming more real with others because
you've been rejected in the past after mentioning your shortcomings. You may be defensive, fearful, shameful, prideful, or choosing isolation because you don't know to whom
to turn for compassion and acceptance. Take a step now and trust a God-sent Nathan in
your life. James 5:16 actually commands us to do so: "Confess your sins to each other
and pray for each other so that you may be healed. The earnest prayer of a righteous
person has great power and produces wonderful results." And who wouldn't want God's
healing, great power, and wonderful results—not to mention a nonjudgmental friend,
confidant, and prayer partner?

SOUL SEARCH

To what James 5:16 accountability partner or sponsor could you admit your defects and
confide your take-to-the-grave secrets? If you have no one in your life to serve in this
role, what could you do now to find someone?

*Compassionate God, I humbly confess all my sins, especially _____. Reveal to
me any other sins in my life that are delaying my recovery and your one-of-a-kind plan
for me. Send me all the courage I need to confess these things to another person, even
admitting more faults than I ever expected.*

P.U.**R**.P.O.S.E. Principle III: **R**ightly Tell My Recovery Story
Step Six: Entirely Ready
I acknowledge that I'm entirely ready to have
God remove all my character defects.

Create in me a clean heart, O God. Renew a loyal spirit within me.   PSALM 51:10

We ache to be firmly fixed on living a virtuous life, not on the cruel addictions that have blackened our hearts and created disloyalty in us. With the psalmist David, we pray that in spite of our having yielded to temptation, God will restore our former clean hearts and loyal spirits. But the ugliness and nastiness that loom in the darkness, even when we're well into our recovery programs, often make us come undone with sadness.

I can certainly vouch for the ugliness and nastiness of two black witch moths that loomed in the darkness of my living room and made me come undone. Late one evening when I opened my patio door, two supersized moths that looked like well-fed bats flew in and glued themselves to my wall. I feared that leaving the door open would invite more of their clan to come in, but I also worried that closing the door and leaving them unattended for even a second might allow them to hide in the drapes or a lampshade. So with a sheet over my head/body and with my unprotected eyes peering out, I spent one long hour using the straw end of a broom to pry the nasty critters off my wall and swoosh them outdoors. (Admittedly, much of my supposed attack time was actually spent hiding, strategizing, adding to my body armor, and crying.)

When the ugly, nasty beasts of our character defects swoop in to blacken our hearts and stir up disloyal spirits in us, the only proven method of removing them is to confess to God; otherwise, we'll spend frantic, time-consuming energy trying to defeat them in our own strength.

SOUL SEARCH

Are you ready to ask God for a clean heart and a loyal spirit? What can you do to become entirely ready to have your character defects removed so you don't open the door to more sin, stall your recovery, and postpone God's inconceivable dream for your life?

My God, create in me a clean heart and loyal spirit so I can recover and be of steadfast service in whatever way you direct!

P.U.**R**.P.O.S.E. Principle III: **R**ightly Tell My Recovery Story

Step Six: Removing Defects

I acknowledge that I'm entirely ready to have
God remove all my character defects.

We are no longer slaves to sin. For when we died with Christ we were set free from the power of sin. ROMANS 6:6-7

God never ceases to amaze me with his vast array of creative methods that cause sin to lose its power in the life of a believer—someone who has been crucified with Christ and is set free from the power of sin. For example, my friend Paul, who's a believer and a recovering food addict, shared with me how ingeniously God helped him admit that he was a slave to food and become entirely ready to stop the insanity. He said, "As I got to know my elderly, overweight, housebound customers, I learned that they were taking several dozen medications each day to help with diseases that were the downstream consequences of their years of obesity. One day, God impressed upon me, *That will be you in twenty years, if you don't change your eating patterns.* It's as if I'd had a heart attack scare without the actual heart attack. For that reality check, I'll be eternally grateful."

Ask God to give you a "heart attack scare" (without the actual heart attack) so you can admit what's really going on in your life and become entirely ready to have him remove all your character defects. And ask that your ardent willingness to change causes you to act differently—to live rightly in the moment, starting now. Just don't be surprised at how eager God is to respond to such an earnest prayer.

SOUL SEARCH

How has being freed from the slavery of your sins also freed you to live a significance-filled life of God's design (e.g., fewer distractions, purer movites, more credibility, less looking over your shoulder, additional income for ministry use)? What step can you take now to begin or continue to live that freed-up life?

My King, thank you that I finally "get" that I'm no longer a slave to sin, because my old sinful self was crucified with Christ, causing sin to lose its grip on me. Show me how to strip away and throw off anything that gets in my way of proceeding posthaste along the route to recovery you've diagrammed for me.

P.U.**R**.P.O.S.E. Principle III: **R**ightly Tell My Recovery Story

Sifted like Wheat

I have pleaded in prayer for you, Simon, that your faith should not fail. So when you have repented and turned to me again, strengthen your brothers. LUKE 22:32

At the Last Supper, Jesus told Simon Peter that Satan had asked to sift the disciples like wheat, like grain shaken in a sieve to separate the chaff from the wheat (see Luke 22:31). The devil wanted to agitate them with temptations of doubt to see whether a false profession of faith (chaff) or a solid faith (wheat) would remain. Satan has asked to sift you like wheat, too, and you've probably felt many times during your struggle to get clean that your faith was on the brink of failing or had failed.

Peter was about to be sifted/tested by the devil to the point of denying Jesus three times later that night. Ultimately, though, his faith would not fail, because Jesus was pleading for him in prayer. And equally incredible is that Peter's eventual repentance would be used to strengthen others whose faith was under attack.

Satan enjoys agitating you by tempting you to overeat, overspend, overmedicate, or overreact. When you give in to these types of temptation, you conclude that Jesus doesn't care about your everyday struggles and that he's abandoned you. This shakes your faith to its core. At these times, it's important to remember that Jesus is pleading for you in prayer to trust him and that he's sent at least one person (probably more!) to strengthen you. Thank Jesus for his prayers, for whomever he's sent to walk alongside you, and for the privilege you have of strengthening others. And admit to him any hesitancy you have about sharing the story of your shaken faith with others. Can you imagine us not having Peter's story?

SOUL SEARCH

When have you felt that Satan was sifting you like wheat and that you were on the brink of walking away from Jesus for a season or forever? Whom did Jesus send to strengthen you during your time of utmost need, and whom can you strengthen now?

You who plead in prayer for me in all circumstances of my life, thank you! I choose to stay sober out of sincere gratitude and so that I might experience the joy of strengthening others in whatever way you have purposed me to do.

P.U.**R**.P.O.S.E. Principle III: **R**ightly Tell My Recovery Story

Pressing On

Hopefully, our most unfortunate choices are behind us and we have a dynamic process in place to curb further decay. Now we can press on to do the God-glorifying work that's been assigned us and help others do the same!

☀ Meditate on the Assurance of God's Word

I press on to possess that perfection for which Christ Jesus first possessed me.
PHILIPPIANS 3:12

Finally, I confessed all my sins to you and stopped trying to hide my guilt. I said to myself, "I will confess my rebellion to the LORD." And you forgave me! All my guilt is gone. PSALM 32:5

He gave his life to purchase freedom for everyone. This is the message God gave to the world at just the right time. 1 TIMOTHY 2:6

Humble yourselves before the Lord, and he will lift you up in honor. JAMES 4:10

☀ Humbly Talk with the Lord

Take some time to admit to God, yourself, and another human being the exact nature of your wrongs. Pray to become entirely ready now to have God remove your character defects.

Thank God for his astounding and generous gifts of faithfulness, compassion, forgiveness, fellowship, truth, and guidance.

☀ Take the *Life Purpose Coach* Challenge

Add ten years to your current age. After the shock of that number wears off, ask yourself what you hope and pray your life will look like then. Include details about your sobriety, relationships, character, faith, ministry, job, avocation, leadership roles, and passionate life purpose. If you sense this is God's will for your life, choose a spoken, written, graphic, or other creative way to ingrain his vision into your memory.

P.U.R.P.O.S.E. Principle III: **R**ightly Tell My Recovery Story
Working the Program

Help me abandon my shameful ways; for your regulations are good.   PSALM 119:39

It takes a lot for us to humble ourselves and ask God to remove our shortcomings (Step Seven) and also for us to prepare a list of all persons we've harmed and become willing to make amends to them (Step Eight). It's hard to seek help in working a twelve-step program, abandoning our shameful ways, and moving on. Somehow it feels like we're abandoning ship—our ship, the ship of which we've been the Captain, Head Honcho, Supreme Ruler, and Boss all our lives. But every good captain knows that the International Convention for the Safety of Life at Sea requires that he or she exercise professional judgment to protect passengers, even to the point of helping them abandon their sinking ship as an act of survival.

If the thought of abandoning your sinking ship of addiction terrifies you, like a nightmare out of *Titanic*, pause a moment to be encouraged. God, your trustworthy Captain, knows what he's doing, and he's crafted a world-class, personal life raft for you. After all, he chose you before you were born, so he has a vested interest in transporting you to safety. Charles Spurgeon, sometimes called the "Prince of Preachers," adds some humor to this topic of how unconditionally God has loved us for eons: "It's a good thing God chose me before I was born, because he surely would not have afterwards." What a reminder of God's extreme affection for us in spite of our shortcomings.

God is not your Plan B. He was, is, and always will be your only qualified, faithful, and wise veteran Shipmaster, the one who's adept at navigating the stormy seas of your life.

SOUL SEARCH

Are you ready to admit your human limitations and acknowledge your frailties? What might help you with the moment-by-moment decisions you face about choosing God versus choosing the sinking ship of mind-numbing substances or activities?

Captain of my life, you chose me before I was born. Navigate for me now, so I desire to abandon my shameful ways, for I know that your regulations are good. Do for me what I cannot do for myself, which is to change my behavior and arrange a purposeful assignment for myself!

P.U.R.P.O.S.E. Principle III: **R**ightly Tell My Recovery Story

Step Seven: Humbly Ask

I humbly ask God to remove my shortcomings.

Does a clay pot argue with its maker? Does the clay dispute with the one who shapes it, saying, "Stop, you're doing it wrong!" Does the pot exclaim, "How clumsy can you be?"
ISAIAH 45:9

Isaiah shares with us God's analogy about how ludicrous it would be for a clay pot to argue with its maker, which gives us fair warning not to quarrel with our Maker, who can bring down kingdoms and shape us as he sees fit. In fact, Isaiah 45:9 begins with this ominous declaration: "What sorrow awaits those who argue with their Creator." The Lord gave the nation of Israel a similar admonition, complete with an object lesson, through the prophet Jeremiah in a potter's shop. As Jeremiah watched the craftsman at his wheel, he saw the potter mash an unfinished jar back into a lump of clay because it wasn't to his liking. Then the Lord said, "O Israel, can I not do to you as this potter has done to his clay? As the clay is in the potter's hand, so are you in my hand" (Jeremiah 18:6).

These passages remind us of the truth about God's authoritative role in fashioning the world and our lives, too. We're but clay, and he's the one with the power and desire to reshape us daily. Acceptance of this large dose of humility signals a defining, aha moment in our recovery stories. It's a memorable turning point when we finally realize that we're only fragile, marred vessels; that we're powerless to change our character defects, rants, and sins; and that it's wise to agree to be putty in the Master's hands!

Throw yourself on the Potter's wheel, humbly asking him to remove your unsightly shortcomings and remold your character with honesty, compassion, courage, and pure motives. Understand that God already sees you as a finished product; he envisions you just as you'll be when his remodeling work is done.

SOUL SEARCH

In what way could the Potter crush your pride in an instant? For what earthly task does God seem to be reshaping you?

Potter of exquisite work, remold me daily to resemble your Son all the more; then my heart will rejoice in you and in your perfect design for my life.

P.U.**R**.P.O.S.E. Principle III: **R**ightly Tell My Recovery Story
Step Seven: My Shortcomings
I humbly ask God to remove my shortcomings.

The tax collector stood at a distance and dared not even lift his eyes to heaven as he prayed. . . . "O God, be merciful to me, for I am a sinner." LUKE 18:13

In this story (see Luke 18:9-14), which Jesus told to self-righteous listeners, he compared the Temple prayers of a Pharisee and a despised tax collector. The haughty Pharisee thanked God that he wasn't a sinner, cheater, or adulterer, or anything "like that tax collector" (v. 11), even proudly proclaiming that he fasted twice each week and tithed on all his income. The tax collector, however, declared himself a sinner. Jesus showered his praise on the humble man, saying, "This tax man, not the other, went home made right with God" (v. 14, *The Message*). Once again we hear the consistent, biblical message of humbling ourselves before God, of being unpretentious and gentle. We're reminded that Jesus will honor our unassuming spirits when we pray, *O God, be merciful to me, for I'm an addict, a cheat, and a liar. Make me less of a manipulative, selfish sinner. I humble ask you to remove all my shortcomings.*

To cultivate a desire to be meek, we must admit to God when we fall short, instead of trying to measure up by doing good works. In fact, we must live in response to God's grace, not in pursuit of it. This will help us to become humble and positive as we bring into check our previous autoresponses of angry outbursts, self-deprecation, and judgmental undertones. We'll hear ourselves praying, *God, help me to get out of my own way, to communicate respectfully with others, and to conform to your will in all areas.*

SOUL SEARCH

Have you ever felt justified about not repenting for your shortcomings because you attend church regularly or because you're not an odious sinner who's committed heinous crimes? In what way could Jesus' antidote of humility help you with this type of mistaken belief?

Sweet Jesus, I dare not raise my eyes to you, but I want to thank you for your mercy. Fill me with more of you, so I may become a humble vessel for your glory in whatever servant-leader role you carve out for me on earth.

P.U.**R**.P.O.S.E. Principle III: **R**ightly Tell My Recovery Story
Step Eight: The List
I prepare a list of all the people I've harmed and
become willing to make amends to them all.

Plant the good seeds of righteousness, and you will harvest a crop of love. Plow up the hard ground of your hearts, for now is the time to seek the LORD. HOSEA 10:12

Recovery Step Eight, like several others in the process, helps us plow up the hard ground of our hearts and plant good seeds that reap a crop of love. When we reflect on all the people we've harmed, it's not hard to see that our heart's soil may have been backfilled with bitterness, hatred, a critical nature, resentment, defensiveness, spite, negativity, or a refusal to forgive. No wonder people are mad at us. Who wants to hang out with the type of person who's belligerent, unkind, hostile, or passive-aggressive? Being around us is like choosing to live in an exploding minefield. If you mix a truckload of grief and sorrow into our soil, of course we'll reap broken relationships. Hurt people hurt people.

God expects us to prepare ourselves to plant seeds of hope, compassion, grace, and forgiveness with those we've harmed and with those who've harmed us. We're not to worry about the outcome, which might likely include rejection, judgment, and vulnerability. Instead, we're to get our minds ready to focus on forgiving others and ourselves, as well as consider how we are going to make amends to those we've trampled in the dust when we had little or no regard for their feelings or needs.

To prepare a list of those you've harmed, think about your wrongdoings (e.g., financial decisions, neglect, identity theft, relationship schemes) and who was in the wake of each disaster. It's a difficult exercise to do, so pray and remind yourself that the more you seek the Lord now, the shorter your list will be in the future.

SOUL SEARCH

How is God directing you to prepare yourself to make amends—and to whom? How will extending forgiveness propel you into fulfilling God's outstanding plan for your life?

Blameless One, shower your righteousness on me now; I certainly need it to do my recovery work and to answer your call on my life.

Step Eight: Clothed with Compassion

I prepare a list of all the people I've harmed and
become willing to make amends to them all.

Bear with each other and forgive whatever grievances you may have against one another. Forgive as the Lord forgave you.   COLOSSIANS 3:13 (NIV)

This Colossians passage, which is often recited by believers who are in recovery, is telling us not to hold grudges when we've been offended, lest we appear to have forgotten our own need for mercy. It's teaching us to patiently restrain ourselves when we encounter one another's weaknesses, forgiving each other as the Lord forgave us. This message is sandwiched between two verses that represent Paul at his straightforward best, as he relays God's wishes about how we're to treat and forgive others. Colossians 3:12 reads, "Clothe yourselves with compassion, kindness, humility, gentleness and patience" (NIV). And verse 14 reads, "And over all these virtues put on love" (NIV).

In stark contrast, imagine how Satan rewrites Colossians 3:12-14 to goad you into sin, especially into an unforgiving spirit, when you're in a weakened state of addictive behavior: "Chosen by the devil for this new life of hate, dress in the wardrobe he picked out for you: coldness, cruelty, pride, boisterous conduct, chaos, and impatience. Be quick-tempered, aggressive, and ready to blame. Hold a grudge forever, never forgiving. And regardless of what else you put on, wear anger. It's your basic, all-purpose garment. Never be without it. It will reduce all perfect harmony to rubble."

We either follow hard after God or after Satan. Where our loyalty lies will be obvious within minutes to anyone with whom we have a minor tiff or major disagreement. Let your words and actions make it evident that you lovingly forgive others because the Lord lovingly forgives you.

SOUL SEARCH

What are you wearing these days: love or hate, compassion or coldness, kindness or cruelty, humility or pride, quiet strength or boisterous conduct, discipline or chaos, patience or impatience, forgiveness or an unforgiving spirit? How's your wardrobe impacting the list of those you've harmed and your life mission?

Father of mercy, teach me to love and forgive, just as you love and forgive me.

Crossroads

This is what the LORD *says: "Stop at the crossroads and look around. Ask for the old, godly way, and walk in it. Travel its path, and you will find rest for your souls."*
JEREMIAH 6:16

What a beautiful verse to inspire us on the path to recovery—or so it seems at first glance, until we read the rest of it: "You reply, 'No, that's not the road we want!'" Ah, it seems that Israel was rejecting the Lord's way, and we know that never ended well. Jeremiah 6:17 follows the same theme as verse 16, and how did the people respond? "No! We won't pay attention!" Jeremiah cautioned them to listen to the warnings from the Lord, who was about to turn from them in disgust.

Sometimes when I'm babysitting my four- and six-year-old grandsons, they reach an irresolvable impasse with each other. To prevent tension from escalating to Cain and Abel status, I've taught them to stop and call for me. They have my permission to say, "GGRR," (the name my first grandson gave me before he could say *Grandma*) "handle it!" That's my cue to step in as the voice of reason and show them the path they should travel to settle the argument. (If I'm exhausted, I'll be less angelic and simply try to outmaneuver the brother who's in possession of the stolen property.) If all else fails, I'll threaten to implement tough love—stalling long enough, though, to put the onus on their parents, so I can remain the nice Grammie!

Let our passage remind us that God is more than willing to parent us with tough love, handling our rebellion in whatever way will help us change our ways. Nice is not his goal; obedience is. It may sadden us to our core, but it shouldn't surprise us when we read a verse like this: "I will label them 'Rejected Silver,' for I, the LORD, am discarding them" (Jeremiah 6:30).

SOUL SEARCH

Think about a path that God recently laid out for you in regard to your sobriety. What's stopping you from having an ideal response and attitude of cooperation?

Pathfinder, I've stood at the crossroads and rejected your wisdom about which way to travel, and now I'm completely lost. Please come find me and set my feet on your path toward healing and experiencing your passionate plan for me.

P.U.R.P.O.S.E. Principle III: **R**ightly Tell My Recovery Story
Accepting the Challenge

When you humbly accept God's challenge to live a sober life, you learn the importance of asking him to remove your shortcomings and of leaning on him to help you prepare a list of all the persons you've harmed. Harder than that, though, is to learn how to "become willing" to make amends. As millions have done before you, trust God on that!

☀ Meditate on the Assurance of God's Word

Everyone has sinned; we all fall short of God's glorious standard. ROMANS 3:23

If someone borrows an animal from a neighbor and it is injured or dies when the owner is absent, the person who borrowed it must pay full compensation.
EXODUS 22:14

Well then, if we emphasize faith, does this mean that we can forget about the law? Of course not! In fact, only when we have faith do we truly fulfill the law.
ROMANS 3:31

☀ Humbly Talk with the Lord

Offer to God a sin that you're ready to send packing, so you can free yourself up to explore his best plans for you in more detail.

Invite the Holy Spirit to call to mind those to whom you need to make amends; agree now to prayerfully consider any future actions steps you're prompted to take in Step Nine (see May 29–31).

☀ Take the *Life Purpose Coach* Challenge

Write these two character faults, *Pride* and *Impatience*, across the top of a sheet of paper to create two major columns. In each column, write the names of the people you've harmed because of your pride or impatience. (It's okay to put a name in both columns.) Next cross out those headings and replace them with *Humility* and *Patience*, respectively. Reflect prayerfully about the difference the new behavior could make in the lives of those you've listed. Repeat this exercise, as necessary, with any other character faults and corresponding good traits. And don't forget to enlist prayer partners!

P.U.R.P.O.S.E. Principle III: **R**ightly Tell My Recovery Story

Continuing with Wisdom

The wisdom that comes from heaven is first of all pure; then peace-loving, considerate, submissive, full of mercy and good fruit, impartial and sincere.   JAMES 3:17 (NIV)

As James describes in detail, true wisdom that comes from God reflects an understanding of God's holy ways. It's a willingness to yield to others; it overflows with good deeds done humbly; it's compassionate, reasonable, and free from prejudice and hypocrisy. One of its flagship principles is treating others with mercy, dignity, and honor. Without wisdom, we won't get far in making direct amends to people or evaluating whether doing so would injure them or others (Step Nine). And without wisdom, it's nearly impossible to continue taking personal inventory and to promptly admit when we're wrong (Step Ten). Without it, we definitely won't be peacemakers who plant seeds of peace and reap a harvest of righteousness in healthy, energetic community with others (see James 3:18).

Wisdom will help you complete what you started in Step Eight as you earnestly seek the right way to go about the God-led process of making amends to those you've harmed. God will direct your steps about paying back debts, apologizing, and attempting to heal damaged relationships. He'll provide wise and loving input as you resume your personal inventory and set right any new mistakes. He'll also tell you what topics to discuss with a prayerful sponsor or recovery coach who can advise you and even role-play scenarios with you.

God wants to help you examine honestly your actions, reactions, motives, and addiction triggers, not to rationalize them. Ask him for insight, courage, and a vigilant commitment to make amends. And use this prayer of Thomas à Kempis, a Dutch monk: "Give me grace always to desire and to will what is most acceptable to you and most pleasing in your sight." What life purpose in that prayer!

SOUL SEARCH

What valuable pointer could wisdom teach you about making amends—about bringing goodness into a situation where previously you've brought discord? How could your response to that advice create a domino effect of mercy, joy, love?

Wise Counselor, make me wise. I confess my hesitancy to take a step in the direction of vulnerability, which could wallop me with a hard blow of criticism, rejection, and consequences. Walk with me, Lord, as I move forward in your will.

P.U.**R**.P.O.S.E. Principle III: **R**ightly Tell My Recovery Story
Step Nine: Be Reconciled
I forgive those who've hurt me, and I make direct
amends to the people I've hurt whenever possible,
except when to do so would injure them or others.

*If you are presenting a sacrifice at the altar in the Temple and you suddenly remember
that someone has something against you, leave your sacrifice there at the altar. Go and
be reconciled to that person.* MATTHEW 5:23-24

Jesus' instructions about forgiveness in the Sermon on the Mount command us to turn
from our anger and act with humility. We're to "go and be reconciled" to those we have
harmed. This ninth step of the Twelve Steps for Believers instructs us to repair whatever
is broken and to resolve whatever matters are festering, even if others reject our offers.
One caution, though: don't be tempted to work this step earlier than recommended or
without godly guidance. I learned the hard way that to do so is disastrous.

More than two decades ago, I called a Christian woman who had "messed with my
marriage" years earlier than that, to apologize to her that I'd retaliated with unspeakable cruelty. Here's how the conversation went down and how I ended up stirring her
anger pot. I asked her if she had a moment to chat, and she said no. I barreled through
anyway, ignoring her rushed tone, saying, "Well, this will only take a minute. I just
want to apologize for hurting you." I can't remember exactly what I said next, but she
quickly picked up on the fact that my apology was only a clever ruse, a cunning ploy, to
try to get her to feel bad and apologize to me. I wasn't schooled in the concept of poor
motives back then, so I had followed my natural instincts to attempt to manipulate her.

She lit into me, calling me on my forgiveness pretense, and the incident went from
bad to worse faster than a race car can go from zero to fifty miles per hour. When I hung
up, I felt a sense of righteous indignation that she still hadn't apologized to me and that
she was still as evil as I'd thought previously. *Humph.* I declared myself a saint because
I had apologized. Wrong!

SOUL SEARCH

What's your worst- and best-ever "making amends" story? How do heartfelt amends
prepare you to accept an intimidating mission for Christ?

*Forgiving Savior, please help me reconcile with those I've harmed and with those
who've harmed me. I couldn't be more ready.*

P.U.R.P.O.S.E. Principle III: Rightly Tell My Recovery Story

Step Nine: Unfinished Business

I forgive those who've hurt me, and I make direct
amends to the people I've hurt whenever possible,
except when to do so would injure them or others.

*Zacchaeus . . . said, "I will give half my wealth to the poor, Lord, and if I have
cheated people on their taxes, I will give them back four times as much!"* LUKE 19:8

Zacchaeus, a chief tax collector, had become rich through tax fraud. After meeting
Jesus, he offered eagerly to help the poor and to make financial restitution to those he'd
cheated, and Jesus commended him for that. This type of ninth step, taking care of
unfinished business, brings with it great freedom and a clean slate.

It's not easy to make a choice to stop hiding our sins and avoiding those who are
angry with us. After we admit our guilt to God and ourselves, we then need to admit to
the people we've harmed that we understand the pain we've caused them and that we're
committed to changing our behavior. We request forgiveness from them in an effort to
heal our damaged relationships. In recovery terms, we clean our side of the street, which
includes forgiving those who've hurt us!

Back in 1993, I asked God for the courage I needed to right the wrong I'd caused
with my previous boss, the owner of the company where I had worked. The Holy Spirit
was prompting me to pay him back for what I'd taken in the form of office supplies and
personal, long-distance telephone calls over three years of employment. I needed to set
things straight, be forgiven, and forgive myself. I was ready to take action to correct my
past mistakes, regardless of the outcome. I calculated my debt at four times as much
as I'd taken to be $500. I wrote a letter to him, confessing my specific theft, asking for
forgiveness, and enclosing a check that he did cash. (I'm so glad I sent it, because he died
a few years later, and I was able to go to the funeral with a clear conscience.)

SOUL SEARCH

Are you ready for a fresh start that comes from making amends? What small step can
you take now so you can proceed with more freedom and credibility toward God's
uplifting call on your life?

Restorer of my soul, I'm depending on you to strengthen me for this difficult step.

P.U.**R**.P.O.S.E. Principle III: **R**ightly Tell My Recovery Story

Step Ten: Continue Taking Inventory

I continue to ask God to help me to take personal
inventory and promptly admit when I'm wrong.

If we claim we have no sin, we are only fooling ourselves and not living in the truth.
1 JOHN 1:8

John Newton had quite a reputation as a foul-mouthed British sailor and profiteering slave trader. Oral tradition and popular movies about him expose him as a disgraceful backslider with much recurrent sin. If you're living in God's truth, as our passage from 1 John encourages us all to do, you may be able to relate to Newton in some of his robust days of debauchery. Let the rest of Newton's story—of how he finally came to his senses—inspire you.

On March 10, 1748, Newton's ship got caught in a violent storm, which he survived miraculously. More than several decades later, he wrote a song about that experience, which had ever so slowly sparked a religious conversion in him and led him to become a minister and an avowed abolitionist. Recognize this?

Amazing grace! how sweet the sound—
That saved a wretch like me!
I once was lost but now am found,
Was blind, but now I see.

Newton had taken years to do his initial personal inventory and admit that he was wrong, but he eventually did it, and he did it well. If he were alive now, I'm convinced Newton would encourage us to take Step Ten, the maintenance step of character building that prevents us from coming up short too often. And certainly 1 John 1:9 points us in that same direction, "If we confess our sins to him, he is faithful and just to forgive us our sins and to cleanse us from all wickedness." Amazing grace—how sweet it is!

SOUL SEARCH

What have character-forming storms taught you? How could the spiritual discipline of taking stock of your life also reveal God's uncommon, beautiful plan for you?

Mighty Lord, I echo John Newton's prayer: "May the grace of Christ our Savior, / And the Father's boundless love, / With the Holy Spirit's favor, / Rest upon us from above."

P.U.**R**.P.O.S.E. Principle III: **R**ightly Tell My Recovery Story

Step Ten: Standing Strong

I continue to ask God to help me to take personal
inventory and promptly admit when I'm wrong.

If you think you are standing strong, be careful not to fall.   1 CORINTHIANS 10:12

Our passage reminds us that if we think we're standing firm, feeling confident that our minds are steadfast, we'd better pay attention lest we fall into sin. As we grow in our recovery for the remainder of our time on earth, we need to continue taking an honest look at our lives and promptly admitting when we're wrong. It's the personal inventory process that will keep us from unexpected relapses.

Back in 1980, I felt like I was sitting strong and confident in the saddle of a motorcycle when I donned my leather jacket and rode in a biker pack on a 500-mile road trip to the Grand Canyon. Well . . . when I rode on the backseat of a red Suzuki with some middle-aged, off-duty police officers and their spouses. But I'm told that I wasn't really sitting sturdy; apparently, I slept slouched over for much of the trip. The gentle humming of the motor and the great outdoors must have put me into deep coma-like trances. The group didn't know what to do with me, shy of sending me home on a bus or strapping me with a bungee cord to my husband. We were young and foolish back then—arrogantly confident that we'd live forever—so onward we rode with no safety precautions. Now I can only shake my head, aghast at the danger I was in. I wasn't sitting strong at all; I could have splattered onto the highway at any moment.

Sobriety is one long road trip of becoming wise, humble, and honest. We must either choose to act differently as dangers are exposed along the way, or we must prepare to live with the damaging effects of our poor choices. God wants to use our ongoing personal inventories to help us don his greater good for our lives.

SOUL SEARCH

Do you find it hard to admit promptly when you're foolish, arrogant, or lying? What life choice are you currently making that you already know will cause you to be aghast later?

Source of all wisdom, I'm living foolishly, thinking that I'm standing tall, without understanding that I could soon take the worst sin-spill of my life. Watch over me.

P.U.**R**.P.O.S.E. Principle III: **R**ightly Tell My Recovery Story

Forgiveness

The king . . . said, "You evil servant! I forgave you that tremendous debt because you pleaded with me. Shouldn't you have mercy on your fellow servant?"
MATTHEW 18:32-33

Peter asked Jesus a question about how often he should forgive someone who had sinned against him, wondering if seven times was enough. If you've been in a Christ-based recovery program for more than a day, you probably have Jesus' answer memorized: "No, not seven times . . . but seventy times seven!" (Matthew 18:22). To solidify this difficult concept, Jesus told a riveting parable about an unforgiving debtor (see vv. 23-35). Let's take a little creative license and have you insert your name in the following blanks of the story:

Once upon a time, a king forgave millions of dollars' worth of debt owed by _____, his servant. Shortly after, _____ refused to forgive a peer who had an outstanding balance of a few thousand dollars. In fact, the evil _____ grabbed the debtor by the throat and demanded instant payment, ignoring pleas for an extension on the loan and sending the peer to jail until the debt could be paid in full. Witnesses to the incident ratted out _____ to the king, who became furious and ordered jail time and torture for _____ until the debt was paid.

Then Jesus said, "That's what my heavenly Father will do to you, _____, if you refuse to forgive your brothers and sisters from your heart" (Matthew 18:35).

We're required to extend mercy to others just as God has extended mercy to us. It's not our business to ask, "Why don't they have to make amends?" or to worry about how others might respond to our amend-making efforts. God will see our willingness to set our relationships straight as we seek forgiveness from those we've wronged and as we forgive others.

SOUL SEARCH

Recall one of the times you've begged God your King for forgiveness and received it. How did you feel? Besides God, who else has forgiven you multiple times?

My forgiving King, you've let me off the hook more times than I can count. Guide me now to forgive others in the same merciful way you've forgiven me. I understand that this softer attitude of my heart is a foundational requirement to successfully completing my life's work.

P.U.R.P.O.S.E. Principle III: **R**ightly Tell My Recovery Story

Guide My Steps

Rely on the Lord to be your primary guide as you attempt to right the wrongs you've done, so you don't inadvertently end up causing more harm than good. Ask him to maximize your process of daily self-examination and making amends by developing Christlike humility, compassion, wisdom, and courage in you.

☀ Meditate on the Assurance of God's Word

His [prodigal] son said to him, "Father, I have sinned against both heaven and you, and I am no longer worthy of being called your son." LUKE 15:21

If you are a thief, quit stealing. Instead, use your hands for good hard work, and then give generously to others in need. EPHESIANS 4:28

I—yes, I alone—will blot out your sins for my own sake and will never think of them again. ISAIAH 43:25

☀ Humbly Talk with the Lord

Talk to God about your real fear of making amends, which may involve repercussions of jail time; a tarnished reputation; or the loss of a job, friendship, hobby, or recurrent sin that you secretly enjoy.

Ask God to give you encouragement to formulate the everyday habit of accurate self-appraisal, which will make you more forgiving of others' faults and move you closer to his long-term dream for your life.

☀ Take the *Life Purpose Coach* Challenge

Because an inventory of actions can be unbalanced toward the wrong a person has done, jot down three things you've done right—perhaps things you've done to support your sobriety in the past ninety days. Any good action step is fair game, no matter how small it may seem. And don't forget to send up a celebratory prayer of thanksgiving to almighty God for those three successes.

P.U.R.P.O.S.E. Principle III: **R**ightly Tell My Recovery Story

Eyes on Sobriety

He has rescued us from the kingdom of darkness and transferred us into the Kingdom of his dear Son, who purchased our freedom and forgave our sins.   COLOSSIANS 1:13-14

What a phenomenal Scripture passage, telling us that God has rescued us from darkness. *The Message* paraphrase refers to the darkness as dead-end alleys, dark dungeons, and the pit we were in. These are what God has rescued us from when he transferred us into his Kingdom, which was purchased by his dear Son, Jesus. With all the supernatural rescuing going on in Colossians 1, how could we not want to show our gratitude to God by working Step Eleven of the Twelve Steps for Believers program? That's when we get to seek, through prayer and Bible reading, to get to know God and his purpose for our lives, asking him for the power to carry out his will. And how could we not want to work Step Twelve, telling the message of our spiritual awakening to others while continuing to practice these recovery principles in our lives? Frankly, these two steps are like a reward for all the hard work that led up to them, for keeping our eyes on sobriety.

Pray that you'll be strengthened on your recovery journey with God's glorious power, so you'll have all the endurance and patience you need to cooperate with him. Pray that you'll be filled with joy, always thanking the Father, who has enabled you to share in the inheritance that belongs to his people, those living in his light (paraphrased from Colossians 1:11-12). This outlook will prepare you to echo the prayer of a Chinese student who said, "Change the world, O Lord, beginning with me." Shall we add, ". . . beginning right now"?

SOUL SEARCH

What one, small, undeniable action step does Step Eleven suggest to you personally now? Regarding Step Twelve, in what specific way do you think God might intend for you to carry a personalized message of hope to others?

Ruler of the Kingdom of light, I claim the inheritance that belongs to your people who live in the light. My heart's desire is that you'll strengthen me with your glorious power, endurance, patience, joy, and gratitude, so I'm able to help those still living in darkness to see your light.

Step Eleven: Conscious Contact with God

I seek through prayer and Bible reading to get to
know God and his unique purpose for my life,
asking him for the power to carry out his will.

The LORD directs the steps of the godly. He delights in every detail of their lives.
PSALM 37:23

The psalmist explains that the steps of a godly person are graciously ordained in God's loving-kindness, and furthermore, that God delights in those who delight in him. Psalm 37:24 adds, "Though they stumble, they will never fall, for the LORD holds them by the hand."

This raises the question "Are you godly?" That is, are you God-fearing and reverent toward him? Maybe you and I aren't so faithful all the time, but we can let Psalm 37:34 teach us God's recommended process for becoming more devout and upright. It reads, "Put your hope in the LORD. Travel steadily along his path." So, that's it: we're to trust him and travel unswervingly, uncompromisingly down the road he maps out for us, following single-mindedly after him. If we do that relentlessly, God will assuredly help us in every area of our lives, including with our addictions to substances, behaviors, or emotions.

Step Eleven, an expanded version of Step Three, certainly moves us in a godly direction by instructing us to improve our relationship with God, getting to know his purpose for our lives and asking him for the power to carry out his will. Working this step implies that we're praying for endless wisdom about God's instructions. It means that we're crying out to the Lord, like Asaph, the choir leader of the Israelites, did in Psalm 73:25: "Whom have I in heaven but you? I desire you more than anything on earth." Asaph had experienced his own personal demons when he became jealous of the prosperity of the wicked—but he finally confessed his sin to the Lord and found shelter in him from bitterness.

SOUL SEARCH

What's your favorite setting for trying to improve your conscious contact with God? (Maybe a cozy, indoor setting? Outdoors in nature? Or . . . ?) When have you walked in God's will and felt the power of operating at his direction?

My lovingly kind God, I want to be godly so you'll direct my steps and delight in every detail of my life. Give me clarity of purpose and the desire to carry out your perfect will.

P.U.**R**.P.O.S.E. Principle III: **R**ightly Tell My Recovery Story

Step Eleven: Victorious Life

I seek through prayer and Bible reading to get to
know God and his unique purpose for my life,
asking him for the power to carry out his will.

*I will give you the treasures of darkness, riches stored in secret places, so that you may
know that I am the* LORD, *the God of Israel, who summons you by name.*
ISAIAH 45:3 (NIV)

As I write this devotional, a police helicopter is circling above my neighborhood in what
appears to be a fifteen-mile radius, announcing by loudspeaker, "We're looking for a
lost child." The local news has filled in the descriptive details of a little girl's age, hair
color, and clothing. I've gone outside to see if I can be of any help, but in the darkness
of the night I must rely on prayer. God is a lot like that hovering chopper and news
commentator, bent on bringing you home. (Sometimes I even think of him as a ship
convoy battling the enemy or a motorized infantry in full search mode or a skywriter
drawing arrows to point the way.) Do you hear him calling you by name everywhere
you turn? He knows you're lost to addiction, but he misses you, wants you back, and
can't wait to spend time with you.

His welcome-home gift for you, called "the treasures of darkness," is rich treasure
that kings have hidden in obscure, secure places. God, the one true King, knows where
all the secret treasures are that you'll ever need for living a significance-filled, victorious
life—and he's offering to give them to you.

God wants you to live smack-dab in the center of his will under his power. Will you
let him bring you home again and give you the treasure of himself, his unique will for
your life, and his power to carry it out?

SOUL SEARCH

Do you think you're so lost that the God of the universe can't find you by sea, land, or
air? When you do connect with him about his will for your life, will you do what you
can, with what you have, where you are?

*You who summon me by name, how could I be so fortunate as to have the King of all
treasures, goodness, and compassion calling me home! I'm eager to sit with you, Lord,
for some long chats and to return and hear of all your generous plans for my recovery
and life mission.*

P.U.R.P.O.S.E. Principle III: **R**ightly Tell My Recovery Story

Step Twelve: Giving Back

I tell others about my spiritual awakening
using these steps, while continuing to
practice these steps in my own life.

You must show mercy to those whose faith is wavering.   JUDE 1:22

The brief, one-chapter book of Jude implores all who've been called by God to be steadfast in our faith, but verse 22 specifically commands us to show merciful love to those whose faith is wavering. This imperative statement in Jude resonates with the importance of Step Twelve, which involves sharing experience, strength, and hope—as well as sharing the freedom and victory that God has to offer. Another great reminder of this "giving back" principle is in Matthew 10:8, which reads, "Give as freely as you have received!" Out of gratitude, we're to find ways to build others up in their faith—and their recovery.

Both the Bible and wise sponsors tell us to get the word out about living a spiritually awakened life, but both also explicitly warn us not to endanger our own faith or recovery by helping others in an unhealthy way. We're to draw a line in the sand and not assist in any way that might cause us to stumble or relapse into old, codependent behaviors. Jude 1:23 warns us to reach out to others "with great caution, hating the sins that contaminate their lives." Or as *The Message* paraphrase says so well, "Be tender with sinners, but not soft on sin. The sin itself stinks to high heaven." What a critical concept to hold onto tightly.

SOUL SEARCH

Will you bring the hope of Christ to those who are in the prison of obsessions, compulsions, and dependencies? If you were to dream the impossible dream for how you might carry a message of hope to others, what would Jude 1 and Step Twelve prompt you to do with your life?

Powerful Holy Spirit, considering my history, I'm in no position to give advice to anyone, but considering your future plans for me, you've put me in a perfect place to give hope to countless others. Thank you for giving me the hope that saved my life. In gratitude, I choose to serve as your faithful servant the rest of my days on earth.

P.U.**R**.P.O.S.E. Principle III: **R**ightly Tell My Recovery Story
Step Twelve: Light of the World
I tell others about my spiritual awakening
using these steps, while continuing to
practice these steps in my own life.

No one lights a lamp and then puts it under a basket. Instead, a lamp is placed on a stand, where it gives light to everyone in the house. MATTHEW 5:15

Jesus tells us that we're the light of the world, like a city on a hilltop that can't be hidden, like a lamp on a stand that gives light to everyone in the house (see Matthew 5:14-16). We're not to keep God's light under wraps; instead, we have a role as his light bearers who share his brightness with others: "Let your good deeds shine out for all to see, so that everyone will praise your heavenly Father" (v. 16). When we shine for God, letting others know that he's redeemed our past and has used it for a greater purpose in the world, they'll be drawn to his light and begin to praise him for his goodness and power.

To live that type of a spiritually bright life, you must seek a healthy view of yourself, others, and God—a view that enables you to experience more consistent freedom from the bondage of addiction. It's a huge commitment, though, to practice sobriety for a lifetime in all your affairs and help others do the same; it's overwhelming, even if you take it one day at a time, one minute at a time, or one step at a time. To encourage yourself along the way, it helps to remember that living a life of surrender on a more regular basis not only is God's gift to you but also provides directional lighting for those you're called to serve.

SOUL SEARCH

Will you allow God to mature you all the more, so your sober conduct shines a bright light on his goodness? What do you feel is the hardest part of sharing your life and light with others?

Light of the world, because of your beauty I now hate the darkness I once called home. Teach me to invite others into your light with a simple offer to share how you shone your light on me and saved me for a unique purpose.

P.U.**R**.P.O.S.E. Principle III: **R**ightly Tell My Recovery Story
My Seven-Minute Testimony

My entire lifetime is just a moment to you; at best, each of us is but a breath. . . .
And so, Lord, where do I put my hope? My only hope is in you.   PSALM 39:5, 7

Our lives are so short; they're but a breath. Once you take hold of this game-changing concept and decide that God is your only hope for living an intentional life of purpose, people will begin to notice a difference in your behavior. It's then that you'll need to be prepared to share the good news of how God rescued you from drudgery and despair. The devotional on April 15 encouraged you to write and share your "One-Minute Testimony" as God directed you. Today's invitation is to pray about writing your longer testimony of approximately seven minutes. This brief summation of your life is often needed in structured settings, such as church services or recovery meetings, but it's also ideal for one-to-one conversations during which you need to share more details about your story.

To write an effective testimony that's three to four pages, you'll first want to think about what you were like when you lived an addictive lifestyle. Simply recall a few examples of what happened in your life before you knew Christ or began to mature in your faith. Second, bring to mind what happened to cause you to choose recovery—specifically, how God's mercy healed you. (Don't forget to consult your recovery journal for ideas.) And third, gather your thoughts about what you're like now that you're working a faith-based recovery program in community with others and attempting to follow God's plan for your life. As you showcase God's grace in your life to others by sharing it publicly, not just keeping it tucked away in a desk drawer, accept as a privilege God's using you as his vessel to help others.

SOUL SEARCH

In what circumstances do you most need to put your hope in the Lord? In light of God's incredible mercy, what hope do you have about a rewarding and fulfilling future?

Deliverer, focus my eyes on you as I formulate my thoughts about my official testimony and put you at the center of this writing process from start to finish. Bring your listeners to me, as I heal enough to be a credible witness for you.

P.U.R.P.O.S.E. Principle III: Rightly Tell My Recovery Story
Keep Moving Forward

As you move forward in developing a deeper relationship with God and understanding his will for your life, take time to celebrate the joy of your recovery by letting others know about his powerful and welcoming presence.

☀ Meditate on the Assurance of God's Word

Though we are overwhelmed by our sins, you forgive them all. What joy for those you choose to bring near, those who live in your holy courts. What festivities await us inside your holy Temple. PSALM 65:3-4

You won't spend the rest of your lives chasing your own desires, but you will be anxious to do the will of God. You have had enough in the past of the evil things that godless people enjoy—their immorality and lust, their feasting and drunkenness and wild parties, and their terrible worship of idols. 1 PETER 4:2-3

☀ Humbly Talk with the Lord

Praise Jesus that he's your Higher Power and that his patience, compassion, and unconditional love have been your lifeline to hope.

In song, dance, prayer, art, journaling, or some other method, thank God for the miracle of your sobriety and his gift of a captivating life mission that will draw others to him.

☀ Take the *Life Purpose Coach* Challenge

Read Romans 7:14-25, about being freed from your struggle with sin. Then memorize this summary of its comforting concept: "I have discovered this principle of life—that when I want to do what is right, I inevitably do what is wrong. . . . Who will free me from this life that is dominated by sin and death? Thank God! The answer is in Jesus Christ our Lord" (vv. 21, 24-25).

P.U.R.P.O.S.E. Principle IV:
Pursue Positive Practices to Maintain My Sobriety

I'm fully cooperating with God regarding his unique plan for my life.

P.U.R.**P**.O.S.E. Principle IV: **P**ursue Positive Practices to Maintain My Sobriety

Fervent Prayer

Jesus went up on a mountain to pray, and he prayed to God all night.   LUKE 6:12

Jesus demonstrated for us that private, eager, intense prayer is bedrock for living out God's will. Could he have prayed anywhere more secluded than on a mountainside or any more fervently than from dusk to dawn? Jonathan Edwards, a New England Puritan and missionary to Native Americans, personalizes this practice of private prayer for us when he says, "There is no way that Christians, in a private capacity, can do so much to promote the work of God, and advance the kingdom of Christ, as by prayer." But how do we become people of passionate prayer, so we can learn to turn from our compulsive, obsessive ways; promote God's work; and advance the Kingdom of Christ?

One proven method of becoming more enthusiastic about prayer is to learn the art of practicing silence regularly. This works well because it creates memorable, life-changing opportunities of hearing directly from God, which cause us to crave more intimate time with him. It's hard to practice silence, though, because we live in a world that continually bombards us with noise (from the media, music industry, and restaurants); sensory stimuli (from sight, touch, smell, taste, and sound); and information overload (from a glut of decisions—for example, about 350 types of toothpaste!). So to hear God clearly, we must get in the habit of turning off, tuning out, and turning away from the flood of input. To become better communicators with him and doers of his precious will for our lives, we must intentionally disengage from the excessive, loud, screeching craziness of today's world. Like Jesus, we must choose silence wherever and however we can find it.

SOUL SEARCH

What reduction could you make to your surplus of noise, stimuli, and information so you could hear God's plan for your sobriety and life's work? What family member, friend, or sponsor understands the importance of silence and prayer and could help you embrace this prayer practice?

Omnipotent God, you who have immeasurable power, make me into a person of private, fervent prayer so I can boldly and persistently ask you to unleash your power on my recovery efforts and in the world.

P.U.R.P.O.S.E. Principle IV: Pursue Positive Practices to Maintain My Sobriety

Pray without Ceasing

Never stop praying.   1 THESSALONIANS 5:17

You'd think that having a book personally autographed, "Pray, pray, pray, all the time" by Nobel Peace Laureate Mairead Corrigan Maguire, whom I had the privilege of privately interviewing at a 1988 peace conference in Ireland, would help me learn (sometime during that same decade!) the value of praying nonstop. But like many who struggle with issues of pride, control, trust, anger, depression, fear, or stubbornness, I didn't comprehend for many years the enormity of what she'd written or said to me. I sat on the information for a long time, slowly processing what she meant by "Listen to God, perhaps several hours a day, as you go about your work. You'll soon be able to hear him, and not so much your own voice."

Now her suggestions make sense to me. In addition to our dedicated prayer time with the Lord, we're to get in the habit of shooting "bullet prayers" up to heaven dozens upon dozens of times each day. For example, we can pray, *God, thank you for . . . Help me with . . . I'm sorry for . . . I adore you because . . . Bless my friend who . . . Give me wisdom about. . . .* This practice of communing often with God, as we go about our daily routine, shifts our focus off our problems and onto his inexhaustible love and power. It predisposes us to listen closely for his answers and to choose God over selfish, addictive behavior.

Edward B. Pusey, a nineteenth-century English churchman, stated it this way: "Have some arrow prayers to pray during the day, or a psalm. A good watchmaker is one who makes watches and prays; a good housemaid is one who sweeps and prays." Prayer is a must-have habit as we choose sobriety often each day and move toward our God-glorifying, anointed task on earth.

SOUL SEARCH

Who has prayed for you unceasingly, or who do you wish had done so? For whom in your life do you pray nonstop and for what recovery miracle do you pray tirelessly?

Benevolent God, teach me to pray to you with a humble heart and listening ear all day long. I trust you with my everything.

P.U.R.**P**.O.S.E. Principle IV: **P**ursue Positive Practices to Maintain My Sobriety

Private Prayer Life

When you pray, go away by yourself, shut the door behind you, and pray to your
Father in private. Then your Father, who sees everything, will reward you.
MATTHEW 6:6

Nothing that ever has existed, does exist, or will exist can escape God's sight. In regard to our private prayer lives, that's extremely comforting; in regard to our secret lives of sin and addiction, it's disconcerting, to say the least. God knows all and sees all. The only commonsense answer to this dilemma appears to be this: pray more and sin less.

I'm not one to be trapped, though, by a set of *should*s about how to pray. While I know that it's wise to prepare my heart with praise and confession so that gratitude and requests can come spilling out, I never dictate to myself which prayer element (adoration, confession, thanksgiving, or supplication) might totally overshadow another one on any given day. If we find ourselves humbled by the mighty power of God or are burdened with sadness over a recent relapse, we can allow those particular feelings to surface without restraint. And whether we're kneeling with our hands raised in joyful thanksgiving or we've got our faces to the floor beseeching God for a favor, it's our prerogative to express our love to our Maker our way.

I agree with occasionally letting our outdoor, iPod-free, solo exercise time (jogging, biking, swimming) or a long, radio-free, solo commute be part of our designated prayer time when we converse with God—as long as we also make time to read his Word and reflect on it. I've even been known to rely on a furious game of tetherball, me against God, when I'm upset. He's always a gracious opponent, and eventually I calm down enough to take a walk with him and hear his soothing voice.

SOUL SEARCH

How would you describe your private prayer life (e.g., boring, dutiful, energizing, legalistic, intimate, precious)? In what way could you lean into the heart of God more intimately, to welcome him (as you would a lifelong friend) into your personal space and talk to him about your recovery?

Omniscient God, you know all my spoken and unspoken prayers. Draw me closer
to you in prayer, so I might be able to hear your advice about my next steps toward
sobriety and your will for my life.

P.U.R.P.O.S.E. Principle IV: Pursue Positive Practices to Maintain My Sobriety

Practicing Solitude

Very early in the morning, while it was still dark, Jesus got up, left the house and went off to a solitary place, where he prayed.   MARK 1:35 (NIV)

Susanna Wesley, the mother of John and Charles of the Methodist movement, is said to have been a faithful prayer warrior. But how could this be, when she was a pastor's wife with nineteen children—ten of whom survived their infant years? Well, church history tells us that when Susanna couldn't find a private place to pray, she'd put an apron over her head as a sign to her children to be extra quiet while she talked to God. I definitely had it easier than Mrs. Wesley in my child-rearing days. With only two children, who were often at school or on outings with their friends, I could pray nestled on a cushioned, patio swing, sipping tea, with no need to drape a dirty apron over my head. What about you?

Do you have a solitary place where you can go to be alone with God to hear his voice, pour out your heart to him about your sobriety worries, or ask him about his best plans for your life? Where can you have a deep, unhurried conversation with the Lord, melting into his presence, undistracted by the cares of the world? Any rolling hills you can climb in the springtime to sing his praises? Any local gardens you can frequent on summer or fall days to get his input? Any beach or lake you can visit on a wintery afternoon to weep and journal about a loss in your life?

Not only did Jesus find places to meet with his Father, but he also instructed us to do so, saying, "Here's what I want you to do: Find a quiet, secluded place so you won't be tempted to role-play before God. Just be there as simply and honestly as you can manage" (Matthew 6:6, *The Message*). By practicing solitude, our focus moves off ourselves and onto God, and we begin to sense his presence, peace, grace, forgiveness, wisdom, hope, and most highly creative dreams for our lives!

SOUL SEARCH

Where can you go to be alone with God in prayer? What's been your most cherished, solitary time with him that's helped you with your recovery?

Omnipresent God, you who are everywhere, show me a solitary place, a quiet and secluded place, where I can meet with you—and I'll gladly go!

P.U.R.P.O.S.E. Principle IV: **P**ursue Positive Practices to Maintain My Sobriety

Pray for Wisdom

If you need wisdom, ask our generous God, and he will give it to you.   JAMES 1:5

Asking a generous God for wisdom about your sobriety or life path is, undoubtedly, a spiritually mature step to take, but hearing his potentially counterintuitive advice can be disconcerting. In situations when his counsel interferes with your desires, you'll find yourself wrestling with these predictable thoughts: *Why does God's wisdom have to be so different than mine? I like my ideas!*

An unknown Confederate soldier is credited with helping to explain the great chasm between God's eternal perspective and our earthly one:

> *I asked God for strength that I might achieve;*
> *I was made weak that I might learn humbly to obey.*
> *I asked God for health that I might do greater things;*
> *I was given infirmity that I might do better things.*
> *I asked for riches that I might be happy;*
> *I was given poverty that I might be wise. . . .*
> *I got nothing that I asked for but everything I had hoped for.*
> *Almost despite myself, my unspoken prayers were answered.*
> *I am, among men, most richly blessed.*

Knowing how brilliant God is should help you trust him more and encourage you to ask him for more wisdom about your recovery and your future life mission. If you are unwilling to pray for his advice, try to remember Proverbs 3:15: "Wisdom is more precious than rubies; nothing you desire can compare with her."

SOUL SEARCH

What do you desire more than God's wisdom? If Wisdom were a person standing in front of you right now, what wise message might you want to hear so you can pursue God's large plan for your life?

My wise God, grant me wisdom beyond my years. Give me your eternal perspective that causes your glory to be known around the world, and squelch my fear of hearing what you have in mind for me.

P.U.R.**P**.O.S.E. Principle IV: **P**ursue Positive Practices to Maintain My Sobriety
Pray for Equipping

May [the God of peace] equip you with all you need for doing his will.
HEBREWS 13:21

God's power is infinite; he rules supremely over everything you need to maintain your sobriety and to faithfully complete the distinct mission to which he's called you long-term. We can even be so bold as to note that it's actually in God's best interest to equip you immeasurably well, so you can heal and do all the work he's designed you to do for his Kingdom. Whether you need courage, a forgiving heart, self-control, humility, spiritual gifts, skills, resources, experience, wisdom, education, or a network, he's the one who is able to provide it. To avoid being overwhelmed by your perceived lack, you must remember one biblical truth: "What is impossible for people is possible with God" (Luke 18:27).

Also, it may help you to focus on the fact that God doesn't call people because they're independent-contractor types who exude self-sufficiency; he prefers to call humble people who know they must depend on him, and then he equips them exceedingly more than sufficiently to succeed. Your heavenly Father actually delights in your willingness to ask for a full equipping, because it means you're relying on his strength, not your own. So don't be shy about asking!

My prayer for you is best described in the remainder of our passage, which concludes, "May he produce in you, through the power of Jesus Christ, every good thing that is pleasing to him. All glory to him forever and ever! Amen" (Hebrews 13:21). All that remains now is for you to believe that God is able to provide all you need to heal and to serve others well in the name of Jesus.

SOUL SEARCH

What equipping do you need in order to continue recovering from addiction and to do God's work on earth? Is it time to have a nice long chat with him about that, smiling with relief that he's way ahead of you?

Infinite God, your power is without limit and beyond measure. Knowing this gives me the confidence I need to ask you to equip me, exceedingly more than sufficiently, with all I require for doing your will. I ask this expectantly. "Oh, how great are [your] riches and wisdom and knowledge!"*

---
* Romans 11:33.

P.U.R.P.O.S.E. Principle IV: **P**ursue Positive Practices to Maintain My Sobriety

Becoming a Person of Prayer

Learn the art of choosing silence and solitude, of praying without ceasing throughout the day, of praying privately, and of praying for wisdom about your recovery and equipping in your ministry. In all these ways of becoming a person of fervent prayer, desire to be found faithful.

☀ Meditate on the Assurance of God's Word

Early the next morning Jesus went out to an isolated place. The crowds searched everywhere for him, and when they finally found him, they begged him not to leave them. LUKE 4:42

A house is built by wisdom and becomes strong through good sense. PROVERBS 24:3

You guide me with your counsel, leading me to a glorious destiny. PSALM 73:24

☀ Humbly Talk with the Lord

Commit to the Lord that you want to live a quiet life so that you'll have more opportunities to sit with him privately and unpack your pain, paranoia, and patterns, as well as the joys of your life.

Let God know that you can't live without his wisdom, healing, and equipping; that you'll seek times of extended solitude to help you discern his will for your life.

☀ Take the *Life Purpose Coach* Challenge

Several times each year, schedule a definitive appointment with the Lord to get away with him for four to eight hours. This will give you a chance to review your life from a macro-perspective, helping you reassess who you are and what's important to you in light of God's bountiful plan for your life. This time of renewal and refreshment will give you the strength and courage you need to fight the good recovery fight and move toward a life of service dedicated to the Lord.

P.U.R.P.O.S.E. Principle IV: **P**ursue Positive Practices to Maintain My Sobriety

Relationships, Role Models, and Sponsors

A house is built by wisdom and becomes strong through good sense.   PROVERBS 24:3

My friend called me the other day with yet another story of a near mishap triggered by her lack of common sense. Here's the scoop, minus her name: she almost caused a house fire by lighting a bathroom candle under a low-hanging towel rack and then forgetting about it for an hour. As we chatted, she told me she was holding a particularly warm towel in her hand, so I suggested she use it as a hot compress over her eye to help with her headache—and she did!

In a perfect world, with enough common sense to go around for all, we wouldn't need advice from best friends, supportive family members, or wise role models. We'd do just fine on our own, living our Lone Ranger lives. But in this fallen world, we need people for solace, hope, forgiveness, inspiration, unconditional love, and even solid advice about hot-towel compresses. Barbra Streisand sang the lyrics of Merrill and Styne on this topic, "People who need people are the luckiest people in the world," and yet we let our "grown-up pride hide all the need inside." So true.

In addition to needing a variety of friends who do life with us, we need those in whom we can confide our deepest secrets, such as a sponsor, mentor, life coach, therapist, or spiritual director. As you know, "you're only as sick as your secrets." Now I'm no advocate of sharing our innermost stuff with wild abandon, but I do know firsthand that being deeply known by a safe person is liberating. Honesty and vulnerability, which allow us to take the bucket of cement off our shoulders, is always the first step in the healing process. A different analogy that's been used to describe the process of releasing ourselves from secret shame is this: "Shining light on our shadows makes them disappear."

All in all, the consensus is this: we need people.

SOUL SEARCH

Which wise souls could help you lead a recovered life of purpose? What's preventing you from asking them to share their wisdom?

My Sure Foundation, you're my cornerstone. I ask that you send wise people to help me "build my house," so I don't burn it to the ground.

P.U.R.P.O.S.E. Principle IV: Pursue Positive Practices to Maintain My Sobriety
No Record of Wrong

[Love] keeps no record of being wronged.   1 CORINTHIANS 13:5

Those who love us unconditionally are to keep no record of our wrongs. Colossians 2:14 adds that even God canceled the record of the charges against us and nailed it to the cross. The context is that he's forgiven all our sins, and we can include all addiction-related sins in this "Done Deal" category. How are you doing with not keeping a record of those who've wronged you?

When I notice that I'm refusing to let go of how someone's upset me with words or actions, I allow a story about a monkey and a coconut to flash into my mind. Here's why: to capture a wild monkey, people have been known to make a small hole in a green coconut, which they fill with rice, fruit, sweets, or peanuts, and tether to a tree. An unsuspecting, curious monkey squeezes his hand into the coconut and grabs the treat in his little monkey paw, only to discover that he can't get his clenched fist out through the hole. The monkey, refusing to let go of the prize, holds himself prisoner until he's captured. Think about how ludicrous that is! After replaying that scenario in my mind, I say to myself, *Katie, don't be such a monkey; let go of what's in the coconut trap before you die!*

Like the little monkey and me, have you clung to something that's become a death trap for you? Are you so unwilling to release the record of wrongs that others have committed against you that you're adding to your suffering, demise, and inability to do the life assignment God has entrusted to you? The obvious solution is to unclench your fist now and let go of the stuff that's holding you prisoner.

SOUL SEARCH

How difficult is it for you to release your anger and the itemized list of crimes that others have committed against you? Have you been idealizing your self-righteous anger, rather than seeing it for the coconut trap it is?

Tenderhearted God, who made heaven and earth, thank you for loving me enough to cancel the record of my wrongs. Help me release my "angry list," which is keeping me trapped in a self-made prison.

P.U.R.P.O.S.E. Principle IV: Pursue Positive Practices to Maintain My Sobriety

Healthy Church Relationships

Make me truly happy by agreeing wholeheartedly with each other, loving one another, and working together with one mind and purpose.   PHILIPPIANS 2:2

In today's verse, Paul is relaying a message from God, saying that our Creator wants us to live in harmony with other Christians, loving them and working in unity with them—but wait for the clincher: we're to do this by sharing the mind and purposes of Christ. Oh, dear, that's a mouthful of a goal. From the remarks surrounding our passage, it sounds like this means we're supposed to be tender, compassionate, selfless, and humble in all our church-based relationships. We're supposed to quit trying to impress people and instead take an interest in them, lending them a helping hand when they're in need.

I don't know about all this talk, urging us to do the impossible! Church pews are filled with damaged and disgruntled people, and not to mention those addicted to money, power, sugar, booze, drugs, gossip, sex, thrills, and drama. Church politics is loaded with discord, disputes, and divisions. How can Paul expect us to be united in the Holy Spirit, keeping one purpose in mind—the great work of the church, the salvation of souls? How are we supposed to agree wholeheartedly in this common cause when all the murmurings, schisms, and strife among church members breed endless contention and quarrels?

And yet, Paul will not concede. He's adamant that we must show mutual respect to all the saints of the church, which is the body of Christ. It's not a nice-to-have, flowery request. It's the truth of what God wants.

SOUL SEARCH

In what way do you work and play well with members of your church? Why is this important for God's work, your recovery, and the distinctive role he's carved out for you in the world?

Spirit of grace and wisdom, I want to make God truly happy with me by living in harmony with my Christian brothers and sisters, by loving them, and by working together with one mind and purpose to bring all people to Jesus. Grant me success in this important endeavor.

P.U.R.P.O.S.E. Principle IV: Pursue Positive Practices to Maintain My Sobriety

Cord of Three Strands

Two people are better off than one, for they can help each other succeed. If one person falls, the other can reach out and help. ECCLESIASTES 4:9-10

I admit to you that, a long time ago, I was a card-carrying, ten-year member of the Lone Ranger Club, which even excluded any Tonto sidekicks. To put it mildly, people outside my immediate family were difficult for me. I had to pray for six long years to like people—and much longer to love some of them as individuals. As life ripped me to shreds (an unexpected divorce and the death of my ex when our kids were young; being downsized from corporate; multiple single-mothering crises; loss of a dream), I finally came to accept the reality of the rest of our verse: "But people who are alone when they fall are in real trouble."

God was kind to me, though, and he ministered to me by teaching me that a cord of three strands (him, a friend, and me) is not easily broken (see Ecclesiastes 4:12). This three-way partnership is how he helps us face the worst in our lives and enjoy the blessings, too. True friends are loyal, and they love us through all kinds of weather (see Proverbs 17:17). God designed us to want to have and to be that type of friend. Loving, intentional friends are his vessel to help Lone Rangers and others learn to choose sobriety daily, grow spiritually, become credible witnesses for the Lord, and live life on purpose.

When I think about the loneliness of my days gone by, I'm reminded of these words of Pope John Paul II: "The worst prison would be a closed heart." To whom can you say, "You're my person!" and know that the feeling is mutual?

SOUL SEARCH

What best-friend type of relationship do you have now or have you had in the past? Considering a dollar value, what's a best friend worth to you these days?

Lord of all power, I need a best friend with whom to do life. I know I can't recover fully from all that ails me without having a loving support system in place. But even if I could be forever sober on my own, I wouldn't want to be without those you've handpicked for me.

P.U.R.**P**.O.S.E. Principle IV: **P**ursue Positive Practices to Maintain My Sobriety

God's Gift of Role Models

I always thank my God when I pray for you, Philemon, because I keep hearing about your faith in the Lord Jesus and your love for all of God's people.   PHILEMON 1:4-5

Paul was applauding Philemon, a wealthy Christian, for being a role model for others in the church, because his love of God's people overflowed from his deep faith in Jesus. Who's been or could be such a role model for you, helping you grasp the enormity of Christ's goodness? Who's helped you in the past or could help you now to choose sobriety and live out God's design for your life—a parent, grandparent, sibling, spouse, teacher, or counselor? You might say no to those ideas and suggest, instead, your pastor, boss, sponsor, or prayer partner. You might even name a historical figure, Bible character, or modern-day famous person as someone who's had or could have a positive impact on your life.

We all need wise, godly people to invest in our holiness by sharing their testimonies and spiritual growth secrets with us. We need people who exude courage, humility, patience, and God-confidence. We can engage with these trustworthy advisors, either personally or through their writing and speaking, as they ask probing questions, breathe truth into our lives, and encourage us to do personal inventory and live above our circumstances.

One cautionary tale, though, about a role model experience gone bad, as told by Ed, a recovering addict. He shared with me, "I really looked up to him; he taught me so much. But the healthier I got, the more I saw his serious flaws that he was unwilling to address. I'll be forever grateful for his temporary role in my life, but I'm not strong enough to risk getting pulled back down. I'll continue to pray for him, but I definitely needed to release him into God's hands. And what did I learn about myself? That I tend to idolize and then later severely criticize my heroes, so I'm going to try to strike a healthier balance in my own behavior next time!"

SOUL SEARCH

During this season of your life, who'd be the best role model in the world for you, in addition to Jesus? What could a Christ-honoring role model inspire you to do to further God's work on earth?

Spirit of Revelation, send me role models who love you boldly, obey you immediately, and praise you generously. And make me more teachable than I am right now.

P.U.R.**P**.O.S.E. Principle IV: **P**ursue Positive Practices to Maintain My Sobriety

Relationship-Minded Sponsor or Coach

When you follow the desires of your sinful nature, the results are very clear. . . . Let me tell you again, as I have before, that anyone living that sort of life will not inherit the Kingdom of God.   GALATIANS 5:19, 21

We all need someone to guide us through life, someone who respects confidentiality and has our best interest in mind. You may prefer the term *sponsor, mentor,* or *life coach,* or perhaps you prefer *lay counselor, therapist,* or *spiritual director* (one who disciples people in the formation of spiritual habits). Regardless of the terminology or purpose of any support person, we especially need someone when we're dealing with a Galatians level of debauchery, which could range from sexual immorality to hostility, selfish ambition, envy, or drunkenness. Navigating these types of rough seas without godly advice is a disaster waiting to happen. Accountability in these areas is key and is achieved with the help of any type of sponsor who's effective in relational mentoring. This person will be able to help you identify and end those associations that are sucking you into beliefs and behaviors detrimental to your recovery and to the work the Lord has reserved for you.

For example, a recovery coach might say to you, "Scroll back through your distant and recent past to look in the window of where you've lived, worked, played, worshiped, and sinned. Try to recall the face of the first person with whom you involved yourself who wasn't of the mind of Christ or wasn't filled with the purpose of knowing Christ. How difficult did that relationship make it for you to get to know Christ more intimately or move forward with God's will?" Someone who's prayerfully focused on your relationships can help you analyze the exorbitant costs versus abundant blessings of all your friendships.

SOUL SEARCH

In what way has God been nudging you to get help in cultivating or terminating a relationship? How could a God-sent friendship help you develop your character, stay sober, and enjoy the expedition the Lord has planned for you?

Author of eternal salvation, help me connect with a relationship-minded sponsor or coach who cares deeply about your eternal relationship with me.

P.U.R.**P**.O.S.E. Principle IV: **P**ursue Positive Practices to Maintain My Sobriety
Living in Community

Loving family members and long-term, dear friends solidly support you in faith-based, healthy community living, as you do them. Love doesn't subsidize gambling habits, participate in overeating, ignore an extramarital affair, encourage compulsive shopping, do drugs, breathe secondhand smoke, or tolerate drinking and driving.

☀ Meditate on the Assurance of God's Word

Love is patient and kind. Love is not jealous or boastful or proud or rude. It does not demand its own way. It is not irritable.   1 CORINTHIANS 13:4-5

Most important of all, continue to show deep love for each other, for love covers a multitude of sins. Cheerfully share your home with those who need a meal or a place to stay.   1 PETER 4:8-9

☀ Humbly Talk with the Lord

Have a chat with God about how you neglect, abuse, or invest in relationships. Discuss any lingering issue you have about boundaries, distrust, enabling, regrets, bitterness, or codependency.

Confess any bigotry, commitment phobia, and sins of the flesh that are blocking you from Christlike love, new friendships, and a burgeoning life mission.

☀ Take the *Life Purpose Coach* Challenge

Commit to trying—this week—one relational action step that supports your healing:
- ☐ Seek out a sponsor, support group, or clinic for help with an addiction.
- ☐ Go on date nights with your spouse and date outings with your children.
- ☐ Join a business networking group for help finding a job.
- ☐ Socialize weekly in a godly manner to nurture friendships.
- ☐ Seek financial counseling to get a new perspective on spending.
- ☐ Go to therapy for deep-seated relational issues.
- ☐ Join a Bible study to learn more about God.

P.U.R.**P**.O.S.E. Principle IV: **P**ursue Positive Practices to Maintain My Sobriety

Things Hidden

Even Death and Destruction hold no secrets from the LORD. *How much more does he know the human heart!* PROVERBS 15:11

The French novelist André Malraux wrote, "Man is not what he thinks he is, he is what he hides." Whereas we'd like to think we're fairly decent people, the reality is that what we hide in the darkest depths of our souls is who we really are. It's the things hidden in that panicked place—a place known only to God, ourselves, and perhaps a few others—that define us, predict our futures, and weigh us down daily. It's the counterfeit living, including concealed motives, duplicity, veiled emotional payoffs, and secrets, which holds hostage our every thought and dictates our every action. Our secret-self can only emit a silent scream of despair over the fractured relationship between our public personas and private lives.

But Truth stands up and proclaims loudly, "All are imposters!"—and for that, I'm grateful. Nobody wants to be the only one confessing the sham of disingenuous living, when everyone's hiding something, everyone's broken, and all families are dysfunctional. What if the law of the land were that nobody could deny their addictions, whether to adrenaline, power, fame, substances, or behaviors? And what if the fraud-riddled, Bogus Master in us became willing to meet the God of Proverbs 15:11 and to ask for help right now? What if we understood that relief is only a prayer away: *Lord, I can no longer hide my myriad of wrong motives, dark secrets, calculated lies, and phoniness; I ask you to take over now?* We'd all fess up, and the supernatural healing could begin.

SOUL SEARCH

When has a hidden motive (for instance, revenge, self-gratification, hero worship, or selfish ambition) led you into a web of lies or another sin, such as theft, abuse, or passive-aggression? How many times per day do you wish that your sinful secret(s) would be uncovered, so you could be forgiven and forgive yourself—and get on with your life?

My Helpmate, teach me to be who I say I am, do the good things I say I'll do, and speak the truth with love. And if I begin to misrepresent myself or concoct tall tales, stop me in my tracks so I don't jeopardize the world-class task you've given me.

P.U.R.**P**.O.S.E. Principle IV: **P**ursue Positive Practices to Maintain My Sobriety

Duplicity

The integrity of the upright guides them, but the unfaithful are destroyed by their duplicity. PROVERBS 11:3 (NIV)

Our rental car slowed in traffic as my friends and I drove toward the touristy town of Paia, Maui. Out of nowhere, an old woman with arms crossed appeared on the side of the road, staring at us with a shaman-like eeriness. Her matted, gray hair was so long it enveloped her sandals and trailed three feet behind her in the dirt. Because we gawked rudely at her, we interpreted her unrelenting glare to mean that she didn't like haoles (foreigners) in her town. Later, one of the locals explained the truth behind her odd behavior. He said, "Hitchhiking is illegal here, so the wahine [woman] was cautiously asking you for a lift, using her wrinkled brow and the common practice of crossed arms, so she wouldn't get arrested for thumbing for a ride."

No wonder we were confused; she was obeying the letter of the law but ignoring the spirit of it. For us, her actions didn't communicate her real intentions, so we were befuddled. In this case, since nobody was hurt by her duplicity and hidden agenda, we might be tempted to say, "No harm, no foul. We'll just chalk it up to a life lesson about not convoluting facts."

Reflecting on Proverbs, though, we understand that we're not to be duplicitous, make false representation, or twist the truth. So how are you doing with this type of integrity? Have you ever tried to conceal an addiction by arguing that things were not what they appeared to be? Have you purposefully implied one thing but meant another to distract the Al-Anon prayer warriors? Whenever we're faced with a decision to lie or dupe someone, we must remember that God wants to help us change our deceptive ways, and that the challenge we face is never bigger than the God we serve.

SOUL SEARCH

What pretense are you maintaining, and how does that make you feel? When uncovered, what toll will it take on your role as a field worker for the Lord?

You who uncover truth, no more false advertising for me. I'm tired of burying incriminating evidence, changing my story, and being a con artist. I want to think, think, think before I speak or act. Give me your power to change.

Hidden Motives

The LORD searches every heart and understands every motive behind the thoughts.
1 CHRONICLES 28:9 (NIV)

God understands every motive behind our thoughts and actions, every reason for doing or not doing something. He has no trouble deciphering when our prayer request on behalf of a friend is really gossip, when we made a sizable donation to a church building campaign to gain bragging rights, or when our latest pity party is an Oscar-worthy, attention-getting tactic. Do you recall when Jesus exposed the Pharisees as hypocrites because their motive was to gain respect by feigning holiness? He said, "You are like whitewashed tombs—beautiful on the outside but filled on the inside with dead people's bones and all sorts of impurity" (Matthew 23:27). Outwardly they appeared righteous, but inwardly their hearts were filled with evil.

Neither you nor I has ever tried to appear holy while courting hypocrisy, right? We best not say, "Right!" or someone will call us out with Mark Twain's famous phrase: "Denial ain't just a river in Egypt." Whether we're denying an actual addiction or a related wrong motive, it helps to ask ourselves, *Am I all about disguise, illusion, outward appearances, and masks, or do I try to be authentic and vulnerable?* And an equally important question is this: *Am I ready to begin wrestling with my motives, so I can stop the staging of my imaginary idyllic life?*

Consider this: you have a motive for wanting to know your life purpose. Is it to satisfy your curiosity, give you a conversational nugget in church huddles, or reduce your boredom by capturing a feel-good daydream? Or is it to fulfill the word of the Lord in your life and shoot glory up to him? Your answer matters to God. Ask him to show you H.O.W. to use Honesty, Open-mindedness, and Willingness when face-to-face with deciphering your motives.

SOUL SEARCH

What motive in your life isn't as it appears to be to others? In what way does one of your hidden motives surprise you?

God of forgiveness, from my fake smile to my motives of fear, anger, jealousy, and pride—I'm ready to dump all that nonsense in your lap. Help me come clean in all areas of falsehood in my life.

Right and Wrong Motives

People judge by outward appearance, but the LORD looks at the heart.
1 SAMUEL 16:7

When the prophet Samuel was searching for the next king of Israel among Jesse's sons, God told him not to look at Eliab's outward appearance or height. God said that he, the Lord, doesn't see his servants the way others see them; he looks at their hearts, their motives. It follows for us, then, that we should check our hearts in all situations. Granted, it never hurts to comb our hair, brush our teeth, and put on deodorant (since others do judge us on our appearance, breath, and body odor), but we're to focus primarily on godliness!

So what would a pure heart and right motives look like for someone serving in ministry? A desire to glorify God definitely tops the Right Motives List, followed by a desire to be obedient to the point of washing others' feet humbly. We know we're in the right motives ballpark when our hearts break over the things that break the heart of God.

But Alcoholics Anonymous sponsors hear all the time that their sponsorees are leading meetings, serving at events, or making newcomers feel welcome for a whole host of wrong motives. Take your pick from this list: to impress, feel needed, stir up drama, manipulate an outcome, do obligatory penance for public sin, run from loneliness, ignore personal issues, critique coworkers, endear others, or assuage guilt. Sometimes those in recovery even serve to be in the limelight, in the know, or in the "in" crowd—or to be affirmed as sponsor material. And in violation of all that's decent, they might serve in order to troll the dating waters of non-solidly-sober souls. Such cathartic maneuvering, avoidance measures, smug behavior, and mindless acting out aren't the way to honor God while serving. Pray for all sponsors, everywhere, who certainly have their hands full!

SOUL SEARCH

What Grand Canyon exists between your true motives (for serving, caring, giving, healing, praying, or leading) and how you playact? What would it feel like if you didn't have such a gaping disparity in your life?

Pervading Wisdom, you ponder my motives and wish to make my heart right. I'm done with my destructive deceit; bring on the real me to do the work you commissioned me to do on earth.

P.U.R.**P.**O.S.E. Principle IV: **P**ursue Positive Practices to Maintain My Sobriety

Payoffs

Put me on trial, LORD, and cross-examine me. Test my motives and my heart.
PSALM 26:2

All behavior has a conscious or an unconscious payoff—a valuable return for having invested in a specific behavior. Your payoff or reward for doing something is a clear indicator of your motive for doing it. And 100 percent of the time, your motive will point directly to your desire for happiness. To uncover your happiness motive, just ask yourself any one of these truth-serum questions: *What is it I want? What do I hope to gain? How will this action benefit me? What's my motivation? What happiness will this behavior bring me?*

Anyone who's fascinated by human behavior enjoys investigating people's "artificial or true happiness" payoffs by asking questions like these:

- What was his payoff for gang involvement? Possibly vengeance?
- What was her payoff for taking narcotics? Did she achieve temporary freedom from guilt?
- What was their payoff for pursuing a godly life? Was it a reputation for holiness or was it intimacy with Jesus?

Other common happiness payoffs are money, material gain, pleasure, thrill, power, approval, sanity, praise, love, respect, truth, health, safety, security, peace of mind, significance, protection, hope, joy, a jeweled crown in heaven, and magnifying God's name.

Our verse teaches us to ask the Lord to put us on solemn trial to find out if we're living under the delusion that our motives are pure. We're to examine our hearts in a most thorough, ongoing investigation, listening to our consciences. We're not to shrink from any test in this regard, because unearthing the root reasons for our behavior will help us turn from sin, recover from addiction, grow spiritually, and fulfill our unique purposes on earth.

SOUL SEARCH

Which of your disreputable motivations do you find most worrisome? What primo reward or valuable return do you desire on your investment of time, energy, and resources in God's call on your life?

Refining Fire, I desire to have all the motives of my heart purified. Examine me, O Lord, and expose the truth of my behavior.

Secret Shame

God would surely have known it, for he knows the secrets of every heart.
PSALM 44:21

Years ago, one of my longtime friends, whom I love like a sister, kept her adulterous affair secret from me for several weeks. Here's how she acted during that time of holding the huge S.E.C.R.E.T.: Snippy/Sour/Surly, Evasive, Conflicted, Random, Egotistic, and Tense. I should have realized that these are my friend's "tells" when she's hurting. Her avoidance tactics and abruptness were clues enough, but I assumed she was angry with me for some reason. Later, she told me that her secret actually spelled out S.H.A.M.E.: Sad, Humiliated, Afraid, Morally Broken, and Empty. She said that she still loved God with all her heart, but she felt that he couldn't possibly love her, knowing her secret shame.

But God had never stopped loving her, had he? And who among us, sinners that we are, could ever stand in judgment of her? Living a double life had been exhausting and painful for her, and it had filled her with dread of exposure and public ridicule. Much of her angst was that she knew camouflage is a magnet for detection.

When you find that your loved ones are knee-deep in atypical behavior, like I've described with my friend, pray for God to reveal any shame-based secret or cry for help that he needs and wants you to hear. And ask him for a tender heart for those who do confess their shame to you, so you might minister to them with the love of Jesus. Pray for those who've had to wear the scarlet letter *A* for adultery, who've had their suicide attempts whispered about in their church, or who've had their bulimic body-image struggles judged by town gossips. After having lived with smoke and mirrors, they'll need your support to get rid of their guilt and shame, which—as we know—are the gifts that keep on giving.

SOUL SEARCH

What damage has a secret done to someone you know? What secret of your own are you tired of sweating bullets over because you're afraid of the ensuing condemnation?

My Redemption, help me lovingly recognize shame-based behavior in others, so I can be a better minister to them. And send me someone I can trust with my unbearable secrets so I can move forward with your goals for my life.

P.U.R.**P**.O.S.E. Principle IV: **P**ursue Positive Practices to Maintain My Sobriety

Authenticity

Be honest with God and others about your right and wrong motives. You might as well, because God already knows all your secret thoughts, and savvy people can often see right through deceit, charm, contrived answers, and manipulation.

☀ Meditate on the Assurance of God's Word

When you ask, you don't get it because your motives are all wrong—you want only what will give you pleasure.   JAMES 4:3

I, the LORD, search all hearts and examine secret motives. I give all people their due rewards, according to what their actions deserve.   JEREMIAH 17:10

This is the message I proclaim—that the day is coming when God, through Christ Jesus, will judge everyone's secret life.   ROMANS 2:16

☀ Humbly Talk with the Lord

Confess the times you've been aware of your lies, hypocrisy, or disingenuous behavior, but proceeded down that path out of pride, fear, shame, or obstinacy.

Ask the Holy Spirit to motivate you to be authentic in your recovery circles and in your ministry-mission work.

☀ Take the *Life Purpose Coach* Challenge

Take a deep, prayerful breath and schedule a conversation with someone who's known you for quite a while, someone who loves you unconditionally and won't lie to you. Ask for their impression of your past and current default motives. Without rebuttal, record their answers on a paper labeled "Motives Then" and "Motives Now." To get a complete historical view of your modus operandi (MO), shake off the shock and repeat with a second and third individual, as needed! And thank the Lord for such honest, helpful feedback and for your renewed eagerness to live your best purpose-centered life.

P.U.R.**P**.O.S.E. Principle IV: **P**ursue Positive Practices to Maintain My Sobriety

Signposts to Wholeness

May [God] keep us centered and devoted to him, following the life path he has cleared, watching the signposts, walking at the pace and rhythms he laid down for our ancestors. 1 KINGS 8:58 (*The Message*)

God is with us day and night, inclining our hearts toward him. He longs to lead us at his pace and rhythm down the pathway he's cleared for our journey. Jesus says, "Walk with me and work with me—watch how I do it. Learn the unforced rhythms of grace. . . . Keep company with me and you'll learn to live freely and lightly" (Matthew 11:29-30, *The Message*).

To order our steps with the Lord's steps, which keep us from living a random life of despair, addiction, purposelessness, and chaos, I've found these five important signposts valuable: (1) live simply, (2) guard your health, (3) keep yourself physically fit, (4) enjoy levity, and (5) give and receive grace. For each of these neon-blinking billboards you follow, you'll move closer to a well-ordered life that makes it possible for you to participate fully in your recovery program. And if you put all five of these directives into practice, together they bring about a better result than any one of them could accomplish alone.

William Lyon Phelps, an American author and scholar in the early 1900s, wrote this about ordering our lives to get a clear view of where we're going: "A well-ordered life is like climbing a tower; the view halfway up is better than the view from the base, and it steadily becomes finer as the horizon expands." A view from the top of what your sobriety and life mission look like—that's worth following God's signposts every inch of the way.

SOUL SEARCH

Which of God's signposts would help you the most with your recovery? What can you do differently now to live a well-ordered life and enjoy the view of palpable hope on the horizon?

Abiding Presence, I want to learn to live a synergistic life based on your goals for my sobriety and purpose. Teach me to tweak every area of my life until it's well ordered and honors you.

P.U.R.**P**.O.S.E. Principle IV: **P**ursue Positive Practices to Maintain My Sobriety
Signpost 1: Simplified Lifestyle

Don't carry a traveler's bag with a change of clothes and sandals or even a walking stick.
MATTHEW 10:10

While visiting the Calcutta Missionaries of Charity, I was reminded of their vow of poverty, which limits their possessions to a crucifix, rosary, prayer book, pair of sandals, flour-sack undergarments, cardigan, plate and spoon, canvas bag, and three saris for wearing, washing, and mending. Humor me for a moment and consider, hypothetically: How would being that unencumbered make you trust God for everything? Wait a minute; that question is too easy! You'd probably be like the missionaries who wait expectantly in their courtyard for God's daily delivery of rice, beans, milk, medical supplies, clothing, money, lumber, and volunteers.

I withdraw that question and ask you this harder one: How could simplifying your life (financially, mentally, emotionally, physically, and spiritually) strengthen your recovery, by giving you more space for God's will and his ways? For example, with his help . . .

- Financially surrendering all you own, earn, hoard, and dream of possessing could reduce your addictive desire for more, bigger, better, faster, or sooner.
- Mentally disengaging from "garbage" input from magazines, the Internet, television, or clubs could make room in your mind for becoming Christ-minded.
- Emotionally detaching from a pattern of stubbornness, impatience, intolerance, or anxiety could entice you to work your recovery program.
- Physically loosening the grip of gluttony, slothfulness, fatigue, or isolation could radically change the way you see your hopeless situation.
- Spiritually rejecting legalism, guilt-driven service, the notion of earning a place in heaven, or mistaken thinking about your lack of worth could revolutionize your view of your Higher Power, Jesus.

God's work, including your recovery steps and life mission, flourishes in a simplified lifestyle of quiet reflection. Don't let your insatiability for too much be the death of you. Instead, follow your heart that's begging you to simplify all aspects of your life.

SOUL SEARCH

How would simplifying any part of your life strengthen your recovery? What harmful lifestyle idols (any possession, place, or person you've placed above God) need to go?

Living and True God, free me from the mountain of stuff that's hindering me.

P.U.R.**P**.O.S.E. Principle IV: **P**ursue Positive Practices to Maintain My Sobriety
Signpost 2: Health and Wellness

Jesus matured, growing up in both body and spirit, blessed by both God and people.
LUKE 2:52 (*The Message*)

Those seeking sobriety want emotional, physical, mental, relational, financial, and spiritual health. They want to mature in all areas and be blessed by both God and people. They're ready to evaluate a variety of health risk factors, such as their use of nicotine, alcohol, or drugs. In addition, they might want help with their weight, exercise plan, nutrition, stress, insomnia, obsession with plastic surgery, or social skills. These people often seek health-and-wellness coaching because wholeness, peacefulness, authenticity, and intimacy have become primary concerns. Looming large are issues related to body image, fear, self-esteem, depression, anger, perfectionism, or loneliness. In all likelihood, they're dealing with a crisis of faith or serious questions about why they were even born. Does this describe you in any way?

These individuals understand Plato's comment "The part can never be well unless the whole is well." They become ready to function optimally by assuming responsibility for the quality of their lives, which they know begins with avoiding temptations of every type. They're willing to create holistic action plans and establish accountability. Do you find yourself becoming more ready and willing every day to move toward health and wellness?

To be clear, most of these descriptors could be said of Christians and non-Christians alike. The difference for believers, though, is that one of our primary motivators for choosing a healthy lifestyle is that we want to be about our heavenly Father's business. (Read how Jesus modeled this passionate purpose for us in Luke 2:41-52.) Are you looking forward to being about God's business and seeking wholeness to help you fully engage?

SOUL SEARCH

How has your head-and-heart commotion caused you to yearn for health and wellness? What could you do now to move toward an inner calmness, sober choices, and life satisfaction?

God, my ever-present help, I'd give anything to be blessed by both you and people. Help me mature in you, so I might glorify your name with my good character and through all you've designated for me to do during my short stay on earth.

P.U.R.**P**.O.S.E. Principle IV: **P**ursue Positive Practices to Maintain My Sobriety
Signpost 3: Being Physically Fit

Don't you realize that your body is the temple of the Holy Spirit, who lives in you and was given to you by God? You do not belong to yourself. 1 CORINTHIANS 6:19

You already know that God bought you at a high price and that you're to honor him with your mind and body, but did you realize that your body is actually his Spirit's temple? Scripture says that you don't belong to yourself, which raises a question for you to answer: "How can I be a first-rate steward of my physical temple?"

Wouldn't it be nice if seeing our bodies as temples were the secret to instant recovery? Imagine if sobriety were a slam-dunk event after addicts make the connection that because their bodies are the Holy Spirit's temples, they shouldn't abuse them! But, alas, the truth is that recovery is a process, not an event. We must give time, time—and we must realize that the price for serenity and sanity is self-sacrifice.

It isn't enough to make the connection between the responsibility of self-care of your temple and what that could mean to your recovery. You must ask yourself some serious questions like these and then invite God's Spirit to act daily and deliberately to ensure positive results: Do I get enough sleep each night and take one-minute vacations from my work throughout the day? How's my nutrition: poor, good, or great? What form of exercise is fun for me—swimming, rowing, golfing, dancing, skating, biking, hiking, or pumping iron? Have I thought through the benefits of increased muscle tone, healthy weight maintenance, stress relief, and disease prevention?

By taking a methodical, day-by-day approach to fitness, you'll be reminded many times each day that God's Spirit is within you, his temple, to help you with all aspects of your recovery and life's work. You're not alone.

SOUL SEARCH

What can you do to care more lovingly for the temple of the Holy Spirit? How will this contribute to your sobriety and long-term, godly goals?

Resurrected Christ, you referred to your own body as a temple.* Help me to see my body as a temple, too, and to ask for some serious help with my action steps.

---

* See John 2:21.

201

P.U.R.**P**.O.S.E. Principle IV: **P**ursue Positive Practices to Maintain My Sobriety

Signpost 4: The Role of Levity

Thanksgivings will pour out of the windows; laughter will spill through the doors.
Things will get better and better. Depression days are over.
JEREMIAH 30:19 (*The Message*)

When God talked about bringing his people out of Babylonian captivity, he said they'd be filled with such gratitude that it would overflow into laughter. What has been holding you captive lately? Have you been chained to codependency, sugar, wine-induced gossip, or illicit behavior? Imagine that you're being set free right now from that bondage. Let loose your shouts of joyful thanksgiving as you realize that your depression days are over and that you're getting ready to "thrive and flourish," as the next part of the verse says. Hear yourself laughing out loud in utter relief.

What if laughter were actually a prison-door key, perfectly molded by God to free you from your self-imposed incarceration? You know that it could be the key, because you've heard testimonials, as I have, about the therapeutic powers of humor. I'm not just talking about how the sound of a chuckle can bring a smile to your face. I'm reminding you that a good belly laugh can relax your whole body, relieving it of tension by decreasing your stress hormones. Laughter can change your mood and boost your energy by releasing endorphins, which are your body's feelin' good chemicals; it can even increase blood flow to your heart. And when you share a fall-down-laughing moment with someone, it creates a bond between you that helps morph conflict into optimism for a brighter future. When you stop taking yourself so seriously and start laughing at yourself, your perspective shifts from feeling overwhelmed to remembering that God was still God the last time you checked.

Just as parents delight in the laughter of their children, your heavenly Father delights in hearing you laugh.

SOUL SEARCH

Will you try to laugh, smile, or embrace a cheerful attitude more often, out of gratitude to God for being set free from an addiction? When is laughing at yourself hard for you?

You who reign eternally, I'm ready for my depression days to be over! Let thanksgivings and contagious laughter overflow from my household onto my mission field. I'm ready to thrive and flourish!

P.U.R.**P**.O.S.E. Principle IV: **P**ursue Positive Practices to Maintain My Sobriety

Signpost 5: Grace Extended and Received

Look after each other so that none of you fails to receive the grace of God.
HEBREWS 12:15

An aerial view of any community always causes me to pray for those people who are hurting in the homes below. God gives me this sense that I can see widows sobbing in their darkened bedrooms, parents at their wits' end with rebellious teens, children terrified by abuse, and other lonely souls contemplating suicide. However, even if nothing traumatic is happening, people still feel body-slammed by the daily stress of relentless pressures. Compound that with recovery issues, and it spells Dysfunction with a capital *D*.

Don't be tempted to look down at the houses anymore; look upward instead! Cast your eyes on heaven and pray with me for God's free, generous gift of grace to fall on all who are distressed. Ask him to extend his unmerited love, his benevolent favor, to those in need—including you and me, too! Pray by name for individuals to whom you need to offer undeserved grace, and also for those who've been withholding grace from you. As you pray the following Scriptures, tell God you want to learn to extend and receive grace more graciously:

Even before I was born, God chose me and called me by his marvelous grace.
GALATIANS 1:15

God saved you by his grace when you believed. And you can't take credit for this;
it is a gift from God.   EPHESIANS 2:8

I know that giving and accepting grace isn't easy, but we can let these verses remind us that it's only by God's grace we've been saved—and that more of his favor is always available.

SOUL SEARCH

How has grace revealed to you the doting nature of your heavenly Father? How might your lifelong ministry involve giving others the gift of grace?

God of grace, I join all believers in households, as we pray, "Let us come boldly to the throne of our gracious God. There we will receive [your] mercy, and we will find grace to help us when we need it most."*

---
* Hebrews 4:16.

P.U.R.P.O.S.E. Principle IV: Pursue Positive Practices to Maintain My Sobriety

Living the Life

Living a simple, reasonably healthy and fit, laughter-dotted, and grace-filled life is essential to resisting the pull of addiction. If you make a concerted effort to address those five areas, you'll move light-years closer to optimal sobriety choices and dreaming God-sized dreams for your future.

☀ Meditate on the Assurance of God's Word

God bought you with a high price. So you must honor God with your body.
1 CORINTHIANS 6:20

When the LORD brought back his exiles to Jerusalem, it was like a dream! We were filled with laughter, and we sang for joy. And the other nations said, "What amazing things the LORD has done for them." PSALM 126:1-2

☀ Humbly Talk with the Lord

Ask Jesus to give you the courage you need to downsize your life, the vigor you need to maintain a healthy exercise routine, and the audacity you need to live your life with a dash of lighthearted humor.

Remind God that you're in dire need of a belly laugh or two, and challenge him to create such fun opportunities for you sooner rather than later.

☀ Take the *Life Purpose Coach* Challenge

Simplicity, wellness, fitness, levity, and grace have one thing in common: change. They require change on your part and they have the power to change the current reality of your surroundings, health, body, attitude, and character. So when you begin to get frustrated with any backsliding and relapses, think Change! Dial back your need to acquire stuff and to be in control of the universe; physically burn off stress-causing, brain chemicals like cortisol; and enjoy the medicinal benefits of laughter and grace.

Spiritual Habits

"Physical training is good, but training for godliness is much better, promising benefits in this life and in the life to come." This is a trustworthy saying.   1 TIMOTHY 4:8-9

Athletic training is a great simile for spiritual training; both require motivation, inspiration, and disciplined habits to carry their participants to victory, especially if success is only a glimmer in a newbie's eyes. I'll leave sports training to those expert coaches, but I can tell you that no part of godliness training is based on performance, rules, timelines, or stats. Spiritual growth and recovery are intense enough without all that potential legalism and rigidity. Instead, remember that Jesus is your spiritual Coach, and victory is intimacy with him. Invite him to grow you into the person he's designed you to be. With that being our undisputable, basic premise, here are some spiritual habits that can help you connect and cooperate with Jesus: private and community worship, Bible reading and study, Scripture memorization and meditation, prayer and fasting, purity, journaling, forgiveness, servanthood, confession and repentance, accountability, and fellowship. Or these might be among your personal favorites: silence and solitude, simplicity, surrender, intercessory praying and praying the names of God, generosity, or tithing.

With that substantial list, you understand why I wanted to stress upfront that spiritual growth must be all about holding Jesus close, not acquiring head knowledge or performing holy feats of religiosity. Donald Whitney, author of *Spiritual Disciplines for the Christian Life*, offers this encouraging insight, "If your picture of a disciplined Christian is one of a grim, tight-lipped, joyless half-robot, then you've missed the point. Jesus was the most disciplined Man who ever lived and yet the most joyful and passionately alive." Take journaling, for example. It's counterproductive to feel pressured to adopt it as a spiritual habit. Instead, it's better to view it as a golden opportunity to ask your Creator some questions and to record his answers, which gives you a wealth of wisdom available at your fingertips. Whenever you think about spiritual habits, which will help you recover, think about getting to know Jesus.

SOUL SEARCH

Which joy-inspired spiritual habit tunes you into Jesus' sobriety goals for you and his best intentions for your life? Which member of Jesus' spiritual coaching staff on earth might support your training efforts?

My Constant Companion, train me to be more like you.

P.U.R.P.O.S.E. Principle IV: Pursue Positive Practices to Maintain My Sobriety

Reading God's Word

All Scripture is inspired by God and is useful to teach us what is true and to make us realize what is wrong in our lives.   2 TIMOTHY 3:16

Paul shares more about the topic of Scripture in 2 Timothy 3:17: "God uses it to prepare and equip his people to do every good work." What an exceptional gift God has given us—a gift inspired by him to teach and correct us as well as prepare and equip us! What more consistent source of wisdom could anyone desire? Reading and meditating on God's Word is the only safe, logical way to proceed to freedom from sin, self-centeredness, and addiction. Nineteenth-century theologian James W. Alexander adds, "The study of God's word, for the purpose of discovering God's will, is the secret discipline which has formed the greatest characters."

As to where we devour God's Word, I personally think that variety is the spice of life. Some of my holiest friends disagree; they're adamant that we need to have a designated Quiet Time chair, lamp, throw blanket, humongous study Bible, and a plethora of writing supplies. All that structure can make me claustrophobic, so I often prefer to be spontaneous. As for your reading and meditation, it may work for you to crawl back into your unmade bed with instrumental music playing softly, or you might prefer to lounge on your living room floor by your fireplace. You may decide to sit in a straight-back chair at your kitchen table, nibbling on almonds, or you might choose to take refuge in your favorite La-Z-Boy recliner. In fact, you may want to read Scripture aloud in your child's bedroom, thinking of prayer requests from his or her point of view. And never underestimate the joy of having a cappuccino with Christ at a quiet sidewalk café or sitting together to watch the sun go down from the comfort of a bay window. What a privilege to read and meditate on God's Word—wherever!

SOUL SEARCH

How does interacting with Scripture refuel your empty tank and keep you from trying to mastermind your own recovery? What's your favorite location for enjoying the Bible?

Word of Life, teach and correct me, so each decision I make and each relationship I develop moves me closer to you and sobriety. Prepare and equip me to lead the life you destined me to live.

P.U.R.**P**.O.S.E. Principle IV: **P**ursue Positive Practices to Maintain My Sobriety

Fasting

When you fast, don't make it obvious, as the hypocrites do, for they try to look miserable and disheveled so people will admire them for their fasting.
MATTHEW 6:16

I can still recall my anger from thirty years ago when an acquaintance asked me to prayerfully fast with her and others on behalf of their dying friend. I thought, *How dare you put me on the spot with your high expectation for a public, affirmative reply. I feel bad for the woman who's ill, but I don't even know her, and nobody's "guilting" me into anything!*

Since then, I've come a long way in understanding the enormous value of joining with other Christians in biblically based fasts, but I still do much better when the Holy Spirit prompts me privately and is the only one who knows. I'm particularly sensitive to the second half of today's verse, in which Jesus speaks of his disgust for hypocritical, showy fasting, "I tell you the truth, [people's admiration] is the only reward they will ever get." I've also begun to appreciate the wide variety of fasts, one being the Daniel 10 fast with fruits, vegetables, and water for twenty-one days. Another fast, as found in Esther 4, is a cleansing abstinence for three days and nights.

One word of warning: don't let fasting derail your recovery; be careful not to exacerbate any feeling of "being deprived of one more thing." If that's an issue you face, you may prefer one-day or one-time fasts from things like chocolate, caffeine, television, shopping, or optional telephone calls. With this milder expectation, you can focus more on going toward God's strategic plan, rather than going without something. And never forget that prayer is actually the reason for any fast. For example, by skipping a 3 p.m. sugar habit or a 9 to 10 p.m. television-viewing pattern, you're choosing to make more room in your schedule to pray.

SOUL SEARCH

How could the spiritual discipline of prayerful fasting support your sobriety? What could it do for your life's mission assignment from God?

O great and awesome God, please teach me to fast, according to your great wisdom, so I might find more time to pray. And fill me with humble joy when I honor you in this way.

P.U.R.P.O.S.E. Principle IV: Pursue Positive Practices to Maintain My Sobriety

Intercessory Praying

Dear brothers and sisters, I urge you in the name of our Lord Jesus Christ to join in my struggle by praying to God for me. ROMANS 15:30

Like Paul, we're to urge our Christian friends to pray for us, even adding as he did, "Do this because of your love for me, given to you by the Holy Spirit" (more of Romans 15:30). Hopefully, you have loved ones who consider it an honor to pray you through your addictive struggles. As Andrea, who attends a recovery program, just told me recently, "Nothing surprises me anymore about how horribly people are hurting. So many of my friends are dealing with a spouse or loved one who's deep into gambling, alcohol, marijuana, cocaine, pornography, adultery, or an eating disorder. Typically I get so depressed by the endless list of prayer requests, I end up crying out to the Lord to send somebody to pray for me." We all need someone to intercede on our behalf for relief from our debilitating habits and heartaches.

So when God prompts you to pray for someone specifically, you might like to try this method of private intercessory praying: insert the person's first name into a Scripture passage. For example, from 1 Peter 5:8-9, you could pray, *Lord, you know that the enemy prowls around like a roaring lion looking for an opportunity to devour _____. I pray that _____ will be self-controlled, alert, resistant to the devil, and firm in the faith.* You could also pray Colossians 1:9-14, asking God to fill your friend with the knowledge of his will through all spiritual wisdom, or you could pray Psalm 5:11-12, asking God to spread his protection over your friend. And once you're on a roll, don't forget to intercede for your friend's peace, relationships, physical and mental health, studies, employment, obsessions, and compulsions.

SOUL SEARCH

For whom is God asking you to pray, and in what specific area of need (if that's been revealed to you)? Will you ask someone trustworthy to intercede for *you*, regarding *your* greatest area of need?

God of unlimited authority and influence, I pray Colossians 4:12-13, earnestly asking you to help _____ and me stand firm in your will for our lives, so we'll be mature.

P.U.R.**P**.O.S.E. Principle IV: **P**ursue Positive Practices to Maintain My Sobriety

Purity

Run from sexual sin! No other sin so clearly affects the body as this one does. For sexual immorality is a sin against your own body.   1 CORINTHIANS 6:18

A lifestyle of purity is not just abstinence from sins of the flesh, like adultery, prostitution, sexual abuse, deviant sex offenses, and pornography. It's also a desire to reject idols of all kinds, especially anything related to vain ambition; it's a decision to choose holiness and think on pure, admirable ideas—especially on Jesus Christ, the only pure one. We were born impure because of Adam and Eve's Garden sin, but Jesus deemed us pure when we began our relationship with him. Now we're in his lifetime purification class, glad to hear from 1 Corinthians 10:13 that our temptations are the same as what others experience. It further explains, "God is faithful. He will not allow the temptation to be more than you can stand. When you are tempted, he will show you a way out so that you can endure."

Are you tired of feeling guilty and hiding your shame about ambitiously selfish desires and other impure thoughts, words, and actions that degrade your soul? If so, are you willing to do whatever it takes now to stay pure? Prayerfully consider these suggestions: sit in the presence of Christ often; check your motives in all matters; don't stay in a hotel room without an accountability partner; avoid crass, selfish people; say no to strip clubs and strippers at parties; block adult content on your television; get online accountability through a software application; avoid X-rated, magazine stands; drop out of social circles that flaunt provocative clothing; and refuse to engage in emotional adultery.

To help with insidious sins of impurity, you'll want to read God's love letter aloud, searching for and memorizing verses like "Since the Master honors you with a body, honor him with your body!" (1 Corinthians 6:13, *The Message*). This will help sensitize your heart toward uplifting conversations and activities.

SOUL SEARCH

What drastic measures could you implement now to keep yourself out of harm's way of sexual sin? How urgent would God rank this matter: *Extremely* or *Whenever*?

*Pure and Holy God, I choose to stay away from all sexual sin; give me strength. * I want to spend my time following you and fulfilling your phenomenal plan for my life.*

---

* From 1 Thessalonians 4:3.

P.U.R.**P**.O.S.E. Principle IV: **P**ursue Positive Practices to Maintain My Sobriety

Tithing

If you do [bring all your tithes], . . . I will pour out a blessing so great you won't have enough room to take it in! Try it! Put me to the test!   MALACHI 3:10

One Sunday in 1988, I listened intently to a Malachi 3 sermon that introduced a new concept to me. Our pastor was talking about how we rob God by not presenting 10 percent tithes and extra offerings. While I was fascinated by the idea that tithing was a command, I was still reluctant to increase my five-dollar-per-week donation. I felt that was a fair amount, considering the high cost of living as a single mom with two children in Southern California. (Don't laugh or cry.) I was intrigued, though, when our pastor said that if we obey this command, God will throw open heaven's windows for us, with a blessing so great we won't be able to take it all in.

Walk with me now after services, as I gravitate toward the smiling faces of a young couple, my friends who are mingling around the refreshments. Think of the most hard-hearted, self-centered, rebellious, angry-at-God thing you could say to the group of us to disdain the sermon. I want to see if God touches your heart, like he did mine that Sunday, with what the husband said and the wife affirmed: "We love to put God to the test regarding our finances, marriage, and ministry. We've tried to outgive him, but he always gives us back so many more blessings!" I was flabbergasted that real people had actually had the full-blown, Malachi experience—and God made a tithing believer out of me that day.

Think of the beaming smile you'll have when you get to tell someone—perhaps a newcomer at a recovery meeting—about your joy of trying to outgive God.

SOUL SEARCH

How do you feel about taking God's tithing challenge and putting him to the test? How would you feel if the blessing God poured onto you included the funding of your life dream?

Lord, although I'm not in gunnysack and ashes, I come before you to confess my sin of robbing you of tithes and offerings. I do want all nations to call my life blessed*— including my finances, relationships, prayer requests, sobriety, and purpose.

---

* From Malachi 3:12.

P.U.R.P.O.S.E. Principle IV: Pursue Positive Practices to Maintain My Sobriety

Embracing Spiritual Habits

Consider how far a new spiritual habit could take you on your recovery journey. With nothing to lose and everything to gain, wouldn't the results be worth the experiment?

☀ Meditate on the Assurance of God's Word

Your word is a lamp to guide my feet and a light for my path.   PSALM 119:105

Give your gifts in private, and your Father, who sees everything, will reward you.
MATTHEW 6:4

Esther sent this reply to Mordecai: "Go and gather together all the Jews of Susa and fast for me. Do not eat or drink for three days, night or day. My maids and I will do the same. And then, though it is against the law, I will go in to see the king. If I must die, I must die." So Mordecai went away and did everything as Esther had ordered him.   ESTHER 4:15-17

☀ Humbly Talk with the Lord

Ask the Lord to help you recall a time when you witnessed the beauty of a spiritual habit in someone's life.

Praise God that you're only one prayerful decision away from initiating or upgrading a life-renewing spiritual habit.

☀ Take the *Life Purpose Coach* Challenge

The next time you face a difficult decision about your addiction, take one day to pray ardently about fasting from something. Without that preliminary day of prayer, you might feel like you guilt-tripped yourself into a fasting experience, rather than choosing it with your whole heart, mind, and soul. This preparatory time of prayer will also help you ready yourself to enter God's throne room and bow to hear his plans for your sobriety and significance-filled life.

P.U.R.P.O.S.E. Principle IV: Pursue Positive Practices to Maintain My Sobriety

Perseverance and Lifelong Learning

We are pressed on every side by troubles, but we are not crushed. We are perplexed, but not driven to despair. 2 CORINTHIANS 4:8

Before we dive into today's verse, think terra-cotta pots! That's what the apostle Paul likens us to in 2 Corinthians 4:7, when he describes us as fragile clay jars that can be so easily broken. As such frail beings, we could be crushed and driven to despair under the daily trials and emotional battering of our lives; we're simply not able to cope or persevere when hard-pressed, perplexed, terrorized, or knocked down. We're such ordinary, unadorned jars that our weakness and insignificance make it obvious that our great power to overcome troubles, confusion, suffering, temptation, persecution, and addictions couldn't possibly come from ourselves.

This makes us all the more grateful that God has put a great treasure—the light of Christ—in us unworthy containers! By sharing in the suffering and death of Jesus, who is our treasure, our light, and our Savior, we also share in his resurrected life and all-surpassing power (see 2 Corinthians 4:10). And Jesus is the only reason we're able to prevail over all difficulties, including our recovery setbacks.

When you find yourself pressed on every side, perplexed, and on the brink of ominous despair over a looming relapse or your flailing ministry, consider these words of Abraham Lincoln about a nation's persevering efforts to heal, care for those who had fought the good fight, and find peace, "With malice toward none; with charity for all; with firmness in the right, as God gives us to see the right, let us strive on to finish the work we are in."

And also consider making a lifetime commitment to learn all God wants you to learn about staying the course with your spiritual growth, sobriety, and life mission, even when you'd rather give up. Offer this type of dedication: "God will receive more and more glory. That is why we never give up" (2 Corinthians 4:15-16). Never give up.

SOUL SEARCH

How has Jesus' resurrection power helped you persevere when you were hard pressed, perplexed, persecuted, or knocked down? What did you learn from that situation?

Light of the World, shine through me, so all who know me—the fragile me who used to pose as the self-sufficient me—will know for certain that it's your power that helps me persevere.

P.U.R.P.O.S.E. Principle IV: Pursue Positive Practices to Maintain My Sobriety

Staying Power

The judge . . . said to himself, "I don't fear God or care about people, but this woman is driving me crazy. I'm going to see that she gets justice, because she is wearing me out with her constant requests!" LUKE 18:4-5

I'm grateful for the parable Jesus told about a widow who, because of her persistence, was finally granted justice by an evil judge. The story's one main teaching point is that we're to have an expectant faith, as evidenced through continual prayer until the end of time, literally. So, when we hit rock bottom and another intervention doesn't work, or when our God-given plans have been decimated a-g-a-i-n beyond recognition, we're to pray and believe; then pray some more! We're to remind ourselves that one of God's most important goals for us is that we grow in expectant faith, which happens when we persevere.

I personally define *perseverance* as the gift of grace and staying power that God gives us to move toward the vision he's assigned us, even when the situation is obviously hopeless or seemingly endless. It's an uncanny determination to stay the course, fight the fight, hope against all odds, and believe in miracles. I'm actually sad as I type this, because these words flood me with memories of the enormous toll I've paid hanging on for twenty-five years to God's slowly unfolding dream for my life. Is my ministry making incredible strides? Yes. Has it been worth it? Of course. But I've concluded that perseverance is not for the fainthearted. Sometimes I think the only reason I've survived the experience is that I'm so stubborn!

SOUL SEARCH

When have you persevered against all odds, begging God for long-term stamina in your rehabilitation or fresh insight about how to accomplish his will? In what way did you grow closer to the Lord through that experience?

Eternal King, you know how discouraged I get by difficulties that cause me to stumble in my sobriety and that delay your loving plan for my life. Teach me to be a person of persistence, hanging on when I feel that my heart can't care anymore, my mind can't believe anymore, and my body can't cling to life any longer.

P.U.R.P.O.S.E. Principle IV: Pursue Positive Practices to Maintain My Sobriety

Perseverance during Trials

When troubles come your way, consider it an opportunity for great joy. For you know that when your faith is tested, your endurance has a chance to grow. So let it grow.
JAMES 1:2-4

What trouble or challenge have you faced in your recovery that has tested your faith and caused you to grow spiritually? Were you fortunate enough to experience the great joy of knowing that you were developing endurance?

In 2002, a few months prior to the release of my first book, my faith was tested and "great joy" was a joke. My publisher at that time (unnamed) canceled my contract. In stunned disbelief, I read blurry words on a certified letter about a market downturn after the 9/11 terrorist attacks and the cancellation of 75 percent of all author contracts. I knew better than to ask God why he had allowed my life dream to dissipate before my eyes, although I was sorely tempted. He knew that I'd worked for twenty-five years on that book, rewriting each sentence a thousand times, soliciting input from countless friends, and surviving rejection letters from forty-seven publishers.

After two long days of ugly crying and making 1,500-piece puzzles, I stood up, dusted myself off, and said, "I'm either a Hebrews 11 woman of great faith or I'm nothing. God gave me this dream of writing a book, so I will keep moving forward with it. If he chooses to take it away forever, that's his prerogative. I only want what he wants." Today, that book, *Pathway to Purpose*, is a bestseller in twelve languages—but even if that were not true, I can honestly say that maturing in my desire to trust God enduringly has been among his greatest gifts to me.

Whatever setback you're facing in your sobriety or your life's dream, I urge you to choose Hebrews 11 as your faith-renewing prayer. God is faithful.

SOUL SEARCH

What has helped you stay the course when you were feeling utterly defeated by your painful past? What would help you hang on to God's future dreams for you?

Jesus, you who persevered, even to death on the cross, I'm at the end of the proverbial rope. I can't hang on any longer. Unless you choose to reenergize me, I'm done. I'm toast. I'm history. Hear my prayer and make me able to go the distance for you.

P.U.R.**P**.O.S.E. Principle IV: **P**ursue Positive Practices to Maintain My Sobriety
Daily Perseverance

We can rejoice, too, when we run into problems and trials, for we know that they help us develop endurance.   ROMANS 5:3

Romans 5:3 doesn't read "if" we run into problems; it reads "when" we run into them. The good news, though, is that Paul isn't saying we must rejoice in our trials, as is often misquoted. He's saying that we rejoice because we develop endurance by working through our problems. That includes faithfully working through our addiction dilemmas, hysteria, and mania—even when rejoicing doesn't come automatically.

This verse should have been my race motto in 2005 during a half marathon in Tahiti. My younger sister, Mo, who was an avid marathoner, asked me to run with her for her Fiftieth-Birthday-Hurrah! I did so, coming in last place with an eighteen-minute mile. It was a colossal debacle for me, which came as no surprise, considering that I'd gained twenty pounds since my personal best time of a nine-minute mile ten years prior. We never suspected, though, that the temperature at 6 a.m. in February would be ninety degrees and that the humidity would be a smack-you-in-the-face 95 percent! I was in such bad shape by mile seven that the bicycle-medics trailed me, their last-place runner, with great suspicion. Mo stayed with me, assuring me that she wouldn't allow anyone to pull me off the course unless I was actually flatlining. She knew how much I value stick-to-itiveness and "Finisher" medals.

When your recovery feels like a hot, humid, excruciating race, you can still rejoice in the gold medal you'll receive for endurance. Just make sure to enlist a support team who can help you inch forward with your daily commitment to decent living and fulfilling God's daring plan for your life.

SOUL SEARCH

Who encourages you to persevere in a healthy lifestyle of close personal examination? When has that lifeline of support helped you endure tough times?

My Safe Haven from the heat, you know that I'm barely holding it together on a daily basis. Without the hope of you personally pacing me to the finish line, I won't be able to endure. I thank you for the family and friends you've sent me as spiritual, emotional, and physical medics. Teach me how to rejoice in the personal growth I'm experiencing.

P.U.R.**P**.O.S.E. Principle IV: **P**ursue Positive Practices to Maintain My Sobriety

Needing to Learn

The LORD says, "I will guide you along the best pathway for your life. I will advise you and watch over you." PSALM 32:8

God prompts us to learn more about him, his timing, and his ways. He also encourages us to learn more about our talents, spiritual gifts, motives, culture, family history, character, and role models. You might feel like God is nudging you to learn something along the lines of budgeting, sign language, or graphic design. Or his personalized agenda for you might guide you to learn a new concept, practical skill, or leadership style that would enhance your family or ministry dynamics. For sure, God is hoping that you learn to answer these questions about your recovery and his calling on your life:

- Where's my life heading?
- How will I feel when I get there?
- What course correction do I need to make now?

Learning one new idea can point you in a refreshing direction. Recovering addicts have told me that learning one or more of these basic facts has set them on a new path of healing: (1) Life isn't fair. (2) I can never escape the struggle of being human. (3) I can't please everyone. (4) I can't make it on my own. (5) Hurt people hurt people. (6) I may waste my life trying to be worthy of someone's love. (7) Rituals give us a feeling of being in control of our lives. (8) I can't undo and unsay cruel things. (9) Isolation is a danger signal. (10) God doesn't make junk. (11) Those who've abandoned their dreams are discouraging mine.

SOUL SEARCH

Do you feel that you're teachable most of the time? If time, money, and energy were not an issue, what would you decide to learn/study now that could help you with your sobriety and launch you into all God intends for your life?

My Daily Promise, I'm going to hold you to your promise that you'll watch over me and guide me on my life journey. Give me wisdom about what I need to learn during this season to become the best version of my God-honoring self and to accomplish all you desire while I'm on earth.

216

P.U.R.P.O.S.E. Principle IV: Pursue Positive Practices to Maintain My Sobriety

Lifelong Learning

Intelligent people are always ready to learn. Their ears are open for knowledge.
PROVERBS 18:15

The book of Proverbs tells us that we're to be eager learners. That means learning about every aspect of the disease of addiction, including such things as the danger of grandiose thinking and internal bondage, the value of moral inventories, and the necessity of turning our wills and lives over to the care of God. That task can feel overwhelming. Quite honestly, I even have trouble learning the meaning of tech words, like Bing, Vlingo, Wikipedia, Yelp, and Zagat. I was probably the last to know, for example, that the mathematical term *googol* (10^{100}) had been adapted by Google creators to refer to a mindboggling amount of web information. Much of the time, I don't feel particularly intelligent; and I wonder if keeping my ears open for more knowledge triggers an inferiority complex in me about my inability to understand certain topics. At times, learning can be embarrassing and exhausting.

But today's verse says that it's important to stay current in all the areas God has called us to live, work, and serve. He's able to put to good use whatever we learn, whether that's the latest recovery skills, most effective business strategies, most telling market trends, best educational methods, or most proven practices for our spiritual growth and evangelism efforts. At minimum, we're commanded to be lifelong learners about who God is, about how we can become more like Jesus, and about how to hear from the Holy Spirit in our daily walk.

Whether you feel God is leading you to learn new relaxation techniques, time-management skills, communication methods, or discipleship processes, take a deliberate step in that direction. Your godly choices regarding learning opportunities will undoubtedly bless your recovery efforts and lifetime dream. As Proverbs 9:9 reminds us: "Instruct the wise, and they will be even wiser. Teach the righteous, and they will learn even more."

SOUL SEARCH

What new concept, skill, or methodology would encourage your sobriety, cause you to become more effective in ministry, or move you toward God's matchless call on your life? How seriously are you considering an intelligent step?

You who always have my best interest at heart, give me a gentle push toward what you'd like me to learn next.

P.U.R.P.O.S.E. Principle IV: Pursue Positive Practices to Maintain My Sobriety

Going Forward

Don't ever give up on your sobriety or on your "I was born for this" mission. Learn all you can to go the distance and be successful in both areas. God will be glorified by your perseverance and teachable attitude, and you'll be rewarded.

☀ Meditate on the Assurance of God's Word

Blessed are those who persevere under trial, because when they have stood the test, they will receive the crown of life that God has promised to those who love him.
JAMES 1:12 (TNIV)

We want each of you to show this same diligence to the very end, in order to make your hope sure. We do not want you to become lazy, but to imitate those who through faith and patience inherit what has been promised. HEBREWS 6:11-12 (TNIV)

☀ Humbly Talk with the Lord

Be honest with God about those things that cause you to lose hope and stamina in your healing process—things like exhaustion, fear of failure or rejection, negativity from others, misinformation, or overcommitment. Ask him for all you need to counteract the discouragement.

Praise God for all the times you've chosen to learn something new that honored him in your home life, workplace, recovery program, small group, or on the life quest he mapped out for you.

☀ Take the *Life Purpose Coach* Challenge

Make a prayerful and informed decision to claim or reclaim your commitment to life-time sobriety before naysayers surround you once again. Resolve now to be resilient and keep moving forward, even if it takes you outside your comfort zone of familiarity. Choose and enlist three prayer warriors to pray you through.

P.U.R.P.O.S.E. Principle IV: Pursue Positive Practices to Maintain My Sobriety

Gratitude, God-Control, and Boundaries

Show me the path where I should walk, O LORD; point out the right road for me to follow. PSALM 25:4

The road to recovery can feel like a scary, unchartered pathway that's overgrown with knee-high weeds, thorny bushes, and fallen trees—all thwarting your every step. You may fear that the venomous snakes of your past will slither out of hiding and strike when you least expect it, poisoning your mind again. You may see vultures circling overhead, hoping for your demise during times of painful vulnerability. As the psalmist does, why not ask the Lord to show you the best pathway? What do you have to lose by asking God to point out the right road for you to follow? His goal—his joy—is to get you safely to the place of his choosing. In fact, Teresa of Avila was known to say, "God is on the journey, too."

Take some time to consider three positive practices that are guaranteed to help you walk down God's designated pathway for your life:

- living in gratitude,
- being under God's control, and
- setting clear boundaries for yourself.

If you're tired of being afraid of what sobriety and God's long-term mission hold for you, these three proven guidelines can calm your fears. Give them a try. None is rocket science, but each will change your life forever.

SOUL SEARCH

Are you ready to proceed down the path to recovery, no longer veering from your challenging life's work and fearing that risks, ridicule, or trials might overtake you? Which of the three guiding principles do you think you need most and why: gratitude, God-control, or boundaries?

Strength of my heart, you know how much I've struggled with the unknowns about living sober and cooperating with your triumphal vision for my life. So, God, I sincerely want to thank you for going on this journey with me, never leaving my side for a moment.

P.U.R.P.O.S.E. Principle IV: Pursue Positive Practices to Maintain My Sobriety

A Life of Gratitude

Give thanks for everything to God the Father in the name of our Lord Jesus Christ.
EPHESIANS 5:20

Today's verse reminds us to live in gratitude for everything God has done for us, including his redemptive good use of the evil we've caused or experienced. This mind-set of thanksgiving gives us hope for all the good he has in store for our tomorrows.

When I was in high school, I had three reasons to be inordinately grateful to my brother Chuck. First, he had loaned me his gorgeous 1955 Mercury sedan to drive while he was serving in the military for several years. Second, he wasn't livid when he came home and noticed that his white leather ceiling had yellowed due to my secret teenage habit of smoking in his car. (I was flabbergasted that I'd made such a rookie mistake; I hadn't even noticed that it was happening, and I was truly sorry that I'd done that to his beautiful, classic car.) And, third, my sweet brother never asked me to pay for the professional stain removal.

Likewise, in our relationship with Jesus, we constantly do things to harm our beautiful selves or others, often because we don't consider the consequences of our actions. Jesus doesn't become livid; instead, he calmly deals with each situation we bring on ourselves—reminding us that he paid the ultimate price on the cross to wipe the stain of our sins clean. Our gratitude for his generosity and our contrition and desire to stop sinning are the least of what we can offer him.

Think about the story of the ten lepers who were healed (see Luke 17:11-19), and reflect on whether you're more like the nine lepers who never thanked Jesus or the one leper who returned to fall at Jesus' feet and thank him.

SOUL SEARCH

During the nasty, yellowed days of your life, including seasons of grief, suffering, and risky behavior, how did God show you ultrakindness? Have you expressed your gratitude to him for those times and for all the good, magnificent plans he has in store for your tomorrows?

Upholder of all things, I want to live a grateful life and let others know how you have provided for me, forgiven me, and blessed me beyond belief.

P.U.R.P.O.S.E. Principle IV: Pursue Positive Practices to Maintain My Sobriety

Jesus' Power and Kindness

"My rabbi," the blind man said, "I want to see!"... Instantly the man could see, and he followed Jesus down the road. MARK 10:51-52

We're told in Mark 10:46-52 that Jesus cured the blind Bartimaeus. The story unfolds, explaining that the beggar was so extremely grateful for his salvation and his eyesight that he followed Jesus down the road. Because Jesus was on his way to be crucified, I often wonder if Bartimaeus was at the Crucifixion and testified to onlookers about the power and kindness of Jesus. We have access to that same Jesus to save us from our downward spiral of addiction, whether that's to shopping, hoarding, substance abusing, bingeing, or cutting.

I certainly want to testify that Jesus saved me from routinely chasing chocolate and sugar when he opened my eyes to my crazed behavior. Years ago, I'd grab a Dr. Pepper from the refrigerator on any given morning and jump in the car to head for the thrill of a freshly baked Krispy Kreme donut. Or, on a lunch break, I'd run by Fosters Freeze for a chocolate-dipped ice-cream cone or swing by See's Candies to get some Nuts and Chews for the afternoon. Various evenings, I'd descend upon Baskin-Robbins to get a pint of my favorite ice cream for television time. The entire routine was obsessive, fattening, and expensive. I don't miss those days of sugar idolatry, but I'm hauntingly aware that they could overtake me at any time without Jesus as my "very present help" (Psalm 46:1, ESV). Each day that I'm sane now, I'm enormously grateful for God's kind and remarkable intervention.

SOUL SEARCH

In what way has Jesus opened your eyes to the importance of moral, upright, and principled living? Out of gratitude for his rescuing you from life on a slippery slope, what personalized gift would you like to offer to the world in Jesus' name? (If you feel strongly about giving this gift, do you think it's possible that God may have planted it in your heart eons ago?)

My Rabbi, the Great One, if I lived forever on this earth, it still wouldn't be long enough to tell people how grateful I am to you for helping me see truth.

P.U.R.**P**.O.S.E. Principle IV: **P**ursue Positive Practices to Maintain My Sobriety

Controlling My Mouth

Don't use foul or abusive language. Let everything you say be good and helpful, so that your words will be an encouragement to those who hear them. EPHESIANS 4:29

In the late eighties, I struck up a friendship with a lady I'll call Sally, who was a top-notch entrepreneur with lots of marketing savvy. What bothered me about our relationship, though, was that she had a mouth like a drunken sailor, and she profaned the name of Jesus with endless explicative remarks. Her profanity began to break my heart, although truth be told, I had some personal anger issues and had developed a propensity for a few choice curse words of my own. Over time, the Holy Spirit made it perfectly clear that I was to end my relationship with Sally. After numerous attempts to reason with her, I finally did walk away. I know it wasn't my finest hour, because I must have sounded holier than thou, but I'll always be grateful for the strength God gave me to obey him and choose a better path. By the way, my two young children were thrilled at the dissolution of that friendship. It's astonishing how kids know certain things!

To tackle such a sinister and pervasive problem as cursing, it may be helpful to recall times that God directed your steps away from other sins in the past. This exercise has often caused me to exclaim, "Well, if God handled _____ for me; he can surely handle _____!" Try it.

SOUL SEARCH

What would you most like to change about what comes out of your mouth: your vulgarity, tone, bragging, gossip, lies, or judgmental words? In what way is someone tempting you to sin, and what is the Holy Spirit prompting you to do about the ungodly relationship?

Controller of all creation, take control of my mouth—and keep me safe from anyone who's a bad influence on me. I pray that knowing you will lead me to self-control, that self-control will lead me to patient endurance, and that patient endurance will lead me to godliness. *

---

* From 2 Peter 1:6.

Under God-Control

In your great mercy you did not abandon them to die in the wilderness. The pillar of cloud still led them forward by day, and the pillar of fire showed them the way through the night. NEHEMIAH 9:19

God directed each step of the Israelites' escape from their earthly hell in Egypt, and he wants to direct each of your steps out of your living hell of addiction. He faithfully offered them definitive God-control options for them to follow: a pillar of cloud by day and a pillar of fire by night. God's people didn't have to rely on their own wits to figure out which direction to go or when to set up camp or break camp; he was their personal GPS (Global Positioning System). Nehemiah tells us that God did this out of his great mercy, instead of abandoning his chosen ones to die in the wilderness.

Like the Israelites, we must learn to trust God's navigational expertise; otherwise we'll never end up where he intends. In fact, using our own incorrectly calibrated compasses dooms us to crash and burn. Instead, we must allow him to dictate the direction of every aspect of our lives, including our sobriety, spiritual habits, ministry, friendships, and destiny. He provides us a modern-day, reliable GPS (God Positioning System); we only need to set our satellite preference to the "shortest time" default, which most assuredly is the "stop sinning" mode. That will put us on a wide-open, five-lane expressway toward God's goals for our lives, rather than on traffic-jammed side streets strewn with temptation. Buckle up and select God's safe cruise control speed for a ride of a lifetime.

SOUL SEARCH

What in your life is out of control—in a state of perpetual craziness—because you've tried to manage it by yourself? In what way could you start to be piloted by a reliable GPS that takes you into the Promised Land of recovery and significant purpose?

Director of my life, I choose to be under God-control, not self-control. I leave my life in your hands to do with as you will. Heal me and send me wherever, whenever, for whatever reason.

P.U.R.**P**.O.S.E. Principle IV: **P**ursue Positive Practices to Maintain My Sobriety

Boundaries Based on Priorities

Trust GOD from the bottom of your heart; don't try to figure out everything on your own. Listen for GOD's voice in everything you do, everywhere you go; he's the one who will keep you on track. PROVERBS 3:5-6 (*The Message*)

We know the huge value of having balance in our lives versus being frantically busy and overcommitted. We've even been taught to trust God implicitly and to listen to his voice that keeps us on track toward balance, wholeness, and sobriety. Sometimes, though, we rebel and go rogue, refusing to combat the imbalancing agents in our lives out of fear of looking less than superhuman to others. When that doesn't work out so well, we remember that all we really need to do is identify the top priorities God has assigned us and set boundaries to protect them.

Ask yourself, *What are the five most important, seasonal roles I'm managing right now for God, in addition to my spiritual growth, recovery, and long-term life mission?* For example, are you a husband, father, breadwinner, small group leader, and lay counselor at church? Or are you a daughter, sister, student, choir member, and Christian radio host? Now, make a list of each thing you do that doesn't contribute to those categories or to your basic self-care, sustenance, and the completion of your household chores. After cutting yourself a little slack for some much-needed, healthy downtime, decide what you could eliminate from your to-do list that won't impede your sobriety. Pretend that your life depended on it—and do it! Next, run, don't walk, to enroll in a boundary-setting class or to purchase a related book so you can learn advanced techniques to use against off-focus commitments that stall God's custom-made plan for you.

SOUL SEARCH

When have you set priorities based on guilt or other people's agendas for your life? How did that negatively impact your healing process or the mighty work God has reserved for you?

My Boundary Setter, I trust you from the bottom of my heart to help me focus on the priority roles you've allotted me. I want to listen to your voice about everything I do and every place I go. You're the only one who can keep me on track and help me live the balanced, healthy, purpose-filled life you designed for me.

P.U.R.**P**.O.S.E. Principle IV: **P**ursue Positive Practices to Maintain My Sobriety

Trusting God

Without a doubt, a life lived in utmost gratitude, under God-control, and with clear boundaries is a far richer and more significant life than one lived in opposition to those basic principles. Ask any addict in recovery who's done life both ways to verify that truth.

☀ Meditate on the Assurance of God's Word

Whatever you do or say, do it as a representative of the Lord Jesus, giving thanks through him to God the Father. COLOSSIANS 3:17

Rejoice always, pray continually, give thanks in all circumstances; for this is God's will for you in Christ Jesus. 1 THESSALONIANS 5:16-18 (TNIV)

Their mouths are full of cursing and bitterness. . . . They have no fear of God at all. ROMANS 3:14, 18

[Jesus explained,] "The thief's purpose is to steal and kill and destroy. My purpose is to give [my people] a rich and satisfying life." JOHN 10:10

☀ Humbly Talk with the Lord

Be honest with God about how out of control you feel and what frightens you the most about that.

Magnify the Lord by telling him that you trust him and want to cooperate with his incomparable plan for your life.

☀ Take the *Life Purpose Coach* Challenge

Make a list of things for which you, as a Christian, are grateful (for instance, God's grace, goodness, provision, and peace; your sobriety; your ticket into heaven). You can add what others might list (such as family, friends, health, job, safety). It's also important to write out things that pertain only to you and God's mercy in your life. This thanksgiving list takes your focus off you and puts it on God.

Gifts, Qualities, and Personality

Each person is given something to do that shows who God is: Everyone gets in on it, everyone benefits. 1 CORINTHIANS 12:7 (*The Message*)

Peter Wagner, former professor at Fuller Theological Seminary, liked to say, "Just as important as knowing what [spiritual] gift God has given you is knowing which gifts he hasn't given you." Let's add to his comment: just as important as knowing what best qualities and personality God has given you is knowing which he hasn't given you. The more we investigate what God has (and hasn't) given us, the more we'll understand him, our best recovery options, and his magnanimous plan for our lives. By identifying the myriad of giftedness, attributes, and traits he's embedded in us and not bemoaning those we didn't receive, we're able to move toward a life of sobriety and significance. We can begin in earnest to explain to others who God is, how meticulously he made us, and how generously he loves us.

What's the role of God's Spirit in all this? Well, he hands out our gifts and other identifying features and facets. Imagine this scenario: you have just started working in your family's business—that is, in God's business. Unbeknownst to you, the Human Resources Director, also known as the Holy Spirit, has been working behind the scenes from the moment of your birth, assigning you incredible characteristics and a befitting personality. And from the time of your spiritual birth, he has stacked the deck in your favor by granting you specific spiritual gifts so you'd thrive at your Dad's place. The Spirit has known, since before the world began, the tasks you were going to be asked to perform, based on the needs of the entire organization. So he's already made sure you were perfectly suited to succeed, even if you haven't yet become aware of the particulars. Now he wants to let you in on more specifics.

SOUL SEARCH

Are you thrilled, somewhat pleased, or sorely disappointed with the way you were made—and how could that attitude affect your recovery? In addition to living a sober life, what earthly task do you suspect you've been given to do in your Father's business?

Fresh Wind, breathe anew into me a willingness to identify and utilize my spiritual gifts, Christlike characteristics, and fabulous personality, so I might show off the Father's goodness.

My Giftedness

In his grace, God has given us different gifts for doing certain things well. ROMANS 12:6

Imagine that God is whispering to you, "At the time of your spiritual birth, I deliberately and joyously sent my Spirit to deliver congratulatory gifts to you for joining my family! Even as you recover more fully from your addictive behaviors, I want you to sit down and chat with someone about those gifts. That conversation will honor me as you begin to comprehend that your giftedness is a high honor and responsibility."

Look together at this biblically based list of spiritual gifts so you'll realize that God knew which gifts would most precisely bless the body of Christ through you, as you do the work he has given you to do on earth: leadership, encouragement, intercessory prayer, faith, compassion, service, preaching/teaching, writing, counseling, giving financially, evangelism, discipleship, healing, hospitality, keen judgment, organization, prophecy (blessed sayings), modern missionary, wisdom, martyrdom, celibacy, shepherding, tongues and interpretation, voluntary poverty, craftsmanship, and creative communication.

Enjoy the exciting truths about these gifts:

- They're given to you for a particular season. Alternate gifts are given as needed.
- If you don't want them, neglect them, or involve them with sin, God will take them back.
- Your responsibility is to use them to serve the Lord's family with the strength and energy God supplies.
- When you use them as God intends, he will refresh you with effortless joy and amazing desire.
- Your church body grows spiritually every time you use them.
- Mature Christians will be God's messengers to you to affirm your specific gifts.

Always remember that you're only a steward of these beautiful gifts, so please don't become puffed up about them or demand that you keep your favorites for a lifetime.

SOUL SEARCH

In what way does God's Word shed light on how much he wants you to live a sober life and serve his people, utilizing the spiritual gifts he's given you? Will you?

God who passionately gifted me, I'm madly in love with the generous you! Thank you.

P.U.R.P.O.S.E. Principle IV: **P**ursue Positive Practices to Maintain My Sobriety

Grateful for My Gifts

God has given each of you a gift from his great variety of spiritual gifts. Use them well to serve one another.   1 PETER 4:10

On Christmas morning 1987, I got up early to turn on the tree lights, build a crackling fire, and make hot cocoa and cinnamon rolls. In my excitement, I forgot to open the fireplace flue, causing the living room to fill with smoke and set off an alarm. My two groggy-eyed children bounded downstairs, hearts thumping, worried sick that their gifts, house, and family were going up in flames. They were grateful munchkins when they realized all was safe.

How grateful are you for the spiritual gifts the Holy Spirit gave you when you first became a Christian? (See July 31, August 1 and 3.) You might respond, "Look, lady, I've dangled over life's cliff of despair so long, God's never even tried to broach the topic of giftedness with me." But what if you dared to believe that more will be revealed to you now, based on your slow but sure desire to work the steps of a recovery program and focus on Jesus as your Higher Power? What if God's greater plan and specific purpose for your life was really prevailing?

How would you feel if, right now, God surprised you by unveiling one spiritual gift to you, such as mercy, faith, or visual arts? Or what if he told you that buried deep down within you is the gift of carrying people's burdens to him in prayer? What if you discovered that your testimony, with its "Just for today, I'll try" theme, offered God's gift of encouragement to others? And would it be out of the realm of possibility for God to give you the gift of administration, so you could help organize events in your church? Be grateful for any gifts that God's been keeping safe for you and enjoy the surprise of what he reveals.

SOUL SEARCH

How grateful are you for the giftedness of others, which has blessed you? If the Holy Spirit revealed a spiritual gift to you now, how would you express your gratitude?

Still, Small Voice, I'm grateful you've called me to recovery and that you've kept spiritual gifts tucked away safely for me until I was in better shape to follow your road map for my life.

P.U.R.P.O.S.E. Principle IV: Pursue Positive Practices to Maintain My Sobriety

Letting My Gifts Lead Me

God works in different ways, but it is the same God who does the work in all of us.
A spiritual gift is given to each of us so we can help each other.   1 CORINTHIANS 12:6-7

Your spiritual gifts (for example, hospitality, craftsmanship, giving financially, pastoring others) carry you down God's well-mapped-out pathway to purpose. They're his vehicles for getting you where you need to go, a lot like the bicycle I rode to navigate around a quaint, waterfront community for a year. My sky-blue beach cruiser sure made me smile, as I traveled in style to our local chapel or loaded my basket with fresh fruit from a roadside stand. So, too, your gifts will make you smile, even on difficult do-it-sober days, as you trek with God on an adventure of a lifetime, enjoying seasonal and long-term service opportunities.

But you may be filled with fear that prompts you to run from your spiritual giftedness. Please don't let fear or anything else stop you from investigating and using your gifts, because the reality is that many of them, like singing, teaching, or writing, are also natural abilities that are commonplace in the secular world. The difference is that when God divinely ordains abilities for use in Kingdom work, they become spiritual gifts.

I love how Romans 12:7-8 describes such gifts: "If you help, just help, don't take over; if you teach, stick to your teaching; if you give encouraging guidance, be careful that you don't get bossy" (*The Message*). Bravo to the apostle Paul for his honest discussion of giftedness! He continues with more advice about not manipulating people when you're put in charge, about being quick to respond to those in distress, and about not getting irritated or depressed when working with the disadvantaged. God's calling to use our gifts is front-loaded with a call to smile.

SOUL SEARCH

Which two or three spiritual gifts do you feel you've been given to serve the body of Christ? (August 1 has a list of gifts.) How does your unmerited giftedness cause you to want to leave behind your excuses, apathy, addictions, and defeatist thinking?

Faithful and True Witness, hold me accountable to be a good steward of my current and future spiritual gifts. I want your gifts to carry me with hope, joy, and love toward your will.

P.U.R.**P**.O.S.E. Principle IV: **P**ursue Positive Practices to Maintain My Sobriety

My Best Qualities

Never let loyalty and kindness leave you! Tie them around your neck as a reminder. Write them deep within your heart. PROVERBS 3:3

God created you with a number of phenomenal personal characteristics, such as loyalty, kindness, and generosity, to help you develop long-term relationships. He also knew you'd need other great qualities, like courage, gratitude, and persistence, to support your recovery efforts—and still others, like flexibility, intuitiveness, and tactfulness, to fulfill your particular life's work. So what are your best qualities? Would your most supportive family member say that being "perfectly fair in your decisions" is one of your finest character traits (Deuteronomy 1:16)? Would your dear friend say that integrity and honesty protect you (see Psalm 25:21)?

Reflect for a moment on these five personal characteristics: teachability, humility, patience, cooperation, and calmness. Ask yourself which one would most help you choose sobriety on a more regular basis. Then think about how one of your current best qualities could help you live out your unique purpose more boldly and joyfully. Next, hear yourself verbalize what a specific, undeniable trait might allow you to do for God's glory. For example:

- My forgiving spirit could bring hope to addicts who've not yet been able to forgive and forget.
- My authenticity could encourage my friends to confess and repent of their sins.
- My can-do attitude could inspire others to make a difference in the world for God.

Don't think that you're bragging about yourself when you let your most remarkable or endearing characteristics shine brightly. You didn't create you and you don't sustain you! In actuality, you're bragging on God as you count your undeserved blessings.

SOUL SEARCH

Which Christlike quality do you most admire in others? Which quality do you think God most adores about you?

My praiseworthy Maker, I know that I'm wonderfully made, so forgive my false humility when I downplay the personal qualities you've entrusted to me. Help me accept my godly traits and use them to support my sobriety and the life roles you've determined are best for me.

My Personality Type

Make a careful exploration of who you are and the work you have been given, and then sink yourself into that. GALATIANS 6:4 (*The Message*)

The Epistle writer Paul says that you're to investigate thoroughly the truth about yourself and the task the Lord designed for you—and then dive in to complete your assignment. So right now, let's explore your personality type as one aspect of who you are, and see how that information can help you bring your creative best to every area of your life, including your recovery and life's calling.

I'd like my friend Erik Rees, author of *S.H.A.P.E.: Finding and Fulfilling Your Unique Purpose for Life*, to advise us, because the *P* in *SHAPE* stands for Personality. Based on his research and consultation with Pastor Rick Warren (who created the acronym), Erik suggests in chapter 5 of his book that we can assess our personality in a twofold manner: (1) how we relate to others: Are we outgoing or reserved, self-expressive or self-controlled, cooperative or competitive? And (2) how we respond to opportunities: Are we high-risk or low-risk, people-oriented or project-oriented, a follower or leader, a team player or solo flyer, a lover of routine or of variety?

As you consider your innate and learned personality behaviors, you'll understand how to support your sobriety and God-intended destiny. For example, if you're an extrovert (getting energy from people), you can let recovery meetings meet that need. And if you're an introvert (reserved), you'll know why you need to allot substantial downtime to recharge, even from a sponsor meeting! But God's magnificent plan isn't to surround all extroverts with people and all introverts with spa-type quietness; he sometimes pushes us out of our comfort zone for a season to learn a new behavior. After all, extroverts need to learn to be quiet and introverts may even need to learn to work a room like a public relations pro (followed by a nap, of course!).

SOUL SEARCH

How do you relate to others, and how might that impact your sobriety? How do you respond to opportunities, and how might that impact your life mission?

Revered Maker, I invite you to teach me more about how you made me, because I want to sink myself into the work you gave me to do, including my recovery work, and I want the satisfaction of having done my job in obedience to your precious plan for my life.

P.U.R.**P**.O.S.E. Principle IV: **P**ursue Positive Practices to Maintain My Sobriety

Using What I've Been Given

With all humility, appreciate the spiritual gifts, best qualities, and personality type you've been assigned. Only a good and loving God would take such care in matching all these traits to your specific life's calling. And what other god would even care if you lived a productive, enthralling, sober life? Not one!

☀ Meditate on the Assurance of God's Word

These are the gifts Christ gave to the church: the apostles, the prophets, the evangelists, and the pastors and teachers. Their responsibility is to equip God's people to do his work and build up the church, the body of Christ. This will continue until we all come to such unity in our faith and knowledge of God's Son that we will be mature in the Lord, measuring up to the full and complete standard of Christ.
EPHESIANS 4:11-13

They didn't answer [Jesus], because they had been arguing about which of them was the greatest.   MARK 9:34

☀ Humbly Talk with the Lord

Thank the Lord God for blessing you with all you need to live a healthy life and serve those he's asked you to serve.

Ask God to reveal more to you about how your spiritual gifts, best qualities, and personality type can bring glory to him.

☀ Take the *Life Purpose Coach* Challenge

When you feel that your slow recovery is keeping you from flourishing, pray these powerful prayers:

God, I trust you.

Jesus, help me.

Holy Spirit, fall fresh on me.

I'm always amazed at the peace, courage, and insight these three prayers bring me, instantaneously, as I remember who's watching out for me.

P.U.R.**P**.O.S.E. Principle IV: **P**ursue Positive Practices to Maintain My Sobriety

Four Commitments

Commit everything you do to the LORD. Trust him, and he will help you.   PSALM 37:5

God wants us to open up to him, not holding anything back—not our addictive struggles, stinkin' thinkin', disappointments, doubts, goals, joys, or wishes. When we do connect with him at this deep level, he declares that he'll do whatever needs to be done to help us. I take his Psalm 37:5 promise at face value. Unaware of any loopholes hidden therein, I hold him to his Word. And why wouldn't I? This is the God who has designed us and called us. He cares about us so intently that he's personally arranged all the specifics of our natural talents, acquired skills, passions, values, strengths, temperament, spiritual gifts, heritage, opportunities, and life purpose. He's left no blessing to chance, which means that he's magnificent and that we can trust him!

With the Lord's unbreakable promise and mighty power to help us, all that remains is to decide whether or not we'll commit everything we do to him. Consider these four huge commitments that we could make to him out of gratitude:

- appreciate our talents,
- practice kindness,
- resist boredom, and
- guard our strengths.

If we do these things, we're much closer to reaching the goals God has for our lives, including his goals for our healing and life's work. What a shame to stop shy of making these commitments to God, when they can inspire us to live the best life imaginable. As Thomas Edison said, "Many of life's failures are people who did not realize how close they were to success when they gave up."

God wants you to tap into the full measure of who he designed you to be and all you're able to do in service to his people. Commit your ways to him and trust him to help you.

SOUL SEARCH

How have you been doing lately at appreciating your talents, practicing kindness, resisting boredom, and guarding your strengths? How could a firm commitment to the Lord in these four areas support your sobriety, as well as the fascination in your soul?

Light of my life, I commit everything I do to you. I trust you and thank you for being here to guide me.

P.U.R.P.O.S.E. Principle IV: Pursue Positive Practices to Maintain My Sobriety
Natural Talents and Acquired Skills

To those who use well what they are given, even more will be given, and they will have an abundance. But from those who do nothing, even what little they have will be taken away. MATTHEW 25:29

In the often-told story about using our talents (see Matthew 25:14-30), God gives us a proposition of "use or lose them." He doesn't want us to bury our talents but to go all out using them. At minimum, a talent could support your recovery by giving you confidence, joy, hope, creativity, and fresh perspective—and ultimately it's intended to bless the completion of your life's work. As a Life Purpose Coach, I often hear clients talk about talents in one of three disconcerting ways: "I don't have any," "They're distributed randomly," or "Focusing on them is prideful."

It breaks my heart to see people struggling with such misleading facts about their natural bent. God created us with certain identifiable, innate abilities, and he also helps us acquire specific skills along our journey to be used for his purposes. Regarding your natural talents, have you been blessed with a photographic memory, perfect pitch, or athletic ability? Are you a clever inventor, human calculator, artistic soul, or cinematography genius? Or do you have a résumé-type skill, such as landscape artistry, forensic investigating, or technical literacy? Can you sell, negotiate, edit, search and rescue, or organize closets? Whatever your inherent or well-developed abilities, God expects you to use them to heal and to serve his people.

And as for talents being assigned willy-nilly or talents stirring up pride, I say, "Give God credit for being smarter than you and knowing which talents and skills you'd need to bring him extravagant glory. Why not humbly use your intrinsic and learned abilities in your struggle against addiction and in the task he's anointed you to complete?" God created talented individuals, and he has no intention of letting all that giftedness go for naught.

SOUL SEARCH

Which of your natural or acquired abilities could support your recovery? With whom could you examine this topic and outline some invigorating steps to take toward wholeness and purpose?

Divine Designer, it's not by chance that you've blessed me with specific talent and skill. Help me discuss this topic humbly with a friend, sponsor, or coach.

Practice Kindness

Be kind to each other, tenderhearted, forgiving one another, just as God through Christ has forgiven you.   EPHESIANS 4:32

I'm rude sometimes, and it makes me sad. How often do your rudeness nostrils flare, even while you're working your recovery steps, because you're exhausted, lonesome, fearful, angry, or famished? In all honesty, I do need to suggest some additional words for my own condition, because I've noticed a whole host of other meanness triggers. I call my list the A-B-C-D-Es of rudeness: don't let Katie get too Anxious, too Behind schedule, too Cold, too Dehydrated, or too Encumbered with physical pain. It's a basic tenet of human behavior that we act more civil when we're not carting any such bad moods!

So how is it that we're able to practice kindness—ever? Well, on good days we remember our Ephesians verse, which helps us put things into a forgiveness perspective. We are humbled that our gentle, kind Messiah poured out his blood on the cross as a sacrifice for our sins, setting us free from our wretched selves. We realize that he took great delight in showering us with his exorbitant kindness and his impressive plans for our lives. But the precise word in our passage that has most consistently improved my behavior is *tenderhearted*. If I can recall one or more of the circumstances in which the Lord has been tender with me, during times of my sin and repentance, deep grief, extreme brokenness, intense despair, or utter confusion, I find myself filled with the desire to be a kind and tenderhearted woman—at least, temporarily. And I pray faithfully for the day that my default mode will mirror the gentleness of Jesus.

SOUL SEARCH

What robs you of kindness, and in those situations, how do you attempt to protect others from your unkind words and actions? In a perfect world, how would you like to be treated and treat others?

Messiah, your regal plans for my life include sobriety and an assignment that I want to do lovingly and passionately for the rest of my days. I invite you to make the kindness, tenderheartedness, and forgiveness of Ephesians 4:32 the hallmark of the legacy you wish me to leave.

P.U.R.**P**.O.S.E. Principle IV: **P**ursue Positive Practices to Maintain My Sobriety

Resist Boredom

My life drags by—day after hopeless day.   JOB 7:6 (TLB)

You've probably heard that the love of money is the root of all evil (see 1 Timothy 6:10), but boredom sure seems to run a close second. Think about it: a teenager, bored and unsupervised, might steal a car for a joyride. A mother, bored by her incessant routine, might have an affair to reignite her passion. An employee, bored and unchallenged in his cubicle, might siphon off business from the company. A husband, bored with the predictability of his life, might bet the ponies to feel a thrill. I had a client who was so bored with what she called her "dull, insipid, monotonous life" that she began experimenting with drugs and cutting. But I don't think the word *bored* is in God's vocabulary; I'm sure he's had it removed from all heavenly dictionaries. And I can't recall a single Bible story that indicates Jesus yawned because he was bored with a stagnating life.

I could argue that the majestic splendor of nature, alone, should keep our hearts thumping, senses stimulated, and creative juices flowing, but I also know that boredom stems from deep down inside us, from a feeling of purposelessness. When a person past the age of reason says, "I'm bored," it's as if he or she is drifting aimlessly with no life direction, no rudder with which to steer the ship.

To avoid being trapped by the boredom of a stale, idle, and drab existence that has the potential of ending in a gloomy, irreversible despondency, ask for a friend's help to seek and fulfill God's electrifying plan for your life. As Dale Carnegie suggested, "Are you bored with life? Then throw yourself into some work you believe in with all your heart, live for it, die for it, and you will find happiness that you had thought could never be yours." That type of purposefulness, when you're healthy enough not to obsess over it, can bring you enormous cheer.

SOUL SEARCH

From what you've observed in others, what's the worst effect boredom can have on a person? From your own personal beliefs or experience, what's the best outcome God's purpose can give you?

God who assigns purpose, I ask you to keep me from the evil that boredom can cause, by flooding me with the goodness your purpose gives.

P.U.R.**P**.O.S.E. Principle IV: **P**ursue Positive Practices to Maintain My Sobriety

Strengths Can Become Weaknesses

The governor's soldiers . . . stripped [Jesus] and put a scarlet robe on him. They wove thorn branches into a crown and put it on his head. . . . And they spit on him.
MATTHEW 27:27-30

God has given you strengths, whether that's in a physical, intellectual, spiritual, or emotional area. But have you ever considered that your favorite strength could quickly become your greatest weakness? Notice in our passage that the Roman soldiers let their authoritative power turn into abject cruelty. Pilate had ordered them to crucify Jesus, but they took it upon themselves to strip Jesus, crown him with thorns, mock him, spit on him, and strike him on the head with a stick. Given the right set of circumstances in our own lives, we're like those soldiers, only one breath away from allowing a strength to become a weakness.

Reflecting on this idea of nosedive strengths is an important component of the recovery process. Take tenacity, for example, which is a phenomenal strength needed for working a program—until you allow it to turn your healing journey into a crazed obsession. You may even know firsthand how generosity can deteriorate to enabling. What about how encouragement can take a downward spiral into control? And it's easy to see how hospitality can do a backflip into the sin of perfectionism.

Three things will help you guard against the disintegration of your strengths. First, don't deny them; accept them. Self-awareness in the form of personal inventory is always a great first step. Second, thank God for your strengths daily and use them in the manner he intended. For example, if he's blessed you with charisma, smile to bless others, rather than using your good looks to charm others deceptively or flirt inappropriately. Third, ask God to use your strengths for his glory and for his unfathomable, addiction-free plan for your life. You can never go wrong requesting that favor.

SOUL SEARCH

How has one of your strengths turned into a weakness? In what way could that interfere with your sobriety and God's call on your life?

Strength giver, I seek to guard my strengths as strengths and to devote them to honoring you to the highest degree.

P.U.R.P.O.S.E. Principle IV: Pursue Positive Practices to Maintain My Sobriety

Weaknesses Turned into Strengths

By faith these people. . . . shut the mouths of lions, quenched the flames of fire, and escaped death by the edge of the sword. Their weakness was turned to strength.
HEBREWS 11:33-34

This passage is a reminder that almighty God can do whatever he likes; he's able to accomplish more than you could ever dream he'd do. But wouldn't it be audacious for any unworthy recovering addict to ask him to turn a glaring weakness into a strength?

Here's some perspective that might help: Moses, a stutterer, became the mouthpiece of God himself; David, a murderer, became a psalmist with a testimony. Think, too, about Jesus, of whom was said, "There was nothing beautiful or majestic about his appearance, nothing to attract us to him" (Isaiah 53:2)—and yet, he's the one upon whom all eyes rest. Now consider the fear-filled, weak-kneed disciples at Pentecost, who were gathered in an upper room in Jerusalem when the Holy Spirit gave them the ability to speak in other languages. Read Acts 2:11, in which crowds declare about them, "We all hear these people speaking in our own languages about the wonderful things God has done!" These disciples had been forever changed with power from on high.

God wants to turn your weaknesses into strengths, your doubt into faith, your pride into humility—and he's more than able to do so. Reflect on a weakness with which you've struggled relentlessly and now name the strength into which God could transform it (for example, your anger to love, your impatience to patience, or your instigator tendencies to peacemaker traits). To jumpstart the process, thank God in advance for equipping you with all the newly appointed strengths you desire!

SOUL SEARCH

What personal weakness do you pray God will turn into a lively strength? What hope can you draw that he'll do it, based on his prior miracles in your life?

God who is able, I ask you to take my weaknesses and convert them all into strengths. I commit to doing the work it takes to cooperate in this manner, for the sake of my recovery and the furthering of your work on earth.

P.U.R.P.O.S.E. Principle IV: **P**ursue Positive Practices to Maintain My Sobriety

The Recovered Life

Never take your God-given talents and strengths for granted; they're only on loan to you to help you lead a recovered life on mission for Christ. And out of gratitude, commit to practicing kindness and resisting boredom.

☀ Meditate on the Assurance of God's Word

I have strength for all things in Christ Who empowers me [I am ready for anything and equal to anything through him Who infuses inner strength into me; I am self-sufficient in Christ's sufficiency]. PHILIPPIANS 4:13 (AMP)

[God] said to me, "My grace is sufficient for you, for my power is made perfect in weakness." Therefore I will boast all the more gladly about my weaknesses, so that Christ's power may rest on me. 2 CORINTHIANS 12:9 (TNIV)

☀ Humbly Talk with the Lord

Thank God for a talent or skill that has brought you confidence, peace, joy, or energy. Ask boldly for an opportunity to share it with others for his glory.

Promise God that you'll commit all your ways to him for Kingdom-building purposes, admitting that you can't take one step in that direction without his help.

☀ Take the *Life Purpose Coach* Challenge

My friend Garth, who's a licensed counselor for addicts and also a follow-up recovery coach, offers this challenge: "It's important to replace addictive thought patterns and behaviors with healthy alternatives. For example, when tempted to view pornography, have a substitute activity ready. If you can sing, sing. If you can repair something, repair it. If you can memorize Scripture verses, memorize them. If you can run, run. If you can problem solve, problem solve like never before!"

P.U.R.P.O.S.E. Principle V:
Opt Out of Self-Sabotaging Methods

I choose to live a life of recovery and purpose now.

P.U.R.P.O.S.E. Principle V: Opt Out of Self-Sabotaging Methods

Anger, Bitterness, and Doubt

"Don't call me Naomi," she responded. "Instead, call me Mara, for the Almighty has made life very bitter for me." RUTH 1:20

Naomi, which means pleasant and beautiful in Hebrew, had a rough go of it for more than a decade. She was a stranger in a foreign land. Her husband and two sons died. Her life certainly didn't turn out the way she expected. She felt God had dealt her a hard blow, a bitter pill to swallow. Do you notice in our passage how Naomi's bitterness is mixed with anger against the Lord? Now, watch how that deadly combo of bitterness and anger led her to doubt that God even loved her: "I left here full of life, and God has brought me back with nothing but the clothes on my back. . . . The Strong One ruined me" (Ruth 1:21, *The Message*). She felt that the Lord Almighty had caused her demise and stripped her of all hope. When Naomi told her friends to call her Mara, she was playing a dangerous Blame God game, stacked with cards of anger, bitterness, and doubt. Mara is certainly not alone, though, in that perilous, pity-party game; we've all competed at times for the "Woe Is Me" one-upmanship trophy.

Think about how playing those three cards (anger, bitterness, and doubt) can sabotage your recovery and the work God designed you to do. Eleanor Roosevelt even warned us that "anger is one letter short of danger." Although Eleanor gave us no such catchy phrase for bitterness or doubt, be forewarned that those conditions are just as dreadful as anger, and all three are interrelated.

SOUL SEARCH

Have you ever felt that God had it in for you, raining down his wrath unfairly on you, or have you been more inclined to think that life is unfair due to the nature of our fallen condition? How have your feelings caused you to react to hardship?

Strong One, I admit that I've let anger, bitterness, and doubt ruin my own best life. Forgive me. I know that you love me unconditionally and that you want nothing more than to help me with my sobriety, my character, and your most intentional assignment. I'm eager to listen now.

P.U.R.P.O.S.E. Principle V: Opt Out of Self-Sabotaging Methods

Anger and Rage

Stop being angry! Turn from your rage! Do not lose your temper—it only leads to harm.
PSALM 37:8

Anger is said to be a tidal wave of emotion that can maim those in its wake, and it's also been compared to a ticking time bomb. I was best described as a tornado waiting to happen. During some of my single-mothering years, when I was raising two teenagers, I was a rageaholic (person addicted to rage). I'm surprised my adult kids still speak to me, considering some of my angry outbursts of days gone by. Although my children could never predict the path of my destructive vortex, they became experts at hiding out till the storm had passed.

My turnaround began when I devoured Neil Clark Warren's quick-read book *Make Anger Your Ally,* and I learned that my anger didn't always have to lead to sin. Instead it could reveal truth and invite me to take civilized action steps to remedy all sorts of situations. A lightbulb went on for me when I began to understand that anger is intended to be God's gift to motivate us toward positive change in our lives. Since then, I've learned that I used it as a retaliation device, as my deadly mechanism of choice when I perceived that I'd been offended, wronged, provoked, or denied something. All this information helped me recover from my addiction to rage.

Understanding what types of circumstances rile you—like delays, excuses, clutter, losing paperwork, or excessive noise—can certainly help you take preventative measures to avoid the triggers. Your pre-knowledge also buys you time to cry out in prayer before your anger turns into a sin—like lying, cheating, selfishness, greed, or rage. And knowing who pushes your buttons—like a parent, teenager, coworker, or neighbor—can help you pray for them before, during, and after any flare-up of anger.

SOUL SEARCH

How do you feel when you're the victim of someone's unbridled anger? What can you do to curb your anger so you're able to focus on your sobriety and God's intriguing plan for your life?

My Sure Victory, I ask you to keep my angry thoughts from spilling into unkind words and deeds. Please reveal to me the next step you recommend in my anger-management efforts.

244

P.U.R.P.O.S.E. Principle V: **O**pt Out of Self-Sabotaging Methods

Root Cause of My Anger

"Don't sin by letting anger control you." Don't let the sun go down while you are still angry, for anger gives a foothold to the devil. EPHESIANS 4:26-27

You're well on the way to recovery when you start to unpack the underlying or root cause of your anger. Take some time now to think about what's really causing you to be so angry about random things. Are you humiliated, frustrated, disgusted, in pain, or afraid of intimacy? Has your pride been hurt, or are you afraid that you're about to be "found out"? Are you jealous, exhausted, inebriated, or insecure? Is your anger rooted in issues about overcommitment, loss of control, intense grief, or broken promises?

Personally, I've traced most of my anger issues to what I call the What a Waste of My Time Syndrome (WAWMTS), whose root cause is typically impatience. I used to get really angry, for example, over incompetent food servers, long lines at poorly staffed retail stores, computer crashes, endless chatty phone calls, and complicated recipes with more than two ingredients. Much of my WAWMTS has been treated now with favorable results, but I'm still haunted by another root cause of it: namely, pride that often lurks in the darkness of my soul. My pride has been known to re-trigger the syndrome if I experience consistent, unnecessary interruptions during times of intense focus. I'm usually good up until the sixth or seventh silly disruption, then *bam*, it's WAWMTS!

It's crucial to learn to ask yourself, *What's really going on with me?* This simple practice will increase the amount of anger-free time you can devote to your critical recovery care and your God-glorifying life mission.

SOUL SEARCH

What do you feel might be the underlying cause(s) of your anger toward yourself, your family, society, or God? What has to change in your heart, mind, and behavior to keep you anger-free more often?

Never-Failing One, tell me what's causing my anger and what to do about it, even as it's happening. And give me the courage to share the truth about the deepest root cause of my anger with someone I trust, so it's hidden no more.

P.U.R.P.**O**.S.E. Principle V: **O**pt Out of Self-Sabotaging Methods

Bitterness Hurts

Get rid of all bitterness, rage, anger, harsh words, and slander, as well as all types of evil behavior.   EPHESIANS 4:31

Ephesians directs us to say good-bye to all sorts of evil in our lives, and it cites bitterness at the front of the list. So let's say au revoir, cheerio, ciao, vale, farewell, and so long to bitterness right now, since it's known to be a major cause of recovery setbacks. My favorite "good riddance" send-off for it is from the Spanish, adiós (a Dios—to God). Loosely translated, let's give our bitterness to God.

The tendency of human beings to lean toward this gnarly sin was obvious to Peter when he admonished Simon, the greedy sorcerer: "I see that you are full of bitterness and captive to sin" (Acts 8:23, NIV). It may have been a long time or only a few minutes since you've lived in harmony, agreement, pleasantness, unity, accord, and consensus with a particular person. You can start right now, though, to leave all that friction, conflict, dissension, and discord behind by confessing your bitterness to God.

I recently saw a cartoon of a woodpecker on Noah's ark with this anonymously written caption: "The woodpecker might have to go." What a way to sink a ship fast! It made me reflect on the fact that we can be such busy woodpeckers at times—drilling deep holes of bitterness into our relationships. We do this to the demise of our emotional health and sacred calling—causing our own, well-built ship to sink. God wants to rid us of such destructive behavior, which might even feel like second nature to us now. We need only to bid adieu to it before it becomes ingrained as our "new normal."

SOUL SEARCH

How has bitterness interfered with your recovery attempts and also with God's wish for you to soar? What can you resolve now to do differently the next time you feel compelled to act in a spirit of bitterness?

Light unto my feet, you know how my bitterness has exhausted me and stalled my recovery and the launch of my sweet life mission. I'm ready to change my ways and turn this negativity over to you. I want no part of it anymore.

P.U.R.P.O.S.E. Principle V: Opt Out of Self-Sabotaging Methods

Doubting Thomas

[The disciples told Thomas,] "We have seen the Lord!" But he replied, "I won't believe it unless I see the nail wounds in his hands, put my fingers into them, and place my hand into the wound in his side." JOHN 20:24-25

Our passage reveals that Thomas wrestled with an obstinate adversary, Doubt. So when the disciples gathered eight days later, Jesus appeared to them and then said to Thomas, "Put your finger here, and look at my hands. Put your hand into the wound in my side. Don't be faithless any longer. Believe!" (John 20:27). And finally Thomas believed.

You may be struggling with doubts about your salvation or about your ability to move forward with your recovery. You may doubt that God could love a sinner like you, that he created you for a specific purpose, or that your family will ever forgive you. If so, soak in Jesus' words: "Don't be faithless any longer. Believe!" Form an alliance with God to outwit, outplay, and outlast (*Survivor* style) the clever foe, Doubt. Make up your mind now to be the sole survivor in that game.

My twenty-four-year-old nephew, Eric, told me that before he suited up in his brown belt gi—his uniform for a judo tournament—he had to make sure that he'd already pinned his toughest opponent, Doubt, to the ground. He ended up winning four out of four matches by a full point, each time within one minute, and he was promoted that day to first-degree black belt. Eric couldn't risk doubting that he'd win—not even for a second. His gutsy decision to be victorious has helped me go the distance lately in times of my own doubting. I've realized that faith is a choice we make to believe God's promises, well before we get into the throes of the situation.

SOUL SEARCH

Do you believe that God has a miraculous recovery and a beyond-belief destiny for you to claim? What overcomer's strategy works best for you when Doubt tries to pin you to the ground?

My Victory Coach, when doubts fill my mind, let your comfort give me renewed hope and cheer. *

---

* From Psalm 94:19.

P.U.R.P.O.S.E. Principle V: **O**pt Out of Self-Sabotaging Methods

Still Doubting?

The eleven disciples left for Galilee, going to the mountain where Jesus had told them to go. When they saw him, they worshiped him—but some of them doubted!
MATTHEW 28:16-17

We read in Matthew's story that even at the nth hour, as Jesus was preparing to give the Great Commission to his eleven disciples, some "held back, not sure about *worship*, about risking themselves totally" (Matthew 28:17, *The Message*). We're quickly informed that Jesus was undeterred by that risk-adverse doubt, and that he instructed his motley crew to go and make disciples of all the nations, baptize them, and teach them to obey all his commands. Then he specifically addressed their greatest doubt, assuring them that they'd be okay without his bodily presence: "And be sure of this: I am with you always, even to the end of the age" (v. 20).

Considering this tough world we live in, what a great reminder we have in verse 20, knowing that Jesus will be with us always, till the end of the world, till Kingdom come. This unshakable belief will carry us through our times of doubt about having a child, finding a job, developing a healthy friendship, saving our marriage, or getting a clean bill of health. This firm belief that Jesus is with us is what brings people back from the brink of self-destruction and from their obsessive fears, post-traumatic stress disorder, or unspeakable abuse. Jesus is with us; of that we can have no doubt.

Invite Jesus to abruptly interrupt your doubt cycle before it spins you out of control into worry and anxiety. Ask him to set you up with a four-pronged default cycle of trusting him, his timing, his ways, and his wisdom. And count on him to be with you to showcase the fascination he's placed in your soul.

SOUL SEARCH

Abandoning all doubt, what small step (not a quantum leap) are you willing to take toward what you believe to be true about your sobriety, Jesus, and his call on your life? What's the value of taking a small step sometimes, instead of an Indiana Jones leap?

My Comforting Promise in times of doubt, please speak poignantly to me. I care only about praising you with my life. I trust you when you say that you'll be with me always, even to the end of the age.

P.U.R.P.O.S.E. Principle V: Opt Out of Self-Sabotaging Methods

No Looking Back

Walk away from the angry, bitter, doubt-filled you. Have no more of that madness. Instead, head in the opposite direction toward love, peace, and hope, never to repeat the insanity of yesteryear.

☀ Meditate on the Assurance of God's Word

You must all be quick to listen, slow to speak, and slow to get angry. Human anger does not produce the righteousness God desires. JAMES 1:19-20

Watch out that no poisonous root of bitterness grows up to trouble you, corrupting many. HEBREWS 12:15

Jesus told them, "I tell you the truth, if you have faith and don't doubt, you can do things like this and much more. You can even say to this mountain, 'May you be lifted up and thrown into the sea,' and it will happen." MATTHEW 21:21

☀ Humbly Talk with the Lord

Verbalize a short prayer to thank Jesus for the gift of his calming presence, unconditional love, much-needed peace, and boundless hope.

Ask the Holy Spirit to help you work the next step in your recovery program and life mission without being haunted by any doubts; ask him to fill you with patience and faithfulness.

☀ Take the *Life Purpose Coach* Challenge

Imagine that John Quiñones, the host of the television show *What Would You Do?*, has come to your hometown with his hidden-camera crew. You agree to participate in a scripted scene, playing the role of a particularly angry person. An unsuspecting passerby (who happens to be a twenty-year-sober, kind, discerning believer) steps into your scene and gently encourages you to change your ways. What grace-filled words of his might be a lifeline to you?

P.U.R.P.O.S.E. Principle V: **O**pt Out of Self-Sabotaging Methods

Heavy-Duty Issues

Nothing in all creation is hidden from God. Everything is naked and exposed before his eyes, and he is the one to whom we are accountable. HEBREWS 4:13

Our passage reminds us that we can't hide from God, that he sees everything—the good and the bad of our lives. Jeremiah 23:24, along with many other Scriptures, confirms that idea with the Lord asking, "Can anyone hide from me in a secret place? Am I not everywhere in all the heavens and earth?" Knowing that our thoughts and actions are already an open book to God, it's foolish to try to hide five of the most heavy-duty issues we face: worry, unconfessed guilt, jealousy, hatred, and self-loathing. These are the very demons that can obliterate your recovery efforts and your God-orchestrated dreams. In fact, it's impossible to name one circumstance in your life that's ever improved because of them, except healing from them.

My friend Sal, who's a believer and a recovering gambler, likens these five, sinful tendencies to phantom energy. (That's the electrical energy that appliances, like toaster ovens and hair dryers, use when they're turned off but still plugged in.) He says that they sap our energy but accomplish nothing. His best advice is this: "It's important to take in a big drink of God's mercy by focusing on how he loves to unplug our life-sapping habits from their demonic power source."

Carl Sandburg reminds us that "time is a great teacher," so hopefully by now time has taught us that enough is enough of these unruly habits that have sucked the life out of us. Let's spend the valuable resource of our personal energy on godly endeavors.

SOUL SEARCH

In what way are you burdened by worry, unconfessed guilt, jealousy, hatred, or self-loathing? What could you do now to make that a thing of your past, so you can live a sober, God-inspired life of purpose?

Kind God, don't let me give one more breath to any of these five conditions. They've all taken their best shot at destroying me, and frankly, I've had it with each of them. I choose you over any and all of these demons. Hold me accountable, Lord.

P.U.R.P.O.S.E. Principle V: Opt Out of Self-Sabotaging Methods

Worry Less

I tell you not to worry about everyday life—whether you have enough food and drink, or enough clothes to wear.   MATTHEW 6:25

Are you addicted to worry? Jesus tells us not to worry about anything, but that didn't stop me in 1972 from becoming a colossal worrier. I was hired to teach second grade at a private school prior to enrolling in teacher credentialing classes, so I was worried sick each day that I didn't know what I was doing. My worrying, though, paled in comparison to that of my worrywart students! I'll never forget one little girl, Priscilla, who sobbed uncontrollably because her only pencil broke. It was at that exact moment I made up my mind that our class would discuss and memorize Matthew's entire passage about worry (see Matthew 6:25-34) for an upcoming Parent Night.

Oh, what a huge difference that experience made for those little tykes and me. Just imagine a chorus of thirty-two munchkins excitedly beginning to recite the passage for their parents. On cue at Matthew 6:26, timid Priscilla stepped out and did an impassioned solo recitation of two verses, complete with hand gestures: "Look at the birds. They don't plant or harvest or store food in barns, for your heavenly Father feeds them. And aren't you far more valuable to him than they are? Can all your worries add a single moment to your life?" There was not a dry eye in the house!

Jesus' audience must have heard his passion, too, when he warned them that unbelievers' thoughts are dominated by worry because they don't know that their heavenly Father is already aware of all their earthly needs. Jesus urged his listeners to seek after God, above all else, and to live well—not to be preoccupied with the many worries of tomorrow. Jesus wants to calm you, to tell you not to be anxious about your recent failed recovery attempts. He wants to remind you that he's actively ruling over his creation and that he's already saved you from your sins and spiritual enemies.

SOUL SEARCH

What's got you worried sick? What's preventing you from releasing your worry to God right now?

The Beginning and the End, I release my worries to you so I can focus on my healing and all you've commissioned me to do with my life.

P.U.R.P.O.S.E. Principle V: **O**pt Out of Self-Sabotaging Methods

Unconfessed Guilt

Finally, I confessed all my sins to you and stopped trying to hide my guilt. . . . And you forgave me! All my guilt is gone.   PSALM 32:5

God is the only member of our grand jury; no one else has the right to sit in judgment regarding our addictive rebellion and our violation of his law. And thank heavens, he has a reputation for handing down Psalm 32:5 verdicts of "No longer guilty" once we admit our offenses.

I pity the man on trial for murder who nearly got me as a jury member in 2008. I had sat in the jury pool for three long days while my son and his wife were packing to move out of state for his new job. My heart was breaking because I wanted to be with my two grandsons, spoiling them, before they left. No murder suspect deserved to have me—an anxious, sad, distracted mother and grandmother—deciding if he was guilty and deserved a severe sentencing. As time inched along, 273 potential jurors were interviewed before the prosecutor and defense attorney agreed to impanel 12 candidates. I was #274, and I made it out of the courthouse just in time to get three hours of hugs before I waved good-bye and watched the moving van drive away.

It's God's providence that he's the only one to judge us. And Psalm 51:1-2 reminds us of how easy it is to plead our case: "Have mercy on me, O God, because of your unfailing love. Because of your great compassion, blot out the stain of my sins. Wash me clean from my guilt." No long trial with disgruntled jurors—just God and his instantaneous mercy.

SOUL SEARCH

What guilt are you trying to hide that's eating you alive and needs to be released to almighty God? How do you imagine you'll feel once you've confessed your wrong-doings to him?

Friend of tax collectors and sinners, I ask for your mercy. Remove the stain of my guilt, which I no longer wish to try to hide from you. Immerse me more deeply in the miracle of my recovery and the joy of doing your ultimate-warrior will.

P.U.R.P.O.S.E. Principle V: **O**pt Out of Self-Sabotaging Methods
Say No to Jealousy

A peaceful heart leads to a healthy body; jealousy is like cancer in the bones.
PROVERBS 14:30

Nobody wants cancer in their bones, but that's how Proverbs describes jealousy that resides in us—contrasting it to a peaceful heart and a healthy body. And later, in Proverbs 27:4, the plot thickens when jealousy is said to be even more hazardous than anger or wrath: "Anger is cruel, and wrath is like a flood, but jealousy is even more dangerous." That's scary! Honestly, I didn't know that truth before digging in to study this topic.

What I did know was how easy it is to be envious of another person's blessings, abilities, resources, small group, ministry, or grand life calling. And I know, too, that I'm not the only one who feels this way. Jealousy is a problem common to many, including those in Twelve Step programs who are green with envy over someone else's sobriety. If it weren't a common denominator for humans, God wouldn't have devoted an entire commandment to it when he had only ten spots on the stone tablets! The tenth commandment says, "You must not covet your neighbor's house. You must not covet your neighbor's wife, male or female servant, ox or donkey, or anything else that belongs to your neighbor" (Exodus 20:17). And what else belongs to our neighbors? Their fame, wealth, family's love, friendships, accomplishments, talents, health, reputation, spiritual gifts, and faith, among much else—all of which can be enviable.

We need to guard our hearts against jealousy, using the three best methods known to work well: First, pray for those individuals about whom you're jealous—that God will be with them. Second, rejoice with those who rejoice (assuming their endeavors are pleasing to God). And third—which is definitely the most challenging—take time to personally help them succeed in their God-honoring endeavors. If you allow these types of actions to replace your time spent being jealous, God will shine favor on your recovery and life mission.

SOUL SEARCH

Of whom are you jealous and why? How do you plan to rid yourself of that disease?

Faithful and True One, I know it's hard to watch me live so much of my life envious of others. I refuse to be that person anymore. Make me brand new.

P.U.R.P.O.S.E. Principle V: Opt Out of Self-Sabotaging Methods

Hatred Has No Place

People may cover their hatred with pleasant words, but they're deceiving you.
PROVERBS 26:24

My daughter and I stood aghast and speechless on Christmas Day 2006, as we stared at the Dachau Crematorium (more aptly called group incinerators) that was used for the mass disposal of deceased prisoners in the first Nazi concentration camp in Germany. We learned that the atrocity and monstrosity of Dachau actually became a model, a prototype, for other bestial, sadistic Third Reich camps that followed. How could Führer Adolf Hitler have been filled with that much hatred to allow such irrational and unconscionable treatment of human beings and their corpses?

The truth is that at times we, too, have been filled with hatred for a people-group or an individual, even if the world hasn't read about our sins in history books and toured our "people incinerators." Proverbs outs us when it says that many are actually experts at covering up their hatred with pleasantries. But we must never forget that our undocumented hatred has killed some of our relationships, decimated our recovery efforts at times, annihilated new opportunities, and attempted to suffocate God's ideal outcome for our lives. Our prideful tirades and dreadful deeds against others, if written in books for all to read, would appall and disgust people.

The biggest difference right now between Hitler and us is that we're still alive, which means that God isn't finished with us yet. He wants to redeem the bad in our lives for good. He wants us to think with the mind of Christ. He wants us to be God-controlled in all we say and do. Hatred has no place in our sober lives or in God's unparalleled plan for how we'll contribute to his work on earth. Quite simply, hatred incinerates our efforts.

SOUL SEARCH

How would you complete this sentence: "My hate for _____ feels like _____"? Is the pain caused by your hatred so intense that you need to seek professional counseling to address it?

Man of Sorrows, take this enormous sorrow from me. Release me of all hatred, so I may serve you with a clean and healed heart in the precise way you'd love for me to serve.

P.U.R.P.O.S.E. Principle V: **O**pt Out of Self-Sabotaging Methods

Pandemic of Self-Loathing

That's why I take pleasure in my weaknesses, and in the insults, hardships, persecutions, and troubles that I suffer for Christ. For when I am weak, then I am strong.
2 CORINTHIANS 12:10

When Paul wrote about his weaknesses, including his "thorn in the flesh" (2 Corinthians 12:7) and the cruel, public torments of his life, he explained that his strength in all things came from being united with Christ. Our minds, though, tend to camp on the fact that we feel troubled, tempted, afflicted, and alone. We're disgusted with our weaknesses and beat ourselves up over them because we don't feel holy enough, smart enough, equipped enough, attractive enough, wealthy enough, gifted enough, or worthy enough. We use every self-flagellating whip we can find (self-inflicted abuse via drugs, alcohol, food, pornography, or shopping, for example).

I really think somebody should write a book entitled *The Insufficiency Syndrome: The Self-Loathing Disease with Severe Side Effects*. I'm convinced it would be a best-seller. I believe it's the secret addiction of 80 percent of our world's population, including Christians. Our pastors rarely mention this self-hate pandemic, but it's quite evident in our everyday words and actions. Job says it best: "I loathe my very life" (Job 10:1, NIV).

Instead, what if, like Paul, we saw our blatant weaknesses as cause for celebration—a reason to rejoice that Jesus is enough and that without him we can do nothing? If only we would allow one another to shout out loud, "I'm not enough—and that's a good God-thing!" Overcoming the deeply ingrained issue of a self-loathing pattern must be addressed as a systemic problem, possibly with professional help, but Paul's words are a great place to start. On our own, we're not enough; we're simply not. May a chorus ring out, "Amen to that!"

SOUL SEARCH

How could you rejoice (in a Christ-honoring, rip-roaring way) that you're not enough on your own? How could that help you with your recovery work and eternal contribution?

You who love me unconditionally, teach me to take pleasure, as Paul did, in being weak—because it'll free me to rely on the power and grace of Jesus Christ to make me strong.

P.U.R.P.O.S.E. Principle V: **O**pt Out of Self-Sabotaging Methods

Five Guaranteed Life Killers

Can you imagine a life without worry, unconfessed guilt, jealousy, hatred, and self-loathing? Your thoughts would definitely shift from addiction-laden despair to a life of infinite, godly possibilities.

☀ Meditate on the Assurance of God's Word

Don't worry about anything; instead, pray about everything. Tell God what you need, and thank him for all he has done. Then you will experience God's peace, which exceeds anything we can understand. His peace will guard your hearts and minds as you live in Christ Jesus. PHILIPPIANS 4:6-7

Where is another God like you, who pardons the guilt of the remnant, overlooking the sins of his special people? You will not stay angry with your people forever, because you delight in showing unfailing love. MICAH 7:18

If you are bitterly jealous and there is selfish ambition in your heart, don't cover up the truth with boasting and lying. JAMES 3:14

Repent of your wickedness and pray to the Lord. Perhaps he will forgive your evil thoughts, for I can see that you are full of bitter jealousy and are held captive by sin. ACTS 8:22-23

☀ Humbly Talk with the Lord

Let God know that you're done with the five guaranteed life killers; that you'd rather focus on him, your sobriety, and the divine urge he's placed in your heart.

Ask God for an embrace of his unrestricted love whenever you begin to worry or if he catches you leaning in the direction of self-hate.

☀ Take the *Life Purpose Coach* Challenge

Interview a "wise Solomon" in your recovery leadership circle. Ask specifically about how God freed him or her from one of the guaranteed life killers.

P.U.R.P.**O**.S.E. Principle V: **O**pt Out of Self-Sabotaging Methods

Facing Fears

God has not given us a spirit of fear and timidity, but of power, love, and self-discipline.
2 TIMOTHY 1:7

Fear—we try to stuff it down, mask it, numb it, drown it, control it, or throw money at it. We ruminate about it; rage against it; run and hide from it; or succumb to anxiety, paranoia, sleep disorders, and depression over it. These types of reactions to fear are more commonplace than butter on toast. Dare we even talk about the fears and acting out that surround the terrifying setbacks in our lives? Who does God think he is to make us wait and wait and wait for answers about recovery, finances, jobs, soul mates, or even the life dreams that he's placed in our hearts?

According to 2 Timothy 1:7, the way for us to conquer our fears is to focus on three things: God's almighty power, loving him and others, and self-discipline. First of all, God's almighty power reminds us to trust that he will frustrate our enemies, carry us through our trials, and guide our decisions. Next, love makes the timid among us bold and fearless, it inspires us to be courageous for the sake of our loved ones, and it gives us hope that everything will work out. And self-discipline, which is acting with a sound and sober mind, helps us see things correctly from a godly perspective. With a prudent, well-balanced mind, we see things accurately, not anxiously. By implementing these three solutions (power, love, and discipline), we begin to manage rightly our thoughts, words, and deeds in times of fear. In these specific ways, we prevent fear from deterring us from our recovery work or the Lord's work.

Adrian Rogers, an author and pastor who died in 2005, wrote these words that had a profound impact on me: "Don't be afraid of the will of God. The will of God will not take you where the power of God cannot keep you." Good to know!

SOUL SEARCH

How fearfully nervous are you about your sobriety? How has fear made you apprehensive and hesitant about God's call on your life?

Holy Spirit, my encourager, I'm feeling fearful about my next recovery steps and timid about my life's work. I ask now for a spirit of power, love, and self-discipline.

P.U.R.P.O.S.E. Principle V: Opt Out of Self-Sabotaging Methods

What Fear Does to Us

Be strong and courageous! Do not be afraid and do not panic before them. For the LORD your God will personally go ahead of you. He will neither fail you nor abandon you.
DEUTERONOMY 31:6

A Congolese believer wrote, "Dear Lord, You be the needle and I be the thread. You go first, and I will follow wherever You may lead." I've struggled for fifteen minutes now to figure out how to say that better, fearful that my words about the importance of following God's plan could never measure up. Amazing, isn't it, how we trap ourselves in fear nearly every time we blink—even when writing a devotional about the fears that prevent us from pursuing God's will for our lives?

Is your biggest fear that of rejection, bodily harm, illness, loneliness, powerlessness, purposelessness, moral failure, going through withdrawals, or humiliation? Try this multiple-choice quiz to check how you tend to react to such fears. Question #1: If you were afraid your secrets were going to be exposed, would you lie to cover your tracks, become defensive, shift the focus to someone else, or take a different approach? Question #2: If you were afraid your spouse was cheating on you, would you worry yourself sick, run up your credit cards out of spite, drink yourself into oblivion, or employ another strategy? Question #3: If you were afraid of home foreclosure, would you go to a casino to try to double your cash, commit insurance fraud, isolate from your friends, or choose another way of coping?

Hopefully you provided some saintly answers, because the unhealthy ones are pure insanity. Fear makes us crazy. It even leads to health issues like high blood pressure, as well as an endless list of paralyzing phobias. You've heard about commonplace fears, like flying or public speaking, but how'd you like to be a recovery coach or counselor dealing with your clients' fears of germs, the moon, the color purple, or feet?

SOUL SEARCH

What's one of your greatest fears, and what has it done to you? If you could kick fear to the curb right now, how would that enhance your sobriety or life purpose?

God the Father, rescue me from my fears that are blocking your intentional plan for my life. I want to live out the rest of my days fearless, sober, and on purpose.

P.U.R.P.O.S.E. Principle V: Opt Out of Self-Sabotaging Methods

Being Courageous

I trust in God, so why should I be afraid?   PSALM 56:4

I was filled with agonizing dread on September 19, 1990, as I headed into my children's school, but I put on a brave face. I needed to tell my third-grade daughter and fifth-grade son that their father, whom they adored, had just died after quadruple bypass surgery. It's still tough to flash back on their faces, their shock, as I shared the news with each of them separately and privately in the principal's office. And after that sad, frightening day, I only had two real options for facing my fears for the future. The first was to trust God with every fiber of my being, and the second was to curl up and die. I preferred the latter, but chose the former, only for the sake of my kids. Somewhere, years earlier, I had learned that courage was a fearless trusting of God who is able, and during this painful season, I needed all the courage a faithful God would offer.

In what way have you needed to be courageous and trust God to see you through or save you? Perhaps, as a member of Al-Anon or Alateen, you needed to be brave when staging an intervention for an alcoholic family member, when facing financial ruin, or when escaping with your life. What if you had allowed fear to overtake you?

And what about now, when you need courage to tell the truth, face an illness, defend a belief, confront a psychological fear, stand up for yourself, or walk alongside someone else who's terrified? Like Peter, will you step out of the boat and walk on water toward Jesus, in spite of being deeply afraid? Matthew 14:31 tells us that when Peter began to sink, Jesus immediately reached out and grabbed him, saying, "You have so little faith. . . . Why did you doubt me?"

Will you cry out as Peter did, "Save me, Lord!" when strong wind and waves begin to petrify you? (see Matthew 14:30).

SOUL SEARCH

What scares you about your life, recovery, or ministry-mission opportunities? In what specific, God-inspired way can you take courage now?

Captain of the Lord's host, thank you that when I pray to you, you answer me and free me from all my fears. *

---

* From Psalm 34:4.

Fear God

For you who fear my name, the Sun of Righteousness [Christ] will rise with healing in his wings. And you will go free, leaping with joy like calves let out to pasture.
MALACHI 4:2

How is it possible that fear can lead to freedom? Yet that's what today's verse promises. The fear that Malachi prophesies about is not the debilitating *FEAR* that (as it's said in recovery circles) equals Frustration, Ego, Anxiety, and Resentment. No, the fear that brings freedom is the reverence for God and his name that the Bible refers to as "the fear of the Lord."

Really soak up our passage, and then pray, *My holy, righteous, and tenderhearted God, your name is worthy to be revered and honored. How could I not stand in awe of you and respect the power you wield? Thank you that I don't need to cower around you like I would around an abusive, alcoholic spouse or an irrational, unpleasable parent. Rather, because of the glory due your name, I desire to bow humbly to you, obey you reverently, and worship you with all aspects of my life.*

God wants you to know that the Sun of Righteousness, Jesus, will rise with wings of grace to heal you as surely as the sun's rays bring warmth, light, restoration, and cheer. You shall go forth bursting with energy, full of health, and overflowing with life satisfaction. What do you think of that offer? Would you like to be healed from your sins, obsessions, and compulsions? If so, get out your pen to sign and date a contract to "fear the LORD your God, and live in a way that pleases him, and love him and serve him with all your heart and soul" (Deuteronomy 10:12).

And at the signing party, thank God for sending his Son, our sunshine, to diffuse on you blessings of grace, healing, and significance-filled living.

SOUL SEARCH

What does it mean to you to fear God? How ready are you to be freed from addiction and go leaping with joy like a calf let out to pasture?

Sun of Righteousness, help me remember that "fear of the LORD is the foundation of true knowledge, but fools despise wisdom and discipline."* You might have to mention this idea more than once before it sinks in, but I invite you to do so.

---

* Proverbs 1:7.

Syndromes That Scream Fear

Even when I walk through the darkest valley, I will not be afraid, for you are close beside me. Your rod and your staff protect and comfort me. PSALM 23:4

Some of the darkest, most dismal valleys we ever traverse are the gloomy, sad, and dangerous places of our minds and souls where fear lurks and pounces on us. That's why God's Great Shepherd waits there to guide believers out, to be our Light on the right path. We don't need to fear any psychological and emotional horrors in the valleys, because Jesus is with us.

What fear-filled darkness lurks inside you as a syndrome (life pattern), waiting to ambush your recovery and your life mission? For example, consider the Middle Child Syndrome of those who crave attention and stop at nothing to get it; the Authority Figure Syndrome of those who sabotage the plans of leaders; the Passive-Aggressive Syndrome of those who camouflage deeply buried anger with mixed messages; or the Stuff It Down Syndrome of those who overeat to cram down all sorts of emotions. If one of these is you, cry out to the Great Shepherd to lead you out of that perilous place.

Pray, too, against these syndromes that I've identified in my recovery clients and Life Purpose Coach clients: the I'm Comfortable Syndrome of those who enjoy being unchallenged, even though God didn't create us to be comfortable. Or the Imposter Syndrome of those who specialize in hiding their inadequacies, so people won't figure out that they're faking it. Or the Unforgiven Syndrome of those who self-flagellate, saying, "I'm completely unlovable."

Sobriety and purpose are daring, risk-filled adventures that can't be saddled with the insanity of fear-laden syndromes. Let God have all traces of any such madness now.

SOUL SEARCH

How is a syndrome really a confession of fear? Which of the seven syndromes listed have you seen played out in full Technicolor among your friends or in yourself?

Great Shepherd, I know that I'll live in your house forever, but right now, I surely need your goodness and unfailing love to pursue me all the days of my life.* Specifically, I ask you to run some monster syndromes out of my earthbound temple!

---
* From Psalm 23:6.

Other Unhealthy Syndromes

The LORD frees the prisoners. The LORD opens the eyes of the blind. The LORD lifts up those who are weighed down.   PSALM 146:7-8

Most people are locked in an addict's prison of some type; they are spiritually blind or weighed down by sin, guilt, or fear. Think about these unhealthy syndromes that fuel their misery: they're trapped in an Addicted to Affluence Syndrome, one that causes them to brag and be judgmental. How God must grieve seeing anyone behind those prison bars. Or they struggle with the I Don't Fit Syndrome, saying, "I don't know why people don't seem to like me." The truth is that they've latched onto a self-righteous excuse for not developing relationships. God yearns to open the eyes of those in this dangerous territory, helping them see the light of his divine way.

Or one of the most deadly syndromes, which sabotages recovery and a person's life work: what I call the No Voice Syndrome. Sufferers are afraid to speak up or are insecure about their opinions, but they lobby for sympathy about their loss of personal power. The truth is that complaining about not having a voice is actually easier than participating in life. How God must mourn the acceptance of this weighty albatross around their necks, which keeps them bowed low. He yearns to refresh their souls.

Other conditions that can keep people stuck in addictive behavior are the Spirit of Poverty Syndrome, of not trusting God to provide. Or the Trophy Spouse Syndrome; that's when a perfectionist covers up insecurities by looking good at all cost, while others ask, "What warts is this person hiding?" And never forget the Class Clown Syndrome of those whose loud behavior stems from low self-esteem. Invite the Lord to free you from any prison you might be in, to open your eyes wide to his perspective on all topics, and to lift you up from the sins, guilt, and fear that are crushing you.

SOUL SEARCH

What fear-laced syndrome do you notice most in others, and why do you think you notice it? What syndrome dictates your own addictive behavior and may be blocking your life's contribution to the world?

Lord who frees prisoners, I'm trapped in a crazy-making syndrome, and my only hope is for you to rescue me, open my eyes to the truth, and lift me up from the depths.

P.U.R.P.O.S.E. Principle V: Opt Out of Self-Sabotaging Methods

God's in Charge

Living gloriously sober, for even one more moment, requires that God be in charge of your world, just as he rules the entire universe. Otherwise your efforts will be fatefully futile. It's only with his courage, strength, and timing that you'll live your best life.

☀ Meditate on the Assurance of God's Word

Well-formed love banishes fear.   1 JOHN 4:18 (*The Message*)

I prayed to the LORD, and he answered me. He freed me from all my fears.
PSALM 34:4

Uzziah sought God during the days of Zechariah, who taught him to fear God. And as long as the king sought guidance from the LORD, God gave him success.
2 CHRONICLES 26:5

☀ Humbly Talk with the Lord

Run to God for the courage you need to face your out-of-control fears.

Seek guidance from the Lord regarding your friendships, job, sobriety, and life role as a missionary to the hurting.

☀ Take the *Life Purpose Coach* Challenge

Complete this exercise about a syndrome you have, replacing the sample answers below. Name your own syndrome or borrow one from September 1 or 2.

1. Name and explain a syndrome: <u>Doctor Syndrome: trying to fix others.</u>
2. What's your motive for holding onto that syndrome? <u>To earn admiration and rewards.</u>
3. List at least one characteristic of a person with the syndrome: <u>Has little margin or balance; ignores own emotional and physical needs; often a people-pleaser; needs to learn to play more; might have God complex.</u>
4. What's the payoff you feel the syndrome gives you? <u>I'm seen as a saint.</u>

If this syndrome describes you, pray for guidance as to what to do about this insight.

P.U.R.P.O.S.E. Principle V: **O**pt Out of Self-Sabotaging Methods

God Is Good, All the Time

They do not fear bad news; they confidently trust the LORD to care for them.
PSALM 112:7

Few people would disagree that God is good, but I love saying in unison with others, "God is good—all the time!" He's our Armor; he's the God who sees us; and he's our Banner and our Strength. We can confidently trust the Lord to care for us, even in the face of bad news, rumors, and repercussions from our foolish, addictive choices. William Law, an English cleric and theological writer (1686–1761), said of God, "It is much more possible for the sun to give out darkness than for God to do or be, or give out anything but blessing and goodness."

If you feel like you're circling the drain, spiraling out of control, spinning like a top, or living underground, don't despair. God is good all the time, and he loves you like crazy. Don't quit five minutes before the miracle he's planned for you happens, but remain relaxed and unperturbed, even amid all that frightens you. I can recommend that course of action because Jesus promises, "I am leaving you with a gift—peace of mind and heart. And the peace I give is a gift the world cannot give. So don't be troubled or afraid" (John 14:27). God's generous affection toward you will leave you peaceful and your enemies speechless.

I've heard it said that a human could live without air seven minutes, without water seven days, and without food seven weeks. That's because God, our Maker and Sustainer, arranged it that way. The fact of the matter is that we wouldn't survive even one second without the sterling goodness of God.

SOUL SEARCH

In what particular circumstance regarding your recovery or the unfolding of your life mission has God been good to you? How would you describe how much God loves you and how much you love him?

God of incomparable goodness, you know that troubles related to my addictions swirl around me, terrifying me. Each day, I feel bombarded by more bad news, challenges, and hard decisions. I'm finally willing to swap my fear for the peace you promise. Send your goodness now in the form of peace, protection, provision, and an understanding of my unique purpose in life.

P.U.R.P.**O**.S.E. Principle V: **O**pt Out of Self-Sabotaging Methods

God Is My Full Armor

Put on all of God's armor so that you will be able to stand firm against all strategies of the devil. EPHESIANS 6:11

God impressed our passage for today on my heart many years ago at the home of my dear friends Chaundel and Tom Holladay. It happened when their young son Luke joined us, dressed in an Ephesians 6:10-18 outfit depicting the full body armor of God's righteousness! He enthusiastically described each part of his attire to me, along these lines, "This is my belt of truth, and my shoes are the gospel of peace. See my shield of faith? It stops the fiery arrows of the devil. And this is my salvation helmet and my sword of the Spirit, which—hey, Mommy, is my sword the Word of God?" I was mightily blessed by Luke's explanation, and I'm humbled to know him as the godly man he is today. How God must delight in us when, like a child, we put on his full body armor.

Have you donned God's armor so you're able to stand firm against all the schemes and skulduggery of the devil? You know that Satan is prowling around, plotting ways to undermine your recovery and also God's exquisite plan for your life. To the evil one, no type of subterfuge is off limits in this life-or-death battle, if it'll bring you down.

For right now, think about God, specifically as your protecting Shield of Faith, as the one who'll extinguish all the blazing arrows of the evil one during this fight to the finish. Reflect on Psalm 18:30: "He is a shield for all who look to him for protection." And hold God to this commitment, moment by moment, as you face choices about your addiction.

SOUL SEARCH

Which spiritual habit helps you claim your assurance of divine protection against Satan and his angels when they attack your sobriety? If you stay strong in the mighty power that the Lord has over your life mission, what sweet spot of service could you envision for your future?

My Armor, I'm grateful that your faithful promises protect me and make me unafraid of the terrors of the night and of the arrow that flies in the day. Though a thousand victims fall at my side, though ten thousand are dying around me, evil will not touch me. *

---

* From Psalm 91:4-5, 7.

The God Who Sees Me

[Hagar] gave this name to the LORD who spoke to her: "You are the God who sees me," for she said, "I have now seen the One who sees me." GENESIS 16:13 (NIV)

My cuddly pound-rescue pup, Chubby, grew into a strapping German shepherd–boxer who loved to take me on walks. One fine day in 1984, as he was galloping up a sidewalk and dragging me behind, I fell into an uncovered water-meter hole and sprained my ankle. Chubby seemed to be the only one who saw me that day, as I lay on the side of the busy thoroughfare writhing in pain. Cars sped by, oblivious to the fact that I needed some assistance—more than I was getting from my dog, who wouldn't stop licking my face! With Chubby's nose-nudging encouragement, I finally hobbled the several blocks home.

God is not like the motorists who rushed by me that day, and his heart is even bigger than any "man's best friend" ever born. He's the God Who Sees You, so he knows when you're hurting and when you need a lift from a passerby, a helping hand from a neighbor, or a hug from a family member. He delivers all you need, including strength, grace, mercy, hope, healing, and peace to carry you through. If you find, for example, that you're writhing in emotional pain, stuck on your story, enabling others, broken by scandal, or addicted to intellectual superiority and criticism, give God a chance. You'll find yourself saying to him, as Hagar did when she was running away from Sarai, who'd mistreated her, "You are the God who sees me." And you'll be amazed at the wisdom of his restorative plan.

SOUL SEARCH

How often each day do you spend wishing that God didn't see you contemplating disobedience, committing sin, and dealing with the consequences of your stubbornness, addiction, and other poor choices? Before the world began, what do you imagine God saw and declared to be true about your loving and fruitful service to his people?

The God Who Sees Me, keep me under your watchful eye and gracious protection, especially during times of sin, relapse, fear, uncertainty, ill treatment, and loneliness, when all I want to do is run away and hide.

P.U.R.P.O.S.E. Principle V: Opt Out of Self-Sabotaging Methods

The Lord Is My Banner

Moses built an altar there and named it Yahweh-Nissi (which means "the LORD is my banner"). EXODUS 17:15

Today's soldiers fight under their country's flag and direction. The Israelites fought under Yahweh's banner and direction; in his name, truth, and power they conquered nations. Let this remind you that Christ was lifted up as a banner, when his arms were stretched out on Calvary's cross. His battle cry was that souls would know him. Those who enlist in his army are instructed to prepare for battle against spiritual enemies, following every command he issues. Marching under the authority of his standard, his ensign, identifies us as his people; it assures us of his protection.

When you're paranoid, trapped in approval addiction, feeling vulnerable, or obsessively pursuing feeling good, no matter how bad it makes you feel . . . run back and march under the protection of Christ's banner.

When you're living a lie, feeling desperate for relief from physical or emotional pain, withdrawing from people, or unable to pull yourself up out of the muddy mire of a sinful lifestyle . . . run back and march under the protection of Christ's banner.

When you realize that you're becoming the town crier of juicy gossip, spinning out of control like a whirling dervish, sleep-walking through life, or wallowing in the bitter morass of self-pity over your hardscrabble childhood . . . run back and march under the protection of Christ's banner.

Under his royal heraldry, your victory is certain. The inscription of his glorious name on the standard ensures that. Ask that he lead you to his banquet hall and that his banner over you be love (from Song of Songs 2:4, NIV). It's one decision you'll never regret.

SOUL SEARCH

In whose army are you marching daily, and under whose banner are you standing: the Lord's or Satan's? How will living under Yahweh's banner ensure your remarkable recovery and the fulfillment of your God-envisioned life's work?

My Banner, "as for me and my household, we will serve the LORD."* Show my family and me (especially me!) how to follow all your commands, so we might please you and enjoy your protection.

---

* Joshua 24:15 (NIV).

P.U.R.P.O.S.E. Principle V: **O**pt Out of Self-Sabotaging Methods

God's Strength against Enabling

The Sovereign LORD is my strength! He makes me as surefooted as a deer, able to tread upon the heights.   HABAKKUK 3:19

Are you a codependent family member or friend who's taken responsibility and blame for the behavior of others addicted to such things as alcohol, drugs, power, attention, sex, plastic surgery, or materialism? Do you need God's strength in the form of emotional toughness, fortitude, and staying power to stop enabling others, so they can finally experience the consequences of their behavior?

Only God can give you his strength to stop this sticky-wicket behavior, this glue pot of difficult circumstances, which is causing dysfunctional behavior in others and yourself. Pray for godly determination, saying, *Lord, I don't want to be an enabler who tries to control the addictive behavior of others and ends up perpetuating it. I want to be a vital part of the solution, and for that I ask you to be my strength.*

Pray that God will provide a pattern interrupter to change your attitude. Ask for the resolve to stop cleaning up addicts' messes, keeping their secrets, and making excuses to shield them from the harm they've caused. Ask for the tough love you need to allow them to be found out, so others can hold them accountable. Pray that you'll no longer tolerate verbal, emotional, physical, or sexual abuse; that you'll refuse to fudge on what you know is right; and that you'll stop rehearsing the guilt, which has made you physically ill, depressed, and anxious.

Only God can help you in such circumstances. When you're tempted to back down and avoid your difficult decisions, turn to him as your strength, and trust him with all your heart.

SOUL SEARCH

How desperately do you need God's strength now to move away from enabling others and to move into your true life's calling? Do you believe with all your heart that God will make you as surefooted as a deer in this regard?

My Sovereign Strength, stand with me in my hour of need. Look down in triumph on all my enemies;* rid me of my delusion that I can make an addict change. I'm so sorry for the damage I've caused, and I vow to stop interfering in your business now.

---

* From Psalm 59:9-10.

P.U.R.P.O.S.E. Principle V: Opt Out of Self-Sabotaging Methods

Praying the Names of God

Praise the name of God forever and ever, for he has all wisdom and power.
DANIEL 2:20

Praying the names of God takes your focus off your sorrows, worries, and addictions, shifting it to the majesty of God. If you need healing from obsessions and compulsions, for example, you can pray to God as the Great Physician. For money troubles, you can pray to God as the Provider of all things. For help with temptations, you can pray to God as your Protector. Allow your recognition of who God is to enlarge daily, especially when you're struggling with pain or destructive patterns

Try this rewarding prayer routine, which I've thoroughly enjoyed for years:

While driving by yourself with your car radio off: if you see a tree, call God your Shade from the heat; a stop sign, call him the Law Giver; a bird, call him the Maker of all things; a rock, call him your Rock.

While enjoying a meal in a restaurant: as you taste the bread, think of him as the Bread of Life; as you take a sip of water, know he's the Living Water; as you notice the candlelight, remember he's the Light of the World.

While piddling around at home: if you see a clock, reflect on God as the Alpha and Omega; a bed quilt and he's your Comfort; an e-mail and he's your Answer; a piano and he's your Song.

I urge you to spend your days and nights inhaling and exhaling the names of God, because you'll find that he's all things to all people at all times! He's all you'll ever need. As Joseph Scriven penned in an 1855 poem to comfort his mother when her health was failing, "What a friend we have in Jesus, all our sins and griefs to bear! What a privilege to carry everything to God in prayer!" For everything you're facing, God is your Everything.

SOUL SEARCH

Which name of God best supports your recovery? Which name of God reminds you of his power to launch the life dream he put in your heart?

You whose name is worthy to be praised, I'm certainly blessed to have you fill each need I have at any given moment. You're amazing.

P.U.R.P.O.S.E. Principle V: Opt Out of Self-Sabotaging Methods
God Is Mine and I'm God's

You know that God is your Armor, he's the One Who Sees You, and he's your Banner and Strength. He's your Everything. What else is there to know in life? Nothing much! Your entire life, including your critical recovery and daring mission, are all well covered.

☀ Meditate on the Assurance of God's Word

The name of the LORD is a strong fortress; the godly run to him and are safe.
PROVERBS 18:10

GOD said, "My presence will go with you. I'll see the journey to the end." Moses said, "If your presence doesn't take the lead here, call this trip off right now. How else will it be known that you're with me in this, with me and your people?"
EXODUS 33:14-16 (*The Message*)

☀ Humbly Talk with the Lord

Tell the God who sees you that you prayerfully plan to honor him from now on with your thoughts, words, and deeds.

Thank God that his Son holds you securely, and therefore, the devil can't touch you (see 1 John 5:18).

☀ Take the *Life Purpose Coach* Challenge

In addition to praying the names of God and remembering who he is, it's also important to reflect on these scriptural truths about who you are. Decide which one will be a good go-to thought when you're asking God for peace, purpose in life, or his power to stay sober. Choose one idea and reference to memorize:
- I'm an enemy of the devil (see 1 Peter 5:8).
- I'm the salt of the earth (see Matthew 5:13).
- I'm a citizen of heaven (see Philippians 3:20).
- I'm hidden with Christ in God (see Colossians 3:3).

P.U.R.P.O.S.E. Principle V: Opt Out of Self-Sabotaging Methods

Enemies of the State

I am not afraid of ten thousand enemies who surround me on every side.   PSALM 3:6

An enemy of the state is a person who's accused of a crime against a government, such as treason. Similarly in recovery, certain behaviors are like public enemies of your sober state, legitimately endangering you. Such things as judgmental criticism, gossip, grudges, stubbornness, and lousy life scripts can bring down an addict as fast as any well-planned espionage can bring down a political entity. Psalm 55:3 says of the foes that terrorize us, "My enemies shout at me, making loud and wicked threats. They bring trouble on me and angrily hunt me down." Our only hope against all opposition is to sit with God regularly to hear about the bigger picture of our victorious destiny in Jesus.

William Shakespeare wrote, "'Tis best to weigh the enemy more mighty than he seems."

I concur. 'Tis best to weigh sobriety's Public Enemies #1 through 5 more mighty than they seem:

- Public Enemy #1: Judgmental criticism. Making an offhanded remark about an addict's lax recovery efforts, rather than offering prayerful, constructive criticism, can lead to irreparable damage.
- Public Enemy #2: Spreading gossip in a recovery meeting, rather than having a private conversation spoken in love, can stir up years of distrust among friends.
- Public Enemy #3: Grudges held, rather than released, can escalate poor behavior to unconscionable retribution.
- Public Enemy #4: Stubbornness, rather than a spirit of humility, can cause lengthy delays in life lessons learned.
- Public Enemy #5: Faulty scripts or mistaken thinking, rather than biblically based beliefs, can make us crazy—literally!

What damage have these enemies of your sober state done to your psyche, soul, and efforts to pursue God's will for your life?

SOUL SEARCH

What enemy of your sober state do you fear most? Has your critical spirit toward others or your slander of them ever become a case of "You can dish it out, but you can't take it" and "Turnabout's fair play" with others criticizing you or spreading rumors about you?

Jesus, as God's Word and Wisdom, protect me from all that can bring down my fragile state of recovery. I feel like I'm under terrorist attack, but because of you, I won't be afraid of ten thousand enemies who surround me on every side.

P.U.R.P.O.S.E. Principle V: Opt Out of Self-Sabotaging Methods
Judgmental Criticism

Judgmental criticism of others is a well-known way of escaping detection in your own crimes and misdemeanors.   ROMANS 2:1 (*The Message*)

Years ago, I kept a "Ripley's Believe It or Not" file, as a place to dump the mean-spirited things people said about me via e-mail or mail. A reader told me, for example, that I'm going to hell because I don't share her religious beliefs; another said that I'm a selfish sinner because I'm paid to do ministry; and a third said that I wasn't a good mom because I bribed my kid to go to church camp in 1989. You get the gist—you've felt the fiery darts of judgmental criticism sent against you about such things as how evil you are; how slow your recovery has been; or what a disappointment you've been to your family, school, or employer.

My original intent in saving the correspondence was to allow myself time to process the comments for any truth therein, because I'm a firm believer in constructive criticism. I actually love getting solid advice about how to improve my character or my work for the Lord. After all, Proverbs 29:1 says, "Whoever stubbornly refuses to accept criticism will suddenly be destroyed beyond recovery." But I don't save such condemning, judgmental remarks anymore, because I don't want to be tempted to ruminate over the outlandish accusations, retaliate tit for tat, or allow depression to creep into my soul. I don't have time for that nonsense, nor do you. We must be wise about knowing when to ignore or embrace criticism.

Like Barnabas, whose name means "Son of Encouragement" (see Acts 4:36), we're called to be an encouragement to others. Pray that others will speak the truth to you in love and that you'll speak the truth in love to those to whom God directs you. And always pray that all sinners will work their own programs with their own sponsors.

SOUL SEARCH

What's in your Ripley's file of judgmental criticism that has nearly crippled your recovery efforts or life dream? What critical-spirited, sinful opinion have you added to someone else's file?

Judge of all those who judge me, I know that in your justice, you'll punish anyone who self-righteously dares to judge me under a guise of Christian conviction.* Thanks for handling these types of matters, Lord!

---

* From Romans 2:1.

P.U.R.P.O.S.E. Principle V: Opt Out of Self-Sabotaging Methods

Ugliness of Gossip and Grudges

May the words of my mouth and the meditation of my heart be pleasing to you,
O LORD, my rock and my redeemer.   PSALM 19:14

Gossip is not pretty under ordinary circumstances, but have you ever witnessed ugly, explosive gossip mixed with liquor, stress, exhaustion, fear, or jealousy? If so, you know the damage it leaves in its wake. Imagine a Friday night party in Every Town, where guests have been unwinding from the stress of their workweek, and booze has been flowing freely for hours. Exhausted Ethel says to Impressionable Ida that Fearful Frieda is jealous of Drunken Debby's job promotion. Word spreads like wildfire through the various rooms of the house, escalated by a false rumor that Frieda said Debby slept with her new boss to get the job. The next thing you know, Debby and Frieda are in a screaming match, and—wait for it—in a catfight. Then the prolonged grudgefest starts and relationships go downhill with resentment and insults flying back and forth for years. What a mess!

The best prevention for toxic gossip and grudges is to get in the habit of saying, "Not my business." If you make that your all-time favorite phrase, it takes so much weight off your shoulders. Hearing yourself say it makes you realize that you're not part of the problem or the solution, so you get to stay out of it and, in fact, you've *got* to stay out of it. Billy Graham said, "A real Christian is a person who can give his pet parrot to the town gossip," and God's Word echoes that. Psalm 15:1, for example, asks a simple question about who's allowed to enter the Lord's presence on the holy hill. God's answer comes back loud and clear: "Those who refuse to gossip or harm their neighbors or speak evil of their friends" (v. 3). We must be those people whose words and actions are pleasing to God.

SOUL SEARCH

In what way can gossip destroy families, friendships, jobs, sobriety efforts, ministries, and long-term mission work? How does holding a grudge harm you?

My Rock and my Redeemer, I've had my fair share of being the one gossiped about and being the gossiper. Keep me now from hanging around chatterers* and from carrying a grudge against any of your people.**

---

* From Proverbs 20:19.
** From Leviticus 19:18.

P.U.R.P.O.S.E. Principle V: **O**pt Out of Self-Sabotaging Methods

Headstrong Stubbornness

I know how stubborn and obstinate you are. Your necks are as unbending as iron. Your heads are as hard as bronze.   ISAIAH 48:4

Young siblings who are stubbornly refusing to take instruction from their older brother or sister might defiantly holler, "You're not the boss of me!" Their tense muscles, stiff neck, and steel jaws emphasize their attempt to limit the number of people barking orders at them. They're seeking a modicum of control in their powerless world. But for adults, God labels such obstinate ways as the willfulness of iron-necked, hardheaded people. It grieves him that we never make the connection between our stubbornness and our addictive lifestyles, let alone between our inflexibility and the destruction of our larger-than-life legacies that he has arranged for us. He's saddened by the calcified safety measures we employ to ward off change.

Romans 2:5 spells out the consequences for such rebellious, disobedient behavior: "Because you are stubborn and refuse to turn from your sin, you are storing up terrible punishment for yourself. For a day of anger is coming, when God's righteous judgment will be revealed."

I have a lifelong friend who's a recovering cutter and Vicodin addict. She often refuses to obey those in authority over her or even those who can teach her something important. I've said to her many times, "Pigheadedness is going to be the death of you, relationally, vocationally, financially, and spiritually. God may be slow to become angry, but you're presuming on his patience while pushing the anger buttons of a lot of good people." Cures abound for stubborn hiccups, stubborn warts, and stubborn dandruff, but don't hold your breath waiting for a painless remedy for stubborn, self-destructive, irrational behavior. The headstrong person must choose to return to the Lord and submit to his ways. A wise counselor can only exhort prayerfully in truth and love, while relying on God's grace for the transformation.

SOUL SEARCH

Have you ever said to God or an authority figure, "You're not the boss of me!"? How did that work out for you?

Boss of me, please overlook my stubbornness and awful sin, and please change my heart and help me to stop being stubborn. *

---

* Deuteronomy 9:27; 10:16.

P.U.R.P.O.S.E. Principle V: Opt Out of Self-Sabotaging Methods

Lousy Life Scripts

Dear friend, guard Clear Thinking and Common Sense with your life; don't for a minute lose sight of them. They'll keep your soul alive and well.
PROVERBS 3:21-22 (*The Message*)

Our passage instructs us to hang onto logical reasoning and common sense at all costs. And yet, we don't. We entertain Foggy Thinking and Foolish Judgment as if they were honored guests in our home. Why is that? Why do we allow obvious lies and long-held faulty beliefs to cause us to think negatively and to sabotage what God is asking us to be and do on earth? We must muster the courage to challenge our mistaken thinking now.

Reflect for a moment on one of your most self-defeating beliefs, one that's an ingrained life script that you know you must evict for the sake of your recovery and unique purpose. For example, do you say to yourself, *My past addictions have destroyed God's future plans for me?* You can allow a quip like this to trigger other ideas: *I must earn my way into heaven. Keep the peace at all costs. God is a dictator. I stay sober for you. Look out for #1! Control is king. I can fix others.* Or the classic mistaken thinking: *I don't need anybody.* Beth Moore says in her popular book entitled *So Long, Insecurity*, "We're going to have to let truth scream louder to our souls than the lies that have infected us."

You can hear truth scream by writing out several false beliefs you hold, like "I'm stupid." Next, ask God to change your thinking by knocking down the strongholds of your inaccurate, human reasoning. And then rewrite your statements according to the truth he reveals to you, such as, "I'm usually quite smart! I simply choose to act in unwise ways when I get overly tired." Next, ask a good friend to hold you accountable to owning your new beliefs.

SOUL SEARCH

What's the worst thing you say to yourself? Will you erase the lousy script you've been rehearsing and replace it now with God's personalized script for your life?

God of powerful tools for smashing warped philosophies and tearing down barriers constructed against truth, fit every loose thought, emotion, and impulse of mine into the structure of life shaped by Christ. *

---

* From 2 Corinthians 10:4 (*The Message*).

P.U.R.P.**O**.S.E. Principle V: **O**pt Out of Self-Sabotaging Methods

God Luck

The life of every living thing is in his hand, and the breath of every human being.
JOB 12:10

Instead of saying, "Good luck," my friend says, "God luck" or "Lord luck." I now sometimes use those two phrases to add variety to the typical Christian saying "Be blessed." If I get really excited about wishing someone well, and my Irish heritage kicks in, I might share this traditional Gaelic blessing: "May the road rise up to meet you, may the wind be ever at your back. May the sun shine warm upon your face and the rain fall softly on your fields. And until we meet again, may God hold you in the hollow of his hand." That longer comment is definitely overkill in daily conversations, but it does make a beautiful private prayer with a friend who's in serious need of hope and strength.

What type of encouragement—like "God luck," "Lord luck," "Be blessed," or "God hold you" —would help you as you move out of old addictive habits down the pathway to peace, passion, and purpose? Be bold and ask a dear friend or family member to pray godly success into your life, and don't be shy about praying it for yourself. You never know how a dreaded circumstance, relational challenge, or sobriety struggle might turn out in your favor. The road might rise up to meet you; the wind might be at your back; the sun might shine warmly upon your face; and the rain might fall softly on your fields. For sure, though, remember that God certainly does hold you in the hollow of his hand and blesses you, monitoring every breath you take and watching over the life he designed for you.

SOUL SEARCH

In what way would you like God to grant blessings upon your journey to restoration, wholeness, balance, beauty, grace, and forgiveness? How could you offer his hope to someone else who's hurting and in need of Lord luck?

My gracious, ever-present Lord, hold me in the hollow of your hand down this bumpy path to recovery. And draw me close to your heart to lessen the impact of all the potholes that tend to find me.

P.U.R.P.O.S.E. Principle V: Opt Out of Self-Sabotaging Methods

Moving On

Have you been stalled far too long by judgmental criticism, vicious gossip, endless grudges, pure stubbornness, and a lousy life script? Are you ready to move on now? If so, get on with it in earnest.

☀ Meditate on the Assurance of God's Word

An encouraging word cheers a person up.   PROVERBS 12:25

A gossip goes around telling secrets, but those who are trustworthy can keep a confidence.   PROVERBS 11:13

When you are praying, first forgive anyone you are holding a grudge against, so that your Father in heaven will forgive your sins, too.   MARK 11:25

These people are stubborn rebels who refuse to pay attention to the LORD's instructions. ISAIAH 30:9

Pharaoh again became stubborn and refused to let the people go.   EXODUS 8:32

☀ Humbly Talk with the Lord

Thank God for making you brand new, through and through.

Ask God to help you be a more positive influence in your family, church, recovery circle, and community, pointing people in the direction of his fame, power, and unmatchable kindness.

☀ Take the *Life Purpose Coach* Challenge

Confess the sinfulness of your former addictive lifestyle in all its nastiness, specifying how you've harmed others and how you've held grudges against those who've harmed you. Then decide to stop hitting the instant replay button in your mind of all the weaknesses that have been your downfall. Silence the endless debate, once for all, of "Shoulda, coulda, woulda," which has kept you looking in your rearview mirror. Choose to focus forward on how God can use the new and improved you in the unique manner he stipulated eons ago.

P.U.R.P.O.S.E. Principle V: **O**pt Out of Self-Sabotaging Methods

The Troubles I See

I [Jesus] have told you these things, so that in me you may have peace. In this world you will have trouble. But take heart! I have overcome the world.   JOHN 16:33 (NIV)

Do you remember the old spiritual "Nobody Knows the Trouble I've Seen"? In its best-known rendition, Louis Armstrong sang, "Nobody knows the trouble I've seen, nobody knows but Jesus. Nobody knows the trouble I've seen, glory hallelujah." Do you feel like the world has no idea how many troubles, threats, delays, and roadblocks you've encountered to living a peaceful and holy life, let alone how helpless you've often felt about your addictions? I'm glad the song reminds us that Jesus sees what we're going through, even though the world might not.

And I'm glad that our passage, John 16:33, honestly warns us that we will face troubles in life, rather than suggesting that Christians get a free pass on woes, danger, and pain. When's the last time your life was trouble-free from health, financial, relational, or even ministry issues? When's the last time you were free of self-inflicted addictive troubles, such as gorging, hoarding, overspending, drunk driving, or drug sales?

It's true that we already received one golden ticket, a Get Out of Jail Free card to escape eternal damnation, but we don't get any such pass to skip over struggles on earth. Instead, Jesus reminds us that he has overcome the world, which means he's already defeated Satan's power over us, secured our heavenly future, and stands with us now moment by moment, giving us his peace in the midst of our strife. Like Zazu in Disney's *The Lion King*, we can sing, "Nobody knows the trouble I've seen. Nobody knows my sorrow," or we can be more like Scar, who says to him, "Oh, Zazu, do lighten up. Sing something with a little bounce in it." And what a bounce we have, knowing that Jesus understands every detail of our past, present, and future sorrows.

SOUL SEARCH

Which tough circumstances, delays, roadblocks, and heartaches have threatened your recovery efforts or life's calling? In what way have you seen Jesus standing by you during worrisome times?

Jesus, my traveling companion through this world, I take heart because you've defeated the world, triumphing over Satan and death. I take heart because this world is not my final home; I'm heaven-bound. I take heart because I have the peace of your presence.

P.U.R.P.O.S.E. Principle V: Opt Out of Self-Sabotaging Methods

Numerous Threats

O God, listen to my complaint. Protect my life from my enemies' threats.   PSALM 64:1

Be careful about saying to Satan, "Take your best shot at me, Evil One. You're not going to break me. I belong to God, and Jesus' victory is mine!" I've tried it on numerous occasions, and I always rile the devil terribly. That's okay with me, but I thought it best to remind you that he's real and that he has a thousand and one ways to threaten your life, your sobriety, and the desires God put in your heart for making a difference in this world. You ask, "What's the worst Satan could do to me?" Let me begin with answers from Christian theologian Richard Foster, who wrote, "In contemporary society our Adversary majors in three things: noise, hurry, and crowds. If he can keep us engaged in 'muchness' and 'manyness,' he will rest satisfied."

In addition, the devil loves messing in your life by using these types of threats to sabotage your success for the Lord: body image issues, a broken family unit, the comparison trap and jealousy, debt, clutter, ungodly relationships, obsessive use of social media and telephone, abuse of prescription drugs, excessive gaming, compulsive shopping online or on site, physical and sexual abuse, pornography, lies, illness, and lack of funding for your dreams, just to name a few.

In the face of such evil, you can model a prayer after 2 Corinthians 1:10: *God, you rescued me from mortal danger, and you'll rescue me again. I place my confidence in you.* Go ahead and be specific when you pray—asking for protection against your most serious threats, such as exhaustion, mental paralysis, pride, entitlement, distraction, impulsive decisions, guilt, shame, irritability, overcommitment, frustration, embarrassment, fear, anger, sadness, faulty perceptions of God, low self-esteem, isolation, control issues, depression, anxiety, and/or worry.

SOUL SEARCH

What role has God played in helping you succeed in the face of a threat? Without his protection, how could a new threat rob you of his best design for your recovery and lifetime mission?

My Enemy Slayer, defend me against all that threatens to destroy my sobriety, and teach me to stand firm with you to combat the perils aimed against my life's calling.

September 20

P.U.R.P.O.S.E. Principle V: Opt Out of Self-Sabotaging Methods

Maddening Delays

When you came down long ago, you did awesome deeds beyond our highest expectations. And oh, how the mountains quaked! ISAIAH 64:3

Live in utter abandonment to God's perfect timing! For when the timing was right, he came down on Mount Sinai and did awesome deeds, deeds beyond his people's highest expectations. This God, before whom the mountains still quake, is worth waiting for, day after day and year after year. A kid might argue, "But I want what I want, now!" And we adults actually yell our own version of that prideful remark to God all the time, don't we?

Do you feel that God has missed the boat about something that needs to happen now for you to be happy, successful, sober, or on mission? For example, why hasn't he intervened with your rebellious teenager, your profanity-yelling boss, your addictive desire for just one more _____, or your despair over purposelessness? Has this maddening delay been more crazy-making or anger-producing for you?

As a kid, I sat glued to the television during the suburbanite family sitcom *Father Knows Best*. The title gives away the theme of the show, which also needs to be our prayer: *My heavenly Father, you know best. You've known every detail about my life since before the world began. Not trusting you is akin to blasphemy and mutiny. Stop me now, Abba-Daddy, from being suspicious of your infallible timing.*

You know that every day is a gift; that's why we call it the present. You can spend your time fretting about all the ways God has disappointed you by withholding something from you. Or you can raise your hands in praise, smiling about the wisdom of his persistently perfect timing and promising him that you won't get ahead of him.

SOUL SEARCH

In what circumstance have you experienced the blessings promised in our focal passage? Because your faithful Papa really does know best, what miracle can you expect in his one-billionth-of-a-second timing for your life, recovery, and biggest Kingdom dreams?

God of Resurrection Sundays, you raised Christ from the dead after three days. Your timing was perfect then, is perfect now, and will be perfect forevermore. I wait confidently for you to save me, for I know you certainly hear me. *

---

* From Micah 7:7.

P.U.R.P.O.S.E. Principle V: **O**pt Out of Self-Sabotaging Methods

Why the Delay? Part I

For everything there is a season, a time for every activity under heaven.
ECCLESIASTES 3:1

People often blame God for being slow to act in their recovery. They complain that they have to wait on him. To ensure that you're not unnecessarily extending your grueling wait time, try this prayer sequence with "R" designating a typical Recovery Prayer and "P" designating a typical Purpose Prayer. Notice how the two themes run on parallel tracks!

Lord, I ask you to . . .

R: Make me capable of being honest with myself and accepting my fatal flaws. Guide me through a searching and fearless moral inventory. In your mercy, remove the emotional defects that are keeping me trapped in addiction.

P: Grant me a character makeover so I can represent you with self-control, humility, and peace. I'm caught in a vicious cycle of procrastination, distractions, disorganization, and worry in regard to my life mission.

R: Give me meaningful, in-depth contact daily with family and friends, those with whom I can share my deeper-level recovery struggles with complete confidentiality.

P: Lead me to authentic people who will be my community of believers for mutual encouragement.

R: Teach me how to affirm my strengths and inherent abilities to support my recovery.

P: Teach me to utilize my strengths, abilities, and spiritual gifts for the Kingdom-building project you've assigned me.

R: Send me a sponsor or a recovery coach who loves Jesus and "gets me."

P: Guide me to historical, biblical, and modern-day role models and heroes who can teach me how to take my next action steps toward my life mission.

SOUL SEARCH

How might you phrase a prayer about your unhealthy and healthy passions from a recovery perspective? From a life-purpose perspective?

Infallible God, as I wait for your perfect timing, I'm thrilled to notice the parallel tracks on which recovery and life purpose run. It's like I can double-dip-pray!

P.U.R.P.O.S.E. Principle V: **O**pt Out of Self-Sabotaging Methods

Why the Delay? Part II

If [the vision] seems slow in coming, wait patiently, for it will take place.
HABAKKUK 2:3

To continue (from September 21) talking to God about unexpected delays in your life, pray these complementary prayers for your recovery ("R") and purpose ("P"):

Lord, I ask you to . . .

R: Remind me to eat healthfully, get regular exercise, and get enough sleep, so I can keep down my stress level and keep up my energy level.

P: Coach me to look after my health so my body and mind are fully functioning for the bold task at hand!

R: Free me from the dangers of temptation so I don't relapse and get discouraged.

P: Cause me to resist temptation so I may walk more steadily toward your end goal for my life.

R: Give me joy on my recovery journey, as well as in my roles at home, school, work, church, and within my community—that I might do my loving best.

P: Inspire me to enjoy the roles you've assigned me to do seasonally, as I begin to daydream about moving forward in a broader-reach arena.

R: Help me! I can't face any more loss, financial trouble, betrayal, depression, stress, anxiety, or discrimination! I fear for my sobriety.

P: Help me! I'm in crisis physically, emotionally, and spiritually—and losing focus on you.

R: Make me patient with those people who don't yet believe that you've done a mighty work in me.

P: Wait with me until the people you're sending me to serve are ready for me.

R: Give me your profound wisdom for the rocky road to recovery.

P: Give me your glorious wisdom for the demanding pathway to purpose.

SOUL SEARCH

How might you phrase a prayer about your trust in God's power, protection, and provisions from a recovery perspective? From a life-purpose perspective?

God of the nanosecond, I've decided that I'm going to trust you and your timing in my life! I pray expectantly and thank you in advance for all the miracles you've planned.

P.U.R.P.O.S.E. Principle V: **O**pt Out of Self-Sabotaging Methods

Leaping over Roadblocks

What a God! His road stretches straight and smooth. Every GOD-direction is road-tested. Everyone who runs toward him makes it.   PSALM 18:30 (*The Message*)

You've seen barricade signs that read, "Road Closed. Use Detour." Well, as I tried to write this particular devotional, I encountered roadblocks of every imaginable type, from computer nightmares to time-sensitive deadlines to a quirky illness to urgent family matters. I had to laugh about Murphy's Law: "Anything that can go wrong, will go wrong," considering that my maiden name is Murphy! What's been a roadblock for you: a loved one's agenda for your life; no network or leverage; a shortage of time, money, energy, or expertise; your daily struggle to stay sober?

We know that roadblocks can be from the enemy or just part of life, but often they're God's test of our character. We need to decide in advance whether we'll allow hurdles to block our spiritual growth, recovery steps, or life mission, or if we expect the Lord to lead us along his detour route and teach us to leap over roadblocks.

In my own fiasco, I found myself praying one of my favorite prayers, which was written by Isobel Kuhn, a twentieth century Canadian missionary to China and Thailand: "If this obstacle is from thee, Lord, I accept it; but if it is from Satan, I refuse him and all his works in the name of Calvary!" As I reflected on my situation, I made a list of how many roadblocks Isobel had faced to become a church planter, evangelist, and author of nine books. As a young woman, she overcame agnosticism and battled against thoughts of suicide after her fiancé was unfaithful. Later in life, she experienced a long delay in being sent to the mission field, partly due to a poor character reference but also due to the foreign uprising of 1927 and her forced bed rest from overwork. A few too many roadblocks for most people!

SOUL SEARCH

Would you consider yourself a defeatist, one who's stopped dead in your tracks when things go awry in your recovery or with your life assignment? What's been your greatest roadblock so far in any area?

God of the weary, I'm not letting anything stop me from living the sober, adventure-filled life you crafted specifically for me. Stretch your road out straight and smooth before me.

P.U.R.P.O.S.E. Principle V: Opt Out of Self-Sabotaging Methods

Victory in God

Refuse to focus on troubles, threats, delays, and roadblocks. Turn your addictive past and sober present over to God, so you can complete the future work he's assigned you.

☀ Meditate on the Assurance of God's Word

Even if you suffer for doing what is right, God will reward you for it. So don't worry or be afraid of their threats. 1 PETER 3:14

The LORD is a faithful God. Blessed are those who wait for his help. ISAIAH 30:18

I waited patiently for the LORD to help me, and he turned to me and heard my cry. He lifted me out of the pit of despair, out of the mud and the mire. He set my feet on solid ground and steadied me as I walked along. He has given me a new song to sing, a hymn of praise to our God. Many will see what he has done and be amazed. They will put their trust in the LORD. PSALM 40:1-3

☀ Humbly Talk with the Lord

Ask the Holy Spirit to teach you to stand steadfast in the face of delays.

Chat with the Lord about one roadblock that's particularly disconcerting.

☀ Take the *Life Purpose Coach* Challenge

You've heard the saying "Your fifteen minutes of fame." Well, that's milquetoast-living in comparison to having fifteen minutes of insane determination to obey what God is asking you to do for your relationships, recovery, restoration to him, or the realization of your anointed dream. Anybody can be famous for a few fading seconds, but after a few seconds of godly resolve, your life is never the same. Be obediently bold for fifteen seconds.

P.U.R.P.O.S.E. Principle VI:
Surrender All to Christ My King

When I empty myself of self, I'm able to be and do all God wants.

P.U.R.P.O.S.E. Principle VI: **S**urrender All to Christ My King

Surrender All

All kings will bow before [the Messiah], and all nations will serve him.   PSALM 72:11

Surrender is primarily a cognitive decision, not a tearful, fleeting emotion. Many surrender choices require you to go on a fact-finding mission to review all the particulars about them before you make a decision. While gathering information, it helps to reflect often on our passage, which refers to Christ as the Messiah, the one to whom we surrender everything, including our cars, jobs, children, successes, daily troubles, drug stashes, physical abuse, seasonal roles, and custom-fitted life missions. Abraham Kuyper, a Dutch politician and theologian, adds this insight: "There is not an inch of any sphere of life over which Jesus Christ does not say, 'Mine!'" Yes, Christ wants it all.

To get a clear visual of what your surrender looks like, try this: put something (that won't break when you drop it) in the palm of your hand. Now turn your hand over and release the object. Surrender is releasing something into your Creator's big hands and trusting him to catch it and do whatever is best with it. Hopefully, you'll try that exercise with an actual symbol of your addiction—anything from a donut to a credit card, beer can, pair of dice, or sex tape. If you do, reflect on whether, consciously or unconsciously, you expect to take it back later. Ask yourself if you've already placed it on an altar as a sacrifice to the Lord countless other times and then have run back to retrieve it. If you have, pause to pray and ask others to pray with you that this time will be forever.

SOUL SEARCH

Which worries you more about surrendering: that Christ might take what you surrender or that surrendering one thing might cause a domino effect of surrendering all? With what sponsor, recovery coach, or faithful friend could you discuss your answer?

King of all nations, thank you for acknowledging that surrender is a difficult step. You know how I've dreaded this moment, because I've felt you were upset with me for being so slow to investigate this topic. I appreciate your patience as I examine my heart and your glorious will for me.

P.U.R.P.O.S.E. Principle VI: **S**urrender All to Christ My King

Salvation Precedes Surrender

Everyone who calls on the name of the LORD will be saved.
ROMANS 10:13 and ACTS 2:21

The Bible emphasizes that you receive salvation through the one-time step of calling on the name of the Lord, of inviting Jesus to be your Savior, your Higher Power, your only hope of recovery. That's the moment the Holy Spirit first comes to dwell in you to guide you. If you've not yet made a faith commitment, would you like to accept the gift of spending eternity with Jesus in heaven? (See January 3.) If you're already a believer, will you allow God to call to mind the name and face of a specific person who needs Jesus, so you can pray for his or her salvation right now? Salvation is the big step before you begin to live a daily-sanctified life in which you surrender all things, one by one, to the care of Jesus.

In fact, the living proof of your salvation is a personal relationship with Jesus on earth—one in which you get to know him as if sharing a leisurely meal with him. Jesus sent a message to some spiritually poor church members: "Look! I stand at the door and knock. If you hear my voice and open the door, I will come in, and we will share a meal together as friends" (Revelation 3:20). These types of delicious interactions are not to be rushed moments like swallowing a quick snack. Jesus desires relaxed conversations like those that families are encouraged to share, dawdling over meals. He wants to fellowship with you, allowing you to debrief your life's ups and downs, including your character concerns, sobriety efforts, and lifetime assignment.

SOUL SEARCH

If you received Jesus into your heart today, with whom can you share that exciting news? If Jesus is your Higher Power, what stories can you tell of why life doesn't get any better than living a surrendered life of fellowship with him?

Savior of the world, the idea of having leisurely conversations with you sure got my attention, especially the part about you helping me with my character, recovery, and earthly labor of love. I ask for the pleasure of your constant company, your life-giving Presence. I also look forward to dining with you and all believers in heaven eternally at your glorious, beyond-imaginable banquet.

P.U.R.P.O.S.E. Principle VI: **S**urrender All to Christ My King

Surrender—a Lifelong Process

Take your everyday, ordinary life—your sleeping, eating, going-to-work, and walking-around life—and place it before God as an offering.   ROMANS 12:1 (*The Message*)

Surrender is a lifelong series of everyday decisions after your initial step of salvation. It's the sanctifying process of making well-thought-out, intentional choices to grant Christ lordship over all areas of your life—your sleeping, eating, going-to-work, and walking-around life. It's giving to God any person, place, thing, emotion, or behavior that's a tightly held addiction for you. It's a recurrent response to the pursuit of the Holy Spirit, as he teaches you truths that allow you to give up control of your life—and place it before God as an offering. Surrendering something is always a life-transforming step because it takes courage, is done out of loving obedience, and reaps earthly and eternal rewards.

Surrender means that we hand over our possessions, power, and control to someone in authority who demands it. Because Christians have free will, though, God won't force you to surrender your addictions, demigods, horrors, feeble hands, accomplishments, joy, family, or big dreams to him—that is, until he comes to reign supreme at the end of the world. In the meantime, surrender is a continual choice you make to say, "God, all that I am and all the good I have in my life have come from you. Regardless of what it may cost me, I serve at the pleasure of you, my King, offering you my all. I bow to you in humble adoration, asking you to take all my pressures, trepidations, codependencies, and the evil I've caused, as well as the loves of my life and my successes."

SOUL SEARCH

Will you pray faithfully about releasing your ransomed life to God, thus beginning to entrust all future recovery results to him? Will you consider handing over your exciting, strategic plans to him and yielding to his will for your life?

Lord of all lords, thank you for the gift of allowing me to explore this topic of surrender so I can make well-informed decisions rather than emotion-based responses. Show me now what I've been choosing to withhold from you and why.

P.U.R.P.O.S.E. Principle VI: **S**urrender All to Christ My King

Surrender What?

All the nations you have made will come and worship before you, O Lord; they will bring glory to your name.   PSALM 86:9 (NIV)

The United Nations Headquarters in New York flies the flags of 193 member nations from Afghanistan to Zimbabwe. Imagine for a moment that all the peoples of those nations are bowing in humble surrender to the Lord. What an impressive day that will be. Frankly, I want to prepare myself now. I haven't always been so willing, though. For years I begrudgingly asked, "What does God's law require me to surrender?" My personalized hymn was "I Surrender Some." I became an expert at portioning out a surrender tidbit every now and then—to try to stave off the promptings of the Holy Spirit.

Finally, I got it. I knew that God wanted these things in my life to be entrusted into his loving care:

- My smoking, drinking, and cursing. These were a triple threat to the credibility of any ministry he decided to give me, and I made a conscious choice in favor of God's plan.
- My children and grandsons. Eventually I was able to put them in God's capable hands because I understood that he loves them even more than I do.
- My lifetime dream and goals. I came to realize that I didn't really want to fulfill my wishes, but only God's.
- My income. I learned from Crown Financial Ministries and Ron Blue's financial series that I'm only an earthly steward of all God has entrusted to me.

The list of my next possible surrender items is endless, and I freely admit that I'll be working that list until I go home to be with Jesus.

SOUL SEARCH

Why does surrendering something to Jesus bring peace in that area? What seems to be inching its way toward your "Potential Surrender List": your Facebook postings, therapy appointments, exhaustion, church pew, raunchy reading material, self-injury, parent's health, God's breathtaking plan for your life?

Holy Spirit, you've been patient in allowing me to consider my surrender options. Thank you for making your supreme will clear to me along the way without overriding my free will. You're not a cruel dictator, which makes me love you all the more.

P.U.R.P.O.S.E. Principle VI: Surrender All to Christ My King

When to Surrender

At the name of Jesus every knee should bow, in heaven and on earth and under the earth, and every tongue confess that Jesus Christ is Lord, to the glory of God the Father.
PHILIPPIANS 2:10-11 (NIV)

This Bible passage is one of my favorites. Meditating on it has taught me that I'd rather surrender now of my own free will, than at the end of time with Satan and all the fallen angels. To me, the question is no longer *Will I surrender?* but rather *How soon will the Holy Spirit show me the value of surrendering a particular something?* I've learned the hard way that it's a good idea to pray for wisdom, weigh the facts, and lay down my arms when I'm first prompted to surrender. In fact, I can vividly recall when I argued with God for several years about surrendering my expensive zip code. He had begun to nudge me to sell my big home during the height of the real estate boom in 1995, but I stood my ground firmly against his instructions. Finally a few years later, I did agree to sell it—just as a buyer's market reared its ugly head! So when do we surrender? The sooner, the better, which can require checking in with God daily, hourly, and minute by minute.

I think the toughest challenge about surrendering is to remember that we're not bargaining with God. We can't say, for example, *God, I'll surrender my heroin addiction to you if you don't make me go into a treatment facility or if you'll limit my withdrawal symptoms.* Surrender is not a fast-talking, fancy-footwork negotiation. You either do it when prompted or you don't. Your choice.

SOUL SEARCH

What's the Holy Spirit nudging you to surrender: a fleshly sin, DUI, a family member, computer games, a corner office, a comfortable ministry, arrogance? If you were freed from all your fears about surrendering your life to God, what would you do right now to connect with his ordained purpose for your life?

Glorious One, I think the greatest reward of this surrender process is the privilege of getting to know you better as my unrivaled God. I look forward to being able soon to take off my heavy crown as ruler of my own universe. What a relief that will be!

P.U.R.P.O.S.E. Principle VI: **S**urrender All to Christ My King

Cost of Surrender

[Jesus said,] "You cannot become my disciple without giving up everything you own."
LUKE 14:33

While you've been on your recovery journey, has anyone talked to you about the potential cost of surrendering your life to Jesus? It's certainly an important conversation to have. In 1957 my faith-filled parents were actually told by mature believers, "You must prayerfully count the cost of surrendering your lives to Jesus, because he may take all that you offer." After praying, they wrote down everything they had: one car, some furniture, $300 cash, and their jobs. They also listed their six children, themselves, and everyone's friends—and they gave their all to the King of kings.

Within one week, we got unexpected military-transfer orders to move from California to Hawaii. With a promise of immediate housing, my mom quit her nursing job, and we all said good-bye to our friends. Upon arriving in Oahu, we were informed that the housing wait list was eight months and that our possessions couldn't be delivered to a temporary address. Money was soon depleted because of hotel and food expenses for our small tribe, along with repairs on our loaner car, which was a steering-impaired Nash Rambler. Then my toddler sister Mo fell headlong down the stairs, resulting in three days of seizure-type episodes. I later asked my dad, "How did you make it through all that?"

He said, "Jesus knew what we were going through; he'd never taken his eyes off us. He wanted us to learn to depend on him as our loving Papa-Abba-Daddy who would meet all our needs. When our backs were against the wall, he was teaching us the power of prayer, the importance of obedience, and the wisdom of giving him our full attention as the Lord of our lives. Kateness, he wanted us to look at our worsening situation as if he was God and we were not. We simply focused on him as our influential King with authority and troops."

Consider what it might cost you to surrender your life, with all its beauty and addictive insanity, to Jesus, who might take all that you offer.

SOUL SEARCH

What benefit do you see in surrendering these things to Jesus: your relationship struggles, vicious cycles of addiction and sobriety, and your own big plans? What's the cost to you of doing so?

My Papa-Abba-Daddy, help me release these things into your care: _____.

P.U.R.P.O.S.E. Principle VI: Surrender All to Christ My King
Choosing to Submit Humbly

Surrendering to Jesus is extremely difficult, but everything you choose to submit humbly into his care or return to him will work toward your good. Whether he decides to take what you've surrendered or not, you win, because you let go and let God!

☀ Meditate on the Assurance of God's Word

O people of Judah and Jerusalem, surrender your pride and power. Change your hearts before the LORD, or my anger will burn like an unquenchable fire because of all your sins.   JEREMIAH 4:4

The mountains watched and trembled. Onward swept the raging waters. The mighty deep cried out, lifting its hands to the LORD.   HABAKKUK 3:10

The Almighty himself will be your treasure. He will be your precious silver!   JOB 22:25

☀ Humbly Talk with the Lord

Talk to God about surrendering one specific area that's affecting your recovery (for example, your church mask, workaholism, miscarriage, nervous breakdown, gossip, or unrealistically high expectations).

Worship Jesus as the King of kings, who has all the power, influence, authority, and troops needed to help you stay sober and succeed in your humanly daunting life's work.

☀ Take the *Life Purpose Coach* Challenge

With the help of the Holy Spirit, calculate the true cost of surrendering a particular person, place, thing, emotion, or behavior. Ask yourself, *What might change if God decides to take what I've surrendered?* Then formulate a letting-go sentence like one of these:
- Surrendering my overeating to Jesus will cost me my hiding place for raw emotions.
- Surrendering my car to Jesus could cost me my means of transportation.
- Surrendering my cherished life dream to Jesus could cost me all my hope.

P.U.R.P.O.**S**.E. Principle VI: **S**urrender All to Christ My King

Who Has Surrendered?

The earth is the LORD's, and everything in it. The world and all its people belong to him. For he laid the earth's foundation on the seas and built it on the ocean depths.
PSALM 24:1-2

Dr. Bill Bright, founder of Campus Crusade, was asked how he knew what God was calling him to do after he and his wife decided in 1951 that they wanted to be total servants to Jesus. He responded, "We wrote out a contract and fully surrendered everything we owned or would own to Jesus. Approximately twenty-four hours later God gave me the vision we called Campus Crusade for Christ. I'm sure if there had been no surrender and contract with God, there would have been no vision."

Who else has surrendered? Jesus certainly did. The Virgin Mary and the first disciples did. And among countless others, Anna and Simeon, Hannah, the wise men, and hosts of angels have all surrendered. As we walk down Sobriety Street, we come to a crossroads where we, too, are faced with a surrender decision. Like Bill and Vonette Bright and others, we can either try to be the captains of our own destinies, or we can sign up as lifers in the Lord's army. We can predict where both roads will lead: the first into a deep ditch, the second to a life of significance.

We don't want to be Luke 6:49 people, about whom Jesus says, "Anyone who hears and doesn't obey is like a person who builds a house without a foundation. When the floods sweep down against that house, it will collapse into a heap of ruins." You'd think that nobody would willingly choose a ruined life, but billions do, including those trapped by the insanity of addiction. The good news is that "the earth is the LORD's, and everything in it. The world and all its people belong to him"—and he won't quit pursuing us.

SOUL SEARCH

When have you mouthed the words "Christ is Lord" and then stubbornly gone your own way, choosing an addictive idol over him? How do you feel about belonging to the Lord and surrendering to his recovery plan and purpose-filled master plan for your life?

Gracious Lord who reigns eternal, make me according to your heart and cause me to want to surrender all.

P.U.R.P.O.S.E. Principle VI: **S**urrender All to Christ My King

Jesus Surrendered

[Jesus cried out,] "I want your will to be done, not mine."   MATTHEW 26:39

We're told that Jesus surrendered to God the Father when crying out in the Garden of Gethsemane. But just before he said, "I want your will to be done, not mine," Jesus bowed with his face to the ground and actually prayed to be let out of his commitment. He begged, "My Father, if there is any way, get me out of this" (Matthew 26:39, *The Message*). That's how hard his ultimate submission was, and I often thank Jesus for acknowledging how difficult surrender is for humans.

Recently I was praying our focal verse aloud while busying myself in the kitchen. I was trying to soak it into my soul, when I caught myself repeating, who knows how many times, "My will be done, not yours." I didn't mean it—it was a total word mix-up, which I wish I could blame on dyslexia! It did make me pause, however, and think about how often we say, "My will be done" and mean it. Think about your own recovery, for example. Have you ever told God, "I love you, but . . ." or "I want to follow your plan, but . . ."? Does that hesitation step feel vaguely familiar? C. S. Lewis reminds us that a serious surrender process has no room for waffling, when he writes, "The petition, then, is not merely that I may patiently suffer God's will but also that I may vigorously do it. . . . 'Thy will be *done*—by me—now' brings one back to brass tacks."

Many times we hear, "Insanity is repeating the same mistakes and expecting different results." So true, and yet we repeatedly follow our own self-centered wills, which we know will end in sin, heartache, disappointment, and addiction; ergo, isn't it much more sane to surrender to God's will for our lives right away?

SOUL SEARCH

What have you surrendered to the Lord: your recovery, fears, soothing behaviors, financial worries, parents, bitterness, the divine urge he placed in your heart? Like Jesus, have you ever asked your heavenly Father to release you from a surrender commitment?

Jesus of Gethsemane, teach me to pray, "Thy perfect will be done." I truly want nothing more or less than that.

P.U.R.P.O.S.E. Principle VI: **S**urrender All to Christ My King
The Virgin Mary Surrendered

Mary responded, "I am the Lord's servant. May everything you have said about me come true." And then the angel left her.   LUKE 1:38

You know the surrender story that's told every Christmas about the Virgin Mary, the humble girl whose God-sent assignment was to become the mother of Jesus through the power of the Holy Spirit. By agreeing, she endangered her life, knowing that she could be stoned to death for being a pregnant single woman. What was it about Mary that made her able to surrender her plans to the will of God? It had to be her faith, because only abiding faith in the all-powerful one can overcome a fear of surrendering all. As Hebrews 11:1 teaches, "Faith . . . gives us assurance about things we cannot see." In your walk toward recovery, do you have abiding faith in God's power to help you overcome your fear of surrendering all your personal plans, problematic relationships, places of temptation, and pet sins? Many faith-filled people have gone before us to guide us:

"It was by faith that Abraham obeyed when God called him to leave home and go to another land that God would give him as his inheritance. He went without knowing where he was going" (Hebrews 11:8).

"It was by faith that the people of Israel marched around Jericho for seven days, and the walls came crashing down" (Hebrews 11:30).

It was by faith that four friends of an invalid lowered him down through a roof to be healed by Jesus, and "seeing their faith, Jesus said to the paralyzed man, 'My child, your sins are forgiven.' . . . 'Stand up, pick up your mat, and go home'" (Mark 2:5, 11).

It was by faith that the one of the criminals on a cross spoke the truth that was revealed to him about Christ, and Jesus answered him, "I assure you, today you will be with me in paradise" (Luke 23:43).

With faith like Mary's and the others', we can agree to surrender.

SOUL SEARCH

In what way will your faith help you surrender all your plans and problems and accept God's call on your life? Do you firmly believe that God will help you recover?

All-Powerful One, give me the kind of faith that will cure me of my fear of surrendering.

The First Disciples Surrendered

Jesus called out to [Simon and Andrew], "Come, follow me, and I will show you how to fish for people!" And they left their nets at once and followed him. MARK 1:17-18

Simon and his brother Andrew were rugged, unschooled, Galilean fishermen and the first disciples Jesus called to follow him. Shortly thereafter, a little farther up the shoreline of the Galilean Sea, Jesus saw James and John repairing their fishing nets. We're told, "He called them at once, and they also followed him, leaving their father, Zebedee, in the boat with the hired men" (Mark 1:20). Like Simon, Andrew, James, and John, we're called to follow Jesus. Our first step is to accept him as our Savior, but our lifetime commitment is to follow him as our Lord on a daily basis. Will you yield to God's urgent call on your life, including every single recovery step he wants you to take, every seasonal role he wants you to fulfill, and every difficult and joyful aspect of his specific purpose for your life?

Anita, a believer and recovering alcoholic, food addict, and workaholic, recently wrote to me. She shared this insight about surrendering her life to Christ: "What helped me most was this comment from my sponsor: 'The difference between short- and long-term recovery can be summed up in two words: community and surrender. You can't do it alone, but in community with Jesus as your Higher Power, you will succeed!'" The advice worked; Anita's celebrating twenty-one years of sobriety.

Consider surrendering one of these things now: your anger, despair, envy, impatience, legalism, control issues, notoriety, most-convincing excuse, or even your leadership skills, creativity, or talents.

SOUL SEARCH

What one thing are you willing to surrender to help you follow God's sobriety plan for your life? What else do you need to commit into Jesus' loving care so you're better prepared to complete your distinct assignment on earth?

Holy Servant Jesus, it's hard to grasp that the first disciples responded immediately to your call on their lives. I want to be like that. Will you teach me how to surrender things in my life, as if I'm responding to a fire alarm? I'll be eternally grateful.

P.U.R.P.O.S.E. Principle VI: **S**urrender All to Christ My King

One Surrendered and One Didn't

You will keep in perfect peace all who trust in you, all whose thoughts are fixed on you!
Trust in the LORD always, for the LORD GOD is the eternal Rock.   ISAIAH 26:3-4

In 2007, I spoke at a weekend retreat on the topic of surrender, using the words *own* and *loan* to make the point that God owns everything that's good, holy, or useful to him, and he often loans things to us. For example, our health, families, best friends, mission trips, bank accounts, and possessions are simply on loan to us. We're to be good stewards of what we've been given to manage, shepherd, and nurture. The retreat-goers had a private time of twenty minutes during which they were encouraged to consider surrendering one item from a list of one hundred options. Think for a moment about what you might have been willing to surrender, had you been participating: perhaps something on loan to you, like your child, home, earning power, and goals, or something of your own sinful creation that God can use for good, like your addiction crutches, regrets, or stubbornness.

A month after that retreat, I got a phone call from the women's ministry director about a distraught attendee, a woman whose adult son had just died. Apparently, this mother was furious at me for bringing up the topic of surrendering our children. She felt that because she'd adamantly refused to do so in her private time, God had punished her. (Such deep grief talking.) The wife of the deceased man, though, who'd also attended, had a great peace about her husband's passing and said she'd be forever grateful for the opportunity of surrendering him to God.

Our Creator's perfect will is always done, but he invites us to partner with him through our surrender. According to A. W. Tozer, a Christian pastor and author who died in 1963, "We are called to an everlasting preoccupation with God," and that includes surrendering all to him to do with as he wishes.

SOUL SEARCH

What are you refusing to surrender to the Lord? How could surrendering your recovery leadership team, sponsor, meetings, steps, and relapses give you peace and enhance your specific life mission?

Owner of all, I'm only one surrender moment away from living a transformed life.
Guide me through!

P.U.R.P.O.S.E. Principle VI: **S**urrender All to Christ My King

I Surrender My Indifference

Since you are like lukewarm water, neither hot nor cold, I will spit you out of my mouth!
REVELATION 3:16

Woe to the lukewarm and lackadaisical New Testament church in Laodicea (modern-day Turkey)! The Lord was not pleased with the wealthy church's compromised teachings or with its spiritually poor, apathetic members. Jesus described the uncommitted bunch as "wretched and miserable and poor and blind and naked" (Revelation 3:17). Their indifference triggered his comment that he'd spit them out of his mouth. What about your own faith? Have you grown indifferent to spiritual growth or lax in your recovery efforts?

Jesus referred to the disgusting lukewarm water supply that flowed by aqueduct into their city, knowing that they'd get his point immediately. Their water came from the hot mineral springs of Hierapolis, but by the time it reached them, it was nauseatingly tepid and had a nasty-tasting buildup of mineral deposits. If you've ever had tepid, mineral-laden water, you know it's repulsive and can even induce vomiting.

We must look at our own carelessness and laziness regarding those things that are important to God, especially at our relationship with him and our sober living that enables us to do his will. Imagine for a moment that you're a lukewarm Christian, sitting right now in a Turkish café overlooking a river, waiting to meet Jesus. After you chat awhile, he says to you, "Because I correct and discipline everyone I love, I expect you to be diligent in your spiritual growth and in your recovery efforts, turning now from your indifference" (adapted from Revelation 3:19). After you fall off your chair, will you consider surrendering your indifference to him at this very moment?

SOUL SEARCH

In what way have you been lukewarm about such things as growing in your faith, maintaining your sobriety, or pursuing God's dream for your life? What small step could you take now to begin to change that wretched situation?

My Sweet Intercessor, Jesus, pray for me in my hour of need. Quite often I feel so disconnected from committed believers and so unimpassioned about my life that I don't even like my own tepid self. Do whatever you need to do to keep me from living a lukewarm life.

P.U.R.P.O.S.E. Principle VI: **S**urrender All to Christ My King

I Want to Surrender

Surrender is the willingness to entrust both your your healthy and diseased parts—your holy and idolatrous sides—to the care of your Maker. The process involves believing that God will do a better job than you can with such things and then waving a white flag of surrender to release control of them.

☀ Meditate on the Assurance of God's Word

God's way is perfect. All the LORD's promises prove true.   PSALM 18:30

As I learn your righteous regulations, I will thank you by living as I should!
PSALM 119:7

I bow before your holy Temple as I worship. I praise your name for your unfailing love and faithfulness; for your promises are backed by all the honor of your name.
PSALM 138:2

☀ Humbly Talk with the Lord

Thank Jesus for being such an incredible model of surrender for you.

Ask the Holy Spirit to guide you through timely surrender discussions that produce in you a faith that inordinately blesses your continued sobriety and burgeoning life mission.

☀ Take the *Life Purpose Coach* Challenge

Garth Brooks wrote a classic song, "Unanswered Prayers," about a guy who begged God to allow him to marry his high school sweetheart, but it never happened. Check out the chorus about God's great wisdom in knowing what's best: "Sometimes I thank God for unanswered prayers. Remember when you're talkin' to the man upstairs that just because he doesn't answer, doesn't mean he don't care. Some of God's greatest gifts are unanswered prayers." Take a few minutes to think about your unanswered prayers. Ask yourself how surrendering them upfront by praying, *Your perfect will be done, Lord,* would be a great statement of faith.

P.U.R.P.O.S.E. Principle VI: **S**urrender All to Christ My King
How Do I Surrender?

The life you see me living is not "mine," but it is lived by faith in the Son of God, who loved me and gave himself for me. GALATIANS 2:20 (*The Message*)

Living by faith in the loving, generous Son of God means that we trust Jesus to the point of surrendering our lives to him and refusing to doubt his sovereign plans for us. It's only his purpose that will prevail, so the sooner we choose to live by faith, the sooner we can get on with his promised adventure. But how easy to miss God's will when we're filled with vain ambition, refusing to forgive someone, or saying, "Poor me. Poor me. Pour me another drink."

To live a more faith-filled life, try what I call the Five Stages of Surrender: Revelation, Investigation, Realization, Transformation, and Declaration.

- Stage One: Listen to what the Holy Spirit reveals to you about what he'd like you to surrender without compulsion.
- Stage Two: Investigate any surrender topic the Holy Spirit suggests so you can get all the facts to make a well-thought-out decision.
- Stage Three: Prayerfully come to realize that you're in agreement with the Holy Spirit's surrender recommendation.
- Stage Four: Lean in to the transformation process.
- Stage Five: Publicly declare that it was only by God's incomprehensible grace and power that you were able to surrender. (See October 10–14 for how these stages impact your recovery.)

David Livingstone, an early medical missionary-explorer in Africa, summarizes for us that surrender will send us out, burden us with what burdens the heart of God, and cause us to sever ties that bind us to anything but God and God's work. He prayed, "Lord, send me anywhere, only go with me; lay any burden on me, only sustain me; and sever every tie, but the tie that binds me to Thy service and Thy heart." This is a great prayer for us today.

SOUL SEARCH

Are you willing to live by faith and surrender the doubts you have about your ability to recover from your toughest addiction? How will doing so bless your life mission?

Dynamic Spirit of God, I'm ready to live by faith. Teach me to surrender.

P.U.R.P.O.S.E. Principle VI: **S**urrender All to Christ My King

Stage One of Surrendering: Revelation

Listen to what the Holy Spirit reveals to you about
what he'd like you to surrender without compulsion.

It is not by force nor by strength, but by my Spirit, says the LORD of Heaven's Armies.
ZECHARIAH 4:6

The Lord of Heaven's Armies said that no mighty mountain of difficulty would stand in Zerubbabel's way of finishing the Temple (see Zechariah 4:7). We, too, are assured of the providence and power of the Most High. We don't have to face situations by mustering our own force or strength, but we can overcome difficulties by the power of God's Spirit, who sheds spiritual light on how to proceed.

The same applies to how the Holy Spirit can help you surrender an addiction that's overtaken you. You don't need to muscle up; instead, be still and prepare your heart to listen to what he'd like to reveal to you. Through his supernatural power, he might choose to open your eyes wide to the privilege of God's higher calling on your life—your marriage, parenting, grandparenting, ministry, seminary education, or leadership position at work amid believers, seekers, and atheists. These types of noble endeavors beg you to put your sobriety first to make it last. With your mind awakened and your heart readied, he can then reveal what he'd like you to surrender.

God's Spirit has numerous other ways to get you to listen to a surrender opportunity he wants to reveal. For example, he can use your pain, illness, a crisis of faith, a long delay, or tough consequences. You can't blame him for all your negative circumstances, but you can thank him for using problems to reveal truth. He's never shy about taking advantage of such things as a hangover, detox program, arrest, jail time, or financial ruin to get your attention. Regardless of the Spirit's method of revelation, you can look forward to proceeding in his strength to reap the benefits of surrender.

SOUL SEARCH

How can you quiet your soul so you can hear the truth the Spirit would like to reveal to you? What surrender opportunity do you anticipate in regard to how your addictive behaviors are interfering with God's call on your life?

The Lord of Heaven's Armies, thank you for loving me, even when I refuse to surrender what your Spirit has revealed to me. Bear with me, I pray.

P.U.R.P.O.S.E. Principle VI: **S**urrender All to Christ My King

Stage Two of Surrendering: Investigation

Investigate any surrender topic the Holy
Spirit suggests, so you can get all the facts
to make a well-thought-out decision.

It takes wisdom to build a house, and understanding to set it on a firm foundation;
It takes knowledge to furnish its rooms with fine furniture and beautiful draperies.
PROVERBS 24:3-4 (*The Message*)

After Stage One in the surrender process (sensing when God's Spirit reveals a surrender opportunity), you're ready to keep moving forward. Stage Two is an investigative challenge to pursue wisdom, understanding, and knowledge to help you make a wise surrender choice. It's a time of using logic, rather than letting your heart take the lead. To make an informed decision about any surrender topic, you can do such things as make a phone call, listen to a sermon, do online or library research, talk with a therapist, or attend a seminar.

For example, to help you surrender greed, you could do a Bible study on tithing; to surrender nicotine, you could investigate wearing a patch; to surrender your codependency, you could attend an Al-Anon meeting; or to surrender your anger, you could check out anger-management classes. As a recovering Dr Pepper–aholic who wanted to surrender that burden to the Lord, I had to examine what phosphoric acid does to teeth and bones, what sixteen tablespoons of sugar does to insulin levels, what caffeine does to sleep patterns, and what dehydration does to a body and mind. (To investigate what surrender could cost you, see September 30.)

Proverbs 2:1-3 urges us to make insight our priority. We're to collect and guard God's counsel, tune our ears to wisdom, and set our hearts on understanding. The passage continues in verse 4, advising us to go "searching for [insight] like a prospector panning for gold, like an adventurer on a treasure hunt" (*The Message*). Take time to explore anything that's blocking your sobriety, healthy relationships, and the fulfillment of your heaven-sent purpose on earth.

SOUL SEARCH

What recovery topic will you investigate further? What research would help you become all you're designed to be and do all God has reserved for you to do?

Most Gracious Lord, sit with me as I investigate how I can surrender specific things
to you.

P.U.R.P.O.S.E. Principle VI: **S**urrender All to Christ My King

Stage Three of Surrendering: Realization

Prayerfully come to realize that you're in agreement
with the Holy Spirit's surrender recommendation.

Those who have been ransomed by the LORD will return . . . filled with joy and gladness.
ISAIAH 51:11

It's great coming to the realization that you're sick and tired of being sick and tired and that you need to get with the program, literally! But even more important is the realization that you've been ransomed. Jesus paid the ultimate price to ensure your safety. You've been rescued from a dull, monotonous life, from slavery to sin, from the torture of addiction, from hellfire and brimstone, and from naysayers who don't believe you've got an intriguing assignment on earth.

When you truly take hold of the fact that you've been ransomed, your sorrow turns to gladness and you want to do something that shows your gratitude. It's then that you become willing to move into Stage Three of the surrender process—that you prayerfully come to realize that you're in agreement with the Holy Spirit's surrender recommendation. In a healthy world, he might prompt you to surrender something simple, like your education, vacation budget, small-group members, or workout schedule. But in the recovery world, most of his requests are going to revolve around surrendering your solidly embedded defense mechanisms.

Think about it. What do you hold onto most tightly, if not your desire to distort the reality of your addictive behavior enough to allow the behavior to continue? Defense mechanisms separate an addict from reality. They allow you to define the problem as anything but the addiction, so God's Spirit must help you realize the truth about denial, rationalization, justification, minimization, projection, blaming, hostility, regression, repression, fantasy, hypochondria, acting out, emotional displacement, withdrawal, and distractions. When the Holy Spirit comes alongside you with a huge dose of reality, he's prompting you to surrender all that stands in the way of God's best for you.

SOUL SEARCH

When have you experienced the joy and gladness of having been ransomed from an empty life? What has God's Spirit helped you realize about your addictive lifestyle?

My Only True Hope, I think it's past time for me to surrender my "fixing me" to you.

P.U.R.P.O.S.E. Principle VI: **S**urrender All to Christ My King

Stage Four of Surrendering: Transformation

Lean in to the transformation process.

Don't copy the behavior and customs of this world, but let God transform you into a new person by changing the way you think. ROMANS 12:2

I've been upset with the apostle Paul for stating this verse in such a matter-of-fact way, as if it's easy! It's probably the hardest thing we'll ever be asked to do, not just for those with recovery issues but for even the holiest soul. Here's Paul's bottom-line imperative to us:

1. Live in the evil world, but don't be like all the evil people.
2. Allow God to transform us, whatever that really means in non-Christian lingo.
3. Expect that somehow, miraculously, we'll become able to think like Christ.

You can hear my frustration; this is horribly hard. But let me quit complaining and offer what morsels I've found to be true:

1. We—including all those who've ever sinned, felt hopeless, or been addicted— are expected to be good-to-great role models for those who are hurting in this evil world. One of our most important life purposes is to make sure that others will come to know, love, trust, and glorify God.
2. God is in the transformation business; he moves us across all human barriers of evil to form us into the people he wants us to be. He renovates our lives, changes our hearts, makes over our characters, and shifts our thinking.
3. Becoming like Christ and thinking like him is a supernatural process that we have to let God do for us.

Your willingness to surrender to the transformation process can't be a New Year's resolution that's a blip on your radar. Tell God you're in this for keeps. "Then you will learn to know God's will for you, which is good and pleasing and perfect" (Romans 12:2). What a reward to know and live out God's outrageously great plan, including his sobriety plan!

SOUL SEARCH

What do you have to lose by surrendering to the transformation process? To gain?

Creator God, help me surrender to your divine will for my life. Transform me.

P.U.R.P.O.S.E. Principle VI: **S**urrender All to Christ My King

Stage Five of Surrendering: Declaration

Publicly declare that it was only by God's
incomprehensible grace and power
that you were able to surrender.

I have chosen to be faithful; I have determined to live by [God's] regulations.
PSALM 119:30

Have you ever felt that the Holy Spirit was prompting you to surrender something—perhaps a good, evil, or neutral person, place, thing, emotion, or behavior? If so, did you do your homework to investigate all it would entail to surrender that to Jesus, including how much it might cost you if he actually took it from you? Hopefully, you even came to the realization that you wanted to obey the Spirit's prompt faithfully, causing you to set your sights on becoming more like Christ. It's then that you would have allowed God to transform your thinking and alter your behavior patterns, including those related to addiction. After all these difficult surrender stages comes the easiest and final one: to publicly declare that it was only by God's incomprehensible grace and power that you were able to surrender.

This official, humble declaration tells others that you're choosing to give up control of your own will. You might decide to write out a statement in your recovery journal and tell your accountability partner about it, or you might use some other creative method to memorialize your commitment. Just as people declare their love, declare their intentions to run for office, declare war, and declare victory, so it's the same with your public declaration of surrender. You're declaring that you love Jesus and intend to follow his plan for your life; you're declaring war on Satan and claiming the victory that only God can give.

SOUL SEARCH

What public declaration have you made previously (for example, about love or hate, peace or war, perseverance or quitting, freedom or fear) that helped determine your next action step? In regard to your sobriety, what do you wish you'd have the courage to declare as your surrender commitment to the Lord?

Spirit of Life, thank you for walking me through the five stages of surrender. Help me learn to listen to what you reveal and also to investigate the facts, agree with you, allow you to transform my thinking and behavior, and tell others how grateful I am that I didn't have to "go this alone."

P.U.R.P.O.S.E. Principle VI: Surrender All to Christ My King
Letting God's Spirit Lead

Your recovery and your life mission depend on your willingness to trust God to care for you around the clock, as you listen and respond to his Spirit's surrender recommendations. Prepare your heart to trust God and cooperate with his Spirit.

☀ Meditate on the Assurance of God's Word

[The Lord] will order his angels to protect you wherever you go. They will hold you up with their hands so you won't even hurt your foot on a stone.   PSALM 91:11-12

As the deer longs for streams of water, so I long for you, O God. I thirst for God, the living God. When can I go and stand before him?   PSALM 42:1-2

The Spirit teaches you everything you need to know, and what he teaches is true—it is not a lie.   1 JOHN 2:27

☀ Humbly Talk with the Lord

Praise God that you're responsible only for your daily efforts to stay sober and that he's responsible for the results.

Thank God's Spirit for loving you enough to patiently and consistently guide you through the surrender process without bullying you into submission.

☀ Take the *Life Purpose Coach* Challenge

John referred to himself as "the disciple Jesus loved" (John 13:23; 19:26; 21:7, 20). Write down an endearing name you'd like Jesus to call you, so you can reflect on it often when surrendering gets difficult and hope for living a meaningful life is illusive. Some possibilities:

Sarah means "princess" (see footnote to Genesis 17:15).

Peter means "rock" (see Matthew 16:18).

Hephzibah means "my delight" (see footnote to Isaiah 62:4).

P.U.R.P.O.S.E. Principle VI: **S**urrender All to Christ My King
Surrendering Trouble Spots

We don't look at the troubles we can see now; rather, we fix our gaze on things that cannot be seen. 2 CORINTHIANS 4:18

Recently I had an antique chair delivered from a secondhand store, and I immediately nestled myself deep into it to say my nighttime prayers. Out of the corner of my eye, though, my gaze fixated on unmistakable trouble that was heading in my direction. I saw a tiny, white worm crawling out of the fabric, directly toward my flung-open mouth! Sometimes we just don't have much choice about certain, in-our-face troubles—things like creepy crawlers, sudden illness, or natural disaster.

The Bible is clear, however, that we're not to fix our attention on, become obsessed by, and worry ourselves to death about our present, temporary predicaments. It admonishes us to surrender our transitory worries and trials to our King. Because they cause us to look to him for consolation, they will produce eternal glory that will vastly outweigh them (see 2 Corinthians 4:17). Over what earthbound problems are you fretting and making yourself sick: a lawsuit, in-laws moving in, scorn, weariness, clutter, transportation, a court order, an intervention with a loved one?

Our passage is full of wisdom, as it continues in the second half of verse 18: "For the things we see now will soon be gone, but the things we cannot see will last forever." When we internalize this truth, we're able to fix our gaze on the unseen things, like everlasting happiness with God. But how do we learn to focus on such ethereal things? The answer is by taking daily, incremental steps to surrender whatever troublesome areas of our lives are keeping us from God's plan—for example, by accepting our humanness and surrendering our relapses, people-pleasing tendencies, dishonesty, disappointments, and encumbrances.

Socrates used to say, "Let him that would move the world, first move himself." Will you start now to move your focus off your troubles and cast your eyes heavenward?

SOUL SEARCH

Will you fix your gaze on eternity and begin to surrender your today-troubles? How will this perspective support your recovery efforts and God's infinitely wise plan for your life?

Radiant One, I choose to fix my gaze on a life of everlasting happiness with you!

P.U.R.P.O.S.E. Principle VI: **S**urrender All to Christ My King
I Surrender My Humanness and Relapses

To all who mourn in Israel, he will give a crown of beauty for ashes, a joyous blessing instead of mourning, festive praise instead of despair. ISAIAH 61:3

Have you ever grieved deeply—perhaps even wept over—your humanness as it was demonstrated in your judgmental tone or unrestrained anger raining down like blackened ash on an unfortunate recipient? Have you mourned how humanly prideful you've been about refusing to surrender a resource, crisis, or prospect to Jesus? Have you despaired over your loneliness, frustrations, relapses, or loss of faith? Only God's grace can help us come to grips with the vastness of our human frailty and surrender such utter brokenness.

Was there an online tutorial we somehow missed about how to examine our blatant character flaws, weaknesses, and addictions, while simultaneously comprehending that God will always love us unconditionally? It's hard enough to believe that when we're weak, he can show up to make us as strong as a mighty oak (see the last part of Isaiah 61:3). Why would we dare to hope that he'll lovingly top that miracle and make good out of the worst parts of us?

Desmond Tutu of South Africa, an Anglican archbishop who's been awarded the Nobel, Gandhi, and Sydney Peace Prizes, writes about the way God uses a human being's brokenness: "It is through this weakness and vulnerability that most of us learn empathy and compassion and discover our soul." So just as you pray empathetically for others to accept their humanness, pray for yourself. And just as you've shown compassion to others regarding their relapses, show compassion to yourself. Once you admit that you're an imperfect person, you can begin to surrender your denial, blame, and self-hate. In this way, you'll discover that God has exchanged your ashes for a crown of beauty, your mourning for a blessing, and your despair for praise.

SOUL SEARCH

Will you accept your humanness and acknowledge your relapses, surrendering them to the Lord now? What crown of beauty, joyous blessing, or festive praise could God create out of your ashes, mourning, and despair that would allow you to live the life you've only dreamed of living for his glory?

"O Lord, forgive what I have been, sanctify what I am, and order what I shall be."*

---

* The original author of this prayer is unknown, although it has sometimes been attributed to Thomas Watson.

P.U.R.P.O.**S**.E. Principle VI: **S**urrender All to Christ My King

I Surrender My People-Pleasing

Obviously, I'm not trying to win the approval of people, but of God. If pleasing people were my goal, I would not be Christ's servant.   GALATIANS 1:10

Bill Cosby, among others, has said, "I don't know the key to success, but the key to failure is trying to please everybody." How true! That's a Galatians 1:10 principle and a proven adage that is preached in recovery meetings: an addict's sure formula for failure is trying to please everyone. Why's that? Because efforts to please everyone, in lieu of pleasing God, drive up our stress level, causing even the sober to seek artificial relief.

God has not given us relationships so we can kowtow to people in servitude, following their agenda for our lives instead of being Christ's servants. Rather, God has blessed us with relationships for two biblically based reasons, at minimum. The first is for mutual counsel, as Proverbs 27:17 teaches: "As iron sharpens iron, so a friend sharpens a friend." In conversation, we stir each other to reflect deeply, so we each become wiser, healthier, and more loving people. The second reason is best described in Galatians 6:1: "If another believer is overcome by some sin, you who are godly should gently and humbly help that person back onto the right path." Obviously, we must never risk falling into temptation ourselves as we share a person's burdens, but erring Christians have a right to prayerful empathy.

When we surrender our people-pleasing tendencies into Jesus' hands, acknowledging that we're his humble stewards only, we ward off stress-induced addictions. It's then that we can do our boldest lifetime work for the Lord, our only Master.

SOUL SEARCH

In what ways have you been a people-pleaser or held fast to a related stress-causing belief that good works done for lots of people will earn you a place in heaven? Is God asking you to stand by someone in need or run toward self-preservation?

My Altogether Lovely Christ, I think often of what the father of the demon-possessed boy exclaimed to you: "I do believe, but help me overcome my unbelief!"* Lord, allow me to modify his prayer to this: "I do want to surrender my people-pleasing bent, but help me overcome my unwillingness to surrender it." Respond to my cry for help, as you did to his.

* Mark 9:24.

P.U.R.P.O.S.E. Principle VI: **S**urrender All to Christ My King

I Surrender My Dishonesty

Yes, what joy for those whose record the LORD has cleared of guilt, whose lives are lived in complete honesty! PSALM 32:2

Liar, liar, pants on fire. We chanted that as kids on the schoolyard, only to grow up and find fingers pointing at us as the liars. Women fudge about their age, weight, and hair color; men lie about their salaries, golf scores, and secret fears; and teenagers are experts at hoodwinking, fibbing, and posing. Grandpas trump up stories; authors fabricate; and magicians use sleight of hand. Con artists defraud, and churchgoers put up facades and tell little, white lies. What about you? Are you a sweet talker, spin doctor, or image manager? Do you mislead with posturing or fake behavior or by turning on the charm?

Addicts are liars, so the first casualty of addiction is truth. Desperate addicts lie about obtaining, hiding, using, and distributing substances of choice. Cunning addicts weave webs of lies to bury secrets and avoid painful consequences. The catch-22 is that the more they lie, the more they need to lie to cover their tracks, which increases their shame, which makes them want to use even more. Do you still need your lies, or can God have them? I ask because the surrender process involves evaluating what might change if God decides to keep the dishonesty you relinquish. These suggestions can help in surrendering the liar's life:

- Remember that nothing changes if nothing changes.
- If you start to exaggerate, mask, or deceive, correct yourself midsentence.
- Don't ever lie to your family, sponsor, counselor, doctor, or recovery group.
- Be a Proverbs 15:4 encourager: "Gentle words are a tree of life; a deceitful tongue crushes the spirit."
- Choose friends who don't put on pretense or make unwarranted claims.
- Don't err on the side of self-deprecation when being honest.
- Stay out of other people's business, even if you'd rather deflect attention off yourself onto other liars.

SOUL SEARCH

What lie are you telling yourself or others? How will surrendering your dishonesty help you to heal and to serve God wholeheartedly with your life?

Spirit of Understanding, I know that "the LORD detests lying lips, but he delights in those who tell the truth."* Make me genuine.

---

* Proverbs 12:22.

P.U.R.P.O.S.E. Principle VI: **S**urrender All to Christ My King

I Surrender My Disappointments

My work seems so useless! I have spent my strength for nothing and to no purpose. Yet I leave it all in the LORD's hand; I will trust God for my reward. ISAIAH 49:4

Our prophetic passage from Isaiah about Christ gives us insight as to how the Savior of the world felt about his three-year public ministry on earth. Isaiah said, "My work seems so useless!" Christ had been despised and rejected by many who didn't understand him or his life's work. He knew he'd be rewarded for obeying God; he knew that, ultimately, every knee would bow to him; yet the current results of his selfless toil were not proportionate to his rigorous investment. What profoundly impresses me about Jesus' surrender to his Father's will in the garden of Gethsemane is that he did so despite grieving over something that's rarely discussed: his disappointment.

If, like Jesus, you surrender your disappointments regarding criticism of your ministry, defamation of your character, and the allegedly useless investment of your energy, talent, and time, you can take comfort in knowing that your faithful, self-sacrificing work will be honored in due course. If additionally you surrender your addictions, obsessions, and compulsions, despite your discouragement, fatigue, and supposed failure, you'll also be blessed. Our partnership with God is 10 percent our dedication and 90 percent his perfect plan, timing, wisdom, and results. Any courageous effort we exert to support our sobriety and the cause of God will be rewarded in relative amount to our humble attempts.

In the meantime, allow the Spirit to deepen your love for Jesus, which will inspire you to "trust and obey, for there's no other way"—as the familiar hymn states about surrender. This softening of your heart will invite the Holy Spirit to reveal whatever he'd like you to surrender, whether it's your greatest strength or most consequential sin, your happiest day or darkest hour, or your grandest accomplishment or most colossal failure. Regardless of your joys or disappointments, surrender all to him.

SOUL SEARCH

What's been the biggest disappointment of your life? Are you willing to surrender it now, along with your highest expectations for your recovery and life mission?

My All in All, I have no room in my life to store all my disappointments. Like a computer dumping its data, I give all my gigabits of disillusionment to you.

P.U.R.P.O.S.E. Principle VI: **S**urrender All to Christ My King

I Surrender My Encumbrances

Those who use the things of the world should not become attached to them. For this world as we know it will soon pass away. 1 CORINTHIANS 7:31

Don't live for this fading world by making material things the chief objects of your affection; instead, use things rightly, acting moderately with possessions, leisure, sustenance, clothing, and prescriptions. First John 2:16 adds, "The world offers only a craving for physical pleasure, a craving for everything we see, and pride in our achievements and possessions. These are not from the Father, but are from this world." Think for a moment about how material idols, including staples and necessities with which you've become obsessed, have enticed you to sin, hoard, or squander them on things that satisfy you. In the legal jargon of encumbrances, this means that something holds a claim on you, that it's a hindrance.

I've recently taken a traveling-light vow, partly because God created me to be a minimalist who happens to adore decluttering and partly because I know this lightening of my load makes me mobile enough for God to use me anywhere in the world. In 2010–11, he rewarded my mobility mind-set with a renter to take care of my home and car. I'm still floored by how he orchestrated for me to spend a year in Maui writing three books, three weeks in South Africa giving twenty-three speeches, and eight months at my elderly dad's home, taking care of him before he passed away. I actually got the privilege of helping my father sort through all his personal items, paper clip by paper clip, until all he owned was a bed, a recliner, his Bible and devotionals, and some clothes and toiletries. I can't imagine having bowed to encumbrances, which would have caused me to miss God's seasonal plans for my life. Alas, I've started accumulating stuff again, but I'm trying to remember to hold material things loosely, so that the purpose of my life is not affluence but influence to a hurting world.

SOUL SEARCH

How could downsizing your possessions and obsessions increase your sobriety? What seasonal or long-term service opportunity might God gift to the less-is-more you?

God of my life, excess is causing me to stumble. Give me what I need to surrender more humbly and send packing those things that are my appetite's abusive indulgences.

P.U.R.P.O.S.E. Principle VI: **S**urrender All to Christ My King
Surrender Opportunities

Surrendering your troubles to Jesus, to whom praise belongs, is only possible if you love him more than you love a particular idol, such as worry, fear, anxiety, busyness, manipulation, or addiction. You must choose God or a god.

☀ Meditate on the Assurance of God's Word

Moses told his father-in-law everything the LORD had done to Pharaoh and Egypt on behalf of Israel. He also told about all the hardships they had experienced along the way and how the LORD had rescued his people from all their troubles. EXODUS 18:8

Troubles multiply for those who chase after other gods. PSALM 16:4

☀ Humbly Talk with the Lord

Ask God's Spirit to give you moments of incremental surrender for the rest of your life, but only enough at one time, so as not to overwhelm you.

Share with God that sometimes on your sobriety journey you have felt like a salmon swimming upstream. Ask him for rest and relief from your powerful addiction, which has defied all reason and logic in your life.

☀ Take the *Life Purpose Coach* Challenge

Prayerfully think through your surrender opportunities, which might include travel plans, affirmations, people, pets, career aspirations, caffeine, doubts, painful history, intriguing life's work, or things that have an obsessive, sinful hold over you. As an experiment, choose one thing you'd be willing to surrender to Jesus for one day. Think of it as a twenty-four-hour fast from clutching it tightly or worrying about it. Instead, spend the time praying that you'll trust Jesus with it forever. Discuss your thoughts with your sponsor, recovery coach, trusted family member, or dear friend.

P.U.R.P.O.S.E. Principle VI: **S**urrender All to Christ My King

Surrendering My Entire Life

You have decided the length of our lives. You know how many months we will live, and we are not given a minute longer.   JOB 14:5

R. C. Sproul—an American theologian, author, and pastor—tells his audiences that all the moments of their lives belong to God. He says, "We do not segment our lives, giving some time to God, some to our business or schooling, while keeping parts for ourselves. The idea is to live all of our lives in the presence of God, under the authority of God, and for the honor and glory of God." If, indeed, it's God who has authority even over the length of our lives, down to the split second, then we're to stop compartmentalizing activities and withholding parts of ourselves.

At first, it might seem absurd to hear that you're being asked to surrender every segment of your life, including your purposelessness, prized excuses, the easy and difficult things, life dreams, and addictions. On the other hand, why wouldn't we humbly and gratefully choose our Savior as our Lord? He's the one who freed us from the slavery of our exhausting, addictive sins, and he's the one who made us stewards of the remarkable mission work he planned for us. Where else can we turn for a life of significance? We're not foolish enough to depend on our own evaporating willpower, mortal strength, and secular resources. Give us supernatural powers any day!

Topping any serious-minded, entire-life surrender list for someone in recovery are addictive triggers. If we could just let God have those wretched warlords, what a life we'd lead. Now is just as good a time as ever to ask him to take unhealthy people, unholy places and things, and any miserable situations that trigger your cravings. Are any of these your worst nightmare: pressure to perform, despair, being micromanaged, medical treatment that requires painkillers or antianxiety medication? Whatever your triggers, will you surrender them now?

SOUL SEARCH

What rivals your attention to God? What's the most likely thing God would want you to surrender right away?

The One worth worshiping, replace my triggers with supportive family members, trustworthy friends, and distracting yet healthy activities; with "urge surfing" by meditating until the wave of my cravings passes; and with a reminder of the truth and consequences of my addictive behavior.

P.U.R.P.O.S.E. Principle VI: **S**urrender All to Christ My King

Saying Good-bye to Purposelessness

Month after month I have nothing to live for; night after night brings me grief.
JOB 7:3 (GNT)

Job was lashing out against his affliction, speaking in the anguish of his spirit. You've undoubtedly felt the same, when physical, mental, and emotional stress bombarded you during the worst of your hopeless days and nights. The new normal is to feel despondently wearied over the recurrent futility of our lives. My own loss of hope caused me to attempt to track down Dr. Viktor Frankl, a Jewish neurologist and psychiatrist in Vienna, Austria, who survived four Nazi death camps, including Auschwitz. Frankl wrote volumes about the significant impact that meaningfulness and purposelessness have on a person. I even audaciously, albeit naively, sent him one of my early manuscripts about life purpose to read, along with the gift of a necktie for his tie collection—a month before he died of heart failure on September 9, 1997. (To be clear, my book was not to blame!)

Frankl understood that many people experience their lives as empty, purposeless, and aimless. And because nature abhors a hole or vacuum, it rushes in to fill any abyss with comforting and familiar things like pleasure, power, prestige, recognition, food, sex, substances, busyness, conformity, anger, and hatred. He wrote, "More people today have the means to live, but no meaning to live for." During his imprisonment, Frankl observed that those who held tightly to a vision of the future (a dream of being reunited with a loved one, a project to complete, or a solid faith) had a better chance of survival than those who had lost hope in tomorrow.

Before, during, or after we get to that place of prison-yard desperation, Frankl suggests that we focus on the ultimate meaning in life, which is a deep spirituality and knowledge of God. We as Christians understand that our knowledge of God leads us to a relationship with Jesus who rescues us! Say good-bye to purposelessness; surrender it now.

SOUL SEARCH

Have you experienced being adrift in a hollow, pointless life? What can you do now to fill that hole, that cavity, with a deeper knowledge of God and faith in Christ, your Higher Power?

God who assigns purpose, rescue me from my death camp desperation. Be my purpose for recovering and leaving the legacy you intend.

P.U.R.P.O.S.E. Principle VI: **S**urrender All to Christ My King

I Surrender My Prized Excuses

The man replied, "It was the woman you gave me who gave me the fruit, and I ate it."
GENESIS 3:12

Adam blamed his wife, Eve, for his sin in the Garden of Eden, giving men the oldest excuse in the book: "She made me do it!" And Eve blamed the serpent, making sure she modeled the Excuse Me! tactic for females. What's your prized excuse for your addiction: "I had a bad day and deserve a drink or [name your poison]"?

Do these other excuse-laden statements sound familiar? "I drink to be creative and confident." "The doctor prescribed it to help me sleep [or because I suffer from _____]." "Now is not a good time to stop; my spouse left me [or I lost my job]." "If you had my problems, you'd use too." "It wasn't my fault." "It's not the way it looks!" "I am the way I am." "I don't even drink the hard stuff [or that much or in the morning]." "I can stop at any time." "I'd be okay if it weren't for you!" "My parents never loved me." "I'm not hurting anybody but myself."

Jesus doesn't like excuses. Do you remember the parable he told in Luke 14:15-24 about the master who was furious about all the excuses invited guests were giving for not attending his great feast? Excuses don't cut it with him, especially when they keep us from preparing our hearts to attend his earthly and heavenly banquets.

That certainly brings up the topic of excuses people give for not answering God's call on their lives. Have you used any of these? "I'm not creative or confident enough." "I'm not getting enough sleep." "I suffer from _____, so I can't." "With my current problems I can't." "Now is not a good time." "I'm not that smart." "I'm too afraid [or too busy]." "I'm not holy enough [or gifted enough]." "I'm broke." We *gold medal* in excuses, don't we?

SOUL SEARCH

What excuse do you need to surrender now to move forward with your sobriety or life task? How thrilled will Jesus be with your decision to surrender that excuse?

Loving Presence, I know that the only cure for my prized excuses is resting in your comfort and peace on a second-by-second basis. I'm so ready to heal; make me able to surrender now.

P.U.R.P.O.S.E. Principle VI: **S**urrender All to Christ My King

I Surrender the Easy and the Difficult Things

As for me, I know that my Redeemer lives, and he will stand upon the earth at last.
JOB 19:25

According to the *Oxford English Dictionary*, in Roman law *addiction* was a court ruling that bound a person to a master. Today, do you struggle to be freed from the bondage of your ruthless, devious addiction master? If so, you have the freedom right now to enjoy the presence of and surrender to your loving, faithful Redeemer, who lives and will stand upon the earth at last. And the most proven way to start the surrender process is to saturate your days and nights in prayer and reading God's Word. Also critical is to invite the Holy Spirit to give you an impression of an easy first step so you can increase your confidence level before you face the more difficult choices.

Would these surrender opportunities be easy for you: text messages, Twitter followers, awards, ministry recognition, privileges, expensive jewelry, and your driven attitude?

Would these be more difficult for you: self-centeredness, allocation of time, debt, savings, personalized life mission, intimacy issues, safety, motives, revenge, mood swings, self-destructive addictions, and your recovery process?

In what category do these fall: evening glass of wine, exercise plan and doctor's appointments, entrepreneurial endeavors, hobbies, church involvement, group interactions, and your child's college and career choices?

A coaching client wrote to me this week about her surrender journey, "A depression began for me in 1987, as my husband and I struggled for thirteen years to conceive a child. I wrestled with God until I finally surrendered my dream of having a family to him. In 1999, he brought our precious daughter into our lives through adoption." Although you're not guaranteed a happy-dance outcome if you surrender, Jesus will walk with you every step of your journey.

SOUL SEARCH

What easy or more difficult change is on your surrender horizon? Will you surrender your addiction, which has become your telos (telescopic aim, goal, or life purpose)?

Spirit of a sound mind, I want to use my reasoning faculties to arrive at surrender conclusions, but I'm afraid of the enormity of what you might ask of me. If you'd be so kind as to start me off with surrendering some minor things, I'd sure appreciate it! After that, we can tackle the big sobriety stuff.

P.U.R.P.O.S.E. Principle VI: **S**urrender All to Christ My King

I Surrender My Dreams

Even though the fig trees have no blossoms, and there are no grapes on the vines; even though the olive crop fails . . . yet I will rejoice in the LORD! HABAKKUK 3:17-18

So as not to discourage you too much on your read-through of our passage, I deleted the part of it that talks about fields lying barren, flocks dying, and cattle barns being empty. In its entirety, this passage definitely paints a bleak picture of squashed dreams, but it also makes its point clearly. We're to rejoice in the Lord no matter how dismal, rejected, abandoned, hopeless, or washed up our dreams may seem. We're to rejoice in him, even if our addictions are part of the problem and causing the delay of our God-intended vision.

James Hudson Taylor, who was the British founder of the China Inland Mission and who spent fifty-one years evangelizing in China, wrote, "I have found that there are three stages in every great work of God: first it is impossible, then it is difficult, then it is done." Taylor's influence was widespread, thanks to many hundreds of missionaries who helped him start schools and campaign against the opium trade. His faith and perseverance in the face of unbeatable odds inspire me to surrender my highest hopes to God, knowing that my Lord will bring them to fruition in his own timing, if he so desires. I figure that if they are purpose-filled ideas that he instilled in my heart before I was born, he'll keep them safe. If they're not, I don't really want to have anything to do with them anyway.

So what do you do in the interim after you make the huge decision to surrender the dream itself to Jesus? It's optimal to start turning over everything else, too—like your impatience, obsessions, compulsions, past hurts, and distractions, all of which are keeping your life passion from blossoming.

SOUL SEARCH

Are you willing to surrender your greatest aspirations and all their roadblocks to Jesus? And even more challenging than that, are you willing to rejoice in the Lord as you wait for the triumphal entry of your life-purpose pageantry?

My Resident Tutor, God's Trustworthy Spirit, let your joy come to me each morning, so I might learn to trust the impossible-difficult-done process of an unfolding dream. I do acknowledge the wisdom of surrendering my grandest daydreams and all their addiction-prone hindrances to you.

P.U.R.P.O.S.E. Principle VI: **S**urrender All to Christ My King

I Surrender My Addictions

Return, O LORD, and rescue me. Save me because of your unfailing love. For the dead do not remember you. Who can praise you from the grave?　PSALM 6:4-5

I love to pray this psalm over anything good that's dying in my life, whether that's a godly character trait, relationship, life goal, commitment, event, or spiritual habit. It's always my grand-finale, dying-swan prayer to ask God to rescue something valuable that's languishing before it takes its last breath and can no longer be used for his glory. He's so merciful that such code-blue prayers touch his heart.

This psalm actually brings to mind a blur of a 1983 incident, when my young husband was rushed by ambulance to a hospital. As I stood alone in the hallway, watching doctors and nurses rush past, I heard, "Call a code blue and get a crash cart!" Later I was told, "We resuscitated him with chest paddles." That's what being rescued from the grave means to me, and that's why I pray Psalm 6 and urge you to join me.

Before you feel yourself kicking the recovery bucket, pray that God will resuscitate your spirit, strength, and sacred desire against these sinful strongholds: loveless sex, lustful pleasures, idolatry, magic-show religion, paranoid loneliness, cutthroat competition, never-satisfied wants, brutal temper, quarreling, jealousy, divided homes, small-minded pursuits, vicious rivalries, uncontrollable addictions, drunkenness, wild parties, and ugly community (see Galatians 5:19-21, a particularly colorful read in *The Message*). Ask God to send those despicable sins down into the dark abyss right now as you surrender them to him.

To praise the Lord fully with your life, accept his unfailing love and the new life he's breathing into you. Thank him for rescuing you from death by addiction, for saving you from falling off the wagon into an open coffin.

SOUL SEARCH

What good and valuable thing is vanishing in your life that you need resuscitated and rescued from the grave? What horrid thing will you surrender to the pit of death now?

Lord of the living dead, you know that I'm dead inside and that I need you to send your resuscitation squad with chest paddles to restart my heart! Renew my spirit so I might be sober and do your divine will forever. I surrender my addictions.

P.U.R.P.O.S.E. Principle VI: Surrender All to Christ My King

Surrendering All

Begin in earnest to apply the mind of Christ to your upcoming surrender opportunities.

☀ Meditate on the Assurance of God's Word

Not everyone who calls out to me, "Lord! Lord!" will enter the Kingdom of Heaven. Only those who actually do the will of my Father in heaven will enter.
MATTHEW 7:21

Let all that I am praise the LORD; may I never forget the good things he does for me. He forgives all my sins and heals all my diseases. He redeems me from death and crowns me with love and tender mercies. He fills my life with good things. My youth is renewed like the eagle's! PSALM 103:2-5

☀ Humbly Talk with the Lord

Ask the Holy Spirit to keep you from excusing your way through life. Confess to him your most frequent, stubborn excuses for not following God's tremendous plan for you.

Tell Jesus that you want to place everything in his hands and that if he orchestrates it, you'd be honored to help others surrender to him.

☀ Take the *Life Purpose Coach* Challenge

Make a list of three specific surrender opportunities that the Holy Spirit brings to mind under any of these general life domains: spiritual, relational, emotional, mental, physical, vocational, financial, ministerial, or personal (including addictions). Throughout the next seven days, prayerfully read through your short list, asking God's Spirit to give you his perspective on what to surrender. Try to make it a quiet, devout week filled with anticipation about how this exercise could impact your roles and goals. Prepare your heart to surrender one thing commensurate with the grace you've been given to surrender it.

P.U.R.P.O.S.E. Principle VII:
Experience Heart-Pounding Life Purpose

I'm living in the center of God's will.

P.U.R.P.O.S.**E**. Principle VII: **E**xperience Heart-Pounding Life Purpose

Miracles and Leverage

The LORD *replied, "Look around at the nations; look and be amazed! For I am doing something in your own day, something you wouldn't believe even if someone told you about it."* HABAKKUK 1:5

In the passage that precedes our verse, the prophet Habakkuk has openly questioned the wisdom of God by asking him to explain his whereabouts amid all the evil deeds and misery that abound: "How long, O LORD, must I call for help? But you do not listen! 'Violence is everywhere!' I cry, but you do not come to save" (Habakkuk 1:2).

Habakkuk's brazen accusation was his way of begging God for immediate help against an invading army. God's reply—our verse for today—is notably kind. He tells Habakkuk that he does have an amazingly strategic plan, which is being executed against the bad guys and will eventually bring great sorrow upon them for harming his loved ones.

Do you feel a little bit like the insolent Habakkuk, somewhat miffed about the "Wait and See" zone God's got you in? Or would you say that you're already looking in astonishment at the powerhouse miracles and influential leverage he's given you in life and in your war against addiction?

Have you ever prayed specifically for increased faith to believe that God will do the impossible for you? Corrie ten Boom, a member of the Dutch underground during World War II, certainly had prayed for such faith, as she hoped against all odds. Referring to her experience with her family, who had helped many Jews escape the Nazi Holocaust, she wrote, "Faith sees the invisible, believes the unbelievable, and receives the impossible." Do you want to hope against all odds for sobriety and freedom from evil, as well as for a passionate purpose? If so, why not now?

SOUL SEARCH

When have you watched in utter amazement at the healing grace God brought to your compulsions and obsessions? What goodness do you think he's up to now, in regard to "doing something in your own day, something you wouldn't believe even if someone told you about it"?

God of the invisible, unbelievable, and impossible, grant me increased faith that sees more of the miracles and leverage you've planned for my health, well-being, recovery, spiritual growth, and purpose-centered destiny. I ask specifically to receive the impossible from you.

P.U.R.P.O.S.**E**. Principle VII: **E**xperience Heart-Pounding Life Purpose
God of Miracles

Daniel answered, "Long live the king! My God sent his angel to shut the lions' mouths so that they would not hurt me, for I have been found innocent in his sight."
DANIEL 6:21-22

As King Darius granted his administrator Daniel more and more favor, other staffers grew jealous and plotted the admin's demise. They convinced the king to make a law prohibiting people from praying to anyone except himself, knowing that Daniel would continue to pray to God in heaven and that he'd be punished. When the troublemakers reported to the king that Daniel hadn't stopped praying to his God, the king could find no way around his new law. Reluctantly, he had Daniel thrown into the lions' den, saying, "May your God, whom you serve so faithfully, rescue you" (Daniel 6:16). Like the king and Daniel, you've probably prayed for a miracle, even asking to be rescued from your seemingly inescapable den of addiction and guided toward God's precious plan for your life.

As the historical account continues, the lions' den was sealed tight, and the king spent a sleepless night fasting. Insert yourself into this story right here, as a sinner and also as a servant of the living God, whom you try to serve faithfully. From what you know of God and his miraculous interventions in your life to date, would he leave you to be torn apart, limb by limb, by dangerous beasts? No, Isaiah 35:9 says about the future of those who have been ransomed by the Lord, about those who've been redeemed to walk on the Highway of Holiness, "Lions will not lurk along its course, nor any other ferocious beasts. There will be no other dangers." Like Daniel, continue to pray to God in heaven, and you, too, can expect to be rescued.

SOUL SEARCH

When have you experienced a miracle that rescued you from harm's way, kept you sober, or moved you toward a life of character and contribution? What upcoming miracle do you pray will save you from the roaring lion of recovery-related temptations?

Daniel's God, I pray with the believing King Darius, as he declared to people of every race, color, and creed on earth about you, that you're to be worshiped and feared. Your Kingdom will never be destroyed. You're the living God, who reigns world without end.* Thank you for rescuing me miraculously time and again.

---
* From Daniel 6:26-27.

326

P.U.R.P.O.S.E. Principle VII: Experience Heart-Pounding Life Purpose

Expecting Miracles

I am GOD, the God of everything living. Is there anything I can't do?
JEREMIAH 32:27 (*The Message*)

The God of everything living can do all things; no miracle is too hard for him. Whether you require extraordinary assistance with your teenagers, housing, transportation, education, safety, or recovery, nothing is beyond his supernatural ability to help you. After all, we've already witnessed one of his finest miracles: he chose us to spend eternity with him in heaven, despite our sinfulness. And when we hold fast to our faith during times of confusion, we're also promised peace in the midst of trials, victory over addictions, and sustainable spiritual growth.

I was once up to my eyeballs in single-motherhood debt and was out of options to meet my financial obligations, shy of asking relatives to help. Instead, God gave me the idea to leap onto his golden speeding chariot and glue myself to his legs as he charged through my "Red Ink Sea." Waters parted, thunderbolts clapped, people scurried to get out of our way, and at the end of our wild ride, God hugged me and deposited me a safe distance from my woes with a series of just-in-time income miracles. That faith-building experience of years ago was so intense that I still can't talk about it today without getting a lump in my throat.

Satan did his best to plant seeds of doubt and fear in my mind, trying to convince me that God couldn't perform a miracle for me or that he'd prefer to see me writhe in pain. By grace, however, my battle cry became "God is able." But why did the Lord Almighty choose to rescue me from my self-inflicted situation? I believe it was to increase my faith, so that when things got tough in ministry, as he knew they would, I'd remember to expect miracles from him who is able.

SOUL SEARCH

What would a loved one say has been God's greatest miracle in your life? For what miraculous response are you trusting God now?

Performer of miracles, you've been gracious to shower me with miracles beyond measure. I come boldly to you, however, beseeching you for your miraculous power to heal me in every way and to set my feet on your rock-solid pathway to purpose.

Doing the Impossible

Jesus shouted, "Lazarus, come out!" And the dead man came out, his hands and feet bound in graveclothes, his face wrapped in a headcloth.   JOHN 11:43-44

Martha was upset that Jesus had let her brother Lazarus die, but she truly believed that her Messiah Jesus could still bring her sibling out alive from the grave (see John 11:22). After the stone that sealed Lazarus' burial site was removed, Martha panicked and said, "Lord, he has been dead for four days. The smell will be terrible" (v. 39). Jesus responded by calling attention to a far more important matter: "Didn't I tell you that you would see God's glory if you believe?" (v. 40). And then Martha and her sister Mary witnessed their brother being resurrected from the dead.

You might feel like you've been among the addicted walking dead for four days, months, or years—or like you've been gravitating toward a cliff's edge, so depressed that you want to leap off and be pronounced dead. You might even be so sick at heart from sexual abuse or abusing that you've shriveled up and died emotionally. Whatever your personal angst or trauma, it's best to ask Jesus for your own resurrection experience, like he gave Lazarus and like he himself had. Jesus, your Higher Power, wants to bring you back to life again, and he's proven that he's more than able.

Feel free to use any of these sample Instagram prayers to request godly rebirths and humanly impossible feats: *Make my marriage whole again. Renew my love for your church. Breathe life into my spiritual habits. Restore my friendship with my Christian brother/sister. Bring back my zeal for my life mission. Reconnect me with my sponsor. Return me to sobriety.* Admitting any such need can begin the process of making you healthy again. Above all else, though, always pray for God's will to be done in your life and in the lives of all.

SOUL SEARCH

What resurrection miracle seems impossible in your life right now? If you were raised from the grave (figuratively speaking), what would it mean to your sobriety and purpose-filled life's work?

Lord of resurrection miracles, renew my spirit, so I might do your will forever.

P.U.R.P.O.S.E. Principle VII: **E**xperience Heart-Pounding Life Purpose

God's Blinding Speed

With blinding speed and power he destroys the strong, crushing all their defenses.
AMOS 5:9

If you were moving at light speed (186,282 miles per second), you could be slung around the earth seven times in just one second. That's 500,000 times faster than the *Concorde*, which was the supersonic airliner that cruised at twice the speed of sound. No speed anywhere, though, compares to what Amos describes as the "blinding speed" with which God can act. This all-powerful God is the same one who set our complex world in motion, as Amos reports: "It is the LORD who created the stars. . . . He turns darkness into morning and day into night. He draws up water from the oceans and pours it down as rain on the land" (Amos 5:8).

You may have prayed for your Creator God, the all-powerful Maker of the entire universe, to rescue you with blinding speed so you can heal now from your addictions. You might be crying out to him to send you a Christ-centered recovery program, first white chip, or role model. You might be praying for stick-to-itiveness in working the steps, consequences that will get your attention, peace of mind, an intervention, or an outpatient clinic. And what do you need in order to pursue God's work on earth (for example, time, money, energy, credentials, ability, discipline, healthy passions, or spiritual gifts)? Or are you more inclined to ask for a platform, network, proven track record, support system, or Hebrews 11 faith?

The starship *Enterprise* and the *Millennium Falcon* may have their faster-than-light (FTL) propulsion systems, but God was the original inventor of hyperspace, and nothing compares to the speed at which he's able to work! Ask him to be the Force that is with you, so you "live long and prosper." (Moses said those words long before Spock did—see Deuteronomy 5:33.)

SOUL SEARCH

What do you need God to send at blinding speed to support your recovery and life mission? Will you ask for it now, believing in faith that he will act swiftly on your behalf?

You who invented warp speed, I need your help immediately, and I trust you to send it.

P.U.R.P.O.S.E. Principle VII: Experience Heart-Pounding Life Purpose

God's Silence

O LORD, you know all about this. Do not stay silent. Do not abandon me now,
O Lord.   PSALM 35:22

God is famous for his silence. Recall that Zechariah and Elizabeth longed for a child, but God didn't speak of one until they were both very old (see Luke 1:5-25, 57-80). Or recall how the disciples waited ten days in the upper room (see Acts 1–2), a woman waited twelve years for healing from her bleeding (see Mark 5:25); and Paul waited in vain for relief from his "thorn in the flesh" (2 Corinthians 12:7). You may feel like God is staying silent right now about your cancer, food addiction, unemployment, probation status, friend's betrayal, or previously hinted-at life purpose. Personally, I can attest to the fact that waiting for three critical answers from God, over the past four months, has been extremely difficult.

You may have heard of the highly acclaimed two-act play *Waiting for Godot*, by Samuel Beckett, in which two men wait in vain for someone named Godot to arrive. While they wait, they fill their time doing anything they can think of to silence the silence: they argue and sing, eat and sleep, trade hats and exercise, and even contemplate suicide. The play is filled with numerous biblical references, which may or may not be linked to a theme about waiting for God. Regardless, we come to understand that doing nothing is all they *can* do.

So why might God engage us in such a time of waiting, of silence, of doing nothing, of being still—all of which often fill us with the hopelessness of nothingness? Most likely it's because he's calling us to a time of invisible activity; a time of sitting with him to converse and listen; a time of testing, healing, information gathering, closure, illumination, revelation, restoration, and transformation. For these greater purposes of God, we don't need to silence the silence, but to embrace it wholeheartedly.

SOUL SEARCH

For whom or what have you been waiting? What good has come from your wait thus far?

God who uses silence to grow me spiritually, could you send me a whispered reminder that you haven't completely abandoned me? I'm hurting and feeling alone, and I could sure use the assurance that you haven't forgotten about my recovery or the legacy you've called me to fulfill.

P.U.R.P.O.S.E. Principle VII: **E**xperience Heart-Pounding Life Purpose

Ready for More

Get ready for more of God's astonishing power in your life. Be filled with grateful anticipation about the miracles, influence, and leverage he's willing to bring to your recovery and unique work on earth.

☀ Meditate on the Assurance of God's Word

Nebuchadnezzar said, "Praise to the God of Shadrach, Meshach, and Abednego! He sent his angel to rescue his servants who trusted in him. They defied the king's command and were willing to die rather than serve or worship any god except their own God. Therefore, I make this decree: If any people, whatever their race or nation or language, speak a word against the God of Shadrach, Meshach, and Abednego, they will be torn limb from limb, and their houses will be turned into heaps of rubble. There is no other god who can rescue like this!" DANIEL 3:28-29

[Paul wrote,] "In fact, we expected to die. But as a result, we stopped relying on ourselves and learned to rely only on God, who raises the dead." 2 CORINTHIANS 1:9

☀ Humbly Talk with the Lord

Worship God by praying, "I will remember the deeds of the LORD; yes, I will remember your miracles of long ago" (Psalm 77:11, TNIV).

Thank God in advance of receiving the miracle you most need to stay sober and accomplish his will.

☀ Take the *Life Purpose Coach* Challenge

Four game-changing words: *My List of Miracles.* If you give yourself no other gift in life, get in the habit of recording the miracles God performs for you. This quick-reference list will make it easy for you to recall his unfathomable power in times of doubt.

P.U.R.P.O.S.**E**. Principle VII: **E**xperience Heart-Pounding Life Purpose

Slow Down

On the seventh day God had finished his work of creation, so he rested from all his work.
GENESIS 2:2

After creating the world for six days, God took time out of his busy schedule to rest on the seventh day; he even declared that day holy (see Genesis 2:3). But many with recovery issues are heavy laden with performance-based anxieties that cause them to push themselves to their breaking point. It's a vicious cycle: the more inadequate they feel, the more likely they are to compel themselves to do more, often to the detriment of their health, sobriety, and life mission.

Learning to stop or slow down is one of the hardest lessons I've ever had to internalize, and frankly, I'm still no expert in this area. I have learned a few things, though, including the fact that we must each have something we do to quiet our souls and get us off life's treadmill. It should be a given that we look for renewal by spending time regularly with Jesus in conversation and by taking a Sabbath day once a week. In addition to that type of slowed pace, some people like to listen to classical music or bird watch; others prefer to go to a museum, fishing pond, or the countryside. My daughter-in-love enjoys scrapbooking, having coffee and biscotti with her best friend, and curling up on her couch with a good book; her husband, my son, likes to take scenic bike rides, browse through a sporting goods store, and fiddle with the latest techno gadgets. I like to walk along the beach, go swimming, and build Lego forts with my grandsons. Regardless of how we unwind (in a clean-cut way!), actress Lily Tomlin suggests, "For fast-acting relief, try slowing down."

After you must crank it up for a season, ask God to send you gentle reminders to dial it back. Learn to step down, slow down, and sit down—capturing moments of laughter whenever possible. Even Jesus took time out of his important ministry to attend the wedding feast at Cana.

SOUL SEARCH

What healthy manner of "goofing off" helps you slow down and quiet your soul? What new such habit have you daydreamed about trying? (Will you?)

Quieting Presence, teach me to slow down now and again, so I can go the distance in all you've planned for me to be and do long-term without burning out or turning to ungodly relief from all the stress.

P.U.R.P.O.S.E. Principle VII: Experience Heart-Pounding Life Purpose

Rest and Relax More

Jesus said, "Let's go off by ourselves to a quiet place and rest awhile." MARK 6:31

Jesus sought a quiet place for his close friends and himself to rest. In the context of today's entire verse, we understand that "there were so many people coming and going that Jesus and his apostles didn't even have time to eat." I'm grateful that the Gospel writer Mark talked about Jesus' need for physical and mental rest and for nourishment. We all need time to relax and refuel amid the flurry of ministry busyness; he'd already told us that Jesus once took a nap in a boat (see Mark 4:35-38)!

It's counterproductive and sad to let an inner critic, superhero persona, or self-abusive mind-set dictate a grueling, nonstop work schedule, but workaholics do it anyway. They might believe childhood lies that they'll never amount to anything, so they race around proving that they're capable and successful. Or they might have an obsessive need to please others, fix problems, or earn God's love. If that's you, stop it, grab your earplugs, and head to a hammock for a lazy nap—often. Psalm 127:2 adds this wisdom: "It is useless for you to work so hard from early morning until late at night, anxiously working for food to eat; for God gives rest to his loved ones."

Instead of overworking, some addicts embark on the exhausting pursuit of pleasure via shopping, sex, gossip, gambling, extreme daredevil sports, or self-medicating. Some engage in this type of nonstop motion to assuage their wounded child or toxic shame. Instead of succumbing to either type of self-destruction, it's healthier (and less expensive) to simply rest and relax by taking a time-out, as Jesus did. Doing so is not an optional part of God's plan for your recovery and life assignment; it's a critical part. So go ahead and take that walk, tend to your rosebushes, or meditate (not medicate!).

SOUL SEARCH

What sweet-sounding habit of rest and relaxation might Jesus recommend for you? What exhausting pursuit of pleasure is currently sabotaging your sobriety or God's call on your life?

My Rest, take my exhaustion and teach me the art of downtime. I've heard that rest and relaxation create room for inspiration, so I'm looking forward to that gift from you.

P.U.R.P.O.S.**E**. Principle VII: **E**xperience Heart-Pounding Life Purpose

Inhale and Exhale

I'm happy from the inside out, and from the outside in, I'm firmly formed. You canceled my ticket to hell—that's not my destination! PSALM 16:9-10 (*The Message*)

David sang, "I'm happy from the inside out," because he was thrilled to be on God's soul train, confident that heaven, not the grave, would be his final destination! Can you picture the psalmist taking a deep breath and exhaling as he sang the words in our passage? What about you? Have you ever been happy from the inside out about anything (not including an addictive high that was artificially induced)?

At the risk of not sounding as holy as David, I must say that, to me, few healthy pleasures in life compare to buying a ticket for a sleeper compartment on a passenger train and hopping aboard in California to go visit my sister in Washington! I most enjoy the spectacular scenery that flashes past my window, allowing me to breathe in God's majesty and serenity. I detach from my cell phone and computer, choosing instead to inhale-exhale, pray, read, daydream, vision-cast, and journal leisurely. In the evening, though, it's fun to join others in the movie theater and, later, take a quick shower while my car attendant prepares my sleeping quarters. Between the enviable dining service and having escaped the brutal hustle of air travel, I'm a serene breathin' machine when I disembark. I feel like I've followed Oprah Winfrey's sage advice: "Breathe. Let go. And remind yourself that this very moment is the only one you know you have for sure."

Are you long overdue for a train ride or other outing where you'd have time to inhale deeply, exhale fully, and reflect on how much progress you've made on your recovery journey? Are you ready to stop holding your breath, anticipating that something bad is going to happen? David would encourage you to breathe easier!

SOUL SEARCH

How often do you stop to take a deep, regenerating breath and to exhale slowly? If you did so regularly, how might that positively impact your sobriety and life's work?

Breath of Life, if you were any kinder to me, I'd burst. Teach me to breathe in the fullness of you so I might exhale your inordinate kindness to those in need.

P.U.R.P.O.S.E. Principle VII: **E**xperience Heart-Pounding Life Purpose

Enjoy Life

You prepare a feast for me in the presence of my enemies. . . . My cup overflows with blessings. Surely your goodness and unfailing love will pursue me all the days of my life.
PSALM 23:5-6

God prepares a feast for us, even amid trying times; our cup does overflow with blessings; his goodness and unfailing love surely do pursue us all the days of our lives. It's just that we don't always recognize God's kindness to us. Perhaps because we're too distracted by daily-ness, exhausted by crises, or bound up in addiction, we've stopped believing that goodness will find us. Most of my life, for example, I was a driven, type A personality—not proud of it, but I was. When I got focused on an outcome, I had blinders on until completion. Then one day I woke up and decided I'd had enough of self-imposed stress and chose to actively seek out and enjoy more of life's simple pleasures.

That very weekend, my friend's neighborhood had a Garage Sale Extravaganza, and the new me went. Little did I know that God would overflow my shopping bags with a dozen nearly new robot toys (the fifteen-dollar kind) for fifty cents each for my grandsons. And when I got hungry, little did I expect that he'd prepare a feast for me! Out of nowhere, a man appeared selling homemade hot tamales from warming racks in the back of his truck. Oh my, that roving vendor was like an angel dropped down from heaven. What a moment I had of thanking God for all his goodness to me as I savored every bit of a chicken tamale.

Recall one extremely wholesome and enjoyable moment in your life, letting your five senses fill in the details for you. Now, imagine enjoyment surrounding you all the upcoming days of your sober, significance-filled life. That's only a fraction of the goodness and unfailing love that God has reserved for you!

SOUL SEARCH

Assuming that a street vendor isn't available to you, what real-time feast might God design for you (for example, having friends over for a barbecue or sitting leisurely alone at a sidewalk café)? In what way could God overflow your cup with blessings on your recovery adventure and life mission?

My Song, surely your goodness and unfailing love will pursue me all the days of my life.

P.U.R.P.O.S.E. Principle VII: **E**xperience Heart-Pounding Life Purpose

God's Generosity

All praise to God, the Father of our Lord Jesus Christ, who has blessed us with every
spiritual blessing in the heavenly realms because we are united with Christ.
EPHESIANS 1:3

God bestows on believers every conceivable spiritual blessing, including forgiveness from our sins, redemption of our souls, adoption into his family, the indwelling of his Spirit, and peace that passes understanding. Also, he's generous to us with his grace, promises, protection, provisions, and the truth of his Word. But did you know that his generosity isn't limited by a person's haunting past? In fact, he even showers sinners with his loving-kindness in spite of their substance-bound present and notwithstanding their shaky future. And just wait till we get to heaven and discover more glorious gifts for our eternal enjoyment.

God expects us to follow his lead in being extravagantly generous to those in need, including through our emotional and spiritual support—and our good deeds. But has he gone too far by asking us to share our lives and resources? Not at all! Generosity is one of the most life-giving, stress-relieving, and humbling privileges we can ever experience. Recovering addicts who are working a program or getting other help know the tremendous value of giving back.

Paul zeros in on the topic of financial resources with his protégé Timothy, instructing him to teach the rich not to be proud and not to be obsessed with their money, which is so unreliable. He writes, "Their trust should be in God, who richly gives us all we need for our enjoyment. Tell them to use their money to do good" (1 Timothy 6:17-18). Then Paul explains the benefit of releasing our grip on our stuff: "By doing this [you] will be storing up [your] treasure as a good foundation for the future so that [you] may experience true life" (v.19). And what a precious treasure we gain in living a true life of generosity toward our families, ministries, recovery circles, and strangers!

SOUL SEARCH

In what way has God been generous with you, especially in regard to your past and present addictions? In what way might you be more generous to others, specifically serving them by fulfilling the unique plan God has outlined for your life?

Generous God, you couldn't be a better role model for generosity; teach me to enjoy
being more like you.

P.U.R.P.O.S.**E**. Principle VII: **E**xperience Heart-Pounding Life Purpose

The Least of These

The King will say, "I tell you the truth, when you [showed kindness] to one of the least of these my brothers and sisters, you were doing it to me!" MATTHEW 25:40

It's no secret that we're all in recovery from something and that God sees us when we're trapped in the pettiness and selfishness of an addictive lifestyle. He grieves for us, knowing that we're only inhaling shallow breaths of stale air and that we're unable to see his exquisite and dynamic purposes for us. Shy of negating our free will, he tries to alert us to his proven strategy that would enlarge the breadth, width, and depth of our existence, but we hem and haw; many even hit rock bottom before becoming ready to listen.

And then one day we get it! We understand that the world is full of hurting people, those whom Jesus loves as his companions in suffering. We wake up from our blue funk to care about "the least of these my brothers and sisters," the poor, afflicted, imperfect, scorned, and persecuted. We understand that God is calling us to be healthy so we can help those with pain and unholy habits to experience the abundant life that Jesus died to give to all who trust him.

We read or hear, "I was hungry, and you fed me. I was thirsty, and you gave me a drink. I was a stranger, and you invited me into your home" (Matthew 25:35). All of a sudden, we see Jesus' face in the hungry and thirsty; in strangers; and in the naked, sick, and imprisoned. Our hearts break over those situations that break the heart of God. We agree that our self-indulgence, pity parties, entitlement issues, and Lone Ranger Syndrome must go. And God rejoices.

SOUL SEARCH

When has someone done something for you in the name of Jesus? What gift of self is God asking you to give to his hurting world?

Your Majesty, I pray St. Ignatius of Loyola's timeless prayer: "Lord, teach me to be generous. Teach me to serve you as you deserve; to give and not to count the cost, to fight and not to heed the wounds, to toil and not to seek for rest, to labor and not to ask for reward, save that of knowing that I do your will."

P.U.R.P.O.S.**E**. Principle VII: **E**xperience Heart-Pounding Life Purpose

Enjoying the Journey

To enjoy the remarkable plan that God has mapped out for you, choose to slow down, rest, relax, inhale-exhale, and share with those who are hurting, including those who've experienced the horrors of addiction.

☀ Meditate on the Assurance of God's Word

The LORD is my shepherd; I have all that I need. He lets me rest in green meadows; he leads me beside peaceful streams. He renews my strength. He guides me along right paths, bringing honor to his name.   PSALM 23:1-3

This same God who takes care of me will supply all your needs from his glorious riches, which have been given to us in Christ Jesus.   PHILIPPIANS 4:19

☀ Humbly Talk with the Lord

Chat with God about your tendency toward workaholism, perfectionism, people pleasing, hoarding, low self-esteem, chasing wealth, striving to earn someone's love, or anything else that causes you to perform nonstop. Ask him to give you rest for your soul.

Knowing that Jesus lives in your heart, invite him to choose an actual place in your home or community, so you'll have visual access to him for long chats (that is, when he's not on his knees praying for you!).

☀ Take the *Life Purpose Coach* Challenge

Create your own one-sentence poem or proverb to remind yourself to slow down and inhale-exhale more deeply. Use these two examples to trigger thoughts, although rapping is also an option:

We live most life, whoever breathes most air.
ELIZABETH BARRETT BROWNING

Fear less, hope more; eat less, chew more; whine less, breathe more; talk less, say more; hate less, love more; and all good things are yours.
SWEDISH PROVERB

P.U.R.P.O.S.E. Principle VII: **E**xperience Heart-Pounding Life Purpose
My Distinctive Life Purpose

When you obey me you should say, "We are unworthy servants who have simply done our duty." LUKE 17:10

Very few things can block your recovery efforts or your distinctive life purpose more than ignoring Luke 17:10. In this solemn, clarifying verse, Jesus is teaching his apostles about their duty to respond humbly and obediently to all he commands them to do—without feeling entitled to any reward. The example he chooses is of a slave doing his assigned chores with no expectation of being thanked. Our takeaway is that whatever we do for God is to be done out of humble gratitude for all he's done for us. He will not be indebted to us now, or ever, for any reason. So make it a habit to ask yourself this question: Am I serving so I can be duly recognized and rewarded or because Jesus loves me and gave his life to make me whole again?

Clearly your sobriety and life mission will always be about doing promptly whatever the Lord of lords asks of you. That will require your lifetime attention on Step Eleven of the Twelve Steps for Believers: "I seek through prayer and Bible reading to get to know God and his unique purpose for my life, asking him for the power to carry out his will."

In that regard, God may choose to give you immediate marching orders for an urgent task or to reveal a sneak preview to you of a slowly approaching season. You might think you prefer immediate orders, but a sneak preview actually allows you time to get used to his heart-stopping idea so you can learn to walk through your fears, gather necessary resources, cooperate in a character makeover, and nurture key relationships that support your healthy choices. Whatever God's timing, though, remember that he's the boss.

SOUL SEARCH

How do you feel about not being entitled to any thanks for working your recovery program or completing your assigned work on earth? What's been your favorite unexpected reward (e.g., peace, hope, deeper faith, the promise of getting to know Jesus face-to-face, fulfillment, lifelong friendships, prosperity)?

Master to whom I'm eternally indebted, how could I not trust you with my life?

P.U.R.P.O.S.E. Principle VII: **E**xperience Heart-Pounding Life Purpose
A Sneak Preview

[God said,] "Write what you see. Write it out in big block letters so that it can be read on the run. This vision-message is a witness pointing to what's coming."
HABAKKUK 2:2-3 (*The Message*)

God wants you to write out any sneak preview of his vision for your life, because it acts as a witness pointing to what's coming. What an encouragement for living sober—to get a peek at God's will! Here's how he used sneak previews to point me toward his vision: I . . .

- was filled with a fascination to plant, grow, and prune something that would blossom and bear fruit—but I didn't know what;
- couldn't get enough of mystery stories like *The Bobbsey Twins at the Seashore* and *The Adventures of Sherlock Holmes*;
- was addicted to 1,500-piece puzzles and privately chuckled that I should teach others how to assemble them with lightning speed;
- drooled over opportunities to travel the world;
- was drawn to ambience that makes me exhale, including fireplaces, cushy furniture, delicious snacks, and ocean views.

Today, I'm inordinately humbled and excited to travel around helping people grow into "oaks of righteousness" (Isaiah 61:3) by nudging them to put the puzzle pieces of their lives together. I tell them that God's plan for their lives is not a mystery. And, of course, the Life Purpose Coach client sessions are over the top with ambience, which attracts others to want to learn to do the same work.

God has sneak previews galore for you, too, of his brilliant, unfolding plan. Habbakkuk 2:3 confirms it: "[The fulfillment of God's plan] aches for the coming—it can hardly wait! And it doesn't lie. If it seems slow in coming, wait. It's on its way. It will come right on time" (*The Message*). This good news makes the hard work of recovery manageable.

SOUL SEARCH

Treat yourself to some quiet time with these types of questions, which can reveal God's sneak previews for you: *What intrigues me? As a kid, what did I dream of being—and why? What was my favorite vacation or school subject? What talents or spiritual giftedness have others affirmed in me?*

Eternal God, I thank you that slowly, steadily, surely, the time approaches when your vision for me will be fulfilled.

P.U.R.P.O.S.E. Principle VII: **E**xperience Heart-Pounding Life Purpose

My Heroes and God's Plan

Let the wise listen and add to their learning, and let the discerning get guidance.
PROVERBS 1:5 (NIV)

Do you have mentors who add to your learning and discernment with the guidance they give you about family matters, spiritual habits, life goals, or drug dependency? I've found some wise help in unlikely places, such as in the fictional hero Don Quixote, who was the most ingenious, idealistic Spanish knight of La Mancha. It all started when I flunked my college Spanish class, and my professor allowed me to redeem my grade by translating a small book about the life of Quixote. I spent that summer falling in love with DQ, as I learned that he feared God and believed that godly fear was the source of all wisdom. I was motivated by his advice to be thoughtful, virtuous, and compassionate—and to seek the truth. I understood from him the value of truly knowing myself and not becoming swollen like a frog (puffed up and prideful).

Like my other hero, Joan of Arc (see March 25), Quixote dressed in heavy armor and rode on horseback, wielding his sword with the passionate purpose of righting wrongs. His idealized, adventurous missions inspired me, even though he only charged windmills that he imagined to be hulky giants. To the depth of my soul, I dreamed of the day God would appoint me, as one of heaven's officers, to ride on a trusty steed with the passionate charge of helping the hopeless.

God's plan for our lives is a delight to discern. Our only real job is to enjoy the unfolding of the obvious clues that point to his will. And the only real dangers are all addiction related: e.g., the impatience and pride that taunt us to get ahead of him; the choice of worthless idols; and life patterns of worry, bitterness, regrets, fear, and rage.

SOUL SEARCH

In what way has a personal hero (fictional, historical, biblical, or modern-day) given you an inkling of your victorious recovery? How could a hero help you unleash your lifetime dream?

Precious Counselor, you know how grateful I am for the wisdom you've given me directly and through others. I ask you, in your good timing, to reveal a vivid picture of the newly restored me and the inspirational work you've lined up for me to do.

P.U.R.P.O.S.E. Principle VII: **E**xperience Heart-Pounding Life Purpose
Druthers, Hopes, and Dreams

Take delight in the LORD, and he will give you your heart's desires.   PSALM 37:4

Daydream about what you wish your broad-reach life mission looked like. Ignore any mind chatter as to whether it's your own selfish dream, and realize that your greatest hopes might reflect the desires God put in your heart before you were born. And forget for a moment that life has dropped you in a few briar patches of disappointment, confusion, false starts, and lost dreams as you struggled with recovery issues.

Now imagine how you'd feel watching God create a spectacular storyboard for your life dream or draw a detailed rendering of his electrifying vision for you. What if he even did a three-dimensional, lifelike mock-up of it with all the beauty, hope, and sobriety your heart could hold? That's his specialty—to design, build, and implant desires in your heart that will draw your heart to his—and then to grant you what you desire!

But how do you know which desires to follow, since you also have diabolic, addictive ones? Answer: when you "take delight in the LORD," you choose to align yourself with him and his wishes for you. This enables you to flip your focus off yourself and onto how his dream for you benefits his Kingdom! Those who know and love God come to understand that he doesn't want them to manipulate his dream into their own selfish desires.

You can be sure that even those who don't love God have figured out what to do with their lives based on childhood dreams, intriguing opportunities, failures, and career-guidance counselors. Obviously, many people have found what they're passionate about and have calculated how to make tons of money doing what they love. But you can be equally sure that any heart desire that doesn't align with God's desires is one to reject.

SOUL SEARCH

What do you see when you watch God's vision for you come to life—whether your dream is of an actual location, a conceptual process, or a definitive project? With the ingenious help of God's Spirit, will you discuss details with others you trust?

God who put your desire in my heart, withhold nothing I request that sits in the center of your perfect will. I only want to stay sober and follow your vision for my life.

Drowning Out God's Voice

His master replied, "Well done, good and faithful servant! . . . Come and share your *master's happiness!"* MATTHEW 25:21 (NIV)

If you're having trouble discovering your life mission and can't answer the question "What on earth am I here for?"consider whether any of these overwhelming concerns could be drowning out God's voice. Are you . . .
- worried you'll get the assignment you most dread?
- convinced you don't deserve to know the will of God?
- exhausted by your struggle with addiction?
- terrified of "getting what you ask for" and having to step out of your comfort zone toward your destiny?

No matter what your hesitation, the first way to move forward is to do whatever you need to do to stop drowning out God's voice. This is when you invite him to speak clearly to you about his will and your next steps.

The second way to ensure progress is to focus on the Cross. I did that, literally, in Africa a few years ago. I was staring down a dank asbestos mine shaft, which stood in stark contrast to a huge white cross on a nearby hillside. When my mind concentrated on the seemingly bottomless pit of the dreary hole, I felt cold, alone, lost, and afraid— but when my thoughts shifted to the Cross, I felt warmed, embraced, protected, and hopeful. Any trepidation or reluctance you might feel about your unknown future will only trap you in a lonely mine shaft of inner conflict, thus threatening your sobriety. Instead, shift your focus to the Cross to remind yourself that Christ the risen King is with you now and loves you dearly. And to further curb your concerns, rehearse his words of applause about your recovery and life's work: "Well done, good and faithful servant!" Let his words ring out!

SOUL SEARCH

What can you do to live a more recovered and resplendent life? Will you look to the Cross and trust the one who died for you—knowing that he has a personalized, strategic plan for you?

My only Master, despite my concern over the unknowns I face, I care more about *hearing you say, "Well done, good and faithful servant! Come and share your master's* *happiness!" So keep me from drowning out your voice and turn my eyes to your cross.*

My Deepest Longing

All my longings lie open before you, LORD; my sighing is not hidden from you.
PSALM 38:9 (NIV)

My Christian mentor and life-plan facilitator, Tom Paterson, asked me in 1995, "What's your deepest longing—perhaps something you've never told another living soul that you want to do for the Lord?" I burst into tears as his words struck a chord of desire buried in my heart. I exhaled my reply, grateful that someone had finally asked me to verbalize the deepest longing that I felt God had entrusted to me: "To be a published author, delivering the message God gave me for those feeling hopeless." I was stunned when he responded, "Then, let's create a strategy for you to write one book every year. That's what the best authors do."

God has created a deep longing in you, too—a dream that he took from his heart and planted in yours. He's invited you and commissioned you to be part of his glory-story; he wants your life to be a symphony about his dazzling waltz with you. He's waiting for you to show up and believe that he's orchestrated a fantastic future for you with no revolving door of addiction but with a particular and passionate method of helping him care for those in need.

Reflect on what you're hankering to do for him, what you'd consider unbelievably awesome to have the privilege of doing for others, what you'd be eternally grateful to be allowed to do for the world. Whatever it is, remember that if God has purposed it, it will happen—so get ready to get going!

SOUL SEARCH

What's your deepest longing—perhaps something you've never told another living soul that you want to do for the Lord—something that's fueled by healthy, sober living? Are you willing to pray, pray, pray until your deepest-longing miracle arrives and to be faithful in taking steps to see it to fruition?

My One and Only, my longings lie open before you; my sighing is not hidden from you. I release all my hopes to your loving care because I trust you as the one who deposits dreams in hearts. And by the way, thank you so much for the foundational progress I've made with my emotional baggage, defensiveness, pettiness, and other shortcomings. I know that handling first things first matters greatly to you.

P.U.R.P.O.S.E. Principle VII: **E**xperience Heart-Pounding Life Purpose
God-Given Intuition

Learn to trust your God-given intuition when "you know what you know" about what action steps to take next. It's *your* recovery process and *your* life dream; you are in charge. It's time to let your discerning insights move you closer to God's holy plans for you on earth.

☀ Meditate on the Assurance of God's Word

Before I shaped you in the womb, I knew all about you. Before you saw the light of day, I had holy plans for you. JEREMIAH 1:5 (*The Message*)

The King will say to those on his right, "Come, you who are blessed by my Father, inherit the Kingdom prepared for you from the creation of the world." MATTHEW 25:34

☀ Humbly Talk with the Lord

Thank God for all the progress you've made with your sobriety, all the provisions he's showered upon you, and all the indicators he's sent you about his outrageously great plan for your life.

Ask God to forgive you for doubting him, resisting his Spirit, and making excuses every step of the way. Let him know that you're feeling more cooperative now.

☀ Take the *Life Purpose Coach* Challenge

When you can't shake your sneak preview, inkling, druthers, heart's desire, or deepest longing—no matter how hard you try—consider that your passion in that regard might be a noteworthy sign from God. Smile in *knowing what you know*! Enjoy the excitement as you sit with your Maker all the more to learn about him and his anointing on your life, even if your "One Big Thing" seems like it's impossible. (That's a really good thing, because it keeps God your priority!)

P.U.R.P.O.S.E. Principle VII: **E**xperience Heart-Pounding Life Purpose

My Calling

When I give you a message, I will loosen your tongue and let you speak. Then you will say to them, "This is what the Sovereign LORD says!" EZEKIEL 3:27

I wouldn't have wanted to be Ezekiel, who was instructed to deliver a harsh message from the Sovereign Lord to the obstinate people of Israel. Who wants to be the bearer of bad news, telling rebels that God feels they've behaved worse than any of their neighbors had ever thought about behaving (see Ezekiel 5:7)? Not me! Who wants to inform others that God is going to punish them publicly for their sins while all the nations watch—a punishment the likes of which nobody has ever seen (see vv. 7-9)? No thanks! I much prefer my own ministry, which is one of encouragement. I get to be the good gal who helps people discern and fulfill their life's calling while we sit overlooking the ocean and munch on scrumptious hors d'oeuvres.

God's distinct calling on your life raises two soul-stirring questions that pull you naturally toward wanting to live a fully recovered life and engage effectively in his invigorating mission. First, ask yourself to whom you feel called or whose cries pierce your heart. Might it be teenagers, addicts, orphans, engaged couples, executives, unwed mothers, or disaster victims? Second, ask yourself what God is instructing you to say to those people as your life message. (More on both topics November 21–26.)

The overarching premise to keep in mind is that God has called you to himself—to know him, love him, and glorify him. Everything else you do on earth is incidental to that. My prayer for you and for myself is one that Sir Charles Richard Vaughan, a British diplomat, prayed: "Lord, make your will our will in all things." May our lives glorify God!

SOUL SEARCH

What worries you most about defining the target audience God's selected for you and about clarifying your life message? What's the worst and best that could happen, once you're sure of those details beyond a shadow of a doubt?

Sovereign Lord, I ask for your will to be my will in all things, especially about whom you want me to serve and what I'm to say to them. May your revelation of these specifics make me more passionate about my sobriety.

P.U.R.P.O.S.**E**. Principle VII: **E**xperience Heart-Pounding Life Purpose
To Whom Am I Called?

The LORD gave this message to Jonah son of Amittai: "Get up and go to the great city of Nineveh." JONAH 1:1-2

Successful businesspeople ask themselves three strategic questions in order to position their products and reach their end users: Who's our target audience? What message do we want to send to them? And what's the best possible delivery method to get our message out to them? Over the years, I've determined that somebody in corporate actually stole that effective formula from God, who created it originally to reach people for Christ! After all, God assigns each one of us a target audience with whom to communicate a specific message in a particular way. God told Jonah, for example, to announce the Almighty's judgment to the wicked people of Nineveh (see Jonah 1:2). Despite how entrenched you may feel in the anguish of your past and the rebellion of your present, God wants to heal you from all things addictive for many reasons, one of which is so you can accept your assignment to help others.

Let's prayerfully tackle the first of the three business questions right now by speculating about the group God has called you to serve. (See November 22 through December 3 for the other strategic questions.) Could your target audience possibly be single parents, musicians, HIV-infected toddlers, substance-dependent veterans, prisoners' families, educators, immigrants, or new Christians? Ask yourself, *To whom do I relate? With whom do I cry and for whom do I pray, whether that includes my family, friends, ministry, or world-community circles?* Does your heart break, for example, for the Romanian children living in underground sewers? Has God asked you to minister to the blind? Do you feel honored to help the underemployed who are heads of households or to serve adolescents who mutilate themselves?

SOUL SEARCH

To whom do you feel called as your primary target audience? Why do you think God chose that group for you?

God of details, you seem to have put a burden on my heart for this particular group: _____. Could you possibly be calling me to serve them in a bold way? Please be clear with me, especially in light of how inadequate and afraid I feel. And, oh yes, by all means, I do give those things to you.

P.U.R.P.O.S.E. Principle VII: **E**xperience Heart-Pounding Life Purpose

Who's My Audience?

The LORD replied, "Don't say, 'I'm too young,' for you must go wherever I send you and say whatever I tell you. And don't be afraid of the people, for I will be with you and will protect you. I, the LORD, have spoken!" JEREMIAH 1:7-8

Let this scenario play out in your mind for a minute: you hear God telling you, *Go wherever I send you and say whatever I tell you.* You're not too young, too old, too lost, too lacking in discipline, too abused, or too broken. Listen carefully for his instructions regarding where and to whom you're being sent—in your own hometown or even regionally, nationally, or abroad. Bask in knowing that nothing compares with the joy of reporting in at God's designated location (his duty station for you) to lead a group of people or a people group.

Frankly, the geosocial network games crack me up—the ones that have people checking in via a mobile device at a specific location to get "badges" or become the pretend mayor of that locale. How is it that anyone actually cares about being a mayor of an intersection, a mailbox, a gas station, or a lunchroom? But as fun as location-based networking might be for some, you haven't lived until God directs you to check in somewhere as an influencer who ministers to a particular target audience. (For example, he may call you to go serve where you could help atheists, athletes, cancer patients, special-needs children, airline personnel, rape victims, actors, politicians, outpatient alcoholics, or an international people group.) Putting aside for a moment all your faults, suffering, pressures, and inconsistencies, think about the privilege of being involved in God's great work somewhere in the real world.

SOUL SEARCH

Where and to whom might God be calling you as a servant-leader, as a shepherd for the lost? (Allow your response to be a confirmation of your previous insight on November 21, or let it stir a fresh awareness in you.) How would answering God's call impact your addictive lifestyle?

My Guide, reveal to me where and with whom I'm called to serve. Thank you that I'm sufficient to the task, because (and only because) it's you who's called and equipped me.

P.U.R.P.O.S.**E**. Principle VII: **E**xperience Heart-Pounding Life Purpose

A Life Message

The LORD reached out and touched my mouth and said, "Look, I have put my words in your mouth!" JEREMIAH 1:9

Many scholars think that Jeremiah was still a teenager when God called him to deliver a message to his rebellious contemporaries. When the young man spoke up, he was cruelly persecuted as a traitor for urging God's chosen people to surrender to their Babylonian enemies. His wayward listeners didn't like hearing that their captivity was God's punishment for their unrepentant sinning, nor did they understand God's restorative plans.

Later, John the Baptist was beheaded for delivering this message to Israel: "Repent of your sins and turn to God, for the Kingdom of Heaven is near" (Matthew 3:2). No wonder we have the saying, "Don't shoot the messenger!" But we must never forget that delivering a God-sized proclamation is exponentially more dangerous for those unwilling to practice what they preach, that is, for those who love to fix *others* in lieu of getting the help they themselves need (see Ezekiel 3:10).

I'm happy to report, though, that not every significant declaration will get you shot. For example, consider these exhortations: "Take courage," "Forgive yourself first," and "Let God do the impossible." Undoubtedly you recognize one of the most popular and lifesaving recovery mottos: "Keep coming back!" Or you may recall Mother Teresa's uncomplicated yet powerful message: "Jesus loves you." And the Bible tells us that the prophet Haggai delivered this much-needed pronouncement: "I am with you, says the LORD!" (Haggai 1:13).

Years ago God inscribed on my heart a simple statement to claim and to share: "Have hope." His revelation to you may be more along the lines of a great corporate power slogan or tagline like one of these: "The Power of Dreams" (Honda) or "You will never roam alone" (Travelocity).

SOUL SEARCH

What God-assigned message do you feel prompted to communicate to your target audience? In what way will that "slogan" be a blessing to people in your recovery ministry or other life groups?

Author of all good things, I'm a grateful sinner who's humbled that you reserved a message for me to carry into the world. I accept the exciting, yet challenging, opportunity to do so.

P.U.R.P.O.S.E. Principle VII: **E**xperience Heart-Pounding Life Purpose

Expect Illumination

I received my message from no human source, and no one taught me. Instead, I received it by direct revelation from Jesus Christ.   GALATIANS 1:12

Centuries ago, God revealed to Paul and others the Good News that was preserved for us in the Bible. Such trustworthy truth is worth gold to its readers, especially to those in recovery who've been fed lies from Satan for so long. As we set aside time to dig deep into biblical wisdom, we can expect that God's Spirit will illuminate our thoughts and help us discern our hope-bearing life message. That's the surest way to uncover your "message to the world"—just pay close attention to which inspired truth most resonates with you!

For example, consider 1 Corinthians 15:43, which could actually be the scriptural basis for someone's life message about earthly suffering: "Our bodies are buried in brokenness, but they will be raised in glory." The hallmark of the verse is that it's written from an eternal perspective, which is full of resurrection hope. How might it compare to a message about our bodies that's written from a temporal perspective? Well, here's a quip from an American Greetings card that some wisecracking friends gave me at a recent birthday party: "We start out with lots of memory and drive, then we eventually become outdated, crash at odd moments, acquire errors in our systems, and have to have our parts replaced." Although that over-the-hill gibe did create a moment of laughter among some aging beauties, it's purely pessimistic. Duly note that when God entrusts you with a life message to deliver to his people, its purpose will be to bring hope everlasting.

Regardless of your tainted past or soiled present, you have a faith nugget that you're called to communicate to others—before you feel "old as dirt" and your memory starts to fail!

SOUL SEARCH

As a student of recovery, what has God's Word shown you as a pass-it-on truth about life? How might you encourage the hurting and the hopeless with your anointed and passionate message?

You who designed my life so carefully, thank you for the Bible, which is illuminating the ideal message for me to share with those who are hurting and in need of your everlasting hope.

P.U.R.P.O.S.E. Principle VII: **E**xperience Heart-Pounding Life Purpose
Asking for My Heart's Desire

May he grant your heart's desires and make all your plans succeed. PSALM 20:4

My mom never heard about business guru Tom Peters's formula for success: "under promise and over deliver." So I take it as a God thing that she taught her eight kids to speak humbly about our abilities and then to give more than we ever expected to receive. She also taught us to ask God and others for what we wanted and needed. I know my mom was holy and wise, and her first teaching I get, but how could we humans be so audacious as to ask God to grant the desires of our hearts? Who are we to make such egocentric demands on the Ruler of the world? We're nothing but flagrant sinners, embroiled in conflict, schemes, disorder, addictions, and illusions of power.

God-fearing moms are usually right, though! Scripture bears out that we can ask our Lord for what we want and need, even for the privilege of serving him in a particular, heart-pounding way. He doesn't inspire our healthy, passionate daydreams to frustrate and confuse us, but rather to lead us directly into his purpose-filled, blockbuster will for our lives. Feeling compelled to make a unique, godly difference in the world happens because he's breathed that legacy into us. Of course, we fear selfish motives because it feels so good to have our wishes granted. So squelch that fear by surrendering your desires, motives, assignment, and success to your Maker!

Allow yourself to find peace in knowing that God intentionally created you to bring renown to his Kingdom; therefore, it would be counterproductive for him to thwart your dream of an ordained contribution. After prayerful reflection, schedule some time with a mature believer, like your sponsor, recovery coach, or small group leader, to discuss your impressions. It's a conversation you don't want to miss.

SOUL SEARCH

In spite of your shortcomings, what personal impact would you like to have on the world that would make your heart sing? How will you ever be able to thank God for the gift of destiny that he's given you?

God who forms the hearts of all, my heart is overflowing with a desire to leave the legacy you breathed into me. I look forward to working with you to bring it to fruition.

P.U.R.P.O.S.E. Principle VII: **E**xperience Heart-Pounding Life Purpose
Grateful for My Assignment

God's role in young Jeremiah's mission was to form him, set him apart, appoint him as a prophet, be with him, protect him, and put words in his mouth. Jeremiah's role was to go wherever God sent him, say whatever God told him to say, get up and prepare for action, go out, and be courageous. What a formidable task for Jeremiah or for anyone today, especially for those struggling with recovery issues.

☀ Meditate on the Assurance of God's Word

The LORD gave me [Jeremiah] this message: "I knew you before I formed you in your mother's womb. Before you were born I set you apart and appointed you as my prophet to the nations. . . . Get up and prepare for action. Go out and tell them everything I tell you to say. Do not be afraid of them, or I will make you look foolish in front of them." JEREMIAH 1:4-5, 17

☀ Humbly Talk with the Lord

Ask God to make you fearless as he reveals to you what he wants you to say to others and do for him.

Admit to Jesus that your unfaithfulness makes you unworthy of such a high calling. Thank him for his ongoing friendship, which makes you a victorious overcomer.

☀ Take the *Life Purpose Coach* Challenge

Before you charge forward on your life mission, retreat as often as possible to a quiet place to be still with the Lord and to express your gratitude for your assignment. These private times will allow God to speak to you, comfort you, and breathe strength into you before your tough journey ahead.

P.U.R.P.O.S.E. Principle VII: Experience Heart-Pounding Life Purpose
Delivery Method and Pizzazz

Everything I [the LORD] plan will come to pass, for I do whatever I wish. . . . I have said what I would do, and I will do it.   ISAIAH 46:10-11

God is strategic in everything he does; his plans are well thought out in light of eternity and the salvation of the world. Your role on earth is no accident; the good that God intends for you to do was ascribed before you were born (see Ephesians 2:10). He's set up a deliberate life plan for you—but he's given you free will to decide if you'll cooperate with him or attempt to sabotage his plans. You've been called to serve a particular group of people and to deliver a specific message to them in the purposeful way he decided long ago. Whether you feel ready or unable due to relapses in your sobriety, God has made you able and has promised to equip you with all you need to do his work.

We've already discussed your target audience and life message (November 21–24), so now we can turn our attention to the delivery method God expects you to use and how your healthy passions hint at that method. For example, do you love to sing, build, counsel, ride horses, create websites, or play the guitar?

Author Catherine Marshall sets the stage for us about the pizzazz God created in us to help us do his will. She writes, "Whence comes this idea that if what we are doing is fun, it can't be God's will? The God who made giraffes, a baby's fingernails, a puppy's tail, a crook necked squash, the bobwhite's call, and a young girl's giggle, has a sense of humor. Make no mistake about that." God's plan for you is filled with wonder and humor—and you'll need lots of both to balance out the serious side of his call on your life.

SOUL SEARCH

In what way do you feel ready, willing, and able to cooperate with God regarding the way he'd like you to get your life message out to others? What one recovery favor would you like to request of God right now?

Strategic God, in the past I've mapped out my own course; from now on, I want only to follow your instructions for delivering your desired outcomes. Do whatever you wish with me and through me.

God's Delivery Method

God gave Solomon very great wisdom and understanding, and knowledge as vast as the sands of the seashore. . . . He composed some 3,000 proverbs and wrote 1,005 songs. 1 KINGS 4:29, 32

God inspired King Solomon to write numerous proverbs and songs to deliver a unified message to the world about how to live a godly life. God's purpose for doing so is even spelled out for us: "Their purpose is to teach people wisdom . . . to teach people to live disciplined and successful lives, to help them do what is right, just, and fair" (Proverbs 1:2-3). Wouldn't it be reasonable, therefore, to expect that God will guide you (especially when you're trying to live a wise, disciplined, successful, right-just-fair, and sober life) as to how he wants you to deliver his message to a deteriorating world?

Well, he actually has specified your delivery method by embedding an ideal way to reach your target audience in your heart and mind. He's assigned you a way of communicating your life message to the viewers and listeners in your sphere of influence (which will likely include those struggling with addiction). You might be asked to represent God by using your voice, eyes, ears, hands/arms, feet/legs, sense of taste and smell, written word, resources, or public persona. Among many examples from the Bible, we see that the Gospel authors used the written word to spread the Good News; Esther used her beauty, prayerfulness, and powers of persuasion to save her people from destruction; and Jesus often used storytelling to communicate his message.

Perhaps you've been called by God and equipped to host a Christian radio program, lobby to protect the marginalized, raise funds for missionaries, mentor youth, work in hospice care, manage crusades, provide disaster relief, or prosecute sex traffickers.

SOUL SEARCH

What delivery method do you feel God is prompting you to use for the distribution of his message, and why? How could one step of obedience in that regard stir in you a renewed desire for your own recovery?

God who knows best, tell me what delivery method you'd like me to use to communicate my life message, and I'll set about obeying you—even if I'm sorely afraid.

P.U.R.P.O.S.E. Principle VII: Experience Heart-Pounding Life Purpose
Passion: It's Good for My Soul

The room was filled with widows who were weeping and showing [Peter] the coats and other clothes Dorcas had made for them.   ACTS 9:39

Dorcas had a passion for sewing; it was her thing. As a seamstress, she ministered to the poor and widows of her town and was dearly loved by them. As for me, I barely passed high school home economics after a semester-long, colossal debacle of trying to sew one blouse. That's okay, though, because God created each of us with our own particular passions and pizzazz that make us smile. Somewhere deep inside you resides your God-given sizzle. Even if an addictive lifestyle has buried it under a pile of chaos, a close inspection and prayerful investigation can unearth at least a smidgen of it.

Your fun thing might involve a hobby, such as mountain biking, stained-glass-window design, computer programming, car repair, song writing, health and wellness seminars, home remodeling, photography, golf, chess, hiking, calligraphy, or umpiring. It's exciting to discern how God has decided to use your pizzazz specifically for his glory and for the good of those he's sending you to serve. For now, though, remind yourself of a wholesome activity that made you want to jump out of bed some mornings, no matter how long ago that exuberant jumping may have been. Think about how that healthy fascination gave you renewed gusto on tough days, even causing you to lose track of time.

Addicts are driven by reckless, imprudent passions that can destroy all involved, but the souls of recovering addicts are drawn to the God-shaped passions that relax them, cause them to be grateful for one more chip, and orient them toward joy-filled service. That's one much-deserved vote for sobriety!

SOUL SEARCH

What healthy sizzle for life has God given you that sets you free from the worries that bombard you daily? On a scale of 1–10, with 10 being "over the moon," how happy would you be if he surprised you by using your favorite flair with his God-bright flare for furthering his work on earth?

My passionate God, refresh my soul so my healthy passions resurface. I'm tired of missing all the joy you intended for my life. I'm eager to smile again.

P.U.R.P.O.S.**E**. Principle VII: **E**xperience Heart-Pounding Life Purpose

My Pizzazz and Life Mission

I have filled [Bezalel] with the Spirit of God, giving him great wisdom, ability, and expertise in all kinds of crafts.   EXODUS 31:3

The Lord told Moses that he'd specifically chosen Bezalel to help with the building of the Tabernacle, saying, "He is a master craftsman, expert in working with gold, silver, and bronze. He is skilled in engraving and mounting gemstones and in carving wood" (Exodus 31:4-5). God also called into action many other gifted artisans to make everything he commanded for furnishing the Tabernacle and for clothing the priests with sacred garments. God had work for those who excelled as skilled stonemasons and carpenters, as well as those who were experts in ironwork, woodwork, engraving, designing, and sewing fine linen. It appears that our God not only assigns incredible abilities to individuals, but he also uses that giftedness for his purposes when he calls them into service.

Ah, the creative bent, extreme pizzazz, and supernatural talent God delights in entrusting to his children! He has deliberately wired a vim-and-vigor gift into you—a gift that exemplifies his grace toward you and encourages you to walk away from addictive behaviors. This liveliness energizes your ministry and life mission so you can inspire others to crave him and move their lives in his direction. Imagine for a moment how one of your hobbies could pay spiritual dividends when you use it to attend graciously to the needs of another. For example, what if the hospitable chef in you prepared leisurely meals with a shut-in who's struggling with depression and needs to talk? Or if the handy craftsperson in you renovated a home to accommodate a nonbeliever in a wheelchair? No matter what your zest for a craft or hobby, God can use it to bless his work on earth—locally, nationally, and internationally.

SOUL SEARCH

What passions has God instilled in you to enhance the creativity of your church ministry or life calling? How could your joyful zing actually help you with sober living?

Magnificent God, you who breathed such passion into me, I know that my flair is your twofold gift that blesses others and myself. I'm really looking forward to the contribution that my personal pizzazz will allow me to make for your glory.

P.U.R.P.O.S.**E**. Principle VII: **E**xperience Heart-Pounding Life Purpose

Creative Delivery Methods

Draw a picture of the city Jerusalem on [a brick]. Then make a model of a military siege against the brick. . . . Then get an iron skillet and place it upright between you and the city—an iron wall.   EZEKIEL 4:1-3 (*The Message*)

During the prophet Ezekiel's time in Babylonian captivity, God assigned him the role of author-speaker-actor. For example, Ezekiel often role-played illustrative skits, complete with props, to deliver his hope-filled message that God will never stop pursuing his people. As our passage unfolds into a chapter, Ezekiel was told to lie on his left and right sides for a total of 440 days in a public place with the blockaded brick in front of him and to bake his bread over a cow dung fire—as a warning of the coming siege and as a plea to remember God.

In your own church services or recovery events, you've heard speeches and probably even enjoyed skits as God's messengers used these two proven communication methods. Like me, have you observed any creative methods of communicating one's message, such as liturgical dancing, plate spinning, large canvas artistry, tepee assembling, or accordion playing?

You might consider such creativity off-putting for delivering God's message, so let me share a personal story, before I chicken out. My Old Testament seminary professor assigned each student a prophet to "bring to life" for our classmates, and I had the wild privilege of becoming Ezekiel for twenty minutes, in full prophet garb and wig. Would I choose to reenact his eating of a scroll, shaving his head/beard and then burning that hair, or digging through a wall? Well, with my only feasible option being wall digging, picture me doing that as I screamed out Ezekiel's serious message to my belly-laughing classmates. I did what I had to do to pass a course, but Ezekiel did what he was commanded to do, which was to deliver God's message in a dramatic way.

SOUL SEARCH

If the Sovereign Lord instructed you to do something creative to remind those clinging to sobriety that he'll never stop pursuing them, would you do it? What delivery method would you prefer, if asked?

Creative God, if you'd like me to consider an innovative method of delivering the life message you've assigned me, just bring it on and give me fortitude.

God's Return Policy

God's gifts and his call are irrevocable.   ROMANS 11:29 (NIV)

God's gifts of unmerited forgiveness, joy, and peace—as well as his loving call for a sinner to belong to him wholeheartedly—will never be withdrawn. They're his rock-solid favor of grace and eternal life, not some conditional reward based on how much a person loves or serves him. The Amplified Bible further develops today's verse: "He does not change His mind about those to whom He gives His grace or to whom He sends His call." But what if you want to wiggle out of serving him in a particular way, because it's too difficult and time consuming, or it puts the kibosh on certain addictive behaviors? Is that possible? Yes, God's free-will return policy says you can make the choice to ignore his plans for your life.

If you're tempted to bail on God, you'll find yourself thinking things like, *This is too hard; I can't do it. I don't have time. I changed my mind. This isn't what I bargained for. I can't believe I got myself into this. I'm exhausted. Who's going to help me? I quit. Lord, why won't you open doors for me? I can't breathe.*

But if everything is going along swimmingly, you might instead pray, *Lord, thank you for letting me serve in this capacity. This is fun. I'm in my element. I was born for this. This is as natural as falling off a log. What a blast. I'm in sync. Time just flies by. Life doesn't get any better than this. I have a place and a purpose. I fit.*

Each of those frustrated and joyful comments is an actual excerpt from my spiritual journals over a ten-year period. I am living proof that our reactions to God's plan can range from panic to exhilaration. When we're discouraged, though, the solution is not to return our life mission for a new one, as we might a store-bought item, but to cry out to our faithful God for encouragement.

SOUL SEARCH

During times of ministry testing and recovery challenges, how can you remind yourself that God will never rescind his gifts and call? Right now, do you feel like returning your assigned life mission or recommitting to it?

My Every Breath, teach me to pray, "This too shall pass," when I'm feeling discouraged.

P.U.R.P.O.S.E. Principle VII: Experience Heart-Pounding Life Purpose

Win-Win-Win

If you have trouble discerning God's intended delivery method by which your life message will reach your target audience, dig deep under any recovery rubble for clues on reclaiming your healthy passions, creative flair, and life pizzazz. And never be surprised that your divinely appointed passions are a joyful win for your audience, for you, and for God. (But beware of fun activities that become idols!)

☀ Meditate on the Assurance of God's Word

If God is for us, who can ever be against us?   ROMANS 8:31

The LORD is my strength and my song; he has given me victory.   EXODUS 15:2

All craftsmen who make idols will be humiliated. They will all be disgraced together.
ISAIAH 45:16

☀ Humbly Talk with the Lord

Talk to God about his ideal way of using you to get his message out, especially to those who are confused and wounded.

Ask God to help you do his will, even if it means going outside your comfort level to communicate your life message in a creative fashion.

☀ Take the *Life Purpose Coach* Challenge

Allow God to stretch you into his best version of you as you enjoy the exploration of how he always intended for you to deliver his message to his people. Investigate several communication methods (for example, art, music, dance, teaching, poetry, acting, life coaching) to discover which one or two might be ideal for you. Do leisurely, low-cost probes on any method that seems remotely plausible, having fun on this preliminary adventure. Stay tuned, though, for God to say at a moment's notice, "It's time to start in earnest now!"

P.U.R.P.O.S.E. Principle VII: Experience Heart-Pounding Life Purpose

Joy and Peace

I pray that God, the source of hope, will fill you completely with joy and peace because you trust in him. Then you will overflow with confident hope through the power of the Holy Spirit. ROMANS 15:13

Years ago, my friend told me that the girl's name *Rena* means "joyous song" in Hebrew and "peace" in Greek. I wondered, *If only my parents had named me Rena, would I experience joy and peace more easily?* Now I know that by trusting God, I can keep my birth name and still have the joy and peace of Romans 15:13, along with its bonus gift of confident hope through the power of the Holy Spirit.

Joy and peace are often linked as predominant themes in the life of a Christian, and rightfully so, because God sent his Son Jesus as our comforting refuge and security in trying times. Whether you're struggling with unemployment, trauma, the loss of a loved one, an addiction-related crisis, or purposelessness, you can choose joy and peace by letting the love of the Lord enfold you with hope.

During the holiday season, you'll most likely hear a traditional sermon on, "May the joy and peace of Christ be with you all through the new year." You can even expect to see an ornament, a greeting card, or a decorative wall hanging that links the two concepts. And you probably wouldn't be surprised to hear cellist Yo-Yo Ma's 2008 Christmas album, *Songs of Joy and Peace*, playing on the radio! But amid the worst Christmas scenarios—those involving frenetic activity, raucous noise, overspending, family discord, and substance-abusing parties—Jesus' joy and peace are unlikely. It's during all the festivities, gift giving, and caroling that we most need to remember this sage bumper-sticker advice: "No Jesus, no joy. No Jesus, no peace." Choose Jesus!

SOUL SEARCH

What specific changes in your life or holiday traditions might help you encounter Jesus during this holy season and beyond? How could the joy and peace of Christ lead you to more purposeful living?

My Abounding Joy and Peace, I need you with me now and throughout the upcoming year as I work my recovery program and investigate how I can best serve you with my life. Teach me to trust you more, so I can rest more joyfully and peacefully in you.

P.U.R.P.O.S.E. Principle VII: **E**xperience Heart-Pounding Life Purpose

Red Carpet Treatment

Those who live in the shelter of the Most High will find rest in the shadow of the Almighty.   PSALM 91:1

Everyone knows that a healthy, happy, holy home is more than a residence; it's a warm, inviting, joyful, and peaceful dwelling place filled with love. It's a safe, comfortable, and calming place to tarry, to sit with our legs propped up as we enjoy the sweet fellowship of family and friends. This idealistic rendition might stir up memories of all that your household was not, with its madness, sadness, disgrace, antisocial anxieties, unrealistic expectations, homelessness, or parade of moving vans. But what if you could step into a permanent "home sweet home," upgrading your abode to God's most sacred place, where you could sit with him often? How inviting would that sound to you during your worst moments of struggling with your own troubles and shortcomings—and the character faults of others, too?

God Almighty does have a permanent resting place, and the address on his mailbox reads The Shelter of the Most High. He's laying out the red carpet for you, hoping you'll choose to lodge where he abides. There he wants to cover you with the safety of his protective shadow, under the cloud of his glory, like a baby bird under its mama's shielding wing. Believers who desire to live in close fellowship with God (through the resurrecting power of his Son Jesus Christ) are invited to come on in with boldness and make his home our home! If we do, we'll be blessed by God's divine providence that prepares us for our best healthy future in service to him. This free offer couldn't get much better—except that it does. We also have access to God's mercy seat, his place of grace and forgiveness.

SOUL SEARCH

Which feature of God's home is most enticing to you: his joy and peace, his protection, or his divine providence over your sobriety and life purpose? To whom else would you want God to extend an engraved invitation into his welcoming home?

Most High, exalted above the universe, don't roll up your red carpet until I'm "home sweet home" and in your arms. I'm on my way to your heart right now. Teach me how to bring countless others with me.

P.U.R.P.O.S.E. Principle VII: **E**xperience Heart-Pounding Life Purpose
Being Joy-Filled

When [the three wise men] saw the star, they were thrilled with ecstatic joy.
MATTHEW 2:10 (AMP)

Numerous Bible scholars have described the Matthew 2:10 joy that the three kings experienced when they followed the star and found Jesus, their personal Savior. We read that the magi . . .
- could hardly contain themselves (*The Message*);
- were overjoyed beyond measure (HCSB);
- rejoiced exceedingly with great joy (ESV);
- joyed with a full great joy (WYC);
- were filled with indescribable joy (*Phillips*).

How would you describe your joy of being near Jesus, whose presence is the reason for your recovery?

In 1988, during my long, frantic search for joy, peace, and purpose, I had the privilege of chatting with Nobel Peace Laureate Mother Teresa in Calcutta, India. We sat on an old, wooden bench upstairs in the Mother House of the Missionaries of Charity. I blurted out, "How can you do this work in these terrible slum conditions?" I had felt like asking, "Are you crazy, agreeing to this life purpose of working with the poorest of the poor, with those who pee, bathe, and do their dishes in gutter water?" I'm so glad, though, that I had learned to filter my thoughts before speaking!

With a radiating smile and a gentle pat on my arm, Mother Teresa replied, "It's pure joy." Her outlandish comment took me fifteen years to process. Finally, I understood that the wise woman could do the work of Jesus Christ joyfully only because his love overflowed from her heart and gave her peace about it. She had followed his bright star and was thrilled with ecstatic joy, hardly able to contain herself, overjoyed beyond measure at being in his presence.

SOUL SEARCH

In what way do you rejoice exceedingly with great joy, knowing that Jesus cares deeply about your sobriety and every other detail of your life? How has your joy of knowing Jesus spilled into a service area or life's work of his choosing?

My Pure Joy, thank you for filling me with you, so that I can be "joyed with a full great joy," an indescribable joy.

P.U.R.P.O.S.E. Principle VII: **E**xperience Heart-Pounding Life Purpose

I Choose Joy

Tell all the nations, "The LORD reigns!" Let the sea and everything in it shout his praise! Let the fields and their crops burst out with joy!   1 CHRONICLES 16:31-32

David was overjoyed that the Ark of the Covenant (the wooden chest housing the two stone tablets of the Ten Commandments) had been brought home finally to rest in Jerusalem. His song of praise invited the entire earth to join him in worshiping the Lord in bursts of joy. It was such a celebratory event for David that he distributed loaves of bread, slices of barbecue, and cakes of raisins to the Israelites, whom he blessed in the name of the Lord (see 1 Chronicles 16:2-3).

What about your joy level and songs of praise? Has your boatload of pain, grief, disappointment, disorientation, life fallout, and deliberate sin squelched your worship and kept your life mission adrift?

My dear friend Kay Warren, author of *Choose Joy: Because Happiness Isn't Enough*, confesses in her book that joy did not come easy for her. Without her public confession, I would not have been able to admit to you the extent that I've struggled with joy too—especially in light of David's over-the-top, barbecue type of joy! Kay and I are both very serious-minded gals who weep over people's tragedies. This heavy-heartedness made it easy for us for years to be only moderately joyful pilgrims, but the definition of joy that Kay crafted from her own experiences of deep sorrow has helped me choose joy more often. She wrote, "Joy is the settled assurance that God is in control of all the details of my life, the quiet confidence that ultimately everything is going to be all right, and the determined choice to praise God in all things." And she definitely practices what she preaches.

SOUL SEARCH

When have you experienced God's great joy in your daily life, acts of service, or missionary-type work? How does that godly joy compare to your experience of fleeting happiness or mood-elevating substances and behaviors?

God who created me to enjoy you, I want to live a more joyous life on a more regular basis. What would help me lots is if you sent me reminders that you're in control of all the details of my life, that everything's going to be all right, and that I'm to praise you in all things.

P.U.R.P.O.S.E. Principle VII: Experience Heart-Pounding Life Purpose

Peacefulness Checklist

"My unfailing love for you will not be shaken nor my covenant of peace be removed," *says the LORD, who has compassion on you.*   ISAIAH 54:10 (NIV)

The Lord established a binding covenant, a solemn agreement, with us to grant us peace. It's senseless, therefore, to choose four peace killers that assure us a tedious, conflicted existence: people pleasing, keeping up with the Joneses, worrying about things over which we have no control, and anesthetizing our feelings. Instead, we have the option of four surefire peace enhancers: pleasing God, keeping up with God's daily will for our lives, trusting God to be in control, and expressing our myriad of feelings to God. We're so wise to follow the advice of Psalm 34:14: "Embrace peace—don't let it get away! (*The Message*).

Have you read the anonymous cyberspace posting about inner peace? It's loaded with solid truth about what peace looks like, despite its unexpected punch line: "If you can start the day without caffeine, If you can get going without pep pills, If you can always be cheerful, ignoring aches and pains, If you can resist complaining and boring people with your troubles, If you can eat the same food every day and be grateful for it, If you can understand when your loved ones are too busy to give you any time, If you can overlook it when those you love take it out on you when, through no fault of yours, something goes wrong, If you can take criticism and blame without resentment, If you can ignore a friend's limited education and never correct him, If you can resist treating a rich friend better than a poor friend, If you can face the world without lies and deceit, If you can conquer tension without medical help, If you can relax without liquor, If you can sleep without the aid of drugs, If you can say honestly that deep in your heart you have no prejudice against creed, color, religion or politics, Then, my friend, you are almost as good as your dog."

Ah, to be so peaceful.

SOUL SEARCH

What is Jesus, the Prince of Peace, nudging you to do about pursuing peace? Why is peace essential to your recovery and life calling?

*"O God, make us children of quietness and heirs of peace."**

---

* This prayer has been attributed to Clement of Alexandria and to Clement of Rome.

P.U.R.P.O.S.E. Principle VII: **E**xperience Heart-Pounding Life Purpose

The Lord Is Peace

Gideon built an altar to the LORD there and named it Yahweh-Shalom (which means "the LORD is peace"). JUDGES 6:24

My seminary professor opened and closed each of our Hebrew classes with a broad, cheerful smile as he wished his students, "Shalom." Those were my favorite parts of class, the only parts I actually understood! I wish you could've been there to receive his shalom blessings of peace, wholeness, and wellness. The greeting connotes far more than having an inner calm or the absence of outer conflict. It means we're striving to live in harmony with God, others, and ourselves—that we desire health, fulfillment, and well-being for all people. When the Hebrews called upon God with the formal title Yahweh-Shalom, they were beseeching The Lord Is Peace for safety, satisfaction, prosperity, perfection, and completeness. How many pressing problems and addiction-related issues could The Lord is Peace resolve right now in your life if you asked him to give you and your loved ones a fresh start on his worthy plans?

Yahweh-Shalom appeared to Gideon, telling him to go and fight the fierce Midianites, who for seven years had ransacked the Israelites' Promised Land. God called Gideon a mighty warrior, even though this young man felt like he was the least in his family and from the weakest clan. God said to him, "Go with the strength you have, and rescue Israel from the Midianites. I am sending you!" (Judges 6:14). After Gideon's rip-roaring defeat of approximately 135,000 Midianites, using only 300 men, he built an altar to thank the Lord for the peace granted to his nation. I wish I could have been there—that is, for the altar-building part! If I had been, I could have prayed for us and for our families and friends that the powerful, gracious God of Gideon would grant us peace of mind, wholeness of soul, and wellness of body. Join me in that prayer of shalom today.

SOUL SEARCH

Why is a calm, peaceful spirit so important on your journey to recovery and purposeful living? What would you give to have peace of mind more often?

My Yahweh-Shalom, you never cease to amaze me, especially because you're available to me all hours of the day and night to comfort me with your presence, which is Peace.

P.U.R.P.O.S.E. Principle VII: Experience Heart-Pounding Life Purpose

Craving Joy and Peace

We know the inherent dangers of lusting after people, places, things, emotions, substances, and activities. What a refreshing change to crave God's life-sustaining joy and peace on our path to sobriety and purpose!

☀ Meditate on the Assurance of God's Word

Honor and majesty surround him; strength and joy fill his dwelling.
1 CHRONICLES 16:27

Blessed be GOD—he heard me praying. He proved he's on my side; I've thrown my lot in with him. Now I'm jumping for joy, and shouting and singing my thanks to him.
PSALM 28:6-7 (*The Message*)

Since we have been made right in God's sight by faith, we have peace with God because of what Jesus Christ our Lord has done for us.   ROMANS 5:1

☀ Humbly Talk with the Lord

Thank God that you're sitting in his dwelling place, enjoying his honor, majesty, strength, and joy.

Lay your troubles before the Lord, including life's unfairness, a family feud, a chronic illness, or your addiction to people, praise, perfection, or pornography. Ask for exceptional peace and extraordinary power to overcome the challenges of your world.

☀ Take the *Life Purpose Coach* Challenge

Study your face in a mirror for thirty seconds, and notice if you see hope, joy, and peace—or doubt, sadness, and worry. If the former stares back at you, shout, "Way to go, [your name goes here]!" If the latter seems evident, make a cerebral and heartfelt decision to trust God, who is the source of all hope. Then lean into the pure joy of Jesus and the peace of knowing that the Holy Spirit is the original Life Purpose Coach.

P.U.R.P.O.S.**E**. Principle VII: **E**xperience Heart-Pounding Life Purpose

Divine Commission

I am a minister of the Church by divine commission, a commission granted to me for your benefit and for a special purpose: that I might fully declare God's word.
COLOSSIANS 1:25 (*Phillips*)

God wants to reach the world through willing servant-leaders with ready hearts. Like Paul, we've been commissioned by the divine will of God as ministers of his church for a special purpose, which is to fully declare his Word. We're anointed stewards, who've been entrusted with the task of making the invisible God known to others. As witnesses of Jesus Christ and as workers sent to harvest his fields, we must decide if we'll go or not. Our sovereign God, who could summon angels or create robots to carry out his wishes, waits patiently for our free-will decision. He won't force us to serve him.

We often cause this decision to be harder than it needs to be when we succumb to *why me?* pride, *why now?* theatrics, and *what if?* fears. We've also been known to enshroud ourselves in a fog of substances, a lair of sin, and a bunker of excuses, just to avoid God's call on our lives. We respond to his simple yes-or-no question with a lifetime of trying to outrun him, hide from him, and pretend that we didn't hear him. But Psalm 139:12 reminds us that even in darkness, we can't hide from him. And Isaiah 29:15 adds, "What sorrow awaits those who try to hide their plans from the LORD, who do their evil deeds in the dark! 'The LORD can't see us,' they say. 'He doesn't know what's going on!'"

Dietrich Bonhoeffer, a German Lutheran pastor who was hanged for leading a resistance movement against the Nazis, says a responsible person is someone "who tries to make his whole life an answer to the question and call of God." That level of responsibility demands a reevaluation of enticing obsessions and compulsions, which keep us from committing our all to God.

SOUL SEARCH

How does doing the Lord's work take your focus off worldly desires? What practical next step would help you accept God's sacredly prescribed goals for you, even if all the facts aren't yet crystal clear?

My Sovereign Master, I accept your divine commission. Protect me from all that might steer me off track.

P.U.R.P.O.S.**E.** Principle VII: **E**xperience Heart-Pounding Life Purpose

Lord, Speak

Samuel answered, "Speak, Lord, for Your servant is listening." 1 SAMUEL 3:10 (AMP)

Hannah's child Samuel lived and served Eli, an elderly priest, in the Temple of the Lord from an early age; he did minor tasks, like lighting the lamps and opening the doors. One night Samuel, who "did not yet know the LORD" (1 Samuel 3:7), thought he heard Eli calling him by name three times, only to find out that God had been the one summoning him. On the fourth call, and with prompting from Eli about how to respond to God, Samuel replied, "Speak, your servant is listening."

If your God radar is often on the fritz, like mine, you've had countless missed connections with the Lord over the years. So many issues can interfere with our ability to hear him, including cynicism, legalism, prejudice, mayhem, despair, addictions, or a hardened heart. An unresolved, festering conflict; an anxiety-ridden rumination; an illicit, clandestine rendezvous; a dangerous fixation (such as eating deodorant, tires, rubber bands, vapor rub, cat food, or toilet paper)—all of these types of unhealthy behaviors monopolize our attention and deafen us to the Lord's voice.

When we consider that the young lad Samuel had only three failed attempts at connecting with God, we can either cry, "Unfair!" that our parents didn't drop us off at a temple to be raised by a priest (see 1 Samuel 1:28), or we can decide now to take personal responsibility for our communication problems. Like Samuel, who "grew in favor with the LORD and with the people" (2:26), we can have the Lord's favor too. We can begin by listening quietly to what he has to say.

SOUL SEARCH

From your understanding of God's communiqués to you so far, do you think your current recovery steps are in alignment with his present and future goals for you? To respond to God's call as Samuel did, all ears and eager to obey, what needs to change in your life now?

God who calls me by name, I'm your appointed servant who wants to hear from you regarding every domain of my life, including my recovery and life mission. I'm eager to become a more obedient listener, knowing that your favor—your goodness and unfailing love—will follow me all the days of my life.*

---

* From Psalm 23:6.

P.U.R.P.O.S.**E**. Principle VII: **E**xperience Heart-Pounding Life Purpose

Send Me

[Isaiah] heard the Lord asking, "Whom should I send as a messenger to this people? Who will go for us?"
[He] said, "Here I am. Send me." ISAIAH 6:8

When I get to heaven, I want to spend time with the prophet Isaiah, a self-proclaimed sinner. He had the privilege of seeing God seated on a lofty throne with the train of the royal robe filling the Temple (see Isaiah 6:1). Isaiah responded humbly to that vision of the King, crying out, "It's all over! I am doomed, for I am a sinful man. I have filthy lips, and I live among a people with filthy lips" (v. 5). Because of our own uncleanness among an unclean people, we often feel like Isaiah, inadequate and unworthy to sing, "Holy, holy, holy" with the seraphim. But listen to what happens next. Isaiah is told, "Now your guilt is removed, and your sins are forgiven" (v. 7). Do you long to hear those words about your impetuous ways?

At that point, when God asked for a volunteer, Isaiah replied emphatically, "Here I am. Send me." How easy it would have been for him to cower in sheer fear of the great unknown. And how easy it is for us to get caught up in our own wishes, especially when driven by fear, pride, impatience, deceit, or entitlement issues of "the world owes me."

Like Isaiah, we're called to spend time in the presence of God so we can be convicted of and forgiven for our filthy habits. Our willingness to be cleansed of all our sins prepares us to be sent out to deliver God's message to God's people. Isaiah's message was tough: to urge a hard-hearted people to repent and seek the Lord. And tradition suggests that his death was no easier; he died a martyr, being sawed in two in the hollow of a tree. What a role model of serving the Lord faithfully until we die.

SOUL SEARCH

How could God use you to reach people for him in your next thirty days or weeks of sobriety? In your next thirty months or years of sobriety?

Holy, holy, holy God—the train of your robe fills the Temple and the whole earth is filled with your glory! Remove my guilt and send me straight to the Land of Purpose.

Say Yes to Change

His son said to him, "Father, I have sinned against both heaven and you, and I am no longer worthy of being called your son."   LUKE 15:21

Jesus told a series of parables about a lost sheep, a lost coin, and a lost child, all of which illustrate one main point: that a repentant sinner is cause for celebration. In the first parable, about a lost sheep, we learn that there's more joy in heaven over one lost sinner who repents than over ninety-nine others who never strayed (see Luke 15:7). In Jesus' second parable, about a lost coin, we read, "There is joy in the presence of God's angels when even one sinner repents" (v. 10). And in the third parable, about a lost son, the dad in the story reveals the main point: "We had to celebrate this happy day. For your brother was dead and has come back to life! He was lost, but now he is found!" (v. 32). Jesus was certainly clear about the rejoicing that follows repentance.

Let's zero in on the Prodigal Son for a moment. He squandered his entire inheritance on prostitutes and wanton extravagance, to the point of growing so famished that he hoped to eat with pigs. If he, who messed up big-time, can say yes to change and be given a fresh start, we certainly can too. Like the Prodigal Son, we must admit to our heavenly Father that we've sinned and that we're unworthy to be called his child. When we swallow our pride and confess our multitude of sins—which often revolve around greed, anger, vanity, selfish ambition, and addictive habits—God forgives us and throws us a party.

SOUL SEARCH

What sin pattern are you willing to stop now, in exchange for being God's guest of honor at a celebration? How could this shift in your attitude and actions impact your status as a local missionary—a person sent to do God's work on earth?

Compassionate Father, how foolish I'd be to continue resisting your generous offer to forgive me and throw a big party for me. Your doing so is the most ludicrous concept I've ever heard, but I'm going to trust that Jesus wouldn't have told three parables about rejoicing over what was lost and now is found if you weren't genuinely serious about celebrating my return.

P.U.R.P.O.S.**E**. Principle VII: **E**xperience Heart-Pounding Life Purpose

Leap of Faith

When Jesus heard [the Roman officer's faith], he was amazed. . . . He said, "I tell you the truth, I haven't seen faith like this in all Israel!"   MATTHEW 8:10

A Roman officer pleaded with Jesus to heal his young servant, who was paralyzed and in terrible pain, and Jesus agreed to go do so (see Matthew 8:6-7). Skeptic bystanders, who doubted that Jesus could heal someone by his presence or his touch, must have mocked the officer's faith-filled request. And surely those onlookers laughed out loud at the officer's preposterous leap of faith when he proposed that Jesus heal his servant from afar, simply by the power of a commanding word. The officer knew, though, that a single command from Jesus was sufficient, because he understood what it meant to be under someone's authority and have others under his authority. If he said, "Jump," his subordinates asked, "How high?" Or as verse 9 phrases it, "If I say to my slaves, 'Do this,' they do it."

What mockable or preposterous leap of faith do you need to take for Jesus to heal you from such things as an avalanche of debt, adrenaline junkie risks, or the nightmares of childhood molestation? Will you dare to believe and express publicly that Jesus really is the Great Physician (see Matthew 9:11-12), who specializes in healing the sick, wounded, rejected, addicted, discouraged, weak, and terminally ill?

Now let's return to our focal passage that begins in verse 10, when Jesus stands amazed at a level of faith unprecedented in all the land. He then instructs the officer, "Go back home. Because you believed, it has happened" (Matthew 8:13). That profound, six-word truth—Because you believed, it has happened—is what I love to hear Jesus say to others and me when we've stood strong in our faith. I pray that you will believe that our Lord Jesus Christ has the power to heal you from addiction—and that you will be healed.

SOUL SEARCH

When have you taken a quantum leap of faith and asked for a physical, mental, emotional, or spiritual healing for yourself or a loved one? What specific cure do you need to move closer toward your promised life mission?

Great Physician, give me extraordinary faith that results in your saying, "Because you believed, it has happened."

P.U.R.P.O.S.**E**. Principle VII: **E**xperience Heart-Pounding Life Purpose

God's Signet Ring

I will make you like a signet ring on my finger, says the LORD, *for I have chosen you. I, the* LORD *of Heaven's Armies, have spoken!*   HAGGAI 2:23

In Haggai's time, a king's signet ring was a distinctive sign of authority, power, and honor. If the king gave his royal ring to a favored subordinate, he was literally giving the person his seal, his power of attorney, his permission to use his signature on documents like edicts and deeds. Pharaoh, for example, gave his ring to Joseph when he put him in charge of the entire land of Egypt (see Genesis 41:42), and King Xerxes gave his ring to Mordecai when he elevated him to second in command in the Persian Empire (see Esther 8:2).

In our passage, God compares Zerubbabel, the governor of Judah, to a signet ring, to a royal representative who had been anointed with authority on earth. This must have humbled the faithful servant of God, because he'd simply done what needed to be done to get the Temple rebuilt. But God loves to bestow great honor on those who follow his instructions, doing what he says needs to be done. Forget for a moment about being a sinner who's struggling with addiction, and let God's remark about the governor remind you that doing God's work his way pleases him.

Ephesians 3:18 enthusiasts would urge you to remember also the extravagant dimensions of Christ's love for you. They'd pray passionately over you, "May you have the power to understand, as all God's people should, how wide, how long, how high, and how deep his love is." So when you're feeling like your middle name must be Obsession or Compulsion, stop the worrying and find a way to emulate Jesus Christ, who descended in a direct line from Zerubbabel and is the Signet Ring on the Father's right hand!

SOUL SEARCH

What would it mean to you to have God's royal authority, power, and honor evident in all aspects of your life, including your recovery efforts and your unique, long-term assignment? What step could you take now to please God more consistently?

God's Signet Ring Jesus, I want to delight God by being his faithful servant. Teach me how to become more like you and to do what needs to be done for the Kingdom.

P.U.R.P.O.S.**E**. Principle VII: **E**xperience Heart-Pounding Life Purpose

I Say Yes

After you say yes to God's plan for your life, don't be surprised that his priority SOP (Standard Operating Procedure) is to suggest a specific step you can take away from sinfulness and toward his ultimate will for your life.

☀ Meditate on the Assurance of God's Word

The LORD your God will delight in you if you obey his voice and keep the commands and decrees written in this Book of Instruction, and if you turn to the LORD your God with all your heart and soul.   DEUTERONOMY 30:10

You will be successful if you carefully obey the decrees and regulations that the LORD gave to Israel through Moses. Be strong and courageous; do not be afraid or lose heart!
1 CHRONICLES 22:13

How joyful are those who fear the LORD—all who follow his ways!   PSALM 128:1

☀ Humbly Talk with the Lord

Agree with God about giving up an addiction that is preventing you from being his trustworthy representative.

Ask God Most High (El Elyon) for protection from angry Satan, who's not thrilled with your spiritual growth, sobriety, or plans for furthering God's Kingdom.

☀ Take the *Life Purpose Coach* Challenge

God calls us to missional living (from the Latin *missio Dei*, "the mission of God"). This means we're to adopt a missionary mind-set about pointing others to Jesus. To that end, pray about doing some type of church-related outreach, whether it's working in a soup kitchen, collecting jackets for the homeless, doing a puppet show in a hospital, or repairing your pastor's car at no charge. The local, regional, national, and international opportunities are endless; the rewards are priceless.

I'm Ready to Move Forward

I will strengthen you and help you. I will hold you up with my victorious right hand.
ISAIAH 41:10

Are you ready to take several brand-new, bold action steps in your recovery? Despite the enormity of the task before you, God has promised to strengthen you, help you, and hold you up with his victorious right hand. In addition, his offer extends to helping you discover and fulfill your unprecedented life's work. To move forward in both directions—sobriety and purpose—think about how you'll reply to the question God loves to ask: "My child, how can I help you?"

His help menu includes these five options to ensure your victory lap: (1) wisdom in any research you need to do in books, on the Internet, or through interviews; (2) strategy about a low-cost experiment you could do to solve a problem or test an idea; (3) practical insight about the fear that paralyzes you; (4) profound joy that you've been released to move forward; (5) a gentle heart that allows you to show mercy to those who aren't as far along in their recovery work or life-purpose assignment.

God is calling you to respond to his beautifully drawn blueprint for your life, with sobriety being a must-have feature. Make a commitment now to pray your way through any sober-living setbacks so you can complete your unmistakable lifetime task. Never forget, though, that you need to "be careful what you set your heart upon—for it will surely be yours."* So follow God's lead step-by-step and day by day.

SOUL SEARCH

What is your answer to God's question, "How can I help you?" If God is an integral part of what you've set your heart upon, what fear might try to pounce on you now?

My Strong Tower, you are my place of complete security, reinforcement, and rest.
I flee to you as my city of refuge. Protect me against siege from the enemy as I get
ready to take several brand-new, bold action steps toward my recovery and legacy.
Lord, strengthen me and help me be victorious for your glory.

---

* According to James Baldwin, an American novelist in the 1900s

P.U.R.P.O.S.**E**. Principle VII: **E**xperience Heart-Pounding Life Purpose

Research and Interviews

Moses proceeded to do everything just as the LORD had commanded him.
EXODUS 40:16

During the great Exodus from Egypt, Moses obeyed the Lord regarding how to set up the portable Tabernacle. Every curtain, table, utensil, and sacred garment was arranged just as the Lord had commanded. The result was that the glory of the Lord filled the Tabernacle. Believers today can see God's glory filling their lives if they do everything he commands, both on their recovery walks and their journeys toward eternal significance.

As we learn to listen to God's Spirit, trying to differentiate wisely between his will and worldly enticements swirling around us, we'll recognize more often what's from him and what's from saboteurs or bad pizza! To develop discernment, it's critical to embrace God's love letter (the Bible), stay in prayerful community, and substantiate facts through research and experts.

For example, you might decide to investigate the role of stress in relapse. You could talk to your sponsor, go to the library, or make an appointment with a relapse-prevention specialist. Or perhaps, once your sobriety seems to be sticking, you might feel God nudging you to go on a brief overseas mission trip to explore his call on your life. In that instance, you've got a lot of reading and listening to do about your passport, accommodations, the country's culture, and possibly even a visa, travel shots, and raising support.

To me, research and interviews are fascinating; I've certainly had to confess to God my envy of Barbara Walters. But whether investigating is your thing or not, God needs you to familiarize yourself with the basic facts about your destructive tendencies and your life assignment so you can make informed decisions about a bailout plan for the former and an engagement strategy for the latter.

SOUL SEARCH

What don't you know—that you know you need to know—about your control issues, minimization of addictive signs, tools of escape, or coping mechanisms? What research or interview would help you move toward God's preordained call on your life?

Everlasting God, tell me whatever I need to do to get your eternal perspective about my recovery and life's work; I'm eager to capture the facts and ensuing wisdom that will help me honor you with my life.

P.U.R.P.O.S.**E**. Principle VII: **E**xperience Heart-Pounding Life Purpose

Get Back to Work

Be strong and finish the task!   ZECHARIAH 8:9

Throughout the book of Zechariah, that prophet told the Lord's small remnant of people that God was going to bless them with peace and prosperity. I'd like some of that blessing too. What about you? Apparently, the way the deal works is that we must get ourselves ready to be blessed by finishing God's most pressing tasks and by working on our character. The Israelites, for example, were to get back to work on rebuilding the Jerusalem Temple, because Jesus was going to ride into that Holy City on a donkey before his death; he will later return to it one glorious day. In addition, God was commanding them to "tell the truth to each other. Render verdicts in your courts that are just and that lead to peace. Don't scheme against each other" (Zechariah 8:16-17).

What do you need to do or stop doing to get ready for the second coming of Christ, which could be any moment now? Do you need to address a problem, such as dry alcoholism, enabling, an eating disorder, adult-channel surfing, or physical abuse of loved ones? Do you need to become less toxic and more honest, humble, fair, kind, forgiving, or reliable? Whatever it is, God wants you to get on with it, finishing what you start. Let his promise of blessings motivate you to move toward solutions.

In regard to your personalized mission, ask yourself what you need to study, strategize, create, communicate, depict, or rebuild. And how do you begin such an intimidating undertaking? I've been told, "Just like you'd eat an elephant—one bite at a time." Make your endeavors a series of gradual, inexpensive field tests (low-cost probes); don't spend money you don't have to move forward where God's Spirit hasn't prompted you to go yet. Easy does it.

SOUL SEARCH

How can you get your character ready for Jesus' return to earth, when he'll judge the living and the dead (see 2 Timothy 4:1)? What task have you left undone regarding your recovery or outreach to lost souls?

Architect and Builder of all that's good, I needed this reminder to get myself ready for your return. I do want to "get back to work" on my sobriety, character, and others-centered work, so thank you for blessing my commitment to begin again. Keep me strong to the finish line.

P.U.R.P.O.S.**E**. Principle VII: **E**xperience Heart-Pounding Life Purpose

The Lord's Will

What you ought to say is, "If the Lord wants us to, we will live and do this or that."
JAMES 4:15

James warns us about the evil of boasting about our own plans versus the wisdom of following God's plan. Have you ever said something along the lines of "I know best," like we read in James 4:13: "Today or tomorrow we are going to a certain town and will stay there a year. We will do business there and make a profit"? If so, James says that's foolish, because you don't know what your life will be like tomorrow. What we ought to say is, "If the Lord wants us to, we will live and do this or that."

What plans have you found yourself making lately that affect your recovery or life's work but that you haven't confirmed yet with God? For example, are you forming a new relationship with someone, planning a career move, making a financial investment, changing churches, or pulling back from recovery meetings? Who knows what temptations or dangers might lurk around any of those corners. Only God can steer you in the right direction and tell you when and where to stay or go. The key is to develop God-confidence, so you trust him; that lifeline of trust will keep you from running ahead of him on a wild-goose chase or lagging behind him.

Speaking of lagging behind, be careful not to catch the frightening disease called Analysis Paralysis. As a Life Purpose Coach, I see this all the time in clients who are paralyzed by analyzing too many options for too long. They stand frozen in fear, not wanting to act without God's clearest direction. But something's got to give. Don't stay trapped in fear, anxiety, and doubt. Instead, take a baby step—a prayerful, small step—to investigate the general direction you suspect God is asking you to go. He'll see your sincere desire to please him and can open or close any doors that he chooses.

SOUL SEARCH

Regarding your addiction heartaches or life purpose, when have you gone off in a direction of your own choosing without consulting God? When have you succumbed to paralysis by analysis?

Sole Proprietor of my life, teach me to say, "If the Lord wants me to, I will do this."

P.U.R.P.O.S.E. Principle VII: **E**xperience Heart-Pounding Life Purpose
Released to Move Forward

[God] has sent me [Jesus] to proclaim that captives will be released, that the blind will see, that the oppressed will be set free. LUKE 4:18

The Spirit of the Lord was evident when Jesus stood up in the synagogue of Nazareth on a Sabbath day to read Scripture from the Isaiah scroll, announcing the year of the Lord's favor. He proclaimed that captives would be released, the blind would see, and the oppressed would be set free. Are you feeling imprisoned, blind, burdened, or bruised, ready for it to be the year of God's favor toward you? Do you need to ask for pardon for a free-falling lifestyle of denying, lying, cheating, stealing, hoarding, gambling, self-induced vomiting, or bragging? Are you ready to sing *Free at Last*: "Wasted lots of energy worrying 'bout the past. Good God almighty, I'm free at last"?

Rest assured that God's love for you runs deeper than you could ever imagine. He sent his only Son to release you from bondage to unholy things, to open your eyes so you could see his unconditional love for you, and to free you from the oppression imposed by cruel people and soul-harming addictions. He's not waiting to pounce on you at the slightest provocation, but as the common saying goes, "With great freedom comes great responsibility." So prepare your heart to obey GOD, following him in a Good Orderly Direction (as is taught in recovery circles) as you inherit all the blessings that freedom brings.

You've been granted a prisoner's miraculous reprieve to go and live a profoundly joyful, sober life. May your eyes be opened to the fact that your loving God crafted an astounding life purpose just for you! May you freely give as you have freely received, sharing the Good News you've experienced firsthand with others whose minds are held captive to sin.

SOUL SEARCH

Would you prefer to move forward doing your own thing or doing God's One Big Thing for your life? In what way will you take more responsibility for your recovery, out of gratitude for your freedom from captivity, and for your spiritual eyesight?

Spirit of the Lord, fall on me with a new understanding of what it means to live in the freedom of God's love, protection, forgiveness, generosity, provision, insight, and faithfulness.

P.U.R.P.O.S.E. Principle VII: Experience Heart-Pounding Life Purpose

Be Merciful to Others

The faithful love of the LORD never ends! His mercies never cease. Great is his faithfulness; his mercies begin afresh each morning. LAMENTATIONS 3:22-23

For years, preachers have explained that grace is a gift or favor we don't deserve, while mercy is being spared from fair and deserved punishment. So to be merciful toward others means that we forgive them and cancel the punishment they've earned. Has God been inordinately merciful to you over the years, so much so that you're stunned by your lack of mercy toward others, your refusal to forgive them, and your decisions to heap on disdainful punishment?

The apostle Paul loved to talk about God's mercy to him and used the phrase *even though* to highlight his gratitude: He's say that *even though* he used to curse the name of Christ, was insolent, and persecuted Christians, God still appointed him and had mercy on him (see 1 Timothy 1:12-14). And *even though* you've worshiped idols of addiction, God stll appointed you and is gracious to have mercy on you also.

In response to God's mercy in sparing you from an untold number of earthly punishments and from eternal fire, you're required "to do what is right, to love mercy, and to walk humbly with your God" (Micah 6:8). That's not easy to do, and neither is following the advice you'll likely hear in a Twelve Step group:

- Keep the plug in the jug.
- Remember when . . .
- Practice the 7 Ts (Take Time To Think The Thing Through).

These behaviors speak of how grateful you are to the Lord, whose mercies are fresh each morning. All will give you a gentle heart that allows you to show mercy to those who aren't as far along in their recovery work.

SOUL SEARCH

How do you practice an attitude of gratitude for having been spared from fair and deserved punishment on earth and eternally? To whom would you like to show mercy?

Merciful God, it's a good thing I'm not you. My short fuse, judgmental attitude, and reluctance to forgive would have made a mess of your loving plan to redeem the world. Thank you for your mercy to me. I ask you to guide me into a pattern of mercy toward those I meet on my recovery journey and life mission adventure.

P.U.R.P.O.S.E. Principle VII: Experience Heart-Pounding Life Purpose

My Exciting Action Steps

God is crazy about you! He'll never be unfaithful, treat you poorly, or disappoint you. He only wants to see the excitement in your eyes as you discover and embrace his purposeful plan for your sobriety and selfless life mission. Enjoy being with him and listening to his wise, calming voice.

☀ Meditate on the Assurance of God's Word

Be silent before the LORD, all humanity, for he is springing into action from his holy dwelling.   ZECHARIAH 2:13

Remember, it is sin to know what you ought to do and then not do it.   JAMES 4:17

Act with love and justice, and always depend on [God].   HOSEA 12:6

☀ Humbly Talk with the Lord

Be silent before God, perhaps with your head bowed and palms conveying a release-receive posture. Inhale his forgiveness for your problematic behaviors whilst in the grip of addiction. Then express your gratitude for his love that rescued you from harm or the brink of self-destruction.

Thank God's Spirit for the time he's invested in preparing you to make wise decisions regarding your recovery steps and your holy life journey ahead.

☀ Take the *Life Purpose Coach* Challenge

Tell God that you're ready to travel into your sober, purpose-powered future with him. Without hesitation, sign up for his one-of-a-kind, intense, dramatic, and scenic adventure—one on which he promises to take you deep into living the life he meant you to live as a faithful, wise, strategic, courageous, joyful, and merciful believer. And ask a prayer partner (or two or three!) to hold you accountable before you head out each day, so you'll be focused constantly on following God's exciting lead.

P.U.R.P.O.S.**E**. Principle VII: **E**xperience Heart-Pounding Life Purpose

God's Friendship

I [God] speak to [Moses] intimately, in person, in plain talk without riddles.
NUMBERS 12:8 (*The Message*)

Can you imagine having God speak to you intimately, directly, and plainly, the way he did with Moses—"as one speaks to a friend" (Exodus 33:11)? We only need to read Romans 5:11 to understand that God desires that same endearing familiarity with us: "So now we can rejoice in our wonderful new relationship with God because our Lord Jesus Christ has made us friends of God." And if that were not proof enough, listen to this: "Become friends with God; he's already a friend with you" (2 Corinthians 5:20, *The Message*).

God actually talks to us all the time through his Spirit and his Word, as well as through anointed visions and the spiritual insight of mature Christian believers. When we choose to listen, we're filled with the radiant light of truth—even though our faces might not shine brightly, like Moses' did (see Exodus 34:29). I wonder: With that much communication available from God, why don't we keep our antennae tuned at all times?

Is it because we dread hearing what he might say about our sins and painfully slow recovery? Don't ever let God's intimidating authority block the clarity of his sweet counsel to you. He's a friend who loves you unconditionally, despite the results of your last drug test or your court-ordered anger-management program.

Charles Stanley, the respected founder of In Touch Ministries, gives this good advice about having a conversation with God: "To have God speak to the heart is a majestic experience, an experience . . . people may miss if they monopolize the conversation and never pause to hear God's responses." And remember that God who knows everything about you and your future isn't ever going to communicate more to you than you can handle at the time.

SOUL SEARCH

What's God saying to you about his unconditional love for you, regardless of your relationship with addiction? What's he been relaying to you lately about his magnanimous plans for you?

God my friend, speak to me plainly. I want and need to know you so much better than I do now.

P.U.R.P.O.S.E. Principle VII: **E**xperience Heart-Pounding Life Purpose

Humble Obedience

[Jesus] humbled himself in obedience to God and died a criminal's death on a cross.
PHILIPPIANS 2:8

Our verse raises the thorny question of how the innocent Jesus could submit in humble obedience to God the Father and to cruel, earthly authority, when he didn't deserve to die a painful, criminal's death on a cross. The question is mind-boggling for tender-hearted, pain-averse souls, but it's particularly complex for those with addiction-related authority-figure resistance. So what's the applicable truth about how we're to act like Jesus in our daily, pressurized lives under someone else's authority?

First, we're to humble ourselves and submit to God's plan, as Jesus did. All authority in our lives rests with God. We're to fear him, and in so doing, we will learn to obey, love, and serve him with all our heart and soul (see Deuteronomy 11:13). Second, we're to humble ourselves and submit to human authority, as Jesus did. As 1 Peter 2:13-14 instructs, "For the Lord's sake, respect all human authority—whether the king as head of state, or the officials he has appointed." And third, we're to humbly release our pain to God, as Jesus did. Set aside for a moment the pain of addiction, and think instead about the pain of being obedient to God, which can include exhaustion, rejection, discouragement, ridicule, and character defamation. Only he can comfort us in such mental, emotional, spiritual, and bodily anguish.

We can never go wrong imitating the humble character of Jesus, and Luke 14:11 reminds us of the great reward for doing so: "Those who exalt themselves will be humbled, and those who humble themselves will be exalted." We must decide in each minor and critical instance of our lives whether we will humbly surrender our stubborn pride and our anger-infused pain to the Lord or not.

SOUL SEARCH

What step of humble obedience could bless your recovery efforts and unfolding vision from the Lord? Where could prideful disobedience lead you?

Humble and Obedient One, I pray that you'll mold my character to be like yours. Help me submit humbly to the Father's plan and to human authority, as you did, and help me to humbly release my self-inflicted and unavoidable pain to the Father, as you did.

P.U.R.P.O.S.E. Principle VII: Experience Heart-Pounding Life Purpose

Running and Hiding

Jonah got up and went in the opposite direction to get away from the LORD.
JONAH 1:3

When God gave Jonah instructions to go to the city of Nineveh, the disobedient prophet hightailed it lickety-split in the opposite direction! "He bought a ticket and went on board [a ship], hoping to escape from the LORD by sailing to Tarshish" (Jonah 1:3). God had personally called Jonah to preach repentance to 120,000 people of Nineveh who were living in spiritual darkness, but Jonah disliked his assignment. He didn't want to deal with wicked people whom God would undoubtedly forgive, so he ran away. (No judging allowed here regarding the lustful, thieving, drunken Ninevites or the running, hiding weasel of a selfish and stubborn prophet!)

Then God flung what I imagine would have been a sushi-style seaweed-wrapped Jonah into the belly of a big fish, allowing Jonah to reflect for three days and nights. Finally, after God snatched him from the jaws of death, the prophet guardedly answered his Creator's unique call to preach throughout the land of Nineveh. The king and all the people repented to show their sorrow.

To whom do you relate in this story—the Ninevites (either raucous or repentant) or Jonah (either unfaithful or reluctantly obedient)? And how much can you relate to God's compassion toward a hurting world?

Just as God spared Nineveh, he wants to spare the repentant you from punishment for your sins—even those related to addiction, disobedience, and self-absorption. Jonah said it best (although in a miffed tone): "I knew you were sheer grace and mercy, not easily angered, rich in love, and ready at the drop of a hat to turn your plans of punishment into a program of forgiveness!" (Jonah 4:2, *The Message*). What a God!

SOUL SEARCH

Which of God's recovery directives has caused you to sprint in the opposite direction and try to hide? What specific part of God's plan for you to live fully alive is beckoning you to explore it?

God of Jonah, I'm done with selfish rebellion and tired of hearing myself whine. I've got no place to hide from you. Send me now in the unique life direction you command, and I'll gladly go.

P.U.R.P.O.S.**E**. Principle VII: **E**xperience Heart-Pounding Life Purpose

Will You Go Now?

"Get up! Flee to Egypt with the child and his mother," the angel said. . . . That night Joseph left for Egypt with the child and Mary, his mother.   MATTHEW 2:13-14

After the magi visited Jesus in Bethlehem, an angel of the Lord appeared to Joseph in a dream, telling him to flee immediately with his family to Egypt. The bloody tyrant King Herod was slaughtering male infants in Bethlehem, and Egypt was the closest Roman province that wasn't under the jurisdiction of the madman-king. The angel said to Joseph, "Stay there until I tell you to return, because Herod is going to search for the child to kill him" (Matthew 2:13). So that night, the tired Joseph got up and started the miserable sixty-mile trek in the dark and cold with his precious family. It's unthinkable that the loyal, honorable, obedient man of God would have made any other choice or even hesitated.

You, too, have the choice to ignore God or delay when he warns you to flee from heinous people, unholy places, vile ideas, foul play, and corrupt activities. But to keep your family and yourself safe, you will want to obey God without hesitation. Dangerous circumstances dictate the immediate life-saving response of "We will go now!" Even if you feel that the trek will be too long and arduous, you realize at some level that staying put can be a death sentence for one or more of the people you love or possibly for yourself. Will you be faithful to listen for the wisdom of God's always-perfect plan?

SOUL SEARCH

If Joseph's lag time—the miniscule amount of time he spent between hearing and obeying God that fateful night—was T-minus 30 seconds, how does that liftoff time compare with yours in any typical circumstance? (Do you tend to respond to God within seconds, minutes, hours, days, weeks, months, years, or decades?) How would a decreased lag time benefit you and your loved ones?

Trustworthy One, I want to learn to flee from addictive evil immediately—even if you prompt me to do so in the middle of the night. I ask you to warn me of danger against my family and myself, decrease my lag time in responding to your direction, and guide me to live a purpose-blessed life.

God's Ten Commandments

You have declared today that the LORD is your God. And you have promised to walk in his ways, and to obey his decrees, commands, and regulations, and to do everything he tells you.   DEUTERONOMY 26:17

When the people of Israel promised to do everything God had instructed them to do, as is described in our verse, God declared that they were his own special treasure. Moses delivered the good news, telling them that if they faithfully obeyed all God's commands, they'd receive praise, honor, and renown from God, who would set them "high above all the other nations" (Deuteronomy 26:19).

God promises to bless us, too, if we walk in his ways and do everything he tells us. We only need to read Exodus 20:6 for a vivid reminder of that truth: "I lavish unfailing love for a thousand generations on those who love me and obey my commands." To that end, here's my paraphrase of the Ten Commandments, which were given to Moses on Mount Sinai:

(1) Don't let any other god but me capture your heart. (2) Don't worship an idol of any kind, including people, places, and things that offer empty promises of earthly pleasure. (3) Don't use my name irreverently—ever. (4) Keep the Sabbath day holy; rest that day. (5) Honor your father and mother. (6) Don't murder. (7) Be faithful in marriage; don't consider committing even emotional adultery. (8) Don't steal anything. (9) Don't lie about your neighbor. (10) Don't lust after your neighbor's house, spouse, maid, ox/donkey/Porsche, or anything else.

Ask God for his specific help on any of his commands that relate to your most frustrating areas of brokenness, addiction, wrongdoings, or shortcomings. In fact, ask for enough love, obedience, reverence, holiness, rest, honor, gentleness, faithfulness, integrity, and contentment to fulfill his ideal mission for you!

SOUL SEARCH

Which of the Ten Commandments speaks most directly to you—and why? What's the greatest blessing God could bestow on you as a reward for trying to obey his commands daily, claim your sobriety, and accept his call on your life?

Lord who lavishes your love on me, who brought me out of slavery to sin, I choose to have no other gods before you. I declare right now that you are the Lord my God.

P.U.R.P.O.S.E. Principle VII: Experience Heart-Pounding Life Purpose

Jesus—the First and the Last

[Jesus said,] "I am the Alpha and the Omega, the First and the Last, the Beginning and the End." REVELATION 22:13

The first and last letters of the Greek alphabet are alpha and omega, the beginning and the end. They help describe the fullness of Jesus, who is the first and the last of all things. Isaiah prophesied this truth: "This is what the LORD says . . . I am the First and the Last; there is no other God" (Isaiah 44:6). As our Higher Power, Jesus has proven himself to be our all in all. The entire physical and spiritual universe rests in his hands.

He's the reason we're able to get out of bed in the morning. His protection, provision, and sustaining power are how we come to realize that idols in our lives are sheer foolishness. As our Lord says through Isaiah, "Who is like me? Let him step forward and prove to you his power. . . . You are my witnesses—is there any other God? No! There is no other Rock—not one!" (Isaiah 44:7-8).

The beginning of the end of addiction happens when we understand that Jesus is our everything. To please him, we choose to "strip off every weight that slows us down, especially the sin that so easily trips us up" (Hebrews 12:1). We focus forward, running the race that God has set before us. We keep our eyes on Jesus, our Architect and Completer, our Source and Goal, the Author and Finisher of all things, and the Champion who initiates and perfects our faith. He's "the one who is, who always was, and who is still to come—the Almighty One" (Revelation 1:8).

My heartfelt prayer is that Jesus will bring you to full maturity in him as you do the undeniable work on earth that he arranged so long ago for you to do! Amen and amen.

SOUL SEARCH

What step could you take now to continue to make Jesus your all? How will that important step support your recovery and God's amazing strategy for your life?

The Alpha and Omega, your Word tells us, "Look, I am coming soon, bringing my reward with me to repay all people according to their deeds." You are my Great Reward, and I welcome any additional rewards of your choosing!*

---

* Revelation 22:12

P.U.R.P.O.S.E. Principle VII: Experience Heart-Pounding Life Purpose
I'm Obeying Now

God wants us to obey his unchanging will for our lives. Saying yes to him leaves no room for selfish addictive behaviors, which are time-consuming, distracting, blinding, and emotionally costly.

☀ Meditate on the Assurance of God's Word

We ask God to give you complete knowledge of his will and to give you spiritual wisdom and understanding. COLOSSIANS 1:9

He has showered his kindness on us, along with all wisdom and understanding. EPHESIANS 1:8

Why do you keep calling me "Lord, Lord!" when you don't do what I say? LUKE 6:46

☀ Humbly Talk with the Lord

Ask the Holy Spirit to show you one new truth about how your addiction or sobriety has affected your family, friends, coworkers, passersby, or you. No matter how difficult or encouraging the insight, invite him to stir in you a new or renewed commitment to obey God now.

Seek God's wisdom and favor on your diligent recovery efforts and deliberate steps toward a life of significance.

☀ Take the *Life Purpose Coach* Challenge

Set aside some time to reflect prayerfully on 1 Corinthians 9:25: "All athletes are disciplined in their training. They do it to win a prize that will fade away, but we do it for an eternal prize." Decide whether you will seek an earthly crown or an eternal crown. Your earthly crown could be one of power, publicity, purchases, physical prowess, or pleasure, depending on how you define "success" and "happiness." The eternal crown is an imperishable crown. Proceed cautiously to your conclusion, because it will determine how you live the rest of your life—and both crowns require disciplined training and your undivided attention.

Appendix: Major Topics

FINDING P.U.R.P.O.S.E. THROUGH RECOVERY STEPS
How the Twelve Steps for Believers enhance P.U.R.P.O.S.E.

OVERVIEW OF THE TWELVE STEPS FOR BELIEVERS
January 1: Thanking God That I'm Not God. January 2: Being Restored to Sanity. January 3: Humbly Choosing God. January 4: Confessing My Shortcomings. January 5: Agreeing to New Beginnings. January 6: Rethinking My Actions and Reactions. January 7: Making Time to Hear God's Will. January 8: Answering God's Call on My Life.

P.U.R.P.O.S.E. THROUGH RECOVERY STEPS
January 9: **P**ut God First. January 10: **U**nderstand Truths about God's Will. January 11: Rightly Tell My Recovery Story. January 12: **P**ursue Positive Practices. January 13: **O**pt Out of Self-Sabotage. January 14: **S**urrender All to Christ My King. January 15: **E**xperience Heart-Pounding Purpose.

PRINCIPLE I: PUT GOD FIRST
My primary purpose is to worship God with my life.

GOD CALLS ME TO HIM
January 16: Born to Love God. January 17: God Claims Me. January 18: My King. January 19: The Lord Who Heals. January 20: God Is My Refuge. January 21: The Lord Who Bursts Through. January 22: Choosing God.

MY RELATIONSHIP WITH CHRIST
January 23: Knowing Jesus. January 24: Jesus Is the Vine. January 25: Christ Lives in Me. January 26: An Invitation to a New Life. January 27: The Way, the Truth, and the Life. January 28: Jesus Is the Best Gift. January 29: A Relationship with Jesus.

WHO I AM
January 30: God's Beloved. January 31: God's Child. February 1: God's Masterpiece. February 2: A Victor. February 3: A New Creation. February 4: Christ's Friend. February 5: Who I Am

MORE LIKE CHRIST
February 6: Becoming Like Christ. February 7: Humility and Patience. February 8: Boasting and False Humility. February 9: Being Patient. February 10: Patience with Self and Others. February 11: Patience with God's Plan. February 12: Resembling Christ.

LISTENING TO THE HOLY SPIRIT
February 13: Made Perfect by the Holy Spirit. February 14: Filled with the Spirit. February 15: The Holy Spirit Prays. February 16: The Holy Spirit Is Clear. February 17: Bound by the Spirit. February 18: Fruit of the Spirit. February 19: Listening to the Holy Spirit.

PRINCIPLE II: <u>U</u>NDERSTAND BIBLICAL TRUTHS ABOUT GOD'S WILL
I understand my recovery in the bigger picture of how God is redeeming the world.

GOD RESERVED A UNIQUE PURPOSE FOR ME
February 20: God's Plan. February 21: Eight Phases of God's Plan. February 22: Before I Was Formed. February 23: The Lord's Plans for Me. February 24: My Legacy. February 25: My Life Verse. February 26: Cooperating with God's Plan.

GOD ASSIGNS UNIVERSAL PURPOSE TO ALL
February 27: Two Universal Purposes. February 28: Redeeming the World. March 1: Glorifying God with My Life. March 2: Stealing God's Glory. March 3: Be Holy. March 4: God's Holy Priest. March 5: Two of My Universal Purposes.

GOD'S WAY
March 6: God's Will. March 7: Do What Matters Today. March 8: God's Presence. March 9: Stay Connected. March 10: Gather in Churches. March 11: No Eye Has Seen. March 12: God's Plan Is My Plan.

SERVING GOD AND HUMANKIND
March 13: An Approved Worker. March 14: Bear Fruit. March 15: Don't Lose Heart. March 16: Share the Gospel. March 17: Proclaiming the Gospel. March 18: Strategically Placed. March 19: Committing to God.

WHAT THE BIBLE SAYS ABOUT MY UNIQUE PURPOSE
March 20: "This I Must Do" Assignment. March 21: Mission in This World. March 22: Completing My Work on Earth. March 23: God's Good Work. March 24: What the Lord Wants. March 25: Days Ordained for Me. March 26: Purpose-Filled Living.

GOD'S PURPOSES IN THE OLD TESTAMENT
March 27: Old Testament Purpose. March 28: Noah, Build an Ark. March 29: Abram, Go. March 30: Sarah, You'll Be the Mother of Nations. March 31: Moses, Free My People. April 1: Joshua, Cross the River. April 2: God's Call to Service.

GOD'S PURPOSES IN THE NEW TESTAMENT
April 3: New Testament Purpose. April 4: Stephen, Testify about Jesus. April 5: Philip, Follow Me. April 6: John the Baptist, Prepare the Way. April 7: Peter, Feed My Sheep. April 8: Mary Magdalene, Proclaim the Resurrection. April 9: God's Plan to Redeem the World.

PRINCIPLE III: <u>R</u>IGHTLY TELL MY RECOVERY STORY
I turn my past and present over to God to complete my future life's work.

MY PAST POINTS TO MY FUTURE
April 10: God Works for Good. April 11: Using My Grief. April 12: Tiptoeing through Life. April 13: My Extra Baggage. April 14: My Successes and Accomplishments. April 15: My One-Minute Testimony. April 16: Use All of Me.

THE TRUTH OF THE MATTER
April 17: Consequences, Regrets, and Ungodly Values. April 18: Tough Consequences. April 19: Escaping Consequences. April 20: My Biggest Regret. April 21: Future Regrets. April 22: Pearls of Great Value. April 23: A New Beginning.

GETTING PERSPECTIVE
April 24: Right, Wrong, Confused, or Missing. April 25: What's Right in My Life? April 26: What's Wrong in My Life? April 27: What's Confused in My Life? April 28: What's Missing from My Life? April 29: A Do-Over. April 30: Give Me Insight.

A LIFE OF SOBRIETY
(STEPS ONE AND TWO OF THE TWELVE STEPS FOR BELIEVERS)
May 1: Living Sober. May 2: Step One: I'm Powerless. May 3: Step One: Seeing Truth. May 4: Step Two: Choosing Sanity. May 5: Step Two: Second Chance. May 6: Rest for the Weary. May 7: My Higher Power.

A LIFE OF SOBRIETY
(STEPS THREE AND FOUR OF THE TWELVE STEPS FOR BELIEVERS)
May 8: Faithful God. May 9: Step Three: Care of God. May 10: Step Three: 180-Degree Turnaround. May 11: Step Four: Searching and Fearless Inventory. May 12: Step Four: Carpe Diem. May 13: Rewards of Repenting. May 14: In Relation to Him.

A LIFE OF SOBRIETY
(STEPS FIVE AND SIX OF THE TWELVE STEPS FOR BELIEVERS)
May 15: Becoming Ready. May 16: Step Five: I Admit. May 17: Step Five: Admitting More. May 18: Step Six: Entirely Ready. May 19: Step Six: Removing Defects. May 20: Sifted like Wheat. May 21: Pressing On.

A LIFE OF SOBRIETY
(STEPS SEVEN AND EIGHT OF THE TWELVE STEPS FOR BELIEVERS)
May 22: Working the Program. May 23: Step Seven: Humbly Ask. May 24: Step Seven: My Shortcomings. May 25: Step Eight: The List. May 26: Step Eight: Clothed with Compassion. May 27: Crossroads. May 28: Accepting the Challenge.

A LIFE OF SOBRIETY
(STEPS NINE AND TEN OF THE TWELVE STEPS FOR BELIEVERS)
May 29: Continuing with Wisdom. May 30: Step Nine: Be Reconciled. May 31: Step Nine: Unfinished Business. June 1: Step Ten: Continue Taking Inventory. June 2: Step Ten: Standing Strong. June 3: Forgiveness. June 4: Guide My Steps.

A LIFE OF SOBRIETY
(STEPS ELEVEN AND TWELVE OF THE TWELVE STEPS FOR BELIEVERS)
June 5: Eyes on Sobriety. June 6: Step Eleven: Conscious Contact with God. June 7: Step Eleven: Victorious Life. June 8: Step Twelve: Giving Back. June 9: Step Twelve: Light of the World. June 10: My Seven-Minute Testimony. June 11: Keep Moving Forward.

PRINCIPLE IV: PURSUE POSITIVE PRACTICES TO MAINTAIN MY SOBRIETY
I'm fully cooperating with God regarding his unique plan for my life.

BEDROCK PRACTICE OF PRAYING
June 12: Fervent Prayer. June 13: Pray without Ceasing. June 14: Private Prayer Life. June 15: Practicing Solitude. June 16: Pray for Wisdom. June 17: Pray for Equipping. June 18: Becoming a Person of Prayer.

GOD'S PEOPLE
June 19: Relationships, Role Models, and Sponsors. June 20: No Record of Wrong. June 21: Healthy Church Relationships. June 22: Cord of Three Strands. June 23:

God's Gift of Role Models. June 24: Relationship-Minded Sponsor or Coach. June 25: Living in Community.

PURE MOTIVES GUIDE ME TO MY PURPOSE
June 26: Things Hidden. June 27: Duplicity. June 28: Hidden Motives. June 29: Right and Wrong Motives. June 30: Payoffs. July 1: Secret Shame. July 2: Authenticity.

ESSENTIALS TO GOD'S PLAN
July 3: Signposts to Wholeness. July 4: Signpost 1: Simplified Lifestyle. July 5: Signpost 2: Health and Wellness. July 6: Signpost 3: Being Physically Fit. July 7: Signpost 4: The Role of Levity. July 8: Signpost 5: Grace Extended and Received. July 9: Living the Life.

SPIRITUAL HABITS CARRY ME TO GOD'S WILL
July 10: Spiritual Habits. July 11: Reading God's Word. July 12: Fasting. July 13: Intercessory Praying. July 14: Purity. July 15: Tithing. July 16: Embracing Spiritual Habits.

SUSTAINING MY MISSION
July 17: Perseverance and Lifelong Learning. July 18: Staying Power. July 19: Perseverance during Trials. July 20: Daily Perseverance. July 21: Needing to Learn. July 22: Lifelong Learning. July 23: Going Forward.

HEADING TOWARD MY UNIQUE PURPOSE
July 24: Gratitude, God-Control, and Boundaries. July 25: A Life of Gratitude. July 26: Jesus' Power and Kindness. July 27: Controlling My Mouth. July 28: Under God-Control. July 29: Boundaries Based on Priorities. July 30: Trusting God.

HOW I'M MADE
July 31: Gifts, Qualities, and Personality. August 1: My Giftedness. August 2: Grateful for My Gifts. August 3: Letting My Gifts Lead Me. August 4: My Best Qualities. August 5: My Personality Type. August 6: Using What I've Been Given.

STAYING COMMITTED
August 7: Four Commitments. August 8: Natural Talents and Acquired Skills. August 9: Practice Kindness. August 10: Resist Boredom. August 11: Strengths Can Become Weaknesses. August 12: Weaknesses Turned into Strengths. August 13: The Recovered Life.

PRINCIPLE V: OPT OUT OF SELF-SABOTAGING METHODS
I choose to live a life of recovery and purpose now.

WHAT STOPS ME
August 14: Anger, Bitterness, and Doubt. August 15: Anger and Rage. August 16: Root Cause of My Anger. August 17: Bitterness Hurts. August 18: Doubting Thomas. August 19: Still Doubting? August 20: No Looking Back.

FOILED AGAIN
August 21: Heavy-Duty Issues. August 22: Worry Less. August 23: Unconfessed Guilt. August 24: Say No to Jealousy. August 25: Hatred Has No Place. August 26: Pandemic of Self-Loathing. August 27: Five Guaranteed Life Killers.

BLOCKED BY FEARS AND SYNDROMES
August 28: Facing Fears. August 29: What Fear Does to Us. August 30: Being Courageous. August 31: Fear God. September 1: Syndromes That Scream Fear. September 2: Other Unhealthy Syndromes. September 3: God's in Charge.

REMEMBERING GOD'S GOODNESS
September 4: God Is Good, All the Time. September 5: God Is My Full Armor. September 6: The God Who Sees Me. September 7: The Lord Is My Banner. September 8: God's Strength against Enabling. September 9: Praying the Names of God. September 10: God Is Mine and I'm God's.

STALLED
September 11: Enemies of the State. September 12: Judgmental Criticism. September 13: Ugliness of Gossip and Grudges. September 14: Headstrong Stubbornness. September 15: Lousy Life Scripts. September 16: God Luck. September 17: Moving On.

THREATS, DELAYS, AND ROADBLOCKS TO GOD'S PLAN
September 18: The Troubles I See. September 19: Numerous Threats. September 20: Maddening Delays. September 21: Why the Delay? Part I. September 22: Why the Delay? Part II. September 23: Leaping over Roadblocks. September 24: Victory in God.

PRINCIPLE VI: SURRENDER ALL TO CHRIST MY KING
When I empty myself of self, I'm able to be and do all God wants.

SAVED AND SURRENDERED
September 25: Surrender All. September 26: Salvation Precedes Surrender. September 27: Surrender—a Lifelong Process. September 28: Surrender What? September 29: When to Surrender. September 30: Cost of Surrender. October 1: Choosing to Submit Humbly.

SURRENDERED PEOPLE
October 2: Who Has Surrendered? October 3: Jesus Surrendered. October 4: The Virgin Mary Surrendered. October 5: The First Disciples Surrendered. October 6: One Surrendered and One Didn't. October 7: I Surrender My Indifference. October 8: I Want to Surrender.

HOW DO I SURRENDER?
October 9: How Do I Surrender? October 10: Stage One of Surrendering: Revelation. October 11: Stage Two of Surrendering: Investigation. October 12: Stage Three of Surrendering: Realization. October 13: Stage Four of Surrendering: Transformation. October 14: Stage Five of Surrendering: Declaration. October 15: Letting God's Spirit Lead.

EMPTYING MYSELF OF SELF
October 16: Surrendering Trouble Spots. October 17: I Surrender My Humanness and Relapses. October 18: I Surrender My People-Pleasing. October 19: I Surrender My Dishonesty. October 20: I Surrender My Disappointments. October 21: I Surrender My Encumbrances. October 22: Surrender Opportunities.

SURRENDER IT IS!
October 23: Surrendering My Entire Life. October 24: Saying Good-bye to Purposelessness. October 25: I Surrender My Prized Excuses. October 26: I Surrender the Easy and the Difficult Things. October 27: I Surrender My Dreams. October 28: I Surrender My Addictions. October 29: Surrendering All.

PRINCIPLE VII: <u>E</u>XPERIENCE HEART-POUNDING LIFE PURPOSE
I'm living in the center of God's will.

FULFILLING MY LIFE MISSION
October 30: Miracles and Leverage. October 31: God of Miracles. November 1: Expecting Miracles. November 2: Doing the Impossible. November 3: God's Blinding Speed. November 4: God's Silence. November 5: Ready for More.

EXHALING AND REGROUPING
November 6: Slow Down. November 7: Rest and Relax More. November 8: Inhale and Exhale. November 9: Enjoy Life. November 10: God's Generosity. November 11: The Least of These. November 12: Enjoying the Journey.

WHAT'S MY UNIQUE PURPOSE?
November 13: My Distinctive Life Purpose. November 14: A Sneak Preview. November 15: My Heroes and God's Plan. November 16: Druthers, Hopes, and Dreams. November 17: Drowning Out God's Voice. November 18: My Deepest Longing. November 19: God-Given Intuition.

TO WHOM AM I CALLED AND WHAT DO I SAY?
November 20: My Calling. November 21: To Whom Am I Called? November 22: Who's My Audience? November 23: A Life Message. November 24: Expect Illumination. November 25: Asking for My Heart's Desire. November 26: Grateful for My Assignment.

WHAT GOD WANTS
November 27: Delivery Method and Pizzazz. November 28: God's Delivery Method. November 29: Passion: It's Good for My Soul. November 30: My Pizzazz and Life Mission. December 1: Creative Delivery Methods. December 2: God's Return Policy. December 3: Win-Win-Win.

THE LIFE TO LIVE
December 4: Joy and Peace. December 5: Red Carpet Treatment. December 6: Being Joy-Filled. December 7: I Choose Joy. December 8: Peacefulness Checklist. December 9: The Lord Is Peace. December 10: Craving Joy and Peace.

SAY YES!
December 11: Divine Commission. December 12: Lord, Speak. December 13: Send Me. December 14: Say Yes to Change. December 15: Leap of Faith. December 16: God's Signet Ring. December 17: I Say Yes.

STEPS TOWARD MY PURPOSE
December 18: I'm Ready to Move Forward. December 19: Research and Interviews. December 20: Get Back to Work. December 21: The Lord's Will. December 22: Released to Move Forward. December 23: Be Merciful to Others. December 24: My Exciting Action Steps.

OBEYING GOD'S CALL
December 25: God's Friendship. December 26: Humble Obedience. December 27: Running and Hiding. December 28: Will You Go Now? December 29: God's Ten Commandments. December 30: Jesus—the First and the Last. December 31: I'm Obeying Now.

Author Contact Information

To contact bestselling author KATIE BRAZELTON, PhD, MDiv, MA, in regard to a referral to a certified recovery coach, upcoming certification trainings for recovery coaches, a downloadable small-group book study, a private two-day intensive Life Plan, or a consultation to start a coaching ministry that uses the P.U.R.P.O.S.E. Plan and the Twelve Steps for Believers, use the contact form on the website www.LifePurposeCoachingCenters.com or e-mail her at Info@ LifePurposeCoachingCenters.com.

DR. BRAZELTON is the founder of Life Purpose Coaching Centers International® (LPCCI). She is following her passionate dream of opening 200 Life Purpose Coaching Centers (with coaching toward God's plan, recovery, marriage and family, finances, career, health, etc.) in churches, parachurch ministries, and private coaching practices. To ensure the highest possible training standards and to offer continuing education units, which many colleges accept as transfer credits, LPCCI holds extensive professional credentials in the coaching world:

- Board Certified Coach (BCC) training provider for the Center for Credentialing and Education (CCE)
- Authorized training provider for the International Association for Continuing Education and Training (IACET)
- Approved training provider for the International Coach Federation (ICF)

To learn more about LPCCI and Katie's God-given dream, visit the website www.LifePurposeCoachingCenters.com.

AMBASSADOR SPEAKERS BUREAU in Tennessee manages Katie's keynote and retreat speaking schedule (only). Her audiences have included such groups as the Salvation Army, the American Association of Christian Counselors, the Navigators, Swaziland's Bulembu orphanage staff, and denominations and churches around the world.

To book an event, call Ambassador at 615-370-4700.

Katie is a featured guest on television (e.g., *100 Huntley Street* and TBN Africa) and radio (e.g., *HomeWord* and *Midday Connection*). Her articles have appeared in various publications (e.g., *Christian Coaching Today* and *Extraordinary Women Magazine*). Dr. Brazelton is a board member for the International Christian Coaching Association and also for Rockbridge Seminary. She has interviewed Mother Teresa in Calcutta, countless influential leaders, subject-matter experts, addicts, and prisoners to seek advice for the readers of her numerous books. Katie is the educational dean for Full Circle Outreach (a substance abuse treatment center) and a church consultant; she was previously a licensed minister through Saddleback Church.

To book a television, radio, or print interview (or to request an article), please contact Katie at Info@LifePurposeCoaching Centers.com.

Katie resides in Southern California and has two adult children, a daughter-in-love, and two precious grandsons. She enjoys walking and swimming at Laguna Beach—and making jigsaw puzzles.

Connect personally with Katie on Twitter (@KatieBrazelton), Facebook, LinkedIn, or her blogs.